**Older
Women**

The Boston University Series in Gerontology

Boston University Gerontology Center

The Gerontology Center is a multidisciplinary organization that integrates the biological, psychological, socioeconomic, medical, and humanistic concerns of aging and of the elderly.

Older Women

Issues and Prospects

Edited by
Elizabeth W. Markson
Boston University

LexingtonBooks
D.C. Heath and Company
Lexington, Massachusetts
Toronto

To Alison Markson,
who one day will be an older woman

Library of Congress Cataloging in Publication Data
Main entry under title:

Older women.

Includes bibliographical references and index.
1. Aged women—United States—Addresses, essays, lectures. 2. Middle-aged women—United States—Addresses, essays, lectures. I. Markson, Elizabeth Warren.
HQ1426.089 1983   305.2'6'0973   81–48025
ISBN 0–669–05245–0

Copyright © 1983 by D.C. Heath and Company

Published simultaneously in Canada

Printed in the United States of America

International Standard Book Number: 0–669–05245–0

Library of Congress Catalog Card Number: 81–48025

Contents

Tables

Preface and
Acknowledgments

Older women are an important and growing segment of the population of industrialized nations. Although they share the common denominator of sex, older women vary immensely in their occupations, personalities, socioeconomic status, and life-styles. The purpose of this book is to capture some of the social diversity of growing old, female style.

To edit a book on a single theme is always risky, especially when the theme is as large as older women. One must steer between the Scylla of overspecificity and the Charybdis of overgenerality. In soliciting original contributions for this book, I looked for authors who would bring the perspectives of their particular research and place them in a context relevant to issues and prospects confronting older women today. I have been fortunate in their contributions, for they have provided continuity without undue overlap of material on older women.

The book is organized into four sections: changes beginning in mid-life, occupational and retirement patterns, variations in families and life-styles, and selected health issues confronting older women. Following the introduction, which provides an overview, each section is preceded by a brief review of material pertinent to the articles following. A short epilogue with a review of key issues concludes the book.

I am particularly grateful to the individual authors who made this book possible by providing their chapters. Knight Steel, M.D., director of the Gerontology Center, and Richard Egdahl, M.D., academic vice-president for health affairs at Boston University, provided encouragement and support of this and other volumes in the Boston University Series in Gerontology.

Special thanks go to Stephen Antler, Helen Mayer Hacker, Beth B. Hess, Louis Lowy, Carol Mueller, Patricia Reuss, Charlotte Green Schwartz, Peter Stein, and Marott Sinex for their input at various stages of this project.

I especially thank Gretchen Batra and Ellen Kane for their invaluable assistance throughout preparation of this book.

I also thank Margaret Zusky, Susan Lasser, and the rest of the editorial staff at Lexington Books for their patience and encouragement.

Introduction

Elizabeth W. Markson

This book is primarily about older women; it does not attempt to look at the situations of both sexes equally. While women have been the subject of much scholarly and popular attention within the last decade, only recently has research focused specifically on older women and the ways in which their aging processes may be similar or distinct from those of men. It was not until 1978 that the Baltimore Longitudinal Study added women to its study of normal aging; it was also in 1978 that the Annual Meeting of the Gerontological Society of America first placed a significant emphasis on aging women. It was in 1981 that the White House Conference on Aging first had a special committee on concerns of older women, the final report from which was subtitled "Growing Number, Special Need."[1] The subtitle of that report, summarizes the purposes behind this book; older women are increasing in number and have special needs.

My interest in a book on older women has a long history. Over a decade ago, when I began fieldwork on the elderly, I was struck by both the demographic reality of the disproportionate number of old women and their heterogeneity. I was also struck with the paucity of interest among most of my colleagues in sex and gender differences in the aging process. Teaching primarily female students, I also was startled to find that almost none of these women was interested in older women and that they could not envisage themselves as ever growing old. While the inability to imagine oneself as old is certainly not restricted to female students, it is women who will be culturally defined as older—and old—sooner and for a longer period of time than men.

That older women have been discovered so lately by gerontologists and the general public is ironic in view of their proportional representation in the population. Every society is affected by the age and sex distribution of its population because age and sex influence size of the labor force and economic well-being, fertility rates, life-styles, and life opportunities. The graying of America is predominantly comprised of women; in 1980, women represented 54.7 percent of the U.S. population 40 years of age and over and 59.7 percent of those 60 and over.[2] A few more statistics are relevant here. In 1900, life expectancy at birth was 46.6 years for white men and 48.7 for white women in the United States. Nonwhites had a lower life expectancy: 32.5 years for men and 33.5 for women. By 1979, life expectancy had shifted dramatically with an increase of 24 years for white men, 29.6 years

1

for white women, and 33 and 41 years for nonwhite men and women respectively. That old age is a territory more traveled by women is clear; on the average, a white woman can expect to live approximately eight years longer and a nonwhite woman nine years longer than her male age peer. These sex differences are most marked among the old-old; among those 65–69, there are approximately 127 women to every 100 men, but by age 85 or older, there are 220 women to every 100 men. Thus does demography shape the destiny of older women.

For example, while slightly more than three-quarters of all men 65 and over are married, only slightly over one-third of women 65 and over are married. It is not surprising that a major trial for women in old age is that of widowhood. Since men have a shorter life expectancy than women, they are likely to die first. Furthermore, elderly men remarry at a higher rate than their female counterparts, and they are likely to remarry younger, rather than same age or older, women.

Not only are older women more likely to be widowed and alone but they are also more likely to be portrayed by the media as passive and nurturant and the victims of violent crime. A 1976 survey of violence on television indicated that murder victims were most frequently poor, urban women[3]; in children's books, older women are more likely than men to be described as "sad," "poor," or "dear."[4] The stereotype of the poor, helpless, old woman is particularly interesting in view of the findings of Neugarten and Gutmann that, as women age, they become more assertive and dominant (qualities usually identified as masculine), while aging men become more nurturant.[5] Older women thus find themselves typecast in a role that no longer fits actual personality changes.

Some social scientists have suggested that our attitudes toward women in general and older women in particular reflect a deeply ingrained cultural ambivalence toward women that is related to the assignment of magical powers to them over the centuries.[6] Contemporary fairy tales and myths are filled with fairy godmothers and wicked witches but relatively few male counterparts. In *The Wizard of Oz,* for example, the Wizard is a benign, bumbling, older man, but the Wicked Witch of the West is a warty old hag, feared for her ugliness and powerful evil. (Even Glinda, the good witch, has stronger magical powers than the Wizard; she is, incidentally, also younger than the Wicked Witch.) Thus is the greater assertiveness of older women trivialized by media and mythology so that she is either witch or weakling.[7]

Cross-cultural studies have indicated that, except through witchcraft, older women seldom held formal power or prestige in pre-industrial societies because they had little or no actual control over goods and resources.[8] Their relative lack of control over power and wealth persists today and is an elaboration of a lifelong pattern. For example, the gap between the earnings of men and women widens with age. While the average employed woman earns 59 percent of what an employed man earns in the United States, women over the age of 45 (the most rapidly growing segment of the labor force) earn only 55 percent.

The incidence of poverty among female-headed families is also a life-long trend. Since 1959, the poverty rate for male-headed families of all ages has dropped twice as fast as for those headed by women. Among those 65 and over, the chances of living below the poverty level are about three times greater if the family head is a woman rather than a man, and women over 65 who live alone are the poorest of the poor. Seventy-three percent of those receiving Supplemental Security Income (SSI) for the aged, a form of coverage designed to help the poor, are women; and 61 percent of all Medicaid recipients are women, many of whom are over 65.

Not all older women are poor, of course; one may find rich widows as well as women whose possessions can be carried in a shopping bag. However, women who rely primarily upon their own resources are likely to have fewer assets such as savings, to have lower lifetime earnings, to rely on social security for their sole income, and to receive low benefits as retirees or disabled workers.

These are some of the concerns of older women: widowhood, economic survival, and positive regard. At the 1981 White House Conference on Aging, the Committee on the Concerns of Older Women adopted a bill of rights elaborating on these concerns. Specifically mentioned were the following issues as rights: to self-esteem; to be seen as a unique, productive, attractive, intelligent, and interesting person; to freedom from stigma if one lives alone; to expression of sexuality; to economic support and health care at an adequate level; to equal employment opportunities; to a positive representation in the media; and to rid oneself of dependence on others.[9]

While the issues raised and language used differ from the Women's Declaration of Independence, passed in Seneca Falls by U.S. feminists in 1849,[10] the basic intent is the same: to guarantee equality and quality of life for both sexes. All of us, whether men or women, need to be concerned with what happens to older women because they are the majority of older people. They are also our mothers, our wives, ourselves, our sisters, and someday our daughters, daughters-in-law, nieces, and granddaughters.

We hope, in this book, partially to redress the balance of emphasis that typically has been placed on older men or, often, simply on the old. The term *older* is problematic to define; at what age does one become older? Aging is a process that begins at birth and ends at death so that we are always growing older. Certainly biological factors associated with chronological age determine one's ability to play certain roles; fertility is an obvious example of a biologically bounded role. However, age also is defined culturally and socially by expectations for appropriate behavior and by life events. That there are distinct social clocks ticking off age-appropriate types of behavior as well as stages of the life course has been demonstrated; for example, among middle-class U.S. samples, a middle-aged woman usually is seen as between the ages of 40 and 50, and an old woman between 60 and 75 years of age.[11] Although the primary focus of this book is on old women, chapters are included on changes occurring among women as early as their fourth decade. These mid-life events influence and often shape the future course of the remainder of life, although they are by no means all determining.

In the following chapters, the ideas of a number of people who have been concerned with issues and prospects for older women are presented. Many of the authors are feminists, the majority women. They share in common a commitment to the well-being of older women and men throughout the life course.

Notes

1. For a summary report of this and other committees, see *Final Report: The 1981 White House Conference on Aging,* vols. 2 and 3 (no publisher or date provided).

2. Statistics presented in this introduction are taken from current governmental sources. For additional references, see chapters by Hess and Waring, Braito and Anderson, Turner and Adams, and Szinovacz.

3. G. Gerbner and M.F. Eleey, "TV Violence Profile Number 8—The Highlights," *Journal of Communication* 27 (Spring 1977):171–180.

4. E.F. Ansello, "Old Age and Literature: A Developmental Analysis," *Educational Gerontology* 2 (1977):211–366; C.T. Horner, *The Aging Adult in Children's Books and Nonprint Media* (Metuchen, N.J.: Scarecrow Press, 1982); and U. Lehr, "The Aging of the Women," in *Adaptability and Aging,* vol. 2 (Paris: International Association of Social Gerontology, 1982), pp. 71–84.

5. B.L. Neugarten, ed. *Middle Age and Aging* (Chicago: University of Chicago Press, 1975).

6. See, for example, F. Livson, "Cultural Faces of Eve: Images of Women" (Paper presented at the Annual Meeting of the American Psychological Association, San Francisco, August 1977; and David Gutmann, "The Cross-Cultural Perspective: Notes toward a Comparative Psychology of Aging," in *The Handbook of the Psychology of Aging,* eds. J.E. Birren and K.W. Schaie (New York: Van Nostrand Reinhold, 1977).

7. For further discussion, see Beth B. Hess, "Older Women: Problems, Potentials, and Policy Implications," in *Public Policies for an Aging Population,* eds, E.W. Markson and G.B. Batra (Lexington, Mass.: Lexington Books, D.C. Heath, 1980).

8. See, for example, Leo Simmons, *The Role of the Aged in Primitive Society* (New Haven, Conn.: Yale University Press, 1945); and T. Sheehan, "Senior Esteem as a Factor of Socio-Economic Complexity," *Gerontologist* 16 (1976):433–440.

9. For the full text of the Bill of Rights for Older Women (Recommendation no. 434A), see *Final Report: The 1981 White House Conference on Aging,* vol. 3, pp. 166–167.

10. See Elizabeth Cady Stanton et al., *History of Woman Suffrage,* vol. 1 (1881), reprint ed. (New York: Arno Press and *The New York Times.* 1969), pp. 70–73.

11. Neugarten, *Middle Age and Aging.*

Part I:
Changing Bodies,
Changing Selves

By mid-life, observable physical changes begin to occur among both men and women. Gray hairs and wrinkles appear with greater frequency, weight changes may occur, and for women, changes in reproductive capacity culminate in menopause. That there are gender and sex differences in the experiential quality of growing old seems evident. In a youth-oriented culture like ours, bodily changes are not welcomed by either sex, but there is some indication that these are less humiliating for men than for women. Susan Sontag commented a decade ago, "For most women, aging means a humiliating process of gradual sexual disqualification"[1]—a limiting condition for women not equally experienced by men who may actually find their power and masculinity increased with maturity. A good-looking woman has been defined in sample surveys by Neugarten as between 20 and 35,[2] and women are entreated by advertisements in the media to conceal the gray, remove unsightly bulges, erase wrinkles, and stay younger looking longer through cosmetics, pills, and girdles. It is unlikely that Katherine Hepburn will be cast in a film as the romantic lead opposite Richard Dreyfus whereas no one was surprised at a film in which Burt Lancaster was romantically involved with Susan Sarandon.

That the mid-life woman also looks her age is typically considered less sexually attractive than a middle-aged man is linked not only to physical signs of aging but also to her reproductive capacity whereby the physical stigma of aging are harbingers of the cessation of fertility. Paradoxically, most North American couples today have married by their early twenties and have on the average two children, spaced within the first ten years of marriage. The childbearing phase of a woman's life is thus usually completed when she is relatively young—in sharp contrast to earlier times when it was not unusal for a woman to be in her forties when the last child was born.[3]

Yet much mythology whereby one's value is linked to one's fertility still surrounds the middle-aged woman. Far less studied than the mid-life man, the cultural stereotype of a woman in mid-life is of a person prone to anxiety, depression, and loss of confidence and sexual interest. If suicide is used as a rough index of depression and anxiety, suicide rates peak at mid-life for women while those of men continue to rise with age. Traditionally, menopause has been blamed for many personality changes associated with mid-life; as one nineteenth-century gynecologist, J.K. Shirk, described the cessation of menses in menopause, "The system is now so thoroughly

7

accustomed to this drain that to stop it suddenly . . . we would naturally suppose to be followed by untoward consequences. This we find in reality to be the case."[4] Contemporary evidence suggests, however, that the decreases in estrogen that characterize menopause play a relatively minor role in the anxiety and depression experienced in mid-life. More important is the lack of social support that women may feel as they grow older.[5] The relaxation of inhibitions that comes about after the demands of motherhood have been met may actually free women, permitting them to express a hitherto unexpressed androgeny.[6] The physical changes that begin to occur in mid-life are the focus of part I.

Cleo S. Berkun, in chapter 1, sheds additional light on women's self-perceptions. She reviews recent literature on mid-life women to provide a framework within which to present research results of her study of the effects of changing appearance on women's experience of themselves. Berkun's findings suggest that the white, middle-class U.S. sample she studied still accepts negative stereotypes of female middle age. Furthermore, distress with age-associated changes in appearance was most strongly felt by those women who were less able to control their social environment to avoid direct or indirect social rejection on account of their aging.

While mid-life has been the topic of popular and scholarly works in the United States during the last decade, this stage of life has received little attention in France. There is, for example, no term corresponding to *mid-life* or *middle age* in French; perhaps the closest translation would be "the second maturity." An alternative translation is "the second half of productive life," although, since for economic reasons the permanent layoff or retirement age has been lowered to age 50 in some industries in France within recent years, this latter translation would seem to refer more to potential for production than to opportunity.[7] Maryvonne Gognalons-Nicolet utilizes French material in chapter 2 to argue that menopause is very much a critical psychosocial event, influencing the course of the remainder of a woman's life.

Ruth Jacobs examines one set of options for women who are seeking to resolve issues of particular salience in mid-life—and beyond—in her analysis of women's health spas in chapter 3. Proposing that women, seeking the promise of restored youthfulness and attractiveness, find a pseudo-community while in their exercise leotards, Jacobs also questions the utility of this solution. While health clubs provide a supportive environment for aging women, they deflect attention from the real issues confronting many women as they age.

A key theme, closely related to perceptions of the meaning of bodily changes and to women's roles in mid- and late life, is that of sexuality. Barbara Turner and Catherine Adams place the sexuality of older women in a life-span context in chapter 4. They emphasize the point that, contrary to

popular opinion, none of the changes in sexual physiology following menopause necessarily limits sexual functioning and response. Noting that experience is more critical than physiological changes in determining sexual
expression, Turner and Adams also discuss gender differences in sexuality
and sexual options for women in later life.

Notes

1. Susan Sontag, "The Double Standard of Aging," *Saturday Review,*
23 September 1972, p. 32.

2. B. Neugarten, ed. *Middle Age and Aging* (Chicago: University of
Chicago Press, 1968), p. 24.

3. See E. VandeWalle and J. Knodel, "Europe's Fertility Transition:
New Evidence and Lessons for Today's Developing World," *Population
Bulletin* 34 (1980), for further discussion of changes in fertility patterns.

4. J.K. Shirk, *Female Hygiene and Female Disease* (Lancaster, Penn.:
Lancaster Publishing Co., 1884), p. 132.

5. See, for example, P. Bart, "Portnoy's Mother's Complaint,"
Trans-action/Society 8 (1970):222–228; B. Turner, "Sex Roles among
Wives in Middle and Late Life" (Paper presented at the Annual Meeting of
the American Psychological Association, San Francisco, August 1977);
M.H. Huyck, "Sex, Gender, and Aging" (Paper presented at the Annual
Meeting of the Gerontological Society of America, New York, 1976); and
W. Cooper, "A Woman's View of the Menopause," in *The Management of
the Menopause and Postmenopausal Years,* ed. S. Campbell (Baltimore:
University Park Press, 1975).

6. See Huyck, "Sex, Gender, and Aging"; Turner, "Sex Roles among
Wives"; and B.F. Turner, "Sex-Related Differences in Aging," in *Hand-
book of Developmental Psychology,* eds. B.B. Wolman and J. Stricker
(New York: Prentice-Hall, 1982).

7. See Xavier Gaullier, "Economic Crisis and Old Age: Old Age Policies in France," *Aging and Society* 2 (1981):165–182 for further discussion
of the emerging new old age among early-terminated wage earners.

Changing Appearance for Women in the Middle Years of Life: Trauma?

Cleo S. Berkun

To ask an adult women in this country her age is to violate a strong taboo. Further, except when under certain legalistic circumstances, women have subtle permission to lie about how old they are, or at least to fudge. The roots for such behavior lie in common attitudes about aging, the association of feminine attractiveness with youth, and the primary social value of women being associated with sexual attractiveness. In 1949, Simone deBeauvoir wrote:

> Whereas man grows old gradually, woman is suddenly deprived of her femininity; she is still relatively young when she loses the erotic attractiveness and the fertility which, in the view of society and in her own, provide justification of her existence and her opportunity for happiness. With no future, she still has about one-half of her adult life to live. [p. 640]

DeBeauvoir described aging for the woman as "eventual mutilation." She believes it is vital for a woman to be attractive in order to hold her husband and to keep most of her jobs.

Lest it seem that this is an outdated sentiment, let me quote Ruth Weg, who said about women in 1977:

> More than man, she must retain her youthful appearance, resorting to the creams, the makeup and even surgery—for "she" as "youth" is the decoration of society. [p. 24]

Women, she stated, find themselves asking many questions when they are older. Among them: Will men still find me attractive? Do wrinkles and other signs of aging turn men off? [p. 10].

If these words are accurate, the middle-aged woman will find it necessary to make major adjustments in her life and in her self-concept. It might be expected that as she perceives diminishing social value, her self-esteem would diminish and the likelihood of depression or depressive thoughts increase. Although it is a common sentiment—a truism, perhaps—a theme that recurs through much writing about middle-aged women is that they suffer from aging appearance, a premise that rarely has been tested.

11

On the whole, there has been little research on physical attractiveness using subjects other than the ubiquitous college population, and relatively little research has focused directly on the lives of middle-aged women. Such research as does exist on physical attractiveness suggests overall that, while not a simple matter, what is beautiful is good, that there are stereotypes about what constitutes female attractiveness and that they hold across the life span (Adams 1977; Berscheid 1974). Until quite recently, research results pertinent to older women emphasized a tendency to depression, low self-esteem, identity confusion, high prescription-drug usage, but with some personality shift toward becoming more instrumental in the mid-years (Neugarten 1968; Cahn 1978). However, after reinterviewing participants in the early mid-town Manhattan study, Srole and Fisher (1978) found considerable positive change in the mental health of women over 40 and Weissman, in an epidemiological study, found that middle-aged women were not the age category of women most vulnerable to depression (Weissman and Klerman 1977).

Thus, in designing research to test the merits of assertions that middle-aged women find changing appearance traumatic and contributory to depression or negative self-concepts, there was little hard data on which to base a hypothesis. The research reported in this chapter, then, was conceived as exploratory and descriptive. In this chapter I describe that research, discuss some of the pertinent findings from a symbolic interactionist and feminist perspective, make some observations about the social status of middle-aged women, and end with speculations about upcoming generations of older women. My observations and the interpretation of my research results are fleshed out by extensive years of practice as a clinical social worker, a great deal of reading (in academia, called a literature search), numerous conversations with friends and colleagues, and my own perceptions as a middle-aged woman. First, however, before discussing the research, I briefly discuss what we mean by middle age and who comprises the population of today's middle-age women.

Middle Age

One of the most dramatic changes of the twentieth century has been the extension of life expectancy, from around the mid-forties at the turn of the century, to the late seventies for white middle-class women today. A protracted mid-life, covering a span of twenty-five years, relatively child free, healthy, and vigorous, is a rather new phenomenon. Labeling of those years, as well as understanding life-cycle processes and tasks during those years, seems to have negative connotations for women. First, one does not stop being adult because of having lived past the fortieth birthday (for some reason the magic year), and the age of 65 for entering old age is known to be arbitrary. Then, when does middle age happen, and is there something different about middle age than adulthood, and then, when does it become old age? Neugarten (1974), among others, has tackled this problem and found that there are social expectations about life tasks that are associated with chronological age but that these expectations may be in a state of flux these days. Typically, studies of attitudes point to negative stereotypes about middle age, especially for women, with vague age boundaries at either end of the category, sometimes starting at 35, and sometimes a bit later. Aware of the negative public opinions about middle-aged women, many women do not want to include themselves in the category (Ward 1977).

It is possible that public attitudes toward women who are obviously no longer in the flush of youthful sexual attractiveness cannot be escaped, because attitudes translate into behaviors. Bell (1970) observed:

> As she approaches middle age, however, she begins to notice a change in the way people treat her. Reflected in the growing indifference of others toward her looks, toward her sexuality, she can see and measure the decline of her worth, her status in the world. [p. 75]

Although little disagreement can be found in any writing in regard to social attitudes toward middle-aged women, there is no single definition of middle age that is used throughout the theoretical, empirical, statistical, or popular work on the subject. The term *middle age* usually refers to chronological age, family stage, and/or work stage. If dealing only with chronological age, then cohort factors and/or the social-life stage of the person are not adequately considered. Regarding the latter, for instance, a 45-year-old woman who has two young children and is concerned with being class mother and with school schedules is dealing with quite different issues than a 45-year-old woman whose youngest child is 20 years old, married, and presenting her with a grandchild. Work in which middle age is examined from the viewpoint of family stage like the empty nest may ignore the biological factors like the advent of menopause and usually ignores the situation of single or childless women.

In critiquing research and theory about women in the middle years, Barnett and Baruch (1978) found that underlying many studies of women in the middle years is a belief in the biological determinism of feminine behavior. They found that a woman's life too often is seen only in terms of her reproductive role, with menopause and the empty nest being viewed as the major events of the middle years. The view that paid employment has not been conceptualized as central to the lives of women is reflected in the selection of subjects for study.

Although Barnett's and Baruch's viewpoint seems to indict the notion that, for women, biology is destiny, biology cannot be totally ignored.

Sometime around the age of 50, unless surgical menopause has occurred earlier, menopause occurs. Other bodily changes occur: It is likely that women need fewer calories to maintain their body weight, it is harder to maintain muscle tone, breasts tend to sag, the inevitable facial wrinkles and gray hair appear. A 55-year-old woman may not be easily distinguishable in appearance from one aged 40 or 45, but she rarely would be assumed to be 25 or 35. She cannot totally ignore physical changes any more than she can totally ignore menopause. In a sense, then, biology is destiny for middle-aged women, if the stereotypes about the importance of youthful appearance for women and the negative attitude about older women as compared with men hold true.

Thus, woman's experience may depend on chronological age interacting with external events within an external as well as internal context. Her internal context may be biological in part but would certainly include the internalized effects of her personal and social history. Women who now fall into that loosely defined age grade of middle age have had a variety of life experience, but they have had some external events in common.

Picture, then, that between forty and sixty-five years ago, about 22.9 million female babies were born in this, the wealthiest nation in the world, and lived to tell about it.[1] From their earliest conscious moments, they knew they were the future mothers of the United States and that there was a sure, tried, and true way to achieve that status. They played with Betsey Wetsey dolls (Barbie came later), Shirley Temple was their model (those with straight hair suffered), they wore dresses or skirts to school (in really bad weather, they wore slacks that were taken off in school), and they pined for the day when they might be permitted to wear high heels and lipstick. They took cooking and sewing in school (while the boys took shop) and learned to sit with their legs together and to bend over without showing their panties (while the boys learned to be peekers). As they got a little older, some were good at schoolwork, but they were encouraged to make themselves beautiful and to learn how to flirt just the right amount so as to attract boys without leading them too far. Sex was to be saved for the so-called right man, and they would somehow know when he came along. Then, they would marry and have his children, be exemplary mothers and wives with sparkling homes, happy husbands, and emotionally sound children through togetherness and personal sacrifice. Being women, they would know how to do all this instinctively and happily, with a little help from women's magazines and advice books. Meanwhile, Mr. Right would work, succeed through his own efforts and his wife's backing, providing for all their material comforts and emotional needs. In later years, when the children were successfully launched on their own careers (if boys) or marriages (if girls), women would sit back, glow with pride, spend their time doing volunteer work and cooking dinner for large family reunions, ending their days surrounded by loving great-great grandchildren as they celebrated a seventy-fifth wedding anniversary.

There were a few who had deviant thoughts or aspirations, perhaps delaying or not marrying at all, or who developed a career (but very likely worrying about how to do that and marry, too). Some even entertained thoughts about loving women in preference to men, but we do not know how many. On the whole, though, life's path looked clear—marriage to one husband, children, financial security, and a march into the sunset holding the husband's hand. Details such as who, how many, exactly when, and how much were major problems to be tackled. Work outside the home was either out of dire financial necessity or to mark time until marriage— and was usually in clerical, sales, or unskilled factory work or as a nurse, public-school teacher, or social worker.

However, conditions in the wealthiest nation of the world mitigated against the probability for those little girls of living life as they had learned they had a right to expect. Some had to overcome the effects of the Great Depression, which meant dropping out of school early to work at whatever job was available and entering marriage hoping for release from drudge work. Relief from the Depression came in the form of war, however, and these little girls grown to womanhood have now lived through three wars that actively endangered brothers, fathers, sons, and lovers. They were pulled into doing so-called men's work during World War II and then were sent back home to be responsible for everyone's emotional well-being. They have experienced rapid social change, related to the civil-rights movement, the women's movement, and the turmoil of the infamous 1960s. They have succored their children through those days with all their hazards including drugs. They have experienced the effects of technological change that bring instant communication and entertainment but also that keep us under daily threat of instant termination. Their children tend to live life-styles quite different from their own when they were young adults, to which they, the mothers, must adjust. They take care of elderly parents, their own and their husband's. They have a span of years of life during which their children are independent and away, and they, the women, are still of sound mind and body. For many, however, there is a new hazard: They find themselves on their own because of widowhood, or, more likely, by the dissolution of the marriages they expected to last all their lives, when their husbands go through socially permissable mid-life crises and leave them for younger women.

Thus, today's middle-aged woman may find herself with mental and physical vigor, but with few role models or guideposts, in a social and economic world for which she was not prepared. Additionally, she may be stigmatized through no fault of her own because of chronological age.

The media remind us daily of products designed to retard signs of aging (if not aging itself), and newspapers see fit to print items like the one about a husband who congratulated his wife on her fortieth birthday with black roses, a casket with a dummy inside, and a poem saying, "Turning 20 is young; Turning 30 is fun; But turning 40 is just plain old."[2]

Research Design

Accordingly, although there is little hard data on which to base a hypothesis about the effects of changing appearance on middle-aged women's experience of themselves, my own expectation was that women would be acutely aware of their changing appearance and unhappy about looking older. Sixty physically and mentally healthy, white, suburban women, aged 40 to 55 were interviewed, using a standardized self-report interview. Structured and open-ended questions in the interview were designed to explore issues about the participants' perceptions of their changing appearance; their attitudes toward aging; their overall affective mood; depressive characteristics they might experience; interactive variables such as marital, maternal, and work status; middle-aged worries; changes since being over 40; security with men; and security within the family. In addition to measures of central tendency, correlations and multiple-regression analyses enabled examination of the associative qualities of the variables. However, because the sample was not random and relatively small for the number of variables, the statistical approach utilized cannot be considered to indicate causality but only to point to the possibility of interactive effects of certain variables in these women's lives.

Who the Women Were

Because of space limitations in presenting this material, I focus more on the results than on methodology or statistical analysis and describe the sample demographics briefly. Of the women interviewed, only three had never married; ten were married for the second or third time; five were divorced; four were separated; and one was widowed. Most of the marriages were long term—one woman had been married for less than 5 years, seven for less than 10 years, but the mean number of years of marriage was 22.9 years. Not surprisingly, most of the women had borne or reared children, with only four childless. Thirty-three (55 percent) of the women were still living with children and husbands, twelve were living with husbands only, and nine with children only. Six women were living alone.

The women studied were well educated relative to other women in their age category.[3] Three had less than 10 years of formal education, but the mean was 14.8 years.

An attempt to find two subsamples, one composed of traditional housewives—that is, those whose lives followed the anticipated patterns—and one composed of women committed to work outside the home, had to be abandoned. As the research went on, not only was it clear that there were few women who could be categorized easily but also that meaningful work outside the home was not necessarily paid and that meaningfulness could not be determined by the number of hours of work. With that impression, a re-examination of literature pertaining to middle-aged women, depression, and work revealed that most researchers and writers tend either to ignore the many variations in work patterns or arbitrarily to decide that current work over twenty hours a week classifies a woman as working rather than as a housewife. Every participant had worked for pay and had done volunteer work at one time or another in her adult life. Every participant in the study had fairly recently made, or was seriously considering making, a shift either in paid work or some other meaningful activity outside the home. Some of the shifts had been related to family factors, others had made changes due to other circumstances, some women were actively engaged in sorting out what changes they wanted to make, while others were aware that they would be making changes but currently were more passive. After listening to these women and examining the data, it seemed that neither the number of hours per week that women work outside the home and whether or not they get paid for their work nor the kinds of work they do exhaust the crucial factors to understanding the impact of work on their lives. Of additional importance were the relationships to husband and children, the importance of working, the importance of the job, how secure they felt in employment, and how they envisioned themselves in relation to work.

Twenty-three (38.3 percent) of the women did not engage in paid work outside the home. The others worked a range of an occasional few hours to more than full time. The number of hours a week the women worked was related to their marital status. All the never-married women worked full time; six of the ten remarried women worked full time. Of the thirty-seven women who were still in their first marriages, only two engaged in paid work full time.

However, statistical data do not entirely reflect real life. For one thing, for the married women, the number of hours worked for pay per week was not equal to the time spent productively outside the home. For example, one woman who was paid for about twenty hours of work per week in the family business also put in an equal amount of time engaged in civic activities to increase the business.

Further, sixteen women worked without pay in occupations that would not technically be considered volunteer work—that is, they worked free in their husbands' businesses, held elective office, or were full-time students. In order to analyze quantitatively data related to work, it is necessary to create artificial arbitrary categories, but those do not reflect real life for middle-aged women. Some of the discrepancies in research that study the effects of work on depression may be artifactual, from incorrect definition of work for women. In this research, such definition remained a problem, but questions also were asked to ascertain the importance of a variety of kinds of work outside the home to the participants, as well as how secure they felt in those endeavors. As it turned out, the differences between working and stay-at-home women may be more related to the totality of their situations, including the importance of activities and whether or not they are in the process of making some change that puts them in a competitive situation with younger women and, to a lesser extent, with men, than to work. Primarily, expectations about the direction and content of their lives affected life outside the home for all the women.

Traditional Lives and Expectations

One participant, aged 51, said the following about aging:

> I can't say that it bothers me all that much because there isn't anything you can do about it. Times does march on. I think I feel approximately the same way about that I did with each varying stage of life. You've got to do the best you can with what you've got. Well, the mere fact of getting older doesn't bother me. The one thing that does worry me is physical, and things that might happen to me. My main concern is a stroke . . . .
>
> I hope we can do all the things we plan to do when the kids are gone. I guess I have the typical hopes and thoughts and dreams of my marching off into the sunset with my hand in Tom's.[4]

The speaker typified the traditionally married, home-focused women of this study: She was aware that her appearance had changed, but she was secure in her life circumstances, had few regrets about no longer having to be "on the sexy side of everything." and worried about old age only if she were to become disabled or widowed. Further, she felt confident and more at ease with herself than at earlier periods in her life. Of course, not all the participants were in her circumstances or completely shared her views. How they varied is shown in the following summary of the major results of the study.

The overall impression from this research was that the women interviewed presented a wide variety of circumstances, characteristics, behaviors, and attitudes. The participants found it difficult to quantify their phenomenological experiences (that is, saying "it depends"). However, there were associations between variables in the data. In spite of individual variations in life-styles, there was a sameness or consistency about the quality of the lives of the participants that was related to their being today's middle-aged women. They were all highly family oriented and, with few exceptions, devoted to being married or to the idea of being married (most of the single women would have preferred not being single). They all had expected to marry and to have children, and with only one exception, they had expected to stay home and not work for pay upon marrying and having children. Thus, their lives at the time of the study had been directed by earlier socialization that was common when these women were young—they said they went into marriage largely because it was the only desirable option they perceived. Earlier education or preparation for work had not been central to their aspirations; those who had made career choices had done so expecting them to be temporary. Although married women in the sample had opted to return to work for pay or to engage seriously in the world outside the home without pay, such decisions came later and were limited by the restraints imposed by both the realities of marriage and deep socialization to the primacy of husband-children. Consistently, the needs of husbands and young children had priority over their own. Most of those who had been married and then became single had been forced through economic necessity to work at whatever they could, without concern over personal interests or long-term career development. Because the married women found their prime efforts were focused on marriage maintenance, they limited their out-of-the-home efforts so that the marriage would not be disrupted. A few used the security of the marriage, without disrupting the marriage, to engage in fulfilling activities like painting without worrying about supporting themselves financially.

Dramatically, the women had thoroughly internalized social imperatives about appearance. The use of makeup was considered normal and vital in order to look clean and neat, healthy, rested, and attractive (see table 1-1). There were occasions on which most of the women would be likely to be seen without makeup, usually by husbands and children but once in a while by friends. Never would the women (with the exception of two who used no makeup) be seen at work with a bare face. Although they thought it unlikely that they would be caught at home without makeup, they commented that if someone caught them without cosmetics, it would serve the other person right. The caller would just have to look at the answerer at her worst.

The two women who used no makeup were notably embarrassed and considered themselves to be deviant in that respect. One had decided that she was homely and that makeup did not improve her appearance; the other felt neglectful of her appearance, putting all her energy into a new business. Both thought they were pushing the boundaries of acceptability, as did five or six of the others who used makeup minimally, and tended to forget to repair it during the day. The degree of internalization of feelings about their

Table 1-1
Feelings about Not Wearing Makeup

	Respondents	
Feelings about Makeup	*Number*	*Percent*
Feels different without makeup		
Yes	41	68.3
Somewhat	12	20
No	7	11.7
Looks older without makeup		
Yes	34	56.7
Same	25	41.7
Younger	1	1.7
Looks tired without makeup		
More	33	55
Same	27	45
Attractiveness without makeup		
Less	51	85
Same	6	10
More	3	5
Looks ill without makeup		
Ill	21	35
Same	37	61.7
Better	2	3.3
Other (includes a variety of descriptions like more intellegent		
Negative	45	75
Same	12	20
Positive	3	5

natural faces could be traced back by the participants to early experiences. For instance, they reported comments by their mothers when they came into her presence without lipstick to the effect, "What's the matter, don't you feel well? You don't look well." Thus, an application of makeup would keep the doctor away. They did not test what would happen in their current lives should they defy convention. Styles of makeup and hair varied, but the basic acceptance of the naturalness of using makeup was ingrained. Women who were busy, particularly those who were actively involved in starting new demanding careers, had established habits that minimized the amount of time and effort needed to present themselves as acceptable, but they did not challenge the standards of acceptability. Whether or not they went to the beauty parlor regularly was determined by expedience—what took the least time for best results—rather than by overconcern with fashion. Of those women who colored their hair, only two reported that it was related to graying. Most of the dyers had begun coloring their hair since young adulthood, having always disliked their own hair color, but had no plans to allow their hair to show up as gray. One woman was an exception: From tentatively letting it grow out, she found that her hair was a magnificent silvery color that improved her appearance. On the whole, the participants were less upset about graying hair (they could cover the gray if they so wished) than about wrinkles (much more difficult to do away with).

For all but three of the women, cosmetic surgery was a thing of fantasy, not to be realized because of expense and risk. Only about ten women maintained much of a fantasy about face-lifts, feeling that they would survive in spite of wrinkles. Three already had had plastic surgery, one had a mammoplasty in a last-ditch attempt to save a failed marriage, and two had bags under the eyes removed.

The sampled women accepted the world view or social reality that requires them to look a certain way—a way that fit earlier in their lives with seeking and finding a mate. After marriage, some of the women found they had to project a prescribed image to improve their husbands' careers. Others found that being homebound lessened their efforts at looking attractive. With aging, as appearance and circumstance changed, modifications in behavior were required or became permissible. Those who earlier had been homebound and were more out in public as they became older found they paid more attention to how they looked. Those whose appearance no longer mattered for career advancement (their own or their husband's) found they had relaxed.

Interestingly, the women who were campers and hikers reported a slightly different pattern. They were comfortable in the woods without makeup, although they might be with the same friends to whom they would not reveal a bare face in the city. Thus, the view that makeup is part of one's face is modifiable, depending on the social circumstances and perceptions of acceptability.

On Being Middle Aged

The world view in which women are expected to look a certain way includes components through which the middle-aged and elderly women are seen in stereotypically negative disfavor. They are attributed certain negative behaviors and attitudes in the mid-years, with appearance no longer an asset.[5] The women in this study gave evidence that they, too, had internalized those beliefs, but they tended to exclude themselves from the category of middle age. They liked themselves and did not consider themselves to look worse or less attractive than they had when younger (see table 1–2). While they had internalized the negative stereotypes of middle-aged women, almost two-thirds (63.3 percent) attempted to exclude themselves from devalued aspects of mid-life as the following excerpt indicates:

> There are things that happen when they get to middle age, like menopause. And you hear of all these middle-age divorces and husbands being not content with their wives that they've had for years. And to me, it's just a stereotype word. I don't want to be considered middle age ever, so I feel I've jumped over middle age. I'm fifty now, so I consider myself an adult. I think the word *middle age* scares, and it could be because you're expecting things to happen in your middle age. It's like the child stages—the terrible twos—well it's the terrible middle age. But you also have to accept it as a phase of life, and I'm doing all I can in my power to keep my appearance up to the best. I think the scariest part that I hope I won't have to worry about would be to be left alone [widowhood].

Women like this one found they had more self-confidence, social ease, and a better, broader, more-serviceable perspective on life than they had held earlier—that is, they were less concerned about pleasing everyone. Along with such confidence was confidence with changing appearance. Some of the women felt unambivalently better about their appearance in spite of aging. As one 50-year-old stated:

> I myself am not that concerned about the inevitable wrinkles and that kind of thing. I think that if a person generally keeps herself neat and clean and is careful about her appearance, that's the main thing. It doesn't have anything to do with aging: You can be thirty and look like a slob if you don't care about your body, and I think the key is if you care about yourself as a person, it will come across in your appearance. No, age isn't the factor, I think it's how you feel about yourself—I didn't like myself very well when I was younger, and therefore it carried over into my appearance.

Most negative about their appearance were those women who were facing a harsh social reality in which they had to deal actively with social views of middle-aged women. Women who were trying to attract men or who needed to find work were unhappy with looking older because they recognized the disadvantages of not fulfilling the stereotype of a young, media-ad woman. A 44-year-old woman said:

> I think that I worry about it extensively. The past six months to a year it's become even more of a problem for me. It seems that all of a sudden the

Table 1–2
Attitudes about Changing Appearance

Attitude	Number	Percent
Desire to look younger		
Great deal	41	23.2
Moderate	10	16.7
Not at all	36	60
Feelings about changing appearance		
Very good	35	58.3
Good	13	21.7
Bad	7	11.7
Feelings about attractiveness change		
Positive	18	30
Same	25	41.7
Negative	17	28.3
Feelings about change in womanliness		
Positive, more	20	33.3
Same	37	61.7
Gain or loss in appearance		
Gain	21	35
No difference	24	40
Loss	13	21.7

neck is going, the eyes are getting puffy, the hair won't do what you want it to, and I just feel extremely conscious that I am starting to show my age, and it's probably because I've always been fortunate in the fact that I've always looked younger than my years. This is really preying on my mind more than it should, and I try to overcome it by saying this is ridiculous, but it is bothering me. I just feel like all of a sudden, here it is, all those years that I have been fighting it off, it has caught up with me.

After her first marriage dissolved, she had gone to work as a general clerk in a new business. As the business grew, her job expanded so that she became personnel manager, but she had no college degree. She received a termination notice because new management was trying to bring in all college-trained people. Her job was saved temporarily, but it was a shattering experience for her. Now she thought about an imposed need to make a change. She worried that she would have difficulty finding fulfilling work because of her lack of formal education and training, compounded by her age. Yet she was not an unhappy woman. One concern did not override the satisfaction from other parts of her life.

Single women found aging appearance particularly worrisome. A 47-year-old never-married woman, who worked at a profession in which she felt interested, successful, and useful, had been involved with men in the past but now found the available men to be increasingly scarce. She dyed her hair, wore heavy makeup to cover the evidence of age, and went to great pains to conceal her age. Only her most intimate friends knew. She feared that if she told anyone else, the information might get back to a potential date. It had been her experience that if a man found out her age, he would leave her. Thus she explained her efforts at hiding her age. She was typical of the single women in her experience of being ditched and in her anxiety about her age showing.

Single women also, however, accepted the inevitability of appearance changes and blamed their failures to find men or work on external circumstances but were not engaged in activity that would be geared to improving the societal world view of middle-aged women. They tended more to make accommodations to develop, for instance, other aspects of their lives, in which age and appearance had less importance. Maintenance of close family and friendship ties were of great importance to them, as was skill development and work outside the home.

A few women found that looking older increased their credibility in their professional worlds. These women also were careful in looking conventional in the way they presented their faces—older, but conforming to social expectation. Those who thought they pushed the boundaries of acceptability in that they used little or no makeup, were also careful not to go too far. They did not abandon convention and attempt to pursue success based on their capabilities alone: Presenting a made-up face and correct appearance was seen as a requirement. Women who are trying to succeed professionally in occupations that place them in the public eye frequently find themselves in a bind between the need to attract and the need for credibility. In the mid-years, the conflict is resolved in favor of credibility.[6]

Although almost all the women nonconsciously accepted stereotypes about appearance and about middle age, more than half were positive in their expressed attitudes toward aging. Social rejection because of aging was not feared. The major worries expressed, both about middle age and old age, were being left alone through widowhood (or remaining alone through no remarriage) and diminishing health to the point of physical disability. A commonly held belief was that with health, a husband, and a positive, youthful mental attitude, old age would be fine. The participants tended to view their middle-age worlds as expanding. Maintaining such expansion into old age and being an interesting person was thought to ensure a positive aging experience.

Depressive Feelings and Appearance

The fear of being without a husband was strong, but the majority of the sample felt secure in their marriages. Although aware that many middle-age marriages dissolve, with men leaving their long-term wives for younger partners, 90 percent of the married participants excluded themselves from that risk. The need to maintain a youthful, sexy appearance to preserve or to improve their marriages was rarely expressed. In fact, the participants thought their husbands approved or did not notice their appearance, except for weight (a topic discussed further in the chapter by Ruth Jacobs). Their certainty about the security of their marriages was based either on the notion that the men were too moral to stray, that the men were so dependent on the wives for their daily comfort that they would not stray, or that there was a strong loving bond. Marriages would be threatened only if the wives behaved in ways that would discomfort their husbands—for example, by consistently not being available as needed.

The subgroup most lacking in depressive feelings was composed of the married women who stayed home and who had positive attitudes about aging and about their changing appearance. They were most secure with the men in their lives, even though the marriages were not all good; were glad not to have to continue being seen as a sex object by men other than husbands; and created for themselves a social world in which they seldom were rejected for any reason. Further, the married women were not overly conscious of their efforts to keep their husbands comfortable. Little awareness was expressed of the myriad ways in which their own options for personal expansion were limited, although the desirability of such expansion was declared.

Sustained contact with grown children was valued but not seen as central to daily life. For the older women with younger children at home, the children at times provided a reminder that the mothers looked older than other mothers; such reminders caused discomfort and led to heroic efforts to overcome aging appearance. Other women found that comments from adult children also could serve as a reminder of aging appearance and cause discomfort. What with one reminder or another, even the happily married women noticed with regret that they were looking older. Statements such as "I will no longer wear sleeveless dresses" or "I no longer care to have the lights on when we have sex" indicated awareness and discomfort. However, notably, fretting about changing appearance was not central to the content of worries about middle age and aging unless aging appearance was incongruent with life needs.

When external reality intruded, the sample found they were measurably unhappy with their appearance, even though their own appraisals might have been positive. Thus, the women who were working, who needed to find work or attract men, or whose children reminded them they were aging tended to hold more negative feelings about their changing appearance and show greater likelihood of overall dissatisfaction. However, the women who worked exhibited fewer depressive characteristics, indicating that work was important and that it countered other negative experiences in their daily lives, but work outside the home did not affect ratings of overall mood or overall life satisfaction. Work varied in degree of importance and was but one factor in the more-global measures of mood. For ever-married women, the commitment to wife and motherhood was primary in importance, as reflected in the work histories of the sampled women.

Important to positive mood and low depressive characteristics in all the participants were security with men and with work, when work was important. Further, the worriers among the sample were the least satisfied overall and had the highest degree of depressive feelings. Untested was the likelihood of some personality factor intervening here. To reiterate briefly, most worries focused on being alone through widowhood, no remarriage, physical disability, or the inability to find work. Thus, there was more perceived protection within the marriage against old age. The married women who felt secure were those least concerned about looking older and expressed the most positive attitudes about aging. They were not necessarily the women with the fewest depressive characteristics; depressive characteristics were somewhat mitigated by work outside the home. Last, it was possible for a woman to have expressed depressive characteristics and still state, on the whole, that her life and mood were completely satisfactory.

The participants were ambiguous in crediting various factors for their high level of mental health. Luck and their own efforts were both credited, with little clear distinction between what might be attributed to luck versus the outcome of their own efforts. Some of the women had been involved politically in community affairs, but none had been involved actively in the women's movement. Nevertheless, more than half spontaneously mentioned the women's movement as having opened new doors for them and for their daughters. They thought their ability to discuss openly things such as enjoying the freedom of children leaving and the opportunities for expansion outside the home was directly a result of the women's movement. They were cautious, however, in how far change should go because they did not want the institution of marriage, or their own marriages, threatened.

Discussion

The finding that, for many of the women, changing appearance was not problematic differs from the suggestion of many authors that change of appearance is likely to be traumatic for most women. There are several possible explanations. First, it is possible and even plausible, given the paucity of research on the subject, that the statements of writers on middle-aged women are only suppositions, based on commonsense reactions to known social stereotypes and conditions. Second, research findings on beauty and appearance with younger people as subjects possibly do not hold into the mid-years. Other factors like broadened life perspective may intervene to modify attitudes. Third, feelings about appearance may be so deep and behaviors so automatic that the women interviewed were possibly not aware of them. Experience in the women's movement points to many issues about which women were not consciously aware until they started talking with other women in consciousness-raising groups. The women studied reported not having given much prior thought about the content of the interview. Awareness of the extent to which their appearance guided their social interactions may have been minimal until some event brought the fact forcibly to their attention. Fourth, it is possible that the women, with a few exceptions, never saw themselves as particularly beautiful or successful stereotypical sex objects. Perhaps as they got older they were relieved to drop an unsuccessful role, found they had satisfactory lives, and that they could then better like themselves and the way they looked. Only three of the participants spontaneously remarked on their use of their earlier beauty as a social tool that had worn out.

The women studied, in their acceptance of the naturalness of the use of cosmetics, their acceptance of negative stereotypes of middle age in spite of their own positive self-appraisal, and their reliance on marriage even when they were dissatisfied with their husbands, reflected the internalized world view to which they were socialized early in their lives and the real world in which they live. Further, they did not question or re-evaluate that view of reality but attempted to maneuver their lives within it. Behaviors regarding their appearance, their families, and their lives outside the home were guided by their taken-for-granted social reality of which they were a part through their social structure. They constructed, as much as possible, their own smaller social worlds based on that same social reality.

Whenever possible, the women moved in social circles in which they were accepted, wrinkles and all. They tended to work where age and/or aging appearance did not matter (as long as they were neat and clean) or where looking older added credibility they might not have had as women, particularly if young. The women did exhibit a range of behaviors, but all fell within culturally acceptable limits. There are cultural idiosyncracies and variations within which people may make choices and still maintain a semblance of normalcy (Rose 1962). The women studied were aware of the range of acceptability—that is, they were embarrassed when they thought they might be approaching deviance such as by little or no use of makeup.

According to symbolic interactionist theory, people integrate but never forget what they have learned in their lives; early lessons might not be within conscious awareness (Rose 1962). Although earlier behaviors and attitudes might not be quite appropriate for the women's mid-years, women may persist in them or find changing problematic. However, habitualized patterns, although not forgotten, may be modified continuously as needs and the perceived environment change. The participants did change their habits, depending on their circumstances. For example, women who earlier had the feminine part of a dual carrier relaxed grooming behaviors when career development was not an issue. Because appearance changes gradually, patterns of response from others in the environment may also change gradually and imperceptibly over time. Women may not associate behaviors from others with changes in their own appearance or with their own social status because they are aging. Concurrently, if the people in their important environments are also aging, the environment may be more protective. People who see each other regularly do not notice gradual changes as acutely as they would after a period of absence.

For adults, the consequences of inner biological progression are likely to be social in nature and may be improved or harmed by the social situation of the individual (Riegel 1975; 1976). Women who found themselves in what they perceived to be kind, protective, and secure circumstances were more positive in their attitudes toward their changing appearance and toward aging than were women who had to face a reality that was punitive to older-looking women. The secure women were able to modify their behaviors to suit themselves, always within the bounds of acceptability, while others had to intensify their efforts to suit the preferred social stereotypes. The women put up a personal front and were concerned with impression management. The single women and those looking for work, or even contemplating seeking work, were more concerned about personal-front and front-stage behavior than the others.[7] They were aware (as were all the women) that stereotypes abound about middle-aged women; they shared the stereotypes but were unaware of their own internalization of the stereotypes. Thinking they did not have the negative characteristics associated with the stereotype, they tended to exclude themselves from the stigmatized category. Nevertheless, they and the women who did classify themselves as middle aged had to find ways in which to deal with the chance of being stigmatized. Some tried passing (for example, the woman who told only her closest associates her true age). Others learned new ways of being, to prevent dependency on the attractiveness of youth (for example, learning new skills) and others behaved in ways that would not threaten the worlds in which they were not stigmatized (for example, limiting their activities in order to maintain their marriages or staying in jobs for which they were underqualified to avoid the threat of job hunting). Additionally, they were intent on associating with others like them.[8] The women studied expressed a strong need for contact with other middle-aged women, particularly in circumstances similar to their own.

Conclusions and Speculations

Controlling the environment as much as possible to prevent exposure to direct social rejection was characteristic of the traditional housewives. The management of day-to-day life for most people includes vast numbers of maneuvers, symbols, and interactions that can be engaged in automatically. For comfortable daily living, the meanings of symbols must be shared and the outcome of interactions predictable (Blumer 1962; 1969). Placing oneself in a situation with new, unknown symbolic systems may be risky, especially if stigmatization is also a risk. Such environmental control did not succeed for women who worked outside the home, had young children at home, or needed to find work or attract men. Insulating their social lives was difficult. For them, more reminders of their age were experienced in social interactions, and more negative attitudes about aging and aging appearance were revealed. Although it is methodologically problematic to say that a causal relationship exists, the data of this research strongly suggested that in a supportive environment women did not particularly dwell on their changing appearance or on aging. Further, those women who were not as secure in their environments tended to show more depressive characteristics and lower overall mood, suggesting that the stigmatization may lead to mental discomfort. Many of the women considered themselves to be more attractive in their mid-years than they had been earlier, although they were aware that the so-called generalized other did not so perceive them. The differences in their own perceptions and the social system put them into an asynchronous position, perhaps not to the point of being experienced as a crisis but enough to cause discomfort. Social institutions serve as a framework for the socialization and actions of individuals who act toward situations dependent on their own perceptions (or on the meanings) of the situation to the actors. Further, symbolic interactions find that people are not necessarily consistent in their perceptions, which are based on accumulated past experience as well as present circumstances (Blumer 1962; 1969). All were aware of few supports in the work world and that the world of singles was not supportive for middle-aged women. Some thought that their earlier lives had not prepared them for middle-aged life today. However, they varied in their perceptions of social messages received, of acts toward them, depending on the interaction of individual situations and the commonly held socialization to marriage and motherhood. For instance, a woman with attractive daughters found it natural that men gawked at her daughters rather than at her and did not experience the attention given them as rejection of herself. Her experience was that it was normal that mothers and middle-aged women would not be admired when young, attractive women were present.

To varying degrees, all the women found they had grown in characteristics they found desirable since being over 40. The cause for such growth was not apparent from this study and did not appear to be related to any particular crisis, freedom from crisis, or to any particular environment or life-style (both married and unmarried, working and nonworking women experienced growth). It may be that as women reach the mid-years they are aware of aging and of the need to find a new place in the social structure. They inevitably look older, whether more or less as compared with others their age. Perceptibly for some, and less perceptibly for others, they all adjusted their lives and outlook around getting older. The married women found relief in not being viewed socially as sex objects and pleasure in having nonsexually laden friendships with men. It may be that as women move from being sex objects, and as they overcome various life problems, they find more internal credibility. Even the women who were not entirely confident reported more confidence than previously and anticipated further growth.

Further, it seems that if a woman is depressed, or suffering from other psychologically based symptoms, it may be needless to look for early life deficiencies to explain or change difficulties that arise in the mid-years.[9] This is not an argument that there are no historical, personality, value, or habituated behavioral response patterns or other differences in people that influence how they deal with life's exigencies. Patterns of response always may have been dysfunctional for the person, but other patterns may have been functional earlier and dysfunctional as the external and internal worlds of the woman change. Overwhelmingly, however, crises that occur in middle age may reflect discord between the need of the individual and the demands or provisions of the social environment. While taking into account limitations in the generalizability of the results of this study because of sampling and methodological faults, the data suggest the following:

1. Habituated behavior patterns and early socialization to values and attitudes may prove dysfunctional for middle-aged women. The patterns are likely to fit the feminine stereotype—that is, to be traditionally feminine in appearance and behavior, a potential sex object. Public stress on youth as more acceptable than middle age for women reinforces thinking that is incongruent with the needs of middle-aged women. If one views the major life task of women as that of being feminine, then one may view changes that look as though a woman is becoming less feminine as a disorder in identity (that is, spending as little time as possible on appearance), a search for identity that should have taken place in childhood or adolescence,[10] or the fruition of the masculine side of the personality.

On the other side of that coin, women who are imbued with their own appearance, spending inordinate amounts of time or effort (for example, the woman who had mammoplasty to try to save her marriage, unsuccessfully), may be seen as infantile or narcissistic.[11] Such women may have learned only too well how women are supposed to be in order to succeed. They may be conforming to social stereotypes to a high degree and trying to bring their own self-image into line with their view of the stereotypes. The behaviors may have worked in their younger years but may have become obsolete in middle age.

2. The middle-aged woman may need help in an educational process that involves not only learning new ways of thinking about herself and her behavior but also of understanding that social reinforcements for new behaviors may not be forthcoming. Should she go too far in changing her traditionally feminine ways (for example, by not providing a comfortable home for her husband), she may endanger her place in her social structure. The possibility of that happening (the women studied were aware of that danger) must be seen as real and rooted in social reality rather than as neurotic fear rooted in historical family trauma.

3. The woman who has discarded old patterns of thought and behavior may experience difficulty with others in her environment as a result. If her new ways are not supported or are negated, she may feel uncertain and deviant (for instance, the women who used little or no cosmetics felt different, although they were not interested in using cosmetics).

4. Middle-aged women may cling to marriages that are less than satisfactory or even destructive to the woman's well-being. We have seen that middle-aged women, on the whole, prefer to be married, finding security and a known way of being in marriage. They know that should they become single a new man would be hard to find. Additionally, they would suffer financially. They are aware they would need to find a new way of being in the world, for which they have had little preparation. Their appearance—a former asset—is now a handicap. Such women, especially if less articulate or aware, are subject to being labeled passive-aggressive and/or masochistic. Rather than treatment for a personality disorder, they may need help in developing conscious understanding of their dilemma. Then, and then only, can they actively choose the least costly, or most beneficial, personal action.[12]

5. Concepts of self-actualization may have little meaning for middle-aged women. The women in the study sample were fortunate in being relatively financially secure, healthy, and well educated. All reported some degree of personal growth but were severely limited in the scope of their lives. They were bound by maintaining their own social structure, by the limits of what they perceived as correct female behaviors and attitudes, and by their justified fear of rocking the boat enough to tip it over. The basic

social conditions to increase true self-actualization for middle-aged women may not exist today. Can the woman who must first consider the needs of her husband, or face life alone and poor, work toward self-actualization? Can the woman who likes her face only when it is covered with makeup (or her body only when youthfully slim, firm, and voluptuous) move toward self-actualization? Can any woman move toward self-actualization in a society that acclaims the stereotypical beauty to which only a few may truly aspire?

6. A host of questions and issues is raised for further research. Included would be replication with a random sample, with women from other cultures and races who may be otherwise disadvantaged than the sample, and with efforts to disentangle the cohort effects from the effects of being middle aged. A longitudinal study in which women would examine their attitudes and behaviors as they happen rather than retrospectively would provide harder, more-rigorous data. And what of women who have adopted nontraditional life-styles, like lesbians? What are their experiences in the mid-years?

What then, of upcoming generations of middle-aged women? Are they likely to find their destiny less determined by the biological aging of faces and bodies? If prediction is considered to be just an educated guess, I dare to predict. My own guess is that unless drastic change occurs in women's position in society, they will face the same hazards as women today. The real issues are related to power and social stratification and are not new.

Today, countervailing forces are at play: those that were created by the women's movement through which women's participation in the public world is slowly expanding and those that reflect a reactionary push to keep women in traditional roles (as exemplified by the fight against the Equal Rights Amendment and cosmetic toys for three- and four-year-old girls). College students, both men and women, have a hard time understanding the difference between femininity as expressed by grooming, mannerisms, and clothing and being a woman. Not wearing makeup, high heels, having doors opened (all the old clichés) seem to them to be giving up being female, although they also want a chance at a career and equal pay.

Additionally, I see little evidence that we are, as a society, empowering elderly women more than we have in the recent past. In the private sphere, it is still rare for men to choose women older than themselves as sexual partners for more than a fling or as wives. Perhaps, just perhaps, women who are young today will enter the mid-years with different expectations of life. Perhaps they will not have looked for wifedom to be the center of their lives until death do them part. Perhaps—and this is said with a wish—they will not find it necessary to limit their lives around the needs of others out of fear that unless they do, they will be social discards. The unanswerable question is whether or not sufficient social and political change will have taken place so that the socio-politico-economic environment will support middle-aged and older women as valuable and therefore as attractive personally and physically.

Notes

1. U.S. Bureau of the Census, *Statistical Abstract of the United States* (Washington, D.C.: U.S. Department of Commerce 1980), p. 32.

2. "Today," *Oakland Tribune,* October 15, 1981; p. C-3.

3. *California State Statistical Abstract* (Sacramento: State of California, 1975).

4. All names and quotations about the participants have been changed in the interest of maintaining confidentiality.

5. Many middle-aged female writers, in writing personalized accounts and advice books, include comments about their reactions to their loss of youthful attractiveness and advice on how to improve the ravages of age. Also, see Bell (1970) and Weg (1977).

6. This is not a new conflict. Frances Perkins, the secretary of labor appointed by Franklin D. Roosevelt, was acutely aware of the importance of appearance. She dressed in a "kind of uniform; a simple black dress with a bow of white at the throat and almost invariably she wore a small dark tricorner hat, which she often kept on all day" [George Martin, *Madam Secretary Frances Perkins* (Boston: Houghton Mifflin, 1976), p. 146]. About other women she is quoted as saying, "I sort of sympathized with them. Many good and intelligent women do dress in ways that are very attractive and pretty, but don't particularly invite confidence in their common sense, integrity or sense of justice" (p. 147).

7. Front-stage behavior is guided by the person's desire to put on a front, to act the part she is expected to play, and may be quite different from back-stage behavior, for which the person may be more relaxed. See Goffman (1959) for full discussion.

8. For full discussion on stigma and how people who are stigmatized manage, see Goffman (1963).

9. Note that this discussion does not apply to severe chronic clinical conditions.

10. See, for instance, Lowenthal et al. (1975), who credited "identity confusion" of middle-aged women with unresolved earlier issues. M. Notman (1980) pointed out that the issues confronted in adolescence and mid-life are different and that mid-life changes should not be viewed in terms appropriate to adolescence.

11. For example, C.H. Mann (1980) suggested that "physiological signs of aging are experienced as narcissistic injury by both men and women,

although the psychological impact of this injury varies from individual to individual. It is furthermore important to note that women experience the physical aspects of aging primarily as a threat to their attractiveness to men; . . . '' (p. 131). The implication is that change of appearance is ipso facto to injury.

12. Beck and Greenberg (1974), for example, stated, "But women, both as a group and as individuals, will go nowhere unless a critical decision is reached—that is, despite socialization and precedent, to accept responsibility for their lives, goals, families, careers, and psychological symptoms without falling back on the easy excuses of masculine preference, social appearances, difficult times and circumstances'' (p. 129).

References

Adams, Gerald R. "Physical Attractiveness Research: Toward a Developmental Social Psychology of Beauty." *Human Development* 20 (1977): 217–239.

Barnett, Rosalind C., and Grace K. Baruch. "Women in the Middle Years: A Critique of Research and Theory." *Psychology of Women Quarterly* 3 (1978):187–198.

Beck, A.T., and R.L. Greenberg, "Cognitive Therapy with Depressed Women." In *Women in Therapy,* edited by V. Franks and V. Burtle. New York: Mazel Publishers, 1974, pp. 113–131.

Bell, Inge Powell. "The Double Standard." *Transaction* 8 (1970):75–80.

Berscheid, Ellen. "Physical Attractiveness." In *Advances in Experimental Social Psychology,* vol. 6, edited by L. Berkowitz. New York: Academic Press, 1974.

Berscheid, Ellen, and Ellen Walster. "Beauty and the Beast." *Psychology Today,* June 1972, pp. 20–26.

Blumer, Herbert. "Symbolic Interaction," In *Human Behavior and Social Process,* edited by A. Rose. Boston: Houghton-Mifflin, 1962.

———. *Symbolic Interactionism: Perspective and Method.* Englewood Cliffs, N.J.: Prentice-Hall, 1969.

Cahn, Ann Foote, ed. *Women in Midlife-Security and Fulfillment: A Compendium of Papers,* Comm. pub. no. 95–170. Washington, D.C.: U.S. Government Printing Office, 1978.

deBeauvoir, Simone. *The Second Sex.* New York: Bantam Books, 1949.

Goffman, Erving. *The Presentation of Self in Everyday Life.* Garden City, N.Y.: Doubleday and Co., 1959.

———. *Stigma: Notes on the Management of Spoiled Identity.* Englewood Cliffs, N.J.: Prentice-Hall, 1963.

Lowenthal, M.F., et al. *Four Stages of Life: A Comprehensive Study of*

Women and Men Facing Transition. Monterey, Calif.: Jossey-Bass, 1975.

Mann, C.H. "Mid-Life in the Family: Strains, Challenges and Options." In *Mid-Life Development and Clinical Issues,* edited by W.H. Norman and T.J. Scaramella. New York: Brunner/Mazel Publishers, 1980, pp. 128–148.

Neugarten, Bernice. "The Awareness of Middle Age." In *Middle Age and Aging,* edited by Neugarten. Chicago: University of Chicago Press, 1968.

———. "The Middle Years." *American Handbook of Psychiatry* 1 (1974): 592 601.

Notman, M. "Changing Roles for Women at Mid-Life." In *Mid-Life Developmental and Clinical Issues,* edited by W.H. Norman and T.J. Scaramella. New York: Brunner/Mazel Publishers, 1980, pp. 85–109.

Riegel, Klaus F. "Toward a Dialectic Theory of Development." *Human Development* 18 (1975):50–64.

———. "The Dialectics of Human Development." *American Psychologist* 31 (1976):689–700.

Rose, Arnold. "A Systematic Summary of Symbolic Interaction Theory." In *Human Behavior and Social Processes,* edited by Rose. Boston: Houghton-Mifflin, 1962.

Srole, Leonard, and Arlene K. Fisher. "The Midtown Manhattan Study: Longitudinal Focus on Aging, Gender and Life Transitions." Paper presented at the Gerontological Society Symposium, Dallas, 18 November 1978.

Ward, Russell A. "The Impact of Subjective Age and Stigma on Older Persons." *Journal of Gerontology* 32 (1977):227–232.

Weg, Ruth. "More than Wrinkles." In *Looking Ahead: A Woman's Guide to the Problems and Joys of Growing Older,* edited by L. Troll, J. Israel, and K. Israel. Englewood Cliffs, N.J.: Prentice-Hall, 1977.

Weissman, Myrna, and Gerald Klerman. "Sex Differences and the Epidemiology of Depression." *Archives of General Psychiatry* 34 (1977): 98–111.

2

The Crossroads of Menopause: A Chance and a Risk for the Aging Process of Women

Maryvonne Gognalons-Nicolet

Inseparable both from the sociohistorical context in which it occurs and the individual personality, menopause cannot be viewed merely as a physiological event. In fact, the various developmental changes that occur throughout adulthood are not necessarily linked to bodily changes; rather, they are related to personal- and social-life course events that take place (such as marriage, work, having children, departure of the last child from home, and so on) and their repercussion on each woman's personality and sense of self. Women are particularly vulnerable to crisis at menopause because of the cultural value attached to fertility and motherhood. In the Judeo-Christian tradition, a woman's worth is built upon male values and superimposed upon her; once menopausal, she no longer represents fecundity and is thus obsolete.

Given the cessation of potential motherhood that marks menopause, to what extent do personal and social events contribute to or restrain the development of a woman's personality, the quality of the adaptation to her social milieu, and the diversification of her social activities? For the purpose of this chapter, menopause is evaluated within the chronological period in which it is most likely to occur in the female life cycle (between 45 and 55 years of age) to provide the age frame for key social and personal events within which the processes of female aging will be set.

What are the most significant personal and social resources at a woman's disposal to guide her actions during menopause? How is she prepared for this event, both from a personal and a social point of view? For many women, motherhood may be an all-determining event in their life cycles, and in a parallel direction, its implacable end may appear as a critical period during which women's trajectory of aging will be determined whether on a conscious or unconscious level. Menopause is thus both a risk and a chance for women since they can neither delay nor avoid this biophysiological change. Unlike men who can postpone confrontation with

---

Translated by Elizabeth W. Markson.

their aging bodies by temporal denials (like late fatherhood), women are dealt a relatively swift and nonnegotiable biological ultimatum.[1] Inscribed on her body as the end of menstrual behavior and monthly bodily habits, as the end of concerns related to fertility and contraception, control of reproduction or fatalism, menopause marks the inevitable break with a certain intimacy with one's own physiological functions and forces each woman to search for a new equilibrium with her body and with her self. The cessation of menses thus represents changes in hygiene, in preparation for sexual intercourse, and in monitoring one's physiological, psychological, and social responses to the menstrual cycle.

The severity of the risks incurred by an individual woman at this period of her life will depend, I am proposing, upon the available social choices that allow her to review her behavior, her life history, and her social potential for action—that is, her material, cultural, and relational possibilities available to reinvest in new social roles. Paradoxically, although menopause is a phenomenon as old as humanity, it is mainly within herself that a woman will have to find sufficient resources to mobilize to reorient her personality and change her role repertoire, for society offers very few culturally valued patterns for elders in general, and for older women in particular, who at that time of their lives have to face two inequalities: one of age and one of sex.

Variability of Family and Professional Models

From the recent work of French scholars such as Aries (1973), Flandrin (1976), and Donzelot (1977), questions emerge concerning those sociohistorical factors that determine female choices regarding work, marriage, and maternity at the end of adolescence. Choice, as defined by Bourbieux (1980a; 1980b), is a conscious or unconscious internalized strategy and is shaped by the intertwining of social class and generation. The choices, or illusion of choices, available to women throughout their lives are influenced heavily by both their sociocultural context and the individual woman's position in the status hierarchy.

Within the past century, patterns of production and reproduction have been transformed in a capitalist industrial society so that new divisions of labor, linked closely to gender, have emerged. As part of this process, women's roles were also redefined: No longer were women expected to be involved primarily in economic production as well as childbearing production. Their major roles were confined to the sphere of reproduction, and their major status and sources for personal gratification were derived therefrom. Yet it is far from clear that the maternal pattern, limiting women to childbearing and childrearing only has been the prevalent pattern in all social classes or all societies; the view that biology is destiny and that destiny is motherhood is currently being challenged (Newland 1979; Ehrenreich and English 1978). Women are now discovering their history as unbounded by the conventionally accepted history recorded by men but rather as an independent product of their feminine images (that is, mothers, grandmothers, and the past experiences of all other women in their own personal pasts, interconnected with the values and norms of the socioeconomic contexts of the slice of history in which they lived, loved, worked, bore children, and died). Thus, it is no longer possible for social scientists to assert that all women, as soon as they become young adults, invest the totality of their identities in their maternal role within conjugal life or that those who fail to do so are in some way pathological.

I have stressed the relevance of the sociohistorical context—that one is both a product of one's culture, a member of a specific social class, and of a generation and era—to illustrate the point that the end of fertility will be experienced in different ways depending upon the importance that motherhood has had in women's lives in comparison to all other modes of social participation (for example, worker, militant, professional). Although conventional views of women have seen the wife-mother role as the way in which both female status and gratification are derived, many women indeed play other, concurrent roles. It would be sociological duplicity to view menopause only within the context of motherhood, a duplicity joining the masculine discourse in which the appropriate role of women is emphasized as derived from her procreative function.

To the centrality of childbearing and childrearing in women's lives must be added the temporal limits of these roles, variations in women's ages as they bear their last child and as the last child leaves home (see chapter 11), and significant periods of accumulated pleasures or regrets of different emotionally valued experiences throughout the life cycle.

Women's Perspectives on Menopause

Given the impact of one's sociohistorical context and unique life events upon reaction to the menopause, it is hardly surprising that women view it in different ways. As the work of Neugarten and her associates (1968) has shown, opinions are divided: About half think it is an unpleasant experience. Three-quarters of these women believe that menopause does not really change women's behavior. In contrast, those who are affected by menopause are women with too much free time, who have nothing to do with this free time, or who anticipate age-related health problems before they occur (Neugarten et al. 1968). When women who have not yet experienced menopause were asked what could be the worst thing that could happen to them,

more than half of them answer "to lose my husband," while only 4 percent
mention menopause as a distressing foreseen event. Among the women who
have entered menopause, about half indicate that not to have to worry
about one's menstruation is a good thing while the other half state that
menopause has adverse effects. The meaning and the importance of menopause thus differs according to the family and occupational text in which
any given woman moves (Neugarten 1968).

A description of personal and social difficulties women commonly face
at menopause enables us to define the specificity of the social and relational
context of this unique social period.

Family and Relational Difficulties in the Fourth
and Fifth Decades

The family unit that is set up at the time of the first maturity (between 20 to
40 years old) markedly changes at the time of the second maturity (between
40 to 60 years old), essentially due to the effects of aging. Although
originally socially established and valued for reproduction and the bringing
up and education of children, the family drastically changes as its members
age; this is particularly marked for those women who had forsaken any
occupation or profession, whether temporarily or permanently. When the
last child leaves the parental home, the syndrome of the empty nest most
commonly affects those women who devoted themselves to home and
children.

At the same time the risks of losing one's own father or mother through
death increase, the risks of widowhood also increase due to the lesser life
expectancy of men. Also during this period, those women who are still married may find that their husbands are increasingly preoccupied with their
own careers or with health and concerns about potency—what has been
popularly described in the United States as the male mid-life crisis. Faced
with the prospect or reality of diminished social supports in the menopausal
years, women must reorganize their family lives in the light of threatened or
actual losses of both parent(s) and spouse.

The ways in which such reorganization will occur depend upon a series
of factors: one's ability to change relationships with her children; position
in the familial network and relationships with son-in-law, daughter-in-law,
grandchildren; distance from other relatives; and living situation (alone,
with spouse, or with one of her children). As Roussel's (1976) and Pitrou's
(1976) recent works have emphasized, it seems that in France as women
grow older, their emotional needs for their family increase rather than
decrease. This is especially true among women of lower socioeconomic
status and limited education. As a matter of fact, the more unfavorable are

life conditions and the weaker are material, cultural, and occupational modes of access toward other avenues of action, the more intensive is the flight back into the family. In effect, for a number of women in mid-life, the family represents a tenuous if ambiguous refuge from apparently sudden rolelessness. This flight back into the family may be characterized by adopting a maternal surrogate role. For example, in France, half of the children under one year old and with a mother in the labor force are cared for by their grandmother or other family member at home (INED 1975); this is especially the case when the mother of the young child has a low-status or poorly paid job, as may be seen in table 2–1.

Intensification of family relationships during and after menopause is wished by some women and suffered by some others. It is influenced by other systems of belonging within neighborhood, occupational, political, religious, trade-union, and community spheres.

These systems vary according to the environment. For example, urban and rural settings provide different opportunities for social involvement, and in either locale socioeconomic position increases or restricts participation in formal and informal groups. Thus, the options for postmenopausal women are a result of the roles actually available to them as well as of predisposing aspects of their previous life patterns. Just as it is difficult for a leopard to change its spots, it is problematic for a woman whose major identification has been motherhood to assume new identities with ease. If none or very few other social investments have been made prior to mid-life, the risks of seeing the familial-relation system break down upon loss of one's husband through disinterest, divorce, or death, the departure of the last child, or other increases in family stresses are important. For such women, menopause is likely to be comprised of cumulative negative events, aggravating other crises in mid-life and playing a decisive role that will influence the ways in which they age.

Professional and Economic Difficulties

At a time when the employment market in France and elsewhere offers little flexibility to older workers, women's occupational difficulties are also increasing. Women in the labor force are disadvantaged from the time of their entry because they are more likely to be trained—or hired—for low-paying, sex-segregated jobs where the opportunities to increase one's qualifications or to be promoted to more-lucrative and higher-status positions are limited. An examination of recent official French statistics on unemployment (INSEE 1979) illustrates the difficulties women face throughout their occupational lives. While young women (ages 17 to 24) are more likely to be unemployed than women between 40 and 60 years of age,

Table 2–1

Percentage Distribution of Provider of Child Care for Infants (under One Year), by Occupation of Mother, in France, 1975

			Occupational Category				
Child-Care Provider	Agricultural	Industry, Business, Artisan	High-Level Professional	Middle-Level Professional	White-Collar Worker	Manual Worker	All Categories
Mother of working mother	79	56.1	4.8	4.2	3.2	15.7	15.6
Other family member	18	17.1	14.2	32	37.9	41.5	33.4
Out-of-home baby-sitter	—	9.8	38.1	44.4	44.9	30	36
In-home baby-sitter	—	12.2	30.2	6.8	2.2	0.1	5.2
Day-care center	1.8	2.4	7.9	8.4	9.2	6	7.3
Other	1.2	2.4	4.8	4.2	2.6	6.7	2.5
Total, all	100	100	100	100	100	100	100

Source: INED, *Enquete INED aupres des meres ayant un enfant de moins d'un an* (Paris, May-June 1975).

older women are more likely to be unemployed for longer periods of time. Futhermore, labor-force data indicate that mid-life women are more likely to be unemployed than men in the same age group. In part, this is due to the syndrome of the displaced homemaker—that is, women who have withdrawn from paid employment in order to raise children find their housewife skills difficult to translate and market to employers. In essence, they are disqualified professionally by their long tenure as homemakers and mothers. If the mid-life woman does succeed in re-entering the labor force, she is more likely to have a low-paying job and is at a higher risk of being laid off than a male worker; quite often she may be unable to find a job at all. Thus are the gender-based disparities in occupational opportunities exacerbated by age for women. A similar pattern has been observed in the United States. Recent data indicate that the average unemployed American women over 55 remains jobless for about nineteen weeks, almost twice the average of younger women (Gabe 1981). The number of discouraged older female workers who retire after months of fruitless job searches is, however, almost entirely overlooked by unemployment statistics.

Few Valued Models during Menopause

The life cycle of the individual is punctuated by different systems of social expectations, each of which is determined by culturally valued social patterns. At the present, to be a fiftyish woman offers few attractions. Most women are deprived of their role as mother and nurturer (so strongly valued during youth) and also of much of their sexual charm. The role of grandmother, when it coincides with reality, may very well appear a bit premature or unattractive. In France, at any rate, publicity mainly fosters the images of a traditional rural housewife as grandmother, an image that fits relatively few contemporary women in their forties and fifties. Political, trade-union, or religious commitments remain rarely mentioned as legitimate mid-life attachments, even though the last few decades have increased their visibility for women. As a worker, the woman's occupational career often has been jeopardized and broken. If she is a widow, divorcee, or a woman bringing up her children by herself, she profits from very few supportive opinions or help from her social milieu. It is in this unfavorable, insecure social atmosphere that women must face the turning point of menopause.

Menopause: A Critical Period for the Self

Menopause thus is a critical period during which, more than at any other period of the feminine life cycle, the turning point where the future course of her life will be determined. A biophysiological transformation of the body and a death knell to motherhood, menopause is a period when the chances to become a mother are lost forever. Of course, one's stake in lost fertility will depend heavily upon the personal and social history of any given woman; those who have achieved their desired maternal career or who have forgone being a mother by conscious choice will be less affected facing this eventuality. However, what of all those women who, in conformity to prevailing social norms, will have invested all of their social or psychological resources in maternity and, conversely, those who have denied or concealed the advent of the menopause for whatever reason?

It is not by accident that psychiatric troubles associated with the aging process increase in mid-life. Table 2–2 shows that women 45 to 54 years begin to be represented disproportionately among psychiatric-hospital patients as compared to the general French population, a pattern that continues throughout the remainder of their lives. While rates of psychiatric hospitalization also increase for men in mid-life, my primary concern here is with menopause as a strategic crossroads for aging in women's lives. For both sexes, albeit for different reasons, mid-life is a period, if unsuccessfully negotiated, that affects later life adaptation.

Mental troubles often come with physical troubles. In France, women at greatest risk for either physical or mental illness in mid-life are, contrary to general opinion, primarily married. Single, widowed, or divorced women are able to protect themselves and adapt earlier to feelings of isolation and loneliness than married women of the same social status. They settled in occupations younger and have invested in more-autonomous, varied ways of life than married women whose children are grown up and have left home, who are all at sea, anxious about their free but empty time. Often bereft of meaningful activities outside their family circle, a majority of those who had relied upon their family for a source of identity and self-realization find themselves questioning their very way of life, a real existential crisis in which they face the passage of time and a life plan that has worn thin and that provides very few social or personal options.

Concentration upon one's own body and its most minute sensations increases for those women who see it as a refuge or an escape from a difficult painful present that is often void of meaningful activities. Excess bodily preoccupation, whether physical or mental, illustrates a retreat within oneself in which one's ability to communicate meaningfully with others is blocked. At this point, a woman may turn to her physician, and her relationship with him (or, less often, her) will become salient in her life.

Often unable to meet a new sexual partner due both to the differential mortality rates that make older men scarce and social norms that make finding a younger man taboo, often unable to find a new or more-gratifying occupation outside the home, and seldom prepared to forge new family

Table 2-2
Percentage Distribution of Female Psychiatric Patients in Mental Hospitals and the Female General Population, by Age Group and Sex, in France, 1974-1975

Age Group	Female Psychiatric Patients	Female General Population
15 to 24	7.3	20.1
25 to 34	9.5	16.8
35 to 44	13.4	15.2
45 to 54	18.4	15.9
55 to 64	14.3	11.1
65 to 74	19.6	12.1
75 to 84	15.4	7
85 and over	4.1	1.8
Total	100	100

Source: INSERM, *Statistiques médicales des etablissements psychiatriques,* (Paris: INSERM, 1976). Data for psychiatric patients are as of 31 December 1974 and for the general population as of 1 January 1975.

relationships with her children and grandchildren, a woman may turn to her physician to find solace. Bodily preoccupation fosters this search for medical attention, someone to listen to one's complaints. This, however, is no panacea because how can a woman describe the daily, painful, and sometimes amorphous experiences she has? What is there to narrate as a medical history about her physical, psychological, and social changes during this critical period? How can she be listened to during this critical period except by placing emphasis on physiological changes or problems that are really echoes of other complaints, perhaps a series of wounds deeply hidden from others—and perhaps herself—throughout her life? Only by presenting physical symptoms can she attract attention.

In this respect, medicalization of sexuality during the life cycle becomes more pronounced during menopause through a reinforcement of the somatic basis of one's troubles. In France, preference of the public toward general practioners and internal-medicine specialists is often found with such women so that family doctors and internists rather than gynecologists or psychiatrists often hear this register of complaints. Does their education and the structure of their medical practice prepare them to provide the kind of sympathetic counsel, rather than medical treatment or tranquilizing drugs, that the adrift woman may require at menopause?

The term *disguised depression,* often used by clinicians, clearly indicates this state of sadness and generalized apathy in which physical symptoms take an almost reassuring role compared to the narcissistic wound felt by the mid-life woman caught in existential crisis. Balier (1976) has described the symptoms of disguised depression as follows: a feeling of emptiness, suffering—whether expressed or not—from feelings of loneliness, anxiety concerning the future, incidence of physical illness, loss of self-esteem, and somatic complaints usually expressed by problems in sleeping or digestion and feelings of generalized tiredness. However, most of the time, these symptoms are regarded as commonplace and normal during this period of life and are placed in the background. Thus, instead of recognizing disguised depression, physical symptoms are stressed both by the woman and her physician. Menopause is, however, far more than a cessation of menses with variable physical symptoms. It is an active period of confronting one's own death with an accompanying resurgence of old fears, accumulated regrets and remorses; it is a feeling of fleeting time and of awareness that one is closer to death than to birth. The absence of substitute activities accentuates this process of questioning one's identity.

Menopause is thus both a risk and a chance for women's aging because it is upon this confrontation to death, starting with loss of reproductive capacity and feelings of destruction of part of one's body, that the stakes one will have to play in old age depend. Menopause is an unsettling event because of the disequilibrium it presents to one's self-image and to one's roles. Faced with this change in balance, women may feel threatened by emotional breakdown. Menopause presents an opportunity for introspection and for self-reflection upon one's past and one's probable future. As part of this introspective process, old attachments and motives may be reviewed and assessed and all those little deaths resulting from losses of earlier attachments faced. How will each woman redefine or discover her sense of self after so many changes in her previous way of life? What physical and mental integrity will she preserve to rebuild a self that is one and complete despite the loss of previous attachments?

Conclusion

It is obvious that all women do not experience the event of menopause in the same way and that, as I have noted, women's reactions will depend greatly upon the resources of their social environment and abilities for action, on activities (familial, marital, professional, community, activist, and so forth), or on every other field of action where they find personal gratification from active engagement. It is also obvious that the impact of menopause will depend closely upon the importance given to the maternal function as compared to other social undertakings and upon the future of this function in the relationships with children and grandchildren.

Some women will make these transitions easily because they will have been able to extend and transform their earlier patterns of family or conjugal activities. Others, prepared by early adaptation to loneliness, will feel relieved of menstrual constraints or, on the contrary, will question all their way of life on this occasion. This critical period upsets a certain intimacy of the body in a necessary change in the biologic life cycle; whether or not one accepts or rejects the occurrence of menopause at a conscious or unconscious level, it is an inevitable change. Menopause is thus a double-edged sword, one side of which is risk, the other chance. The risk of menopause stems from the burden that this biophysiologic event may impose upon an already constricting social world. No woman can postpone the deadline menopause places upon her body. Menopause thus forces one to redefine what she will make of the remainder of her life. Herein lies the chance for women: It is a chance that is both a gamble and an opportunity. When I have interviewed older French women, I have been impressed with the insistence with which the majority described menopause as a critical period and of the vital struggle it created for them—and often, alas, to observe their depression.

At the same time, the increased longevity of women emphasizes that menopause often represents a new start. More resistant, better prepared for old age despite lesser opportunities for social participation throughout her life, the woman who has negotiated menopause successfully has skills and energy that may be channeled in new directions. Unfortunately, our kind of society provides few opportunities for her to exercise these skills. That older women have had relatively few options open to them emphasizes the importance of studying the mid-life and older women. By calling attention to older women, a series of useful research questions, illuminating studies of the life course of both sexes, may be formulated.

Note

1. See, in particular, B. Neugarten and D. Gutmann (1968), who discuss the difficulties in evaluating the masculine process of aging inasmuch as men are less tied to precise chronological events.

References

Aries, Phillipe. *L'Enfant et la vie familiale sous l'ancien regime,* 2d ed. Paris: Le Seuil, 1973.

Balier, Claude, "Troubles névrotiques de la sénescence." EMC psychiatric clinique et therapeutique 11(1976).

Bourbieux, P. *Le sens pratique.* Paris: Ed. de Minuit, 1980a.

————. *Questions de sociologie.* Paris: Ed. de Minuit, 1980b.

Donzelot, J. *La police des familles.* Paris: Ed. de Minuit, 1977.

Ehrenreich, Barbara, and Deirdre English, *For Her Own Good.* New York: Anchor Books, 1978.

Flandrin, J.L. *Familles, parenté, maison, sexualité dans l'ancienne societé.* Paris: Hachette, 1976.

Gabe, Tom. *Social Characteristics and Economic Status of the U.S. Aged Population.* Congressional Research Service Report N81-32. Washington: CRS, January 27, 1981.

INED, *Enquete INED aupres des mères ayant un enfant de moins d'un an.* Paris, 1976.

INSEE. *Données sociales, 1978.* Paris: Ministère de Travail, 1979.

Newland, K. *The Sisterhood of Man.* New York: W.W. Norton, 1979.

Neugarten, Bernice (ed.) *Middle Age and Aging.* Chicago: University of Chicago Press, 1968.

Neugarten, Bernice, Vivian Wood, Ruth Kraines, and Barbara Loomis. "Women's attitudes toward the menopause." In *Middle Age and Aging,* edited by Neugarten, pp. 195–200. Chicago: University of Chicago Press, 1968.

Neugarten, Bernice, and David Gutmann. "Age-sex roles and personality in Middle Age: A Thematic Apperception Study." In *Middle Age and Aging,* edited by Neugarten, pp. 58–71. Chicago: University of Chicago Press, 1968.

Pitrou, A. *Relations entre genérations et insertion social.* Paris: Centre National de Recherche Scientifique, 1976.

Roussel, L. "La famille après le mariage des enfants." *Travaux et documents, INED PUF,* no. 78, 1976.

3

Out of the *Mikvah,* into the Sauna: A Study of Women's Health Clubs

Ruth Harriet Jacobs

Just before marriage and after menstruation, orthodox Jewish women were expected to cleanse themselves thoroughly at a community ritual bath called a *mikvah.* The custom still exists though it has declined markedly, especially in the United States where Jewish orthodoxy has been outstripped by less-ritualistic forms of Judaism.

Although men could and did use the mikvah at the Jewish New Year, women all year predominated, and their use of the mikvah was tied to their sexuality. Though the manifest purpose of the mikvah was to purify the women before sexual relations, the latent functions included socialization, social control, and reinforcement of the centrality of gender in regulating and constraining a woman's activities and status.

Today, new houses of women exist in the multiplying women's health clubs utilized by American women of many religions and no religion. These health clubs, as is explained, have the same latent functions of the mikvah and some additional functions reflecting inadequacies in U.S. social institutions.

Before the early 1970s, health clubs were almost exclusively the milieu of men, being part of athletic clubs, male college clubs for graduates, YMCAs, and so forth. In the mid-1970s, a widespread change occurred and has been escalating since. Separate facilities for women now exist in what were exclusively male bastions, and women's health clubs have multiplied as commercial ventures. My hypothesis is that these clubs have less to do with health seeking than with societal functions. I present my conclusions based on extensive participant-observation research in seven health clubs. Two years were spent in one club and three in another, at least three times a week. Other clubs were visited from one to twenty times each.

In talking with and observing 300 women at these clubs, I found that the majority, a decade earlier, had been involved in a prior functional equivalent to the mikvah—namely the emotive and control groups flourishing in the late 1960s and early 1970s.

During these years, a vast range of emotive and control groups sprang up in U.S. society. The popularity of such therapy, encounter, rap, and self-help and consciousness groups could not be explained simply by the reputed success of psychoanalysis and modalities derived from it and other psychological theories. Rather, as I have maintained elsewhere (Jacobs 1981), such groups functioned as mutated new U.S. utopian communities.

Nineteenth-century disenchantment gave rise to considerable full-time communitarian utopianism, repeated to a limited extent in the U.S. twentieth-century communes. However, in the mid-twentieth century, the escape from mainstream U.S. rationality, for many people, was encapsulated in a few hours a week of expressive or control-group meetings.

Unlike earlier utopian communities, most emotive and control groups in the 1950s, 1960s, 1970s, and early 1980s were and are part time, but their part-time nature is consistent with the segmented structure of modern life. Utopias compensate for felt difficulties—in this case, the lack of personal satisfactions in mass culture and the paucity of emotive, integrative, and control mechanisms. Utopias can incorporate recessive cultural genes; enclose deviance or institutionalize it; offer solidarity, catharsis, control, and hope for members; and sometimes serve as change models.

Women predominated in many emotive and control groups of the last few decades. For many of them, the group involvement was with a woman's consciousness-raising group or a support or therapy group. Such groups are less prevalent today for a variety of reasons including loss of funding, leadership, and hope and changing fads. Many women seek to have their needs met in whatever setting is available to them.

Perpetual seekers, they form a clientele for those who offer change for their lives that are boring and disappointing because the work available to them is often boring and demeaning and because they must strain to attract and hold men from whom they acquire support and status.

In the late twentieth century, in the health clubs, entrepreneurs have provided, usually for a substantial but affordable fee, the reality of the illusion of instant hope, community, and support. Promise is offered that by changing one's appearance, one's life will be transformed. Meanwhile, the staff offers encouragement that this is possible. If nothing else, the health club provides a place to be with others. Clubs tend to attract the unintegrated, the anxious, and those who are faded beauties, social rejects because they are aging.

One in two or three marriages, depending upon the locality (40 percent nationally), now end in divorce, and many of the divorcees are older women who suffer social rejection because of what I have called the Noah's ark syndrome—two by two (Jacobs 1979). There has also been a dramatic rise of female-headed households and women living alone. Because of the double standard of aging, men can date and remarry younger women, and the heterosexual older woman has great difficulty in becoming recoupled if she so desires. Also, she is undervalued typically in her work, being underpaid, overqualified, and often realistically anxious about employment prospects as she ages. (The Women's Bureau of the Department of Labor has frequently demonstrated this problem in its statistical bulletins; for example, see their report on the national seminar on low income women, 1978.)

She has limited options for relief. She can pay a therapist or beautician and many do. She can patronize bars, dating or otherwise, and an increasing number of women do. She can receive medication from her physician, and physicians write the largest number of prescriptions for mind-altering drugs for such women. Or, her doctor may change her life by more-dramatic interventions such as a hysterectomy often prescribed for pre-, menopausal, or postmenopausal women. As the April 1980 *Women & Health Roundtable Report* pointed out, hysterectomies are second only to dilation and curettage as the leading surgical procedure in the United States and increased by 50 percent between 1966 and 1975.

Most women, however, would prefer not to go the route of illness, physical or mental, given choices. Indeed, their great fear is dependency, aging, and ill health, and many older women lack the finances to assure good care. On the surface, the health club seems to offer a chance for improvement and self-control in the same way the fad for jogging among both men and women does. Unlike jogging, however, which tends to be a solitary venture, the health club offers companionship and support. Alienated by their work, and often alone, the women seek gemainschaft in the sisterhood of the leotard.

Dressed alike and sweating together, all are friends though strangers. As George Simmel points out in his essay "The Stranger" (1950), the stranger provides a chance to unburden safely precisely because she is one. Women can share confidential information and be assured that their personal crises are common and understood. For the price of membership, empathy is as instantly available as the juice machine. The drink of both fruit juice and empathy is intoxicating to the very thirsty, and older women thirst for what life denies. Faced with structural inopportunity when sexism and agism join, they exercise together and are caught up by group enthusiasm that a better life awaits once the so-called goal is achieved.

Almost all health clubs make use of the goal—loss of an agreed upon number of pounds or inches conforming to the media concept of the perfect female figure. This goal is usually as utopian as the goals of other kinds of utopian communities and crueler than most. However, what is important is not the realization of the goal but the dream of realizing it. When this is imbedded in a part-time community, the package becomes irresistible.

One health-club member put it this way:

> Before I joined this health club, I hated to leave work much as I hated my secretarial job. At least I was with people and my apartment is damn lonely. My former husband decided he wanted to be married to a woman half my age, and the divorce settlement didn't make it possible for me to

maintain my house. I hate my small apartment. I can come to this club and bask in the luxury. Here I am a MEMBER and people are good to me because they want me to join again next year. I don't have to take any crap here and there is always someone to talk to and tell if I had a rough day at the office, which I usually do. Besides, I'm going to be a new me when I get to my goal.

The club offers the prospect of eternal beauty in a society that devalues women who are neither young nor meet standards of beauty. Like the mikvah, it emphasizes women's sexuality. Additionally, it offers help in a society where men are a scarce resource. Mary says:

I get all my needs met here. As a widow, I am unable to get my sexual needs met so I work out my frustration. I live alone and am lonely, and here I have people to talk to. There are other women here who have been widowed, and they tell me how to manage and what benefits I can go after. Why, I saved the cost of the membership by hearing from another widow about something I was entitled to that I didn't know about.

This widow's account shows that the health club provides a functional equivalent to the old backyard fence over which neighbors shared information. In mobile urban society, people do not always get neighboring in their residence units and find new ways to get it. Many of women's neighborhood interactions are around children. When the children grow up, they lose these. Like the men's bar or the adolescent hang-out or other such institutions, the health club provides a surrogate, if transitory, network. Mutual, if limited, friendship and aid is given, but major commitment is avoided on the part of those not in a position or prepared to offer it.

Older women who have suffered relational losses cannot always make new friends at a deep personal level, at least not immediately. The health club can provide a transitional community and support for the many women in transition. As the bloom has worn off for many emotional and control groups such as psychotherapeutic ones, a new form of pseudo community has arisen in a society in which community is in short supply, especially for certain problematic groups like older women.

It may seem therefore, that the clubs have entirely positive functions. Some that have been mentioned or alluded to include the draining off of libidinal energy and the provision of a unit of belongingness, support, socialization, and social control.

However, a closer look is necessary at the functions of the clubs for social control. Many of the women interviewed mentioned that working out at the clubs helped them to deal with their anger. The anger was dissipated both by strenuous physical exercise and by the fact that other women listened to their outbursts and comforted them. One woman put it this way:

I dump all my garbage here. The town where I live doesn't have garbage removal, and I don't want to pay a trucker or spend money and time driving to the dump. So I put my garbage in the dumpster behind the health club. I also dump my other garbage here—my anger that my ex-husband doesn't pay child support and I have to kill myself at a crummy job doing my boss's work to support myself and the kids while my ex-husband and my boss live it up.

A sociologist from Mars looking at the health clubs might suggest that if private entrepreneurs had not seen a way to make money, the government might have done well to set them up as a cheap way of draining the anger of older women denied meaningful roles, work, and services in the society. Frustrated in their efforts to achieve their personal goals or to affect social change, women have retreated to the new kind of women's house where they support each other in their segregation, low status tied to gender and lack of opportunity.

While the physical exercise and companionship indeed have private benefits to the women, the women's energy is diverted from their real anger. Social interaction and comfort are valuable and exercise beneficial, but social-movement involvement might be more effective to redress the women's deprivations.

The health club, like the cult of the joggers, provides a kind of release and recreation and sense of expurgation for improvement in health for individuals, but mainstream social structures proceed in unhealthy ways. Some part-time utopian communities, like some full-time ones, do indeed point toward social change. However, the health clubs, in the opinion of this researcher, are like types of utopian communities that encapsulate deviance and criticism and allow the overall society to disregard it, laugh at it, or pay it lip service.

The cuts in government spending drastically have injured the chances that displaced homemakers and other needy women may be integrated into the economy at more than token wages. Most training programs continue to prepare women for the lowest paid jobs, and this is especially true for older women. The mikvah and the sauna may give a glow of warmth, but often older women are frozen out once their childrearing functions are done. The health club may function to give hope where none exists. Hence, it is clearly a mechanism of social control as well as of social support. Like the mikvah, it has rituals reinforcing women's preoccupation with their biology rather than their social situation.

Righteous anger against individuals and society is worked off and soothed. Those who might otherwise be radicalized sweat. They may indeed sleep better but perhaps too well in view of societal trends. Those who turned inward earlier in the century in est and other emotive and control groups now concentrate on the body instead of the body politic.

References

Jacobs, Ruth Harriet. "The Emotive and Control Groups as New Mutated Utopian Communities." *Journal of Applied Behavioral Sciences* 7 (1981):234–251.

———. *Life after Youth: Female, Forty, What Next?* Boston: Beacon Press, 1979.

Simmel, George. *The Sociology of Georg Simmel,* translated by Kurt H. Wolff. New York: Free Press, 1950.

Women and Health Roundtable. Washington, D.C.: Women and Health, April, 1980:1.

Women's Bureau, U.S. Department of Labor. *Employment and Economic Issues of Low Income Women: Report of a Project.* Washington, D.C.: U.S. Department of Labor, 1978.

The Sexuality of Older Women

Barbara F. Turner and
Catherine Adams

In recent years, Americans have placed more and more emphasis on sexuality as an avenue to self-actualization and an expression of successful adjustment. The outpouring in the popular press, during the last fifteen years, of books and magazine articles on sexuality reflects the curiosity about sexuality among adults of all ages. Older adults are especially interested in information about normal sexual behavior among older people and about the changes in sexual expression that occur with age.[1] Many individuals are dismayed by, but nevertheless believe, the cultural myth that impotence is an inevitable and natural phenomenon of aging.[2] The particular focus in this chapter is on how the sexuality of women is influenced by gender (the social-psychological dimension of sex status) and by aging.

Sexuality in middle and old age cannot be understood without reference to the first half of the life span. To set the sexuality of older women in context, it appears that patterns of sexual behavior and attitudes about sexuality are more variable among women than among men at all ages.[3] Thus, it is very difficult to formulate general statements about the sexuality of older women. Primary emphasis in this chapter is upon the aging process, which includes changes in sexual physiology and in health, and generational or historical shifts over time in sexual attitudes and practices. Gender differences permeate these topics and are discussed throughout this chapter.

Sexuality refers primarily to sexual behaviors and fantasies. In research on older people, behaviors typically studied are heterosexual intercourse and frequency of orgasm[4]; less often, frequency of masturbation, homosexual contacts, kissing and fondling, and attitudes like interest in sex have been assessed. As several writers have pointed out, researchers have tended to focus on frequency counts and have underemphasized the emotional context of sexuality, despite the importance of this facet of sexuality to most women (and men).[5] More generally, sexuality refers to any sensual experience that has erotic overtones for a particular individual and also to those aspects of interactions with others that affirm a person's sense of femininity or masculinity.[6]

Although we are especially concerned with development and change in sexuality over time, it must be noted that virtually all studies are cross-sectional, indicating age differences rather than age changes. The findings of longitudinal studies, which follow one group of respondents over a period of years, may not be applicable to younger cohorts who, as a result of historical change, have different attitudes, practices, and expectations of sexuality. A striking characteristic of the literature on sexuality in old age, furthermore, is its atheoretical nature. Although published findings on sexual activity provide some view of what is common in later adulthood, we know less about normal developmental transformations of sexuality in later life.[7] For this, an adequate life-span theory of sexual motivation would be helpful. Person suggests that a useful theory of sexual motivation should account for the power and plasticity of sexuality—that is, for the enormous strength of the sexual urge as it may be experienced, the variability of intensity of sexual desires, the diversity of stimuli that elicit sexual arousal in different persons, the intermingling of sexual and nonsexual meanings in sexual and nonsexual behavior, and the preoccupation of our culture with sexuality.[8]

Huyck adds that a life-span theory of sexuality should articulate with evidence about developmental changes in other areas of functioning.[9] In particular, Huyck suggests, it is reasonable to expect considerable continuity over the adult life span in the phrasing of sexuality, although new meanings may also emerge. To date, however, research has tended to focus rather narrowly on the frequency of specific sexual activities and has only tangentially addressed issues of stability and change in broader developmental patterns. Developmental changes in other areas of functioning also lead us to expect considerable interindividual variability in patterns of change in sexual attitudes and behavior. Such variability has, indeed, generally been found.[10] At least some of the women between 40 and 80 years of age who responded to Hite's questionnaire reported that their desire for and enjoyment of sex had increased with age, while others reported decreases.[11] In a six-year longitudinal study of respondents aged 60 to 94 at the first point of contact, decline in sexual interest and in incidence of heterosexual intercourse over the six years of the study was the modal pattern for those who reported any interest or activity at the first point of contact.[12] About one-fourth of the men as well as a few of the women, however, reported rising interest and activity.

As a first step toward a life-span theory of sexuality, it is worth pointing out that our experiences of sensuality begin in the first months of life. In object-relations theory, the physical skin contact between infant and mother is the critical factor in bonding the infant to its mother and significant others[13]—that is, sensual pleasure is the vehicle of object relationships in infancy and, therefore, throughout life. Hence, for both women and men, sexuality remains an expression of love for and intimacy with another person—certainly a powerful incentive for engaging in sexual activities. However, because sensual pleasure is first granted to the helpless infant by a powerful adult, sexuality in later life never can be completely free of connotations of dominance and submission. Thus, sentiments other than love are expressed by sexuality: Themes of hostility and dependence, as well as those of love and affection, are played out in bed. The attachment of sexuality to such a variety of sentiments or motives helps to explain the force of sexuality.[14] We know very little, however, about patterns of stability and change over time in motives for sexual behavior. That sensual pleasure ties us to others from the earliest months of life may also help to explain why relatively few women and men regard masturbation, a solitary sexual activity, as their favorite sexual activity.[15] The physical pleasure of orgasmic release is an important incentive for engaging in sexual behaviors,[16] and women are considerably more likely to reach orgasm through masturbation than through intercourse.[17] Self-masturbation also produces a more-intense orgasm in women than do other sexual activities.[18] That relatively few women prefer masturbation to other sexual activities may also indicate the primacy of the interpersonal aspects of sexual expression.

Physical Changes that Affect Sexuality

Researchers agree that none of the changes in sexual physiology that occur in women following menopause necessarily limits the sexual functioning or responsiveness of older women.[19] Menopause brings about a dramatic decrease in estrogen production, which leads to a thinning of the vaginal walls and decreased lubrication. Older women who engaged in intercourse on a regular basis, however—once or twice a week over several decades—lubricated effectively despite the thinning of their vaginal walls.[20]

The sexual functioning of older women is far more affected by the changes in sexual physiology that accompany aging in men. For most women, sex is heterosexual; hence, decline in the sexual functioning of men inevitably produces the same effect in women. For this reason, we devote considerable attention to physiological changes in men.

Compared to young men, older men are slower to achieve an erection and the erect penis is often less firm. The refractory period in men over 60 is much longer than in younger men; following ejaculation, at least several hours and, in some men, several days are required before full erection again can be achieved.[21] Because, in our society, the cultural standard of satisfactory performance of sexual acts such as heterosexual intercourse requires end-product ejaculation, the average frequency of heterosexual intercourse is considerably less among men (and, hence, also women) over 60 than among younger men. The majority of men over 60, it appears, are satisfied with one or, at most, two ejaculations per week.[22] Individual differences in frequency of ejaculation, however, as in other aspects of sexual behaviors, are great.

Rates of impotence increase steadily with age. Kinsey and his associates, who defined impotence as total absence of orgasm from any source whatever, reported 2 percent impotence among 35-year-old men, 10 percent at age 55, and 50 percent at age 75.[23] Verwoerdt, Pfeiffer, and Wang, who defined impotence as cessation of heterosexual intercourse, reported that about 80 percent of the men they studied who were in their late eighties and nineties were impotent.[24] Authorities nevertheless agree that impotence is not a natural or inevitable part of the aging process. Irreversible impotence having a physiological basis is related to pathology in the central nervous system or to prolonged alcohol abuse but is thought to account for only about 10 percent of cases of reported impotence.[25] Most cases of impotence are thought to be caused by psychological factors and thus are potentially reversible. Many men who believe themselves incapable of attaining an erection sufficient to permit heterosexual intercourse, for example, still wake up in the morning with a spontaneous erection. Such morning erections indicate the presence of the physiological ability to attain an erection sufficient enough for intercourse[26]; the felt inability, therefore, is psychogenic. Thus, it is not surprising that, in a study of sexuality among persons aged 60 and over, married women and men who had stopped having intercourse almost always agreed that they had stopped because the husband stopped.[27]

Even if an older man believes himself incapable of intromission or ejaculation, sexual activities other than heterosexual intercourse are, obviously, possible. Kissing, fondling, or total bodily massage may give sensual pleasure to both women and men, and a man may still provide pleasure, including orgasmic release, to his female partner by oral or manual means.[28] Self-masturbation is always an option. The problem is that, in our society, many people view intercourse as the only real sex. In the view of many, intercourse is the main course; other sexual activities, even if pleasureable, are hors d'oeuvres. Three-fourths of both women and men over 60 in one study, for example, regarded heterosexual intercourse as their favorite sexual activity.[29] When older married men stop having intercourse, therefore, at least some wives view their own sex lives as over. Some women, of course, are satisfied or even happy that their sex lives are behind them, but the majority regrets its passing.[30]

What factors account for the fairly high incidence of psychogenic impotence among older men? An important contributing factor is lack of information about normal changes in sexual physiology that occur with aging. One man in his sixties, for example, sadly concluded that he was impotent because, unlike previous years, it now took several minutes for him to attain an erection sufficient to engage in intercourse.[31] There is substantial agreement, however, that neither a slower nor a less-firm erection should be interpreted as synonymous with or precursors of impotence.[32]

Many men and women apparently do not know that ten minutes of oral or lubricated manual stimulation of the penis is quite likely to result in an adequate erection.[33] Anxiety about the length of time it takes to attain an adequate erection may lead many men (and their partners) to give up the attempt. The man's self-esteem and even his sense of masculinity may be threatened by the inability to produce the rapid, reflex erection of youth. Similarly, a less-firm erection may be experienced as personally threatening and interpersonally humiliating. The older woman may conclude that the slow erection is a sign that she is no longer physically attractive to her partner, that he no longer loves her, and/or that he has found another woman. Secondary impotence is an entirely understandable result of such intra-psychic and interpersonal conflicts.

A second contributing factor is the discomfort with which many women in the generation now over 60 regard oral sex in particular.[34] Women in this generation often learned when young that fellatio was unclean and reprehensible; many cannot bring themselves to engage in this activity even when they know that it might benefit the sexual performance of their partners, thereby increasing their own ultimate enjoyment. More generally, both women and men must understand that alterations in sexual techniques may be necessary to minimize the performance changes that often accompany aging in men.[35]

A third contributing factor, among some older men, is the belief that their sexual performance is inferior if it is not like that of young adult-hood.[36] A similar phenomenon occurred among some couples over 60 who had successfully participated in a sexual-therapy program designed to help them become sexually liberated. After an initial period of delight with their improved sexual enjoyment, some participants suddenly avoided all sexuality. Upon exploration, this avoidance was found to be a "psychological defense against depression elicited by sexual liberation in confrontation of sexual limitations due to the physiological changes of aging."[37] As Huyck has commented, the sexual performance of young men, entailing strong sexual desires, frequent intercourse, and end-product orgasm, is now viewed in our culture as the single standard of ideal sexual behavior for all individuals.[38] Measured against this standard, women of all ages and older men tend to be relatively deficient (but see Person, who argues that the sexuality of young men should be viewed as driven rather than normative[39]).

Finally, depression is quite common among older persons, and depression often diminishes sexual desire and performance.

Changes in Health that Affect Sexuality

Good health is important to sexual desire and performance. The malaise and discomfort of acute and chronic illnesses lowers sexual interest and responsiveness in women and men of all ages.[40] Several physical conditions, more common at older ages, are related to diminished sexuality. A number of these are discussed in a book edited by LoPiccolo and LoPiccolo[41]; in this chapter, we address sexual difficulties related to heart disease and cancer.

Cardiovascular disease is the leading cause of morbidity and mortality at older ages in the United States,[42] and myocardial infarction, or heart attack, is among the most common forms of the disease.[43] Men are more likely than women to suffer heart attacks; in general, cardiovascular disease appears to take a more-benign course in women, producing less behavioral and psychological decrement than in men.[44] The results of many studies indicate that many men who survive heart attacks experience sexual difficulties ranging from reduced activity to total impotence.[45] Authorities in the field of sexual rehabilitation agree that heart-attack patients do not get adequate advice or help from their physicians.[46] Apparently, most men receive no advice whatever from their physicians on when they may resume sexual activity following their heart attacks. Fear of dying from another attack leads many men to curtail sharply or entirely to forego sexual activity, even when they have resumed other physical activities that require greater energy expenditures than that involved in sexuality. A widely cited study of middle-aged, middle-class male heart-attack survivors concluded that the oxygen cost of marital sexual intercourse was approximately equivalent to that involved in climbing a flight of stairs.[47]

Dying while having intercourse is, apparently, a rare event. A rigorous study using coroners' reports from Japan found that less than one-half of 1 percent of sudden deaths were attributable to heart attacks during or following intercourse.[48] Furthermore, 80 percent of these deaths occurred during or following extramarital intercourse.

Advice for patients with congestive heart failure is quite different from that given to heart-attack patients. Sexual activity is contraindicated until the heart failure is controlled.[49]

There are almost no data on the sexual difficulties of women who have had heart attacks.[50] Heart function during orgasm, however, has been shown to be similar for women and men, so that the cardiac costs of marital intercourse to long-married women are probably similar to those for men.[51] Depression has been found to be quite common among women who have had heart attacks, however, and depression is likely to impair sexuality.[52]

Cancer of the primary or secondary sex organs may have a negative effect upon sexual functioning. Hysterectomies are unlikely to have deleterious effects,[53] but mastectomies—removal of one or both breasts—may. As one woman mourned, "My mastectomy ruined my sex life with my husband."[54] Counseling of both the mastectomy patient and her husband may help to prevent this outcome.

Many men past middle age undergo surgery to correct benign or cancerous enlargement of the prostate gland. Even radical perineal prostatectomies, however, are not invariably followed by impotence.[55] A man is most likely to find himself impotent following surgery if his surgeon tells him to expect this outcome, thus producing an iatrogenic effect.

The increasing incidence of chronic health problems in middle and old age is accompanied by increased consumption of a variety of drugs prescribed for these conditions. Many types of widely prescribed drugs, however, are known to have deleterious effects on sexual interest, desire, and performance in both women and men.[56] Sexual difficulties caused by drug or alcohol intake are thought to be very common among older people.[57]

Two other phenomena related to physiological health changes in later life—sex-related mortality differentials and the physical attractiveness of women—have decided effects upon the sexual opportunities of older women.

Women live longer than men. Expectation of life at birth in the United States in 1976 was 76.7 years for women and 69 years for men, a difference of nearly 8 years.[58] A large part of this difference is accounted for by differential death rates for women and men over the age of 65. In 1975, white women at 65 could expect to live for another 18.1 years and nonwhite women for 17.5 years, but men, regardless of race, could expect only 13.7 more years.[59] The mortality differential between men and women over 65 has widened since 1900 and is expected to continue to do so for at least the next two decades.[60] In 1975, there were 69 men aged 65 and over for every 100 women of that age group in the United States.[61] This ratio is expected to fall further by the year 2000 to 65 men per 100 women. Due to the female-male difference in life expectancy and the social expectation that women will marry men older than themselves, the ratio of married women increases sharply in later years. Over the age of 65, 75 percent of men but only 37 percent of women are married.[62] Single women thus find fewer men available for remarriage, while single men have many women from whom to choose. In 1970, there were fewer than 3 brides per 1,000 single women age 65 and over, compared to 17 grooms per 1,000 single men in this age group.[63]

For most older women today, sexual expression is viewed as possible and acceptable only within a marriage or a committed love relationship.[64] Unfortunately, as Huyck has commented, "there aren't enough men to go around—and they go around younger women."[65] Many women over 60 are discouraged by the stiff competition for the attention of the few available and healthy older men.[66] Indeed, 10 percent of women between 40 and 60 in a recent study similarly remarked that they could not find a suitable sexual partner since the men their age were attracted only to still younger women.[67] Many women believe that only the unusually attractive older woman can hope to attract men.[68] However, it is possible to overestimate the importance of physical attractiveness. As a 70-year-old widower explained, he preferred the company of women his own age, but "when you ask for a kiss, it's like they're giving up a diamond or something!"[69]

Women's self-esteem rests in part upon affirmation of their femininity, and femininity includes the ability to attract men.[70] Sex-role socialization of girls focuses upon the cultivation of winning charm, but every little girl recognizes, from the frequency of comments upon how pretty she is (or, unfortunately is not), that physical beauty is the critical ingredient in attracting men. Our standards of physical attractiveness are based on the physical attributes of women between the ages of 18 and 25 and are unrealistic even for most women of that age. The physical attractiveness of women past the age of menopause, however, is culturally denigrated.[71] Indeed, impotence in older men has been attributed to the unattractiveness of their wives.[72] Not surprisingly, many women over 60 regard themselves as unattractive; when they do so, they also feel "ignored," "like a failure," that they "do nothing well," and that "others do not enjoy being with" them.[73] There is also evidence that older women view their own attractiveness even more harshly than men usually view them.[74] Such self-denigration is important to sexual functioning; feeling unattractive and fearing rejection, a woman may avoid situations in marriage and out that might lead to a sexual encounter; and it may be difficult to allow oneself sexual pleasure if one feels unattractive.

Gender Differences in Patterns of Change in Sexuality

The literature consistently indicates that women and men develop distinctive sexual styles.[75] The extent to which these differences reflect sex-related biological differences versus the effects of social learning, including social suppression of female sexuality, is of course unclear. Gender distinctions, however, appear to persist throughout life in at least some aspects of sexuality. Women report lower orgasmic frequency than men throughout the adult life span,[76] although orgasmic capacity and frequency rise among women from youth to middle age and then remain steady into the sixties,[77] while falling steadily among men. Person asserts that the quintessential male-female difference in sexual style is that "genital sexual activity is a prominent feature in the maintenance of masculine gender while it is a variable feature in feminine gender."[78] An impotent man feels that both his sexuality and his masculinity are threatened. Physically healthy adult men who have never achieved orgasm are invariably psychopathological.[79] Whether or not a woman is orgasmic, however, bears no relationship to her personality organization or mental health. Unlike men, at least some women may consolidate their gender identity through nongenital routes. Thus, many women—even orgasmic women—feel that the importance of orgasm is overemphasized in today's cultural milieu; more important to many is the emotional context of the sexual relationship.[80]

In general, the greater the sexual interest and activity when young, the greater the interest and activity in later life.[81] These findings support the notion of continuity over the life span in the phrasing of sexuality. Gender differences appear in the early-life determinants of interest and activity in old age. Among men over 60, frequency of intercourse and interest in sex were related to the frequency and degree of interest they recalled having when young; among older women, frequency of intercourse and interest in sex were related to the degree of sexual enjoyment they recalled having when young.[82] Since enjoyment may refer to relationship aspects as well as physical pleasure, these findings again may reflect the relative importance of interpersonal relationships to women.

Gender differences also appear in the life-span trajectories of interest and activity. Kinsey et al. reported that before the middle years of life, wives report more activity than interest in marital intercourse; during middle age, wives report more interest than activity.[83] Bossard and Boll explained the increased marital dissatisfaction of wives in their forties, not by the empty nest or menopause but by sexual frustration due to their husbands' waning potency.[84] Pfeiffer and Davis interpreted part of the sexual disinterest of many of the older women they studied as a defensive response to the realistic difficulties they faced in finding a suitable sexual partner.[85]

There are important exceptions to the overall picture of declines in activity and interest drawn in the literature. Interindividual variability is prominent; while many individuals decline, others remain stable and some increase over time in sexual activity and interest. Contradictory findings have appeared regarding gender differences in patterns of change. In a six-year longitudinal study of respondents aged 60 and over at the first point of contact, Verwoerdt, Pfeiffer, and Wang found that men were more likely than women to report rising interest and activity over the six years of the study.[86] However, in a study that asked respondents over 60 to recall attitudes and activities during their twenties, women were considerably more likely than men to report increased sexuality from young adulthood to old age: 38 percent of the women, compared to 14 percent of the men, reported increases in one or more measures tapping frequency of orgasm, subjective pleasure, satisfaction with sex life, interest in sex, sexual urge, and incidence of participation in a broad range of sexual activities.[87] In many cases, the perceived improvement occurred in middle age or even later. Such findings make it clear that positive change in sexuality can and does occur in late middle age and beyond.

One reason why women may be more likely than men to report increased sexuality over time is that women tend to begin from lower levels than men. Respondents offered a great variety of explanations for the positive changes they noted.[88] Of particular importance was a new relationship (an affair or remarriage) or the end of a sexually unsatisfactory one through death or divorce. Both women and men commented on the sexually improving effects of a good relationship with a loved partner.

Historical Shifts over Time in Sexual Attitudes and Practices

Cultural attitudes and expectations for sexual behavior have changed markedly over the present century. Women born in the opening decades of the twentieth century were socialized quite differently regarding sexual values and practices than women now in their twenties. Thus, differences in attitudes and practices between women of different ages may reflect historical shifts more than developmental effects related to aging.

By and large, women now over 60 learned when young that sex was for men. Once married, a woman engaged in intercourse to please her husband, to show love for him, and to procreate; female orgasm was not expected. Women were not perceived as having sexual needs of their own. Women now between 40 and 60 learned, especially if they attended college, that vaginal orgasms (vide Freud) were desirable, that women could have sexual desires of their own, and that husbands had an obligation to attend to the physical pleasure of their wives. As the findings of Masters and Johnson, documenting the existence of clitoral orgasms and the multiorgasmic capacity of women, were widely disseminated in newspapers and mass magazine articles, women now between 20 and 40 learned that female sexuality, like that of men, was an expression of biological need and that orgasm—indeed, multiple orgasms—was not only desirable but mandatory.[89] Thus, social suppression of female sexuality has diminished gradually during this century, and cultural standards for the sexuality of women have been assimilated increasingly to those for men. The effects of sexual liberation, including demands for top-quality performance, have not been entirely salubrious for women, as feminists have pointed out.[90]

Attitudes and expectations for sexual behavior learned when young tend to have lasting effects over the life span. Conversely, it is clear that many middle-aged and older women (and men) have been affected by current cultural expectations for sexual behavior, although it is to be expected that they would have most impact on the young who do not have to unlearn expectations imparted earlier.[91]

Options for Sexual Expression among Older Women

Genital sexuality is not, and for some has never been, important to the well-being or psychological health of some older women. [92] Such women can do without sexual expression of any type without diminution in self-esteem or well-being. Other women have experienced relationships with men so destructive that they foresee little pleasure in sexuality.[93] For many women, however, sexual expression improves the quality of life. Moreover, for most women, sexuality is heterosexual. Given the shortage of male partners for many older women, what are their options for sexual expression? Suggestions that have appeared in the literature include masturbation, lesbian relationships, polygyny, relationships of older women with younger men, extending the health and life span of older men, re-education of older men to make them more-satisfactory sex partners for older women, and for future generations of older women, changes in the early-life socialization for sexuality of boys and men.

Masturbation

Besides the pleasure it may provide, masturbation is linked to feelings of autonomy and high self-esteem among adolescent girls and may increase feelings of autonomy among adult women as well,[94] in addition to preserving sexual function when no appropriate partner is available.[95] Older women of all marital statuses—never married,[96] married, widowed, and divorced[97]—masturbate. It is not the favorite sexual activity, however, of the majority of those who engage in it.[98] Even for the women over 60 in this study who reported that masturbation was their favorite sexual activity, masturbation was far from a sure route to orgasm. All of these women reported achieving orgasms from this source only some of the time. That reported masturbation occurred more among the unmarried suggests that respondents viewed it as a substitute sexual activity.[99] Such findings suggest that masturbation is far from an all-purpose solution to the unmet sexual needs of the majority of older women (and men) with such needs. In old age, as earlier, sex is an interpersonal activity.

Lesbian Relationships

Long-term lesbian relationships exist, and many such women have grown old together, although we know little about them. Women outnumber men at any older age, and women are more likely than men to be capable of the kind of emotionally intimate relationship prized by many women.[100] It would thus be practical for previously heterosexual women to turn to lesbian relationships in later life. At this time, however, we cannot assess the extent to which such a radical change in sexual preference is possible.

Polygyny

The notion of an older man living with and servicing the sexual needs of several older women seems to be an exclusively male fantasy. Few older men are capable of such demanding sexual activity, and in all probability, even fewer men and women could overcome the cultural conditioning that effectively prohibits such a ménage.[101]

Older-Woman/Younger-Man Relationships

Older men with the social and personal power that accompanies money have always been attractive to much younger women. As more women filter into high-prestige, high-paid occupations, they too will radiate the confidence and social power than can attract younger men. Given the unbalanced sex ratio after the age of 30, however, such relationships are likely to remain uncommon.

Extending the Health and Life Span of Older Men

Demographic projections to the year 2000 indicate that women over 65 increasingly will outnumber men. Thus, increments in vigor and longevity among men, should they occur, are unlikely to benefit women now past 50.

Re-Education of Older Men

Such possibilities, and the sources of resistance to them, have been discussed throughout this chapter. The sexual functioning of some older men (and women) has already been affected by exposure to mass-media material on sexuality and aging—presumably for the better.[102] Sexual therapists, however, report that positive change is unlikely for those older couples whose interpersonal relationship has deteriorated seriously over the years.[103] In such marriages, power struggles and hostility in the overall relationship are also enacted sexually. As Sviland notes, "Increased sexual gratification requires a shift in positive feelings for the partner and will not automatically occur from technique improvement alone."[104] Although re-education of older men and women is likely to produce positive benefits for the sexual functioning of older women, the extent of the benefit for many may be small. Moreover, re-education will have almost no impact upon the great majority of older women that has no male partner.

Changes in the Early-Life Socialization of Men

For future generations of older women, very early training of men in the techniques most likely to bring women pleasure would obviate the difficulty faced in overcoming years of bad habits later in life. However, Person has argued that sexuality will continue to be problematic for women as long as sexuality expresses dependent or masochistic trends, which are inescapable as long as women must define themselves vicariously through their relationship to men.[105] More generally, self-actualization via sexuality will be unlikely as long as sexual relationships serve as a vehicle for the expression of nonsexual sentiments with a negative valence—like hostility—among both women and men.

Today's young women will differ in several respects from their older contemporaries when the former become old. As older women, they will use, with pleasure, a greater variety of sexual techniques, and more are likely to be orgasmic. Rising divorce rates may offset any decline in male death rates that may occur, however, so that older women in the future may be no more likely to be married then are older women today.

The literature we have reviewed makes it clear that positive change in sexuality is possible at any age. Experience counts and may be more important than any changes wrought by physiological aging. As a 65-year-old man Adams studied said, "With aging, there is a mutual desire to give pleasure to one's mate and the maturity to experiment with less inhibition than when younger. I believe the most beneficial and important influence on my sex life is the more mature approach one takes to sex as one grows older, and with it more 'mutuality of pleasure' rather than just seeking to satisfy oneself."[106]

Notes

1. E.M. Feigenbaum, M.F. Lowenthal, and M.F. Trier, "Aged are Confused and Hungry for Sex Information," *Geriatric Focus* 5 (1967):2.

2. May Ann P. Sviland, "Helping Elderly Couples Become Sexually Liberated: Psychosocial Issues," in *Handbook of Sex Therapy*, eds. Joseph LoPiccolo and Leslie LoPiccolo (New York: Plenum Press, 1978), p. 352.

3. Helen Singer Kaplan, *The New Sex Therapy* (New York: Brunner/ Mazel, 1974).

4. Jeffrey B. Wales, "Sexuality in Middle and Old Age: A Critical Review of the Literature," *Case Western Reserve Journal of Sociology* 6 (1974):82–105.

5. Catherine Adams, "Sexuality and the Older Adult" (Ed.D. dissertation, University of Massachusetts at Amherst, 1981); Martin A. Berezin,

"Normal Psychology of the Aging Process, Revisited: Sex and Old Age, A Further Review of the Literature," *Journal of Geriatric Psychiatry* 9 (1976): 189–209; Margaret Hellie Huyck, "Sex and the Older Woman," in *Looking Ahead,* eds. Lillian E. Troll, J. Israel, and K. Israel (Englewood Cliffs, N.J.: Prentice-Hall/Spectrum, 1977):43–58; and Huyck, "Sexuality and the Health of Older Women" (Paper presented at the Conference on Health Issues of Older Women: A Projection to the Year 2000, State University of New York at Stony Brook, 1–3 April 1981.

6. Huyck, "Sex and the Older Woman"; Ethel Spector Person, "Sexuality as the Mainstay of Identity: Psychoanalytic Perspectives," *Signs: Journal of Women in Culture and Society* 5 (1980):605–630.

7. Berezin, "Normal Psychology"; Robert N. Butler and Myrna I. Lewis, *Sex after Sixty* (New York: Harper & Row, 1976); Margaret Hellie Huyck, *Growing Older: What You Need to Know about Aging* (Englewood Cliffs, N.J.: Prentice-Hall/Spectrum, 1974); Huyck, "Sex and the Older Woman"; Huyck, "Sexuality"; and Kate Ludeman, "The Sexuality of the Older Person: Review of the Literature," *The Gerontologist* 21 (1981): 203–208.

8. Person, "Sexuality as the Mainstay", pp. 606–607.

9. Huyck, "Sexuality."

10. Shere Hite, *The Hite Report* (New York: Dell, 1976); William H. Masters and Virginia E. Johnson, *Human Sexual Reponse* (Boston: Little, Brown, 1966); and Adrian Verwoerdt, Eric Pfeiffer, and H.S. Wang, "Sexual Behavior in Senescence," *Geriatrics* 24 (1969):137–154.

11. Hite, *Hite Report*.

12. Verwoerdt, Pfeiffer, and Wang, "Sexual Behavior."

13. Person, "Sexuality as the Mainstay," pp. 614–615.

14. Ibid, p. 615.

15. Adams, "Sexuality and the Older Adult,"

16. Huyck, "Sex and the Older Women"; and "Sexuality."

17. A.C. Kinsey et al., *Sexual Behavior in the Human Female* (Philadelphia: W.B. Saunders, 1953).

18. Masters and Johnson, *Human Sexual Response*.

19. Ibid.; and Masters and Johnson, *Human Sexual Inadequacy* (Boston: Little, Brown, 1970).

20. Masters and Johnson, *Human Sexual Reponse*.

21. Masters and Johnson, *Human Sexual Inadequacy*.

22. Masters and Johnson, *Human Sexual Response*.

23. A.C. Kinsey, W.B. Pomeroy, and C.E. Martin, *Sexual Behavior in the Human Male* (Philadelphia: W.B. Saunders, 1948).

24. Verwoerdt, Pfeiffer; and Wang, "Sexual Behavior."

25. Masters and Johnson, *Human Sexual Response;* and E.B. Strauss, "Impotence from the Psychiatric Standpoint," *British Medical Journal* 1 (1950):697.

26. John Reckless and Nancy Geiger, "Impotence as a Practical Problem," in *Handbook of Sex Therapy,* eds. Joseph LoPiccolo and Leslie LoPiccolo (New York: Plenum Press, 1978), p. 305.

27. Verwoerdt, Pfeiffer, and Wang, "Sexual Behavior."

28. Huyck, "Sex and the Older Woman."

29. Catherine Adams and Barbara F. Turner, "Patterns of Reported Change in Sexuality from Young Adulthood to Old Age" (Amherst, Mass.: Unpublished manuscript, 1982).

30. Adams, "Sexuality and the Older Adult."

31. Ibid.

32. Reckless and Geiger, "Impotence," p. 305.

33. Huyck, "Sex and the Older Woman.

34. Huyck, "Sex and the Older Woman"; and Huyck, "Sexuality."

35. Sviland, "Helping Elderly Couples Become Sexually Liberated."

36. Alex Finkle, "Emotional Quality and Physical Quantity of Sexual Activity in Aging Males," *Journal of Geriatric Psychiatry* 6 (1973):70–79.

37. Sviland, "Helping Elderly Couples Become Sexually Liberated," p. 357.

38. Huyck, "Sexuality."

39. Person, "Sexuality as the Mainstay," pp. 620, 626.

40. Masters and Johnson, *Human Sexual Response.*

41. Joseph LoPiccolo and Leslie LoPiccolo, eds., *Handbook of Sex Therapy* (New York: Plenum Press, 1978).

42. M.G. Kovar, "Elderly People: The Population 65 Years and Over." In *Health—United States 1976–1977,* DHEW Pub. no. 77–1232 (Washington, D.C.: U.S. Government Printing Office, 1978).

43. American Heart Association, *Heart Facts* (New York, 1974).

44. U.S. Department of Health, Education, and Welfare, *Health in the Later Years of Life,* Public Health Service, National Center for Health Statistics Pub. no. 1722–0178 (Washington, D.C.: U.S. Government Printing Office, 1971).

45. A. Bloch, J. Maeder, and J. Haissly, "Sexual Problems after Myocardial Infarction," *American Heart Journal* 90 (1975):536–537; E. Dangrove, "Sexual Responses to Disease Processes," *Journal of Sexual Research* 4 (1968):257; Jerry M. Friedman, "Sexual Adjustment of the Postcoronary Male," in *Handbook of Sex Therapy,* eds. Joseph LoPiccolo and Leslie LoPiccolo (New York: Plenum Press, 1978), p. 374; R.F. Klein et al. "The Physician and Postcoronary Invalidism," *Journal of the American Medical Association* 194 (1965):123; H. Hellerstein and E.J. Friedman, "Sexual Activity and the Postcoronary Patient," *Archives of Internal Medicine* 125 (1970):987; and W.B. Tuttle, W.L. Cook, and E. Fitch, "Sexual Behavior in Postmyocardial Infarction Patients" (abstract), *American Journal of Cardiology* 13 (1964):140.

46. Friedman, "Sexual Adjustment," pp. 375–376.

47. Hellerstein and Friedman, "Sexual Activity," p. 987.

48. M. Ueno, "The So-Called Coition Death," *Japanese Journal of Legal Medicine* 17 (1963):535.

49. R. Koller et al. "Counseling the Coronary Patient on Sexual Activity." *Postgraduate Medicine* 51 (1972):133; and Hellerstein and Friedman, "Sexual Activity," p. 987.

50. Friedman, "Sexual Adjustment," p. 384.

51. Masters and Johnson, *Human Sexual Response.*

52. L.A. Abramov, "Sexual Life and Sexual Frigidity among Women Developing Acute Myocardial Infarction," *Psychosomatic Medicine* 38 (1976):418–425.

53. Margaret Hellie Huyck, Caren Eschen, and R. Tabachnik, "Women's Attitudes toward Radical Hysterectomy" (Paper presented at the Twenty-sixth Annual Meeting of the Gerontological Society, Miami, 1973.

54. Adams, "Sexuality and the Older Adult."

55. Finkel, "Emotional Quality."

56. Reckless and Geiger, "Impotence"; and Kaplan, *New Sex Therapy,* 1974.

57. Huyck, "Sexuality."

58. U.S. Bureau of the Census, *Statistical Abstract of the United States: 1978,* 99th ed. (Washington, D.C.: U.S. Government Printing Office, 1978).

59. Kovar, "Elderly People."

60. Barbara F. Turner, "Sex-Related Differences in Aging," in *Handbook of Developmental Psychology,* ed. B.B. Wolman (Englewood Cliffs, N.J.: Prentice-Hall, 1982).

61. J.S. Siegel, *Prospective Trends in the Size and Structure of the Elderly Population, Impact of Mortality Trends, and Some Implications,* U.S. Bureau of the Census, Current Population Reports, Special Studies Series P-23, no. 78 (Washington, D.C.: U.S. Government Printing Office, 1979).

62. U.S. Bureau of the Census, *Social and Economic Characteristics of the Older Population: 1978,* Current Population Reports, Special Studies Series P-23, no. 85 (Washington, D.C.: U.S. Government Printing Office, 1979).

63. National Center for Health Statistics, *Vital Statistics of the United States: 1970, III, Marriage and Divorce* (Washington, D.C.: U.S. Government Printing Office, 1974).

64. Lillian E. Troll and Barbara F. Turner, "Sex Differences in Problems of Aging," in *Gender and Disordered Behavior: Sex Differences in Psychopathology,* eds. Edith Gomberg and Violet Franks (New York: Brunner/Mazel, 1979).

65. Huyck, "Sexuality," p. 1.

66. Adams, "Sexuality and the Older Adult."

67. S. Sheppard and S. Seidman, "Sexuality and Midlife Women" (Paper presented at the Thirty-fourth Annual Scientific Meeting of the Gerontological Society of America, Toronto, 8–12 November 1981).

68. Kaplan, *New Sex Therapy.*

69. Adams, "Sexuality and the Older Adult."

70. Ardyth Stimson, Jane F. Wase, and John Stimson, "Sexuality and Self-Esteem among the Aged," *Research on Aging* 3 (1981):228–239.

71. Carol A. Nowak, "Socialization to Become an Old Hag" (Paper presented at the Eighty-fifth Annual Convention of the American Psychological Association, San Francisco, 26–30 August 1977); and Carol A. Nowak and Lillian E. Troll, "Age Concept in Women: Concern with Youthfulness and Attractiveness Relative to Self-Perceived Age" (Paper presented at the Twenty-ninth Annual Scientific Meeting of the Gerontological Society of America, Portland, Oregon, October 1974).

72. Masters and Johnson, *Human Sexual Response;* and Isadore Rubin, *Sexual Life after Sixty* (New York: Basic Books, 1965).

73. Stimson, Wase, and Stimson, "Sexuality and Self-Esteem," p. 237.

74. Nowak, "Socialization to Become an Old Hag."

75. Huyck, "Sexuality."

76. Kinsey, Pomeroy, and Martin, *Sexual Behavior in The Human Male;* and Kinsey et al. *Sexual Behavior in the Human Female.*

77. Kaplan, *New Sex Therapy.*

78. Person, "Sexuality as the Mainstay," p. 619.

79. Ibid.

80. Adams, "Sexuality in the Older Adult"; and Hite, *Hite Report.*

81. Eric Pfeiffer and Glenn Davis, "Determinants of Sexual Behavior in Middle and Old Age," *Journal of American Geriatrics* 20 (1972): 151–158.

82. Ibid.

83. Kinsey et al., *Sexual Behavior in the Human Female.*

84. J.H.S. Bossard and E.S. Boll, "Marital Unhappiness in the Life Cycle of Marriage," *Marriage and Family Living* 17 (1955):10–14.

85. Pfeiffer and Davis, "Determinants of Sexual Behavior."

86. Verwoerdt, Pfeiffer, and Wang, "Sexual Behavior."

87. Adams and Turner, "Patterns of Reported Change."

88. Ibid.

89. Masters and Johnson, *Human Sexual Response.*

90. Kate Millett, *Sexual Politics* (New York: Doubleday, 1970); and Person, "Sexuality as the Mainstay," p. 628.

91. Adams, "Sexuality and the Older Adult."

92. Person, "Sexuality as the Mainstay," pp. 624–625.

93. Adams, "Sexuality and the Older Adult."

94. Abraham Maslow, "Dominance, Personality and Social Behavior in Women," *Journal of Social Psychology* 10 (1939):3–39.

95. Huyck, "Sexuality."

96. C.V. Christenson and A.B. Johnson, "Sexual Patterns in a Group of Older Never-Married Women," *Journal of Geriatric Psychiatry* 6 (1973):80–98.

97. Adams and Turner, "Patterns of Reported Change."

98. Ibid.

99. Ibid.

100. Marjorie Fiske Lowenthal et al. *Four Stages of Life* (San Francisco: Jossey-Bass, 1975).

101. Huyck, "Sexuality."

102. Adams, "Sexuality in the Older Adult."

103. Sviland, "Helping Elderly Couples Become Sexually Liberated," p. 358.

104. Ibid., p. 359.

105. Person, "Sexuality as the Mainstay," p. 629.

106. Adams, "Sexuality in the Older Adult."

Part II:
Older Women in Labor

In 1960, about 38 percent of all women were in the labor force; by 1980, almost 52 percent were in the labor force—an increase of 14 percent. Women now constitute 43 percent of the labor force, most of whom must work because one in four have never been married; one in five are widowed, divorced, or separated; and three in ten are married with husbands earning less than $15,000 a year.[1] While the number of employed women increased within the past two decades, their earning power has not. In 1960, full-time female workers earned 60.8¢ for every dollar full-time male workers earned; by 1980, women earned 59.6¢ for every dollar earned by men.[2] As women age, the earning gap widens so that women over the age of 45 earn only 55¢ for every dollar men earn.[3]

Sex and age discrimination combine for women in mid-life to exacerbate their employment problems. Job segregation is an important if subtler aspect of both age and sex discrimination; for example, U.S. Bureau of Labor Statistics data for 1981 show that 50 percent of all employed women are concentrated in four relatively poorly paid female occupations: registered nurse, clerk, retail-sales worker, and teacher. Older women often find getting any job problematic; those with little experience other than as a homemaker are likely to be considered unqualified and those with years of experience, overqualified. The average unemployed woman remains jobless for nineteen weeks—almost twice the average of younger women.[4] That age and sex are double disqualifiers in the labor market is still the case despite the passage of the Age Discrimination Act in 1967 and the Equal Pay Act of 1963. The recent suit brought against I. Magnin and Federated Department Stores, in which older workers claimed that they had been laid off to reduce pension costs for the employer, highlights the dilemma of the older woman. Less likely to have many years of continuous employment behind her, she is less likely to have vesting in a pension because the Employee Retirement Income Security Act (ERISA) guarantees vesting only after ten years of job tenure. It is estimated that only 12 percent of working women receive pensions, and their average pension benefit is $1,471 per year less than that for men—$2,186 versus $3,657.[5] These figures reflect both the lower average earnings of women and their discontinuous job histories, a pattern that is repeated in women's social-security benefits. Six of every ten women 65 or over depend upon social security as their only source of income and receive on the average of $1,400 less than men who, incidentally, rarely rely on social security as their sole income in retirement.[6] The chapters in part II explore some of these issues relating to older women in labor.

Ellen Rosen, in chapter 5, explores the work experiences of female factory workers in New England and the ways in which current employment conditions shape the lives of these people. Presenting data from her recent study of older workers in Massachusetts and Rhode Island, she notes that job loss is particularly traumatic for these women as it leads to reduced pensions.

Maximiliane Szinovacz reviews the meaning of retirement to older women in chapter 6. She challenges the popular assumption that retirement is an insignificant life event for women and suggests that retirement needs for women differ from those for men. Adequate retirement programs for women that take account of the many patterns of female retirement need to be developed on the basis of additional empirical research.

Brian Gratton, in chapter 7, examines the life of women who worked outside the home and spent their last days in a home for older women. He focuses on the history of a charity for the aged that sheltered the housekeepers, laundresses, nursemaids, and ethnic sisters to the Brahmins of Boston. A dual analysis of the lot of employed women pre–social security and the hidden functions in private philanthropy, Gratton's chapter is especially timely given the current political emphasis on increased involvement of the private sector in the provision of assistance in old age.

Notes

1. *Statistical Abstract of the United States, 1981* (Washington, D.C.: U.S. Department of Commerce, 1981), p. 381; and National Commission on Working Women, "An Overview of Women in the Workforce," *News about the 80%* (June 1981), pp. 3–4.

2. Women's Equity Action League, *Comparable Worth: A Fact Sheet* (Washington, D.C.: 1981), p. 1.

3. Working Women, National Association of Office Workers, *Vanished Dreams: Age Discrimination and the Older Woman Worker* (Cleveland, Ohio, 1980), p. 5.

4. Tom Gabe, "Social Characteristics and Economic Status of the U.S. Aged Population," *Congressional Research Service Report,* no. 81–32 EPW (Washington, D.C.: Congressional Research Service, 1981), p. 36.

5. Women's Equity Action League, *Fact Sheet: Age Discrimination in Employment . . . and Women* (Washington, D.C., 1981), p. 2.

6. Ibid.

5

Beyond the Sweatshop: Older Women in Blue-Collar Jobs

Ellen Rosen

As advancing age brings changes in women's family lives, as children reach maturity and wives become widows, the meaning and value of work in the lives of low-wage women in working-class jobs is likely to be altered. Today, increasing numbers of women are remaining on the job throughout their adult lives. Furthermore, each cohort of older women now will be facing rapid industrial transformations that will have serious effects on their experience and treatment in the work place. Many of these changes will create a variety of dilemmas for them as they begin to think seriously about and plan for their retirement and beyond. Thus, we need to know much more about the special problems faced by older female workers, women beyond the age of 50 or 55, women who continue to earn their living from low-wage and unskilled jobs.

This chapter focuses on the work life experiences of older female factory workers in New England. First, I discuss the nature and quality of blue-collar women's work experience. Second, I explore the conjunction between aging and industrial transformations: How do current employment conditions shape the experience of older female factory workers? In addressing these issues, I identify the problems blue-collar women face as they approach and prepare for retirement.

The data to be reported here are the result of an extensive study dealing with the work and family lives of blue-collar female workers of all ages in eastern New England.[1] The women studied live and work in the small- and medium-sized industrial cities of eastern Massachusetts and Rhode Island. More than 400 women were interviewed in this research; all were year-round, full-time workers in three major industries that traditionally have employed larger numbers of unskilled and semiskilled female workers: (1) the garment industry, (2) the electrical-goods industry, and (3) the food-processing industry. In the garment industry women operate a wide variety

The material used here was, in part, prepared under Grant No. 21-25-79-19 from the Employment and Training Administration, U.S. Department of Labor, under the authority of title III, part B, of the Comprehensive Employment and Training Act of 1973. Researchers undertaking such projects under government sponsorship are encouraged to express freely their professional judgment. Therefore, points of view or opinions stated in this chapter do not necessarily represent the official position of the Department of Labor.

of sewing machines, stitching together men's and women's clothing. The electrical-goods industry employs primarily women who assemble the components of nondurable consumer goods such as lamps, lightbulbs, and electrical cords and plugs. Women who worked as food processers typically were employed packing and wrapping baked goods and candies.

The women we interviewed included large numbers of older workers. The average age of the women in our sample was 43, with 47 percent—almost half—being 45 or older. Only 10 percent of the women in our sample were less than 25 years of age. Despite these large numbers of older women, our sample was quite comparable to the age distribution of the female blue-collar working population in the same industries in New England as a whole.[2] In this region, women in manufacturing tend to be older than women employed in other sectors of the labor force, especially those in sales, service, and clerical jobs.

The considerable number of older women currently employed in New England's blue-collar jobs is the result of a unique set of social and historical circumstances. Indeed, we can only understand the experience of today's older female factory workers in the context of four interrelated trends.

The first of these trends is New England's long history of employing large numbers of female workers in semiskilled and unskilled factory jobs.[3] Cities like Fall River, New Bedford, Lawrence, and Lowell, Massachusetts, and Providence, Rhode Island, have always provided an employment base first for factory girls, the daughters of New England farmers and tradesmen in the 1830s and 1840s, and later to changing groups of immigrant women and their U.S.-born daughters.[4] The declining textile industry in the 1920s was replaced by the garment industry in the 1930s in much the same way that the new high-technology electronics industry in the 1980s is now replacing some of the old mill-based industries.[5] Indeed, as new immigrant groups continue to arrive, foreign-born women continue to find jobs in New England's factories. Despite popular beliefs that blue-collar jobs may be disappearing from the employment landscape because high labor costs make labor-intensive industries unable to compete with lower labor costs abroad, the past decade witnessed significant increases in the number of blue-collar jobs held by women, especially in Massachusetts.[6]

The second trend accounting for New England's older female blue-collar work force involves the changing employment patterns of female factory workers since World War II. Until that time, the proportion of married women employed in production jobs was relatively small. Although immigrant women were more likely to hold factory jobs, the typical woman employed in production work was young and single, and she worked between school leaving and marriage and childbearing.

The generation of women in this study who are now 55 years or older usually entered the labor force as factory workers around the time of World War II. Although most did drop out of the labor force to bear and raise children, unlike their predecessors, they returned to work when their children were grown or at least able to care for themselves. They returned to their factory jobs, perhaps ten or fifteen years after they left the labor force to raise families: they returned to work when children's growing needs, inflation, and changing attitudes about married women in the labor force generated the emergence of a new work-family pattern, the dual-earner family.

Analysis of the work histories of women 55 and older in my sample illustrates patterns of their labor-force participation. The women left the labor force to bear and raise children; nevertheless, they have spent most of their adult lives working, primarily in blue-collar jobs. Women 55 and over, with an average age of 59.5 years, have spent a mean of 24.4 years in the labor force. A total of 22.5 of these years, or 92 percent of their working lives, has been spent doing blue-collar work.

These figures mark the rich variations in the family patterns and work lives of the women we studied, patterns that have been complicated by employment declines in the industries in which they worked. However, the work histories of two women—Celia Triano and Marcia Penvert[7]—clarify the complex nature of these patterns.

When we interviewed Celia Triano, she was 60 years old and married. She had two grown sons. Celia was employed in a firm that made electrical wires and cords. She had worked there for the past nine years. She had left her job as a file clerk nine years earlier to work at this job because it was full time and paid higher wages. Celia started working at the age of 19 in 1939. She worked in a rubber factory making golf balls for thirteen years until she married, at the age of 32, and left the labor force for eighteen years to be a homemaker and raise her two sons. At the age of 50, in 1970, she went back to work as a file clerk and then moved to the cord-set plant where she was working when we interviewed her. Celia plans to work until 62 when she would like to take early retirement. Her husband does not think women should work but realizes that they cannot get by on his pay. Only with Celia's job could the Trianos put their two boys through college.

Marcia Penvert, 57, is a garment worker who has worked in the same shop for the past eighteen years. She went to work at the age of 17 in a garment shop where she worked for a year before being laid off and another year in another garment shop when she was laid off once more. In 1943 (when she was 20), Marcia married and did not return to work until three years later in 1947. She worked another year as a garment worker until she became pregnant and then withdrew from the labor force for ten years to raise her children. From 1958 to 1961 she worked in a fourth garment shop until it, too, went out of business. In 1962, she got her present job where she has been working the past eighteen years. Marcia was recently laid off again in 1980.

Although some of our respondents reported working thirty and even thirty-five years in one firm, as these stories illustrate, a good deal of employment instability has characterized the working lives of many older women. On the one hand, the instability often has resulted from personal decisions to enter and to leave the labor force—for example, marriage, children, or simply the desire and financial wherewithall to take some time off. On the other hand, hiatuses in employment and job changes also have been the result of labor-market forces beyond the control of the women—particularly the contraction of employment in the industries that have employed them. Nevertheless, as I have shown, older women in blue-collar jobs tend to report a relatively long period of labor-force participation throughout their adult lives, particularly after the prime childbearing and childrearing years.

The structure of employment in New England's manufacturing firms is a third factor that contributes to the high proportion of older women they employ. Here, jobs typically provide full-time and year-round work for women who need full-time and year-round earnings. Many sales and service jobs requiring comparable skills and/or education offer only part-time work that historically has been at lower wages. Although seasonal layoffs are common in many of the industries where women are heavily employed, the availability of unemployment insurance during slack seasons often is felt to compensate for lost earnings—but only when layoffs are temporary and of short duration.

In addition to full-time earnings, full-time work means eligibility for a wide variety of essential fringe benefits. The most significant of these are health insurance and pensions. The extensive unionization of New England's manufacturing industries has established precedents for such benefits, which today many nonunion shops feel obliged to provide for their workers as well.[8] The expectation of receiving pension benefits is particularly important to older female workers and, as we will show, provides an important incentive for them to remain at work until they are eligible, at age 62 or 65, for receipt of their monthly pension checks.

The fourth and final reason that older women are so heavily represented among New England's factory women is because there is little competition for their jobs from young women. As we have already pointed out, women under the age of 25 comprise only about 10 percent of the women in our sample, a number that reflects their proportion in this type of employment regionally. Recognizing the poor employment future that unskilled and semiskilled blue-collar jobs offer, younger women are entering other types of work and leaving the field to older workers.

To conclude, the female blue-collar labor force in New England has a preponderance of older workers because manufacturing traditionally has been an important source of paid employment for women. Post–World War II transformations in women's labor-force participation meant that women who entered factory work during this period continued to work at these jobs well past marriage and childbearing, unlike the generations of factory women before them. As the inflation of the 1960s and 1970s intensified the need for two earners, especially in working-class families, those women who managed to find and keep such jobs, even in a period of employment decline, found them able to provide a stable source of year-round, full-time work.

As this generation of women turns 55, the motivation to continue working until retirement continues to be fueled by current economic need and the expectation of receiving a pension and increasing retirement income. At the same time, few young women are competing with these older workers for their jobs. Employers therefore have no incentive to turn away older women, many of whom have years of skill and experience. The result of these trends is that older women, 55 and older, now comprise a large part of the customary work force in New England's blue-collar jobs.

Women in Production Work—The Lived Experience

Why do women work in factories? Women have worked in factories and continue to do so because they need to earn a living for themselves and their families but lack the skills and education that would enable them to do more-lucrative, prestigious, or satisfying work. Most of the women we studied indicated that they would not work if they did not need the money. A full 75 percent agreed with the statement, "It's better all around if a woman can stay at home and take care of her family instead of having to work." Only 36 percent said they would continue to work if they or their families had enough money. Our respondents were given a list of ten different qualities of a job. They were asked to rank order the five qualities they felt were most important to them. Good pay was by far the most important.[9]

Only a romanticization of factory work would generate expectations that blue-collar women would value their jobs for the intrinsic satisfactions provided. Yet, while measures of overall levels of work satisfaction were low,[10] virtually none of the women expressed the feeling that their jobs were boring or alienating, as many social scientists would have us believe. Instead, the women complained about hazardous working conditions—for example, ill-repaired machinery and dirty work places. They told us about supervisors who pushed them too hard, who showed favoritism, or who treated them in ways that undermined their dignity and self-respect.

Many women were painfully aware of the low-status image of their jobs; they believed people thought of all factories as sweatshops, a characterization they resented as both untrue and derogatory. Nevertheless, they often shared contemporary attitudes about the kinds of work that are thought be be appropriate and desirable for women. Many viewed clerical work, which is clean and where one gets dressed up to go to work, as highly desirable. Others expressed a preference for working with people in a helping role—for example, in day-care centers and nursing homes. Both clerical-work and social-service occupations were seen as providing much more opportunity to experience personal satisfaction. Yet these jobs were also seen as a luxury available to more-affluent women who could afford to trade wages for job satisfaction. In making their choices about the most suitable job for them, the bottom line was likely to be whether it paid enough.

However, women do not always work in factories simply because they have no other choice. Many women are quite conscious that in taking factory jobs they are trading prestige and work satisfaction for higher earnings and benefits. Sylvia Brentano is one of these women. She had done office work and also had been employed as a sales clerk. When asked what attracted her to her job at Condor Electric, she answered quite simply, "Money." Marcia Penvert, a co-worker of Sylvia, told us:

> I worked at [Town] Hospital. I was a dietary aide. The money was lousy and they couldn't give me full time and I wanted full time. So, I quit . . . I had to wait a year to get in there [Condor Electric]. I finally did and the money is terrific.

Sylvia and Marcia are both women with a high school degree. Isabel Mendoza, however, never went beyond the eighth grade. Nevertheless, she feels she can make more money in a low-wage garment shop than she can cleaning office buildings or working as a chambermaid. Her stitching job is a unionized full-time job with health insurance and fringe benefits.

Blue-collar women need full-time work. They bring home almost half the family income. We estimated that employed married women, living with their spouse, employed year round and full time, earned 43 percent of the total family income.

Finally, some women in this study have developed a view that parallels the ideas of scholars that office and factory work are becoming increasingly similar. Despite the low-status image of factory work, which as we have pointed out is often keenly felt, a number of women have no illusions about the real differences between working in office or factory. Caroline Benuto was a packer at Condor Electric. She told our interviewer:

> I think that in clerical work or sales work, you think that because your are not getting dirty that everything is all right, and it really isn't. The women

who work in those jobs are in just as much trouble as we in the factories are in terms of having demeaning jobs. The only thing is they can get dressed up so it's glossed over. And they get paid less.

Most women we studied tended to accept the limited potential their jobs offered for work satisfaction or occupational mobility. Complaints against bosses and supervisors (there were many) focused on failures to provide a culturally acceptable minimum of on-the-job comfort and work autonomy. Job dissatisfaction also focused on the ways these difficult, dirty, and often dangerous jobs left women little time and energy to be with or to do things for their families. Unlike more-educated women who see time spent on family work as competing with time spent in self-improving professional activities, the women we interviewed were four times more likely to report that their work interfered with their doing things for their families (27 percent) than that their families interfered with their work (6 percent).[11]

Factory Work and the Life Cycle

Certainly the structure of factory work in general, as well as the particular characteristics of individual work environments, influences the responses of the women we studied to their jobs. Additionally, we found that women's stage in the life cycle has an important effect on their overall work satisfaction. Older women were decidedly happier with their jobs.

Consistent with a plethora of reports about undesirable working conditions: dirty work place, ill-repaired machinery, and most important, a piece-rate system designed to make it exceedingly difficult to work fast enough to earn beyond the minimum rate—it is not surprising that the most important predictor of work satisfaction was having a job that was physically comfortable. In order to measure work satisfaction, we used the question, "All in all, how satisfied would you say you are with your job?" [Structured responses were (1) very satisfied, (2) somewhat satisfied, (3) not too satisfied, and (4) not at all satisfied.][12] Higher levels of work satisfaction were also associated with higher hourly wages and with opportunities to make friends on their job.[13] In the context of low overall levels of work satisfaction, these relationships suggest the benefits that female workers get from relatively undesirable jobs. These benefits are needed earnings and opportunities to fulfill important needs for social interaction with peers. Yet, even when we control for all these factors, older female workers were still more likely to be satisfied with their jobs than younger ones.

Wright and Hamilton have argued that older blue-collar men tend to be happier with their jobs than younger men.[14] Older workers, they argue, have jobs that are more highly skilled. They also have jobs that pay higher wages. In short, older men have better jobs. Better jobs, however, cannot explain the higher levels of work satisfaction among blue-collar women. First, in general, female factory workers tend to have relatively unskilled and dead-end jobs. Indeed, such unskilled female workers were targeted specifically for inclusion in this study sample. Older women do not have more-skilled jobs than younger women. Indeed, they tend to have fewer years of education and, because of this, earn lower hourly wages than their younger female colleagues.

We are left with the paradox that while wages are important to female production workers, older women are more satisfied with their jobs even though they earn significantly less than their younger work mates. An explanation of this paradox is to be found only in the life-cycle and generational aspects of the lives of these women. These aspects can only be explored by comparing the problems of older and younger workers.

The heaviest burdens clearly fall on women who must both work year round full time and still take care of their families. Women with growing families have the greatest financial need to work; at the same time, they have the greatest pressures on them to balance work and family obligations. Regardless of whether they were married or not, women with dependent children under age 18 were more likely to report higher levels of work/ family tensions. They felt their work was significantly more likely to interfere with their doing things for and with their families.[15]

The ability of women with young children to work full time and year round is made feasible, but hardly leisurely, by the special schedules offered by factory work. In the garment industry the workday begins at 7:00 A.M. and ends at 3:00 P.M., when children return home from school. Many electrical workers worked the second shift from 3:00 P.M. until about midnight. Such a schedule makes it possible for husbands and wives to alternate work shifts and to take turns caring for children. If a woman begins work at 3:00 P.M., she can be home with her preschool children. Her husband can be home at 5:00 to relieve a relative or babysitter, feed the children, and put them to bed.

Yet, while husbands help with child care and family chores, women still do the majority of the family work.[16] As a result of this schedule, the double day of work falls most heavily on these low-income women who must work but who cannot afford to purchase household help (housecleaning, child care, meals in restaurants) because of the marginal difference between their wages and the cost of such services. The necessity of maximizing earnings frequently stretches the women's resources to their limit. Sarah Bellows worked the second shift at Condor Electric Company. She told us:

> I worked 3:30 to midnight. By the time you get to bed it's 1:20. Then I get up early to get the kids to school. Then back to bed and sleep all morning and then I get up to do my housework and then it was time to go to work, and I had absolutely no time to myself.

Angela Cabeiros is a garment worker whose workday is equally full:

> When I'm working, I take the children to my mother's at 7:00 A.M. I pick
> them up at 4:30 or so. I come home, do some chores, do the dinner. I have
> no time really to spend with them. By the time dinner is done, they have
> dinner, they are tired themselves. So there is not time there. During the
> weekend, I have the chores to do, I have the house to clean. There is really
> no time.

Older women, whose children are grown, have neither the family pressures nor the financial obligations of their younger work mates. As a result,
work increasingly becomes something the women do for themselves. Susan
Bridges, a 62-year-old garment worker, told us:

> When I was younger, I had to work to support six children. Now I work
> because I want to be with people. If I stayed home, I feel I would be lonely.

Indeed, when children leave home, as increasing numbers of wives
become widows, the "girls" in the shop frequently become a surrogate
family. Older women with many years of job tenure in a single firm develop
strong friendships. Indeed, 73 percent of women 55 and over said it was
very true that they had a lot of opportunities to make friends on the job.
Only 52 percent of women younger than 35 agreed. One union official
reported how important such friendships are for keeping older workers on
the job. She said:

> And how many girls [sic] have said to me, "You know, I don't have to do
> this for a living." But they have girls they have been friends with for eigh-
> teen, twenty years. They've spent their lives in the shop. They talk about
> their kids from the day they saw their fanny to the day they got married.
> They cry together, they laugh together, and they are happy together. A lot
> of them, just because they don't want to be away from that [companion-
> ship], will stay and work.

As the financial burdens of earning a living and the conflicts between
work and family life become less severe, older women begin to view their
jobs as more intrinsically satisfying. Of the women 55 and over, 44 percent
said it was very true that their jobs were challenging as compared to 32 percent of women 35 to 54 and 21 percent of the women 34 and under. Of
women 55 and older, 62 percent said it was very true that their jobs gave
them a sense of accomplishment. Women 35 to 54 offered this response
only 47 percent of the time, and women 34 and under only 31 percent of the
time.

Pressures in the Work Place

Lest we paint too rosy a picture of the situation of older women in factory jobs, we must remember that the intrinsic satisfactions many older women get from their jobs are offset by a variety of work place pressures. The context of sociability and the sense of accomplishment and challenge these women report is accompanied by the continued need to do hard physical work. For example, the piece-work system can be an extra burden for older women.

Piece Rates

Over half the women we studied (57 percent) worked on a piece-rate system; the remainder received a fixed hourly or standard wage. Although piece rates are calculated differently from firm to firm and in different industries, all involve a system of payment in which workers are rewarded for working as fast as they possibly can. In industries with low levels of technology where women are heavily employed, like the ones we have studied, the workers' speed has a direct impact on the volume of output. Piece-rate systems increase productivity and promise a share of that increase to workers. This is typically accomplished by basing a worker's hourly wages on the amount he or she produces above a defined minimum. Where workers are unionized, collective-bargaining agreements are responsible for setting the rates. Nevertheless, the implementation of the system in each firm varies with respect to a variety of work place factors and can be a bone of contention between workers and management.

In another study of women garment workers in New England, Lamphere found that management frequently manipulated the piece-rate system in its attempts to increase worker productivity.[17] This was done in a variety of ways: by speeding up the work process to shorten the work season, by timing faster workers rather than average workers as they are supposed to do, and by lowering the rates whenever possible. Though management is often successful, Lamphere found that women have developed a number of strategies to resist management's efforts to reduce their real wages and to make them work harder.

Our data confirm these impressions. Many of the women we interviewed complained bitterly about the piece-rate system. A full 67 percent of the women in our sample said they preferred to work on a fixed hourly wage rather than on piece rates. Indeed, the piece-rate system is particularly burdensome for older women.

As we can see from table 5-1, younger women—54 years and younger—report comparable amounts of work satisfaction with their jobs regardless

Table 5-1
Work Satisfaction, Age, and Piece Rate

| Work Satisfaction | 55 and Older | | 54 and Younger | | Total |
	Piece Rate	Standard Rate	Piece Rate	Standard Rate	
Very satisfied	20 (39%)	24 (58%)	68 (34%)	43 (32%)	
Somewhat satisfied	23 (45%)	15 (37%)	85 (46%)	60 (45%)	
Not very satisfied	6 (12%)	2 (5%)	22 (12%)	24 (18%)	
Not at all satisfied	2 (4%)	2	14 (8%)	7 (5%)	
Total	51 (100%)	41 (100%)	184 (100%)	134 (100%)	410 (100%)

Table 5-2
Mean Hourly Wage

55 and Older		54 and Younger	
Piece Rate	*Standard Rate*	*Piece Rate*	*Standard Rate*
$4.21	$4.74	$4.78	$4.89

$F = 5.012$ $F = 0.499$

Level of confidence = 0.0276   Level of confidence = 0.4803

of whether they worked on a piece rate or on a fixed hourly wage. However, older women—women 55 and older—were more likely to report greater levels of work satisfaction if they were employed on a standard rate. Moreover, older women who worked on a standard rate also earned significantly higher than average hourly wages than their age mates employed on a piece-rate basis (see table 5-2), a relationship that is statistically insignificant among younger workers. Older women, then, may prefer to work at standard-rate jobs because such jobs provide higher earnings.

As we can see from table 5-2, jobs that paid a fixed hourly wage tended to pay somewhat more than piece-rate jobs. However, individual women, younger women who feel financial pressures to make money, maybe are more likely than older women to make up more of the differential by working faster—but not without a cost to them. Garvin quotes a harried younger garment worker on a piece-rate job.[18]

> Pressure. There was a lot of pressure. My average pay rate [base rate] is $4.36 to $4.38 per hour. There were days that if I made my incentive, I made almost $5.00. It's a lot of pushing, but I made $1 or 50¢ more . . . that almighty dollar. It takes a lot out of you.

When workers get older it becomes increasingly difficult to sustain such a rapid pace. As financial pressures abate, women may simply stop pushing so hard. An older factory worker told our interviewer:

> Yes, I liked working on piece rate, but I would take standard now because my working days are over. My family is all grown up, and I don't need to rush any more.

However, there is no evidence that older women, workers who have most difficulty working fast, are more likely to have standard-rate jobs. In our sample, 56 percent of older women (55 years or older) had piece-rate jobs, as compared to 59 percent of women aged 54 or younger. Thus, even in this respect, older women do not get the better jobs. Instead, older women who find themselves employed on a piece-rate basis may suffer the most from the pressures the system produces. Unable to work as fast as younger colleagues, they are obliged to accept still lower wages. As we can see from table 5–2, older workers on piece-rate jobs made an average hourly wage of only $4.21 an hour.

Layoffs

Low wages are tolerated because older female production workers have few alternatives in the contemporary labor market. Yet economic contradictions threaten the fragile security these jobs can offer; even a low-wage job is better than not having a job at all.

While blue-collar women of all ages expressed serious fears of the consequences of losing their jobs in an increasingly tight labor market, older women were particularly worried about this. They felt that age discrimination would be an additional barrier to their finding re-employment after a layoff.

However, no evidence was found that this was the case. Among workers who experienced a layoff, six months later older workers were no less likely than younger ones either to have been recalled or to have found a new job.[19] Since older women are a large part of the customary work force in these industries and occupations, employers appear to be just as willing to have an experienced older worker as a younger one.

When industrial contractions and plant closings produce layoffs, female workers who are affected do not change careers or seek alternative types of employment in sales, service, or clerical jobs. They tend to look for other factory jobs in the same or a similar type of industry. However, their chances of finding such a job are only as good as the toss of a coin. Six months after their layoffs, only half of the job losers we studied who had not been recalled had found new jobs, overwhelmingly in unskilled and semiskilled production work.

Moreover, those who did find new jobs tended to lose wages. Except for garment workers, whose wages were lower to begin with, the workers we studied who found new jobs after their layoffs lost an average of $1.00 per hour in wages—a substantial cut. Older women are not alone in having to accept lower wages. Yet their willingness to do so may in part account for the fact that they apparently do not have a harder time than younger women in becoming re-employed. More research is needed to explore this issue.

While job loss and wage cuts hurt younger workers as well as older ones, they can affect older workers in different ways. Perhaps most important is the way wage losses can affect retirement income. The vast majority of the older women we studied were long-term union members and were therefore eligible to receive pensions when they retire. The amount of these monthly pension benefits typically are based on wages earned during the years directly preceding their retirement. Reduced wages during these years will mean smaller pension checks. The value of pensions for women who are unable to find new jobs, even at lower wages, may be even more seriously eroded.

ERISA now requires that pensions be vested with individuals after ten years of service. Therefore, most older job losers probably will not lose their pension benefits entirely. However, the dollar value of these pensions will be frozen at the point at which the women leave their jobs. Pension benefits typically do not become available until women reach retirement age at 62 or 65. The years of inflation between job loss and retirement can make these women's already minimal benefits virtually worthless when they are finally collected. We estimated that full pension benefits for female production workers who retired in 1980 at age 65 were between $125 and $250 per month, depending on their wages and years of service. Should the amount of even full benefits be frozen, in five to ten years they will provide even less financial security than they could at present.

In 1979, Martha Keys, special advisor to the secretary of Health, Education, and Welfare, before the Task Force on Social Security and Women, testified that "The adequacy of retirement income for women is one of the major problems of our society in the next few years."[20] The future loss of pension benefits could pose a serious threat to the well-being of retired blue-collar women who have experienced earnings losses due to declining wages and unemployment—particularly in light of potential cuts in social security. More research is needed on how such women fare economically when they retire.

While the loss of pension benefits worries older women threatened with a layoff, the experience of losing a job can have devastating psychological effects as well. The women's personal responses to job loss varied with their age and their stage in the life cycle. We found that younger women, women with dependent children at home, were significantly more likely to say that losing their jobs made them worry about how they and their families would continue to pay the bills. At the same time, women with young children reported that layoffs gave them more time to be with and do things for their families. Thus, job loss intensified the conflict women with families at home felt between wanting to stay home and care for these families and needing the income their jobs provided. Older women, conversely, were much more likely to report that they missed doing their jobs. They missed being in the work place with the women they had known for so many years. Thus, as aging contracts the network of family relationships and other social involvements, the loss of a job can jeopardize not only financial security but also one's ability to participate in the world at all. Some of our older respondents equated the cessation of work with death. As one older woman put it when she was laid off, "Part of your life seems to come to an end . . . you worked there for so long."

Looking toward Retirement

After a lifetime of working in factories, the vast majority of blue-collar women, like most other workers, do retire at the traditional retirement age of 62 or 65. Also like other workers, it appears that their decision to retire is not related to levels of work satisfaction but to financial considerations. They leave the work force when social-security and pension checks make it possible for them to spend their remaining years in leisure. Before such transfer payments become available, the absence of work can instead mean enforced poverty.

In an open-ended format, we asked the older women, 55 and over, in our sample whether or not they would want to retire at the moment. Only 16 percent said clearly that they did want to retire. Another 36 percent said they wanted to continue working because they liked their jobs. Yet almost half, 48 percent, said they could not afford to retire; among these older women who were single (largely because they were widowed), 53 percent said they could not afford to retire. In conclusion, it appears that while older women who have worked all their lives might want to retire before they reach the retirement age, many fear losing jobs before retirement income becomes available.

Conclusions

Unskilled factory jobs, particularly in the industrial Northeast, historically have provided paid employment for generations of women who needed to earn money. For over 100 years, women employed in such jobs have been immigrants or American women with little education and few skills. Today, new immigrant women from the Portugese Azores, Haiti, Puerto Rico, and Indochina are replacing Italians, Poles, Irish, Greeks, and French Canadians. Unlike their forebears, the post–World War II cohorts of unskilled female production workers have been the beneficiaries of progressive social programs like social security, unemployment insurance, health and safety regulations, and fringe-benefit packages that include health and retirement benefits.

Yet, at the same time, today's blue-collar women need full-time paid employment for more than a relatively brief interlude between leaving school and marriage. As significant contributors to dual-earner families throughout their adult lives, today's female factory workers are becoming increasingly vulnerable to new developments that threaten to undermine their economic well-being. These developments include the erosion of the employment base itself as well as federal cutbacks in social programs like social security and unemployment insurance.

Despite the increasing economic insecurity, today's unskilled production jobs continue to provide stable employment for many older women who need them. Whether or not they can continue to do so by 1990 or beyond, when the older women we have studied have reached retirement age, is still an open question.

Notes

1. Ellen I. Rosen, "Hobson's Choice: Employment and Unemployment among Women Factory Workers in New England." (Draft final report submitted to the Employment and Training Administration, Department of Labor, October 1981).

2. Ibid., p. 51.

3. Alice Kessler Harris, *Women Have Always Worked* (Old Westbury, N.Y.: The Feminist Press, 1981).

4. Milton Cantor and Bruce Laurie, eds. *Class, Sex, and the Woman Worker* (Westport, Conn.: Greenwood Press, 1977).

5. Ellen I. Rosen, "The Changing Jobs of American Women Factory Workers." Paper presented at Conference of Professional and Businesswomen's Foundation, George Washington University and the Service Employees International Union, 5–6 January 1982.

6. Ibid.

7. The names of the women have been changed to protect the privacy of participants in the study.

8. Robert Snow, personal conversation, 1979.

9. Rosen, "Hobson's Choice," p. 90.

10. Ibid., p. 93.

11. Ibid., p. 107.

12. This question was taken from the 1977 Quality of Employment Survey, Institute for Survey Research, University of Michigan.

13. Rosen, "Hobson's Choice."

14. James D. Wright and Richard Hamilton, "Work Satisfaction and Age: Some Evidence for the 'Job Change' Hypothesis," *Social Forces* 56 (June 1978):1140–1148.

15. Rosen, "Hobson's Choice," p. 215.

16. Michele Garvin, "Factory Women: Sexual Equality and the Role of Work" (Ph. D. dissertation, Boston College, 1981).

17. Louise Lamphere, "Working Class Women: Strategies of Resistance in the Workplace" (Boston, Mass.: Unpublished manuscript, 1981).

18. Garvin, "Factory Women . . . ", p. 124.

19. Rosen, "Hobson's Choice, p. 175.

20. U.S. House, Congress, Select Committee on Aging, Subcommittee on Retirement Income and Employment, "Testimony of Martha Keyes," *Hearings before the Task Force on Social Security and Women,* 96th Cong., 1st sess., 16 May, 26 June, 24 July 1979.

Beyond the Hearth: Older Women and Retirement

Maximiliane E. Szinovacz

In their later years, men retire and women remain housewives—or so previous work on aging women would have us believe. Indeed, it was not before the early 1970s that researchers started to discover female retirement, and the number of studies on female retirement is still extremely limited. Why this neglect of women's retirement in the literature? An analysis of recent texts indicates that research on labor-force participation and retirement has been guided by the assumption that retirement constitutes a significant life transition only for men.

Implicitly, this assumption is evident in the conscious exclusion of women in retirement studies. Most investigations on retirement conducted in the United States as well as in other countries relied entirely on male subjects (Simpson, Back, and McKinney 1966; Havighurst et al. 1969). The inherent assumption that research on retirement is necessarily research on male retirement becomes even more obvious when some scholars altogether fail to mention the sex of their subjects in their sample descriptions (George and Maddox 1977; Walker and Price 1975) or do not include a question on sex in their questionnaires (Kimmel, Price, and Walker 1978). Friedman and Orbach (1974) describe this trend well when they state:

> [Women] have been used as a basis for comparisons with men, and almost no study has been devoted to women's attitudes and responses to retirement outside the context of their adjustment to aging per se. [p. 636].

In addition, many texts contain empirically unsustained statements indicating the primary importance of the retirement transition to men as compared to women. Work is believed to constitute a more-prevalent and salient role for men than for women. Since women have discontinuous work histories and are less committed to their work—if they work at all—it is argued, they are unlikely to experience loss of the work role as a significant life event with potential negative consequences to their self-concept, morale, or life satisfaction (Cumming and Henry 1961; Blau 1973). Women are also expected to experience less retirement stress than men because their major

This project was supported by a grant from the NRTA-AARP Andrus Foundation, Washington, D.C.

life interests are believed to center entirely around familial roles and household activities that continue beyond retirement and that offer women socially accepted roles in later life (Blau 1973). For men, retirement is viewed as a significant role loss leading to decreases in social prestige, self-esteem, and a lack of meaningful activities (see Beeson 1975; Lehr 1977; J.H. Fox 1977 for other critiques of this viewpoint).

Applying this perspective to the family literature, researchers also have emphasized retirement as the major family life-cycle transition for aging men but the launching of the children and widowhood as the salient and critical life-cycle transitions for middle-aged and aging women (Duvall 1977; Blau 1973; Troll 1971). The retirement of the husband is assumed to affect the couple and to require adjustments on the part of both spouses (Duvall 1977; Eshleman 1981).

Only within the last few years have some scholars come to question this one-sided view of retirement and started to investigate the incidence and significance of the retirement experience for women. Preliminary findings from these studies seriously question previous assumptions on women's retirement. This chapter reviews the meaning and importance of retirement for women. Given the small number of existing studies and the prevalence of small, exploratory investigations among them, many of our conclusions will have to remain tentative. It is evident, however, that results from the population of retired men cannot be generalized to female retirees. Therefore, investigations dealing exclusively with male retirement (which have resulted in a fair body of literature) are not considered in this chapter.

The Life Situation of Retiring Women

Retirement has been conceptualized as a process, an event, and a role (Atchley 1976a; 1980). As a process, retirement constitutes the transition from the status of worker to that of nonworker and/or recipient of retirement benefits, and it signifies withdrawal from the work role and entry into the rather vaguely defined role of retiree. Viewing retirement as a process implies that its meaning evolves from a person's preretirement experience and life situation. The significance and meaning of retirement thus are tied inherently to the significance and meaning of work within the total life context of retiring individuals. Indeed, it is precisely because researchers attributed little importance to work outside the home in the lives of women that they anticipated retirement to have few if any effects on aging women. In order to understand fully the impact of retirement on women's lives, it is thus necessary to consider major aspects of the life situation of women at the threshold of retirement.

Labor-Force Participation and Retirement

If retirement were a life transition that affected only a minority of women, it surely would be of little social significance. However, during the last decades increasing numbers of women have joined the labor force, and this trend has been particularly pronounced among middle-aged women. In 1950, 25.9 percent of all women aged 55–59 years and 20.6 percent of all women aged 60–64 years were in the labor force as compared to 47.6 percent and 36.2 percent, respectively, in 1970 and 47.7 percent and 31.7 percent, respectively, in 1978 (U.S. Bureau of the Census 1978a; 1978b). For the 54–59-year age group, labor-force-participation rates are even higher (52.4 percent in 1970 and 53.8 percent in 1978).

These increases in labor-force participation among middle-aged women are accounted for largely by changes in the work status of married women. In the period between 1948 and 1979, the proportion of nonmarried women aged 55–65 in the labor force remained relatively stable at about two-thirds of this group, whereas the proportion of married workers more than doubled (16.9 percent in 1948 and 37.4 percent in 1979; U.S. Department of Labor 1980; Schwab and Irelan 1981, p. 22).

These trends in labor-force participation have led to a pronounced increase of female retirees among women aged 57 years and over. Between 1952 and 1978, the proportion of retired women in this age group increased by 29 percentage points, whereas the proportion of homemakers decreased by 31 percentage points (Pampel 1981, p. 70). The exact proportion of retirees among the population of aging women has been difficult to estimate because official data sources often collapse housewives and retirees into the category of nonworkers. Data from the Harris report suggest that the overwhelming majority of women aged 65 and over consider themselves retirees (50 percent) rather than housewives (30 percent). An additional 17 percent of the women in this age group were still employed or looking for employment and can be expected to join the group of female retirees (Harris and Associates 1975).

Given these changes, there can be little doubt that female retirement has become a socially significant phenomenon. It is also clear that participation in the labor force and retirement are no longer restricted to a marginal group of single or divorced women but involve growing numbers of married women, many of whom re-enter the labor force in mid-life (Mallan 1974; Lopata and Norr 1980). Also, as more women combine work and family roles, the image of the aging housewife dreading the empty nest and her husband's retirement characterizes a decreasing proportion of the female population (Sweet 1973; Lopata and Norr 1980).

Work Patterns

Not only are increasing numbers of middle-aged women employed, but also they exhibit more-continuous work patterns than in the past. Certainly, many aging women discontinued employment during their childrearing years. These interruptions have a significant impact on women's social-security benefits and retirement incomes, but they are not necessarily a sign of lacking attachment to the labor force during the women's later life stages. Data from the Continuous Work History Sample (Mallen, 1974) show that the majority of women (65 percent) newly entitled to retired-worker benefits in 1970 had spent over fifteen years of their lives in the labor force. Twenty-five percent worked continuously for fifteen or more years and 40 percent with some disruptions. Census data further indicate a sharp increase in the median number of years spent in their current jobs by women aged 55 to 65 years, from 4.5 years in 1951 to 8.8 years in 1973 (U.S. Bureau of the Census 1978). There is also some evidence that despite breaks in their careers, women remain within similar occupations throughout their working lives (Rosenfeld 1974).

In addition, greater diversity in women's life-styles caused by later entry into and a greater proportion of time spent altogether outside familial roles signifies a "decrystallization of female life patterns" (Lopata and Norr 1980). These trends suggest that more and more women will experience work outside the home as a significant part of their lives and, consequently, are likely to view retirement as an important, though not necessarily critical, life transition.

Work Commitment and Centrality of the Work Role

One reason why retirement has been thought to present fewer problems for women than for men concerns the centrality of work outside the home in women's lives. Increasing labor-force-participation rates and length of gainful employment provide clear evidence that women now spend a greater part of their lives in occupational roles, but they may still attach little significance to their work. If this were the case, retirement may indeed be experienced as a relatively unimportant event or even as a relief.

Data concerning women's work commitment and the salience of work in their lives again contradict previous assumptions. For one thing, women are increasingly participating in the provider role. Single, divorced, and some widowed women often have to work to support themselves and their children. For these women, gainful employment constitutes their major source of income, and insufficient retirement benefits force some women to remain working beyond the usual retirement years. Also, many wives now obtain employment to help pay family expenses and significantly contribute to the family income (Hoffman and Nye 1974; Hesse 1979).

Career women, of course, are known to demonstrate considerable work commitment and to consider work outside the home as a major life interest (Epstein 1970; Fogarty, Rapoport, and Rapoport 1971; Holmstrom 1972; Pepitone-Rockwell 1980). However, even among women in less-specialized and nonprofessional occupations, work motives are not entirely economic. Rather, multidimensionality of work commitment prevails (Haller and Rosenmayr 1971; Lindenstein Walshok 1979; Szinovacz 1979). For instance, in her study of women in blue-collar and service occupations, Lindenstein Walshok identified four major work motives in addition to financial work incentives—namely, the desire to get out and do something, desire for social contacts, desire for challenge and personal satisfaction, and the need for achievement and recognition (1979, pp. 73–74).

Furthermore, because of their interrupted work histories, women's work and career patterns differ from those of men. Middle-aged women who return to the work force after the childrearing years may not be able to accomplish occupational goals by the time of retirement. These women are particularly likely to view retirement as a disruptive experience (Atchley 1976b; 1976c).

Research dealing more directly with women in the preretirement years also supports the notion that work represents a salient role for women. For instance, Streib and Schneider (1971) found women to have less-positive feelings about retirement than men. Women more than men reported that they missed social contacts at work and the feeling of doing a good job. In his study of retired telephone-company employees and teachers, Atchley (1971; 1976b; 1976c) found particularly female teachers to be highly work oriented and to carry this orientation into retirement. Employed women of all age groups investigated by Prentis (1980) not only indicated relative positive attitudes toward retirement but also mentioned missing work, social contacts at work, use of time, and finances as a potential problem at the time of retirement. These findings suggest that women obtain important rewards from their participation in the labor force. In addition to economic independence and security, work provides women with social contacts and a sense of usefulness and accomplishment, the loss of which could seriously hinder adjustment to retirement.

Finally, arguments concerning sex differences in the centrality of the work role fail to consider that individuals of both sexes may attach similar importance to more than one life role. Marital and kin relationships, social contacts, and diverse leisure activities have been shown to play an important role for the life satisfaction of both aging men and women (Campbell, Converse, and Rodgers 1976; Markides and Martin 1979; Palmore and Kivett 1977; Larson 1978). Some research also indicates that work is not necessarily the central life interest of men (Dubin 1956; Fogarty, Rapoport, and Rapoport 1971; Bailyn 1970; Friedman and Orbach 1974; Maddox 1966). Also, with increasing numbers of retirees and the trend toward earlier retirement (Pampel 1981), the retiree role has become more socially acceptable and less threatening in terms of the potential status loss previously associated with retirement (Sussman 1972; Friedman and Orbach 1974; Bell 1976; Maddox 1966; Taylor 1972; Sheppard 1976). We thus may speak of plurality of life interests and diversity of needs among men and women at the preretirement and retirement stages (Neugarten 1977; Kahana and Kiyak 1977; Block et al. 1978). Some of these interests are facilitated by outside employment (for example, social contacts and income), but others are pursued parallel to and relatively independent of the individual's work role. Retirement adjustment is, therefore, not only contingent on the extrinsic and intrinsic rewards gained from work but also on the extent to which participation in the labor force facilitated other life interests.

Income

For most individuals, retirement involves a significant reduction in income (Fox 1979; Friedman and Sjogren 1981; Schwab and Irelan 1981). Even though the reduction in absolute income is highest for married men and lowest for nonmarried women, this reduction means a substantial economic loss, particularly to unattached women (Friedman and Sjogren 1981). Since aging women in general and unattached women in particular have lower incomes than other population groups, an income reduction upon retirement of over 40 percent often leads to postretirement incomes below the poverty level. In 1971, for example, the median income for all nonmarried women aged 65 and over was $1,720; for nonmarried men, $2,270; and for married couples, $3,970 (Thompson 1974). Sixty percent of the nonmarried women, 40 percent of the nonmarried men, and 20 percent of the couples in this age group had incomes below the poverty level. These income differentials by sex have been attributed to a variety of factors including women's discontinuous and part-time work patterns and their overrepresentation in lower-level jobs and in female occupations with lower wage levels (Pampel 1981; Rosenfeld 1974; Mallan 1974; Thompson 1974; Muller 1980; Parnes et al. 1976). Furthermore, women tend to retire earlier than men and are thus more likely to receive reduced social-security benefits (Foner and Schwab 1981). However, with the increasing trend among men to opt for earlier retirement, this difference has been decreasing as have income inequalities between the sexes among the higher age groups (Foner and Schwab 1981; Pampel 1981). Finally, women are less likely to be covered by private pensions, a factor that may also contribute to their lower retirement incomes (Beller 1980).

Not only are women's incomes considerably lower than men's, they also possess fewer assets than both married and nonmarried men. In 1975, the median net worth was $19,359 for married men as compared to $5,621 for nonmarried men and $4,908 for nonmarried women; and the assets owned by nonmarried women were more likely to be tied up in home equities than those of either married or nonmarried men (Friedman and Sjogren 1981).

Particularly, nonmarried women thus face retirement from an especially difficult economic position. While married women also have few independent economic resources, they may and often are better off relying on the higher retirement incomes of their husbands. Indeed, as Hess and Markson (1980, p. 200) point out:

> It is a sad commentary on women's wages that many working wives do better to accept half of their husband's Social Security rather than their own entitlement.

Family Status and Family Roles

Women have also been assumed to experience few retirement difficulties because of the continuity of their familial and household roles. Several arguments can be brought forward against this claim. Women often return to the labor force in their middle or later years in order to escape the empty-nest household. These women gain satisfaction and self-confidence from the newly gained ability to employ their assertive skills and to obtain personal and economic independence (Livson 1976; 1977; Rubin 1979; Spence and Lonner 1971; Barnett and Baruch 1978). Such life changes also can lead to a shift in women's orientations—that is, from relation-centered values to an increased emphasis on their own abilities and feelings (Back 1974). The assumption that women can substitute former work activities easily with increased involvement in household and family roles thus disregards the fact that many women choose to work in order to escape a full-time household routine or because they are not fully occupied with household and family tasks once their children have reached school age or have left the parental home (Sobol 1974). In this case, household activities are unlikely to represent an adequate substitute for former employment status. Being forced to assume full responsibility for an unsatisfactory or at least unfulfilling role might prove as stressful to women as loss of status due to retirement may be to men (Szinovacz 1980). Also, it is quite doubtful that women who preferred to work rather than to remain full-time housewives in their middle years will develop strong interest and find fulfillment in these same activities once they retire. Keeping busy and involvement in meaningful activities thus may become important areas of concern for women at the threshold of retirement (Laurence 1961; Prentis 1980).

It is also often overseen that female retirees are bound to spend the majority of their working lives outside a marital relationship. In 1978, 52 percent of women aged 65 years and over were widowed, and this proportion increases to 69 percent among those aged 75 and over (Older Women: The Economics of Aging). Additionally, 70 percent of all women aged 55 years and over were living alone as compared to only 36 percent of the men in this age group (Older Women: The Economics of Aging 1980). Many women thus may face retirement and widowhood within a relatively short time period, and such asynchronized and/or accumulated life changes have been shown to hinder adaptation processes (Seltzer 1976; Bengtson 1973; Morgan 1977). It is also conceivable that some wives retire early with their husbands, resume work after the husband's death, and then retire again after a relatively short time period in the labor force. However, data to confirm this speculation are currently not available.

The fact that many female retirees are or become widows also implies that their home-centered activities are no longer services for others. Both retirement and widowhood have been described as roles lacking relational content (Rosow 1974). While the young mother may derive a sense of accomplishment and fulfillment from providing services to her husband and children, the widowed retiree performs household activities primarily for herself. While some of her home-centered activities may be intrinsically satisfying, they surely lack the importance of doing things for others (Matthews 1979). Occasional help provided to adult children is unlikely to substitute fully for the daily exchange of services between spouses.

Social Contacts and Leisure Activities

Research on women's work motives as well as on their concerns in regard to retirement suggests that their participation in the labor force provides women with an important source of social contacts; and social contacts have been shown to affect women' psychological well-being greatly (Powers and Bultena 1976; Lowenthal and Haven 1968). One of the reasons why working women may find retirement a difficult transition is that they have developed a network of social contacts among work colleagues rather than or at least in addition to acquaintances made in nonwork activities. Loss of this network at retirement could result in a serious reduction in the women's social contacts and psychological well-being. These contacts cannot be replaced easily by increased attention on the part of the husband because the women's confidant and close contacts are usually same-sex friends and fulfill other social needs rather than those served by the husband (Powers and Bultena 1976; Candy 1977). Specifically, same-sex friends can increase women's sense of status and power (Candy 1977). Furthermore, retirees who become widows shortly after retirement will have to cope with a dual loss in social supports.

Unfortunately, current research provides little evidence as to the prevalence and importance of co-workers within women's social networks. A recent study by Stueve and Fischer (1978) shows that somewhat less than 10 percent of middle-aged women's social networks consist of co-workers (a mean number of 1.7 co-workers among a mean number of 18.4 network persons). Since these data comprise nonworking women, this proportion is probably considerably higher for middle-aged workers. Among women aged 65 years and over, co-workers practically disappear from the social network. Obviously, this decrease could be attributed to the fact that retirees may identify past co-workers as friends rather than co-workers. The author's results indicate, however, that this is not the case:

> [T]here is little evidence that older respondents continue relationships with former work colleagues. . . . This suggests that exit out of the work role tends to syphon off relationships with most of one's former co-workers. [p. 26]

In addition, social contacts at work not only serve as a source for developing new friendships but also provide routine social encounters with a variety of people. While these contacts may remain quite superficial, they still may contribute to a woman's self-concept, feelings of usefulness, and social accomplishment. For instance, in her pilot study of nonprofessional university employees, Szinovacz (1978) found retired women express regret over the loss of former work colleagues as well as the daily contacts with students. This attitude is very well expressed in the comments of one of the women in this sample:

> And I just miss the people. And I knew everybody. After all, if you work in a place for 40 years you can't help but know them. I see them on the street, but it isn't like being in the office. If I'm lonely here, there are various meetings and we enjoy that, but I really enjoyed young people. This is where I miss working more than anything. [p. 7]

Another problem area mentioned by retirees or women at the threshold of retirement concerns their leisure-time activities, or more generally, their ability to keep busy after retirement. While men may face similar problems, married women or widows may be particularly disadvantaged in this regard. Women in general lack socialization for leisure-time activities, and working wives in particular are usually too restricted in the amount of leisure time available to them to develop outside interests and hobbies (Lehr 1978; Szalai et al. 1972; Walker and Woods 1976). This lack of leisure-time socialization may leave female retirees quite literally with a void of meaningful activities. Also, even if they engage in postretirement activities like volunteer work, these activities often cannot substitute fully for paid work (Sommers 1976).

Another reason why married and widowed retirees particularly may have difficulties developing independent leisure activities could be attributed to their socialization into dependence on their husbands as well as to social norms against the participation of unaccompanied women in public places (Rosenkaimer et al. 1976; G.L. Fox 1977). At least some of these suggestions are grounded in evidence. Data from a nationally representative sample of Austrian women ($N = 28,400$) show that female retirees engage more regularly in home-centered leisure activities (for example reading and watching TV) than employed women but are less likely than employed women to participate in outside activities such as going to the movies, eating out, taking walks, or playing sports (Szinovacz 1979). Since U.S. retirees have been noted to be more action oriented than Europeans (Havighurst et al. 1969), these observations may not hold for female retirees in this country. Indeed, some evidence indicates that older women may increase their involvement in socializing activities and organizations (Hendricks 1977), but further empirical research clearly is needed to clarify this issue.

The Retirement Transition

Given current societal norms, most individuals expect to retire. The retirement decision, therefore, centers primarily on the question when to retire rather than whether or not to retire at all (Atchley 1976a). This does not imply, however, that the retirement decision always reflects personal preference.

Individuals retire because they are forced out of the labor force (mandatory retirement), because they are unable to work, or because they feel that leaving the labor force would be appropriate and would offer them the opportunity to pursue other preferred activities. There is clear evidence that women retire earlier and more for voluntary reasons than men (Atchley 1976b; 1976c; Palmore 1965; Mallan 1974; Foner and Schwab 1981) In explaining this trend, Palmore (1965) referred primarily to women's lack of job commitment. Atchley (1976a) criticized Palmore's interpretation and argued that women's earlier retirement may be attributed to a variety of reasons, including societal pressure to retire and take care of retired or ill husbands, their economic support by the husband, lack of job satisfaction among women in lower-level jobs, and a trend toward joint retirement of spouses.

Some more-recent studies on retirement tend to support Atchley's (1976a) statements. In her study of nonmarried women aged 58–63 years,

Sherman (1974) found labor-force participation negatively related to age, widowhood, education, and racial background (black). The racial and age differences were partially a function of the differing health status of women in these groups. These women also were shown to be less likely to work if they had health problems, received social-security benefits, or obtained support from their children (Sherman 1974). For married women, labor-force participation at a more-advanced age seems to be encouraged by economic responsibilities for others and for oneself (support for dependent children, lack of a pension coverage on the part of the husband), the economic resources of the wife (lack of coverage by retirement pensions), and by familial responsibilities (for example, taking care of an ill or disabled husband) (Henretta and O'Rand 1980).

Increasing evidence also shows that couples decide together about retirement and opt for joint retirement. Since wives are usually younger than their husbands, joint retirement may lead the wife to retire earlier at the husband's usual retirement age. However, other evidence suggests that joint retirement is more likely to delay retirement for both spouses (Anderson, Clark and Johnson, 1980; Clark, Johnson, and McGermed 1980). Overall, their economic security and familial considerations tend to discourage labor-force participation among aging married women. In 1976, only 7 percent of all married women aged 65 years and over were in the labor force as compared to 8.3 percent of the widowed, divorced, or separated women and 15.6 percent of the single women (Hess and Markson 1980, p. 186). The importance of economic considerations for the labor-force participation of aging women is also evident from the work motives of these women. In her report on Austrian women, Szinovacz (1979) found over one-third of currently working women over 60 years of age to mention retirement benefits as a work motive. Participation in a family enterprise, interest in the work, social contacts, and support for the family were also relatively common work motives for this group of women.

These and other findings (Barfield and Morgan 1978a) would suggest an overriding effect of health and economic reasons on retirement timing by women, a trend that corresponds with results on retirement timing by men (Clark and Spengler 1980; Foner and Schwab 1981). Women thus retire earlier than men either because they can afford to retire or because they are unable to continue working. In addition, they may feel retirement to be appropriate at a certain age or life-cycle stage (for example, when the husband retires) or obligatory in regard to new family responsibilities (for example, failing health of the husband). There is little evidence that would suggest, however, that women's decision to retire is prompted primarily (or more than men's) by the alternative attractions seen in postretirement activities and a reflection of low work commitment. Of course, some women may be pushed out of the labor force owing to negative job experiences and many do look forward to retirement, but these trends and orientations are expressions of a societal redefinition of retirement and apply to both sexes (Friedman and Orbach 1974; Atchley 1976a).

Recent studies have shown consistently that most people look forward to retirement and expect no major adjustment problems to retirement (Seldon, McEwen, and Ryser 1975; Harris et at. 1975). This trend applies to both sexes, but some studies did find women to express more-negative attitudes than men and to be more anxious about the future (Streib and Schneider 1971; Atchley 1976b; 1976c; Atchley and Corbett 1977; Anderson et al 1978; Jacobson 1974; Laurence 1961). However, contradictory evidence that indicates more-positive retirement attitudes on the part of women rather than men is reported by Prentis (1980) and Beuther and Cryns (1979).

Investigations of determinants of retirement attitudes suggest that high work commitment may increase women's reluctance to retire, whereas financial security and leisure plans for retirement increase positive retirement attitudes. Thus, women in high occupational positions proved to have relatively negative retirement attitudes (Prentis 1980; Streib and Schneider 1971). Low resistance to retirement was found to be furthered by women's financial resources and the number of activities planned for retirement (Johnson and Price-Bonham 1980).

Specific problems and advantages women anticipate for their retirement are reported by Prentis (1980). He found middle-aged women to look forward to leisure activities (travel, hobbies), more free time, as well as a more-flexible time schedule. Loss of social contacts, financial problems, and lack of meaningful activities were among potential problems foreseen for the postretirement period. This author also reports that most of his middle-aged subjects had thought about retirement, although only 24 percent had made serious plans. Retirement plans were made more often by married women and women with higher incomes.

Overall, these findings suggest that women approach retirement with a relatively positive attitude even though they appear to be somewhat more reluctant to retire than men. Women who are strongly committed to their work, whose work provides them with many social contacts, and who have low incomes seem to express more-negative feelings and thus could be expected to experience more adjustment problems than other groups.

Retirement Effects

In evaluating the effect retirement has on individuals, it is essential to differentiate between retirement adjustment and other individual or situational retirement effects that suggest changes in a person's life-style but that have little impact on adjustment or life satisfaction. Research on female retirement focused primarily on retirement adjustment in general and, in a few cases, determinants of retirement adjustment. To what extent women's life pattern changes after retirement is virtually unknown. Indeed, an overview of the literature on the effects of retirement on women reveals one dominant and typically shared opinion—namely, that our knowledge of this phenomenon is too limited to draw definite conclusions (Beeson 1975; Atchley and Corbett 1977; Little 1981). The few studies that have been carried out, however, do provide some interesting insights into women's reactions to retirement and imply important questions for future research.

Adjustment to Retirement

In direct contradiction to previous assumptions that retirement would be a more-difficult transition for men than for women, current studies suggest that women are more likely than men to experience retirement as a stressful life event. While both sexes have been shown to adjust to retirement reasonably well, women were reported to be somewhat less satisfied with retirement than men and to take longer to adapt to the retirement transition (Streib and Schneider 1971; Atchley 1976b; 1976c). Furthermore, women, but not men, who approach retirement with a negative attitude seem unable to adjust to retirement even after a lengthy time period (Levy 1980). In comparison to men, female retirees were more likely to feel useless and lonely and to miss social contacts and the feeling of doing a good job. Perceptions of financial problems were also more pronounced among women than among men (Streib and Schneider 1971; Atchley 1976b; 1976c). Somewhat divergent results are reported by Sheldon, McEwan, and Ryser (1975). These researchers found women to be more anxious about retirement and to show less preference for the retirement status than men but to adjust better and more quickly to this life transition.

Studies comparing different groups of aging women (employed, retired, housewives) further support the notion that retirement may have negative effects on at least some women. For instance, retirees proved to have lower morale and affect balance than employed aging women (Jaslow 1976; J.H. Fox 1977). Comparisons of retirees and housewives resulted in somewhat contradictory evidence. Whereas Jaslow (1976) found housewives to have lower morale than either retirees or employed women, J.H. Fox's (1977) data indicated that retirees score lower on affect balance than housewives.

Even though the overall effect of retirement may be somewhat more negative for women than men, retirement always entails positive as well as negative consequences. In-depth analyses from a small sample of married female retirees show that positive effects of retirement are attributed primarily to the decrease in women's role obligations and the increased opportunity to engage in new and interesting activities. Some of the negative retirement experiences mentioned by these women included feelings of wasting their time, feeling cut off and useless, lack of stimulation and achievement, fear of becoming dull, being bored and lonesome, missing people at work, and difficulties in settling down to daily chores (Szinovacz 1978).

Determinants of Retirement Adjustment

Inquiry into the factors that affect retirement adjustment is important not only because it offers explanations of differential adaptation among divergent population groups but also because it provides an important basis for social intervention. Knowledge of the conditions that hinder retirement-adaptation processes can help us to identify specific risk or target groups for intervention, and it can serve also as a guideline for program development. Given our extremely limited information on female retirement, current retirement programs must rely primarily on the evidence obtained for male retirement. However, the problems and needs of female retirees may differ substantially from those of men (Johnson and Price-Bonham 1980; Levy 1980).

In addressing the effects of retirement on individuals, one must consider both direct and indirect consequences. Retirees may miss their work, but also they may experience problems because retirement deprives them of means essential for the fulfillment of other life goals. For instance, the loss of income that often is associated with retirement could force retirees to forego some of the social or leisure activities they could afford while they were still working. Furthermore, retirees may be faced with problems that are age related and not a direct function of the retirement transition but that can affect adaptation processes and adjustment to retirement.

Income. Research on male retirement provides clear evidence that income constitutes one of the most potent determinants of retirement adjustment and morale after retirement. Indeed, Atchley (1976a; 1980) suggests that most individuals will experience few negative retirement effects if they can afford meaningful leisure roles. As was indicated in the previous sections, women usually suffer a significant reduction in income after they retire from the labor force, and nonmarried women have lower postretirement incomes and assets than any other group of aged individuals. These differences in income at least partially account for the relatively low morale of retired women. For example, Jaslow (1976) reports that controlling for income greatly reduces the positive relationship between employment and morale found in his sample of aging women. Indeed, within the highest income group, retirees proved to have a higher morale than the employees. In her study of 115 female retirees, Szinovacz (1982a) also discovered a clear relationship between income and retirement satisfaction. Furthermore, women with a retirement income of less than $10,000 were somewhat more likely than women with higher incomes to state that they would have preferred to retire later than they did. Finally, women not only have lower incomes than men, but also they are less likely than men to perceive their retirement incomes as adequate (Atchley 1976b; 1976c).

Income provides retirees with the means to engage in diverse social and leisure activities. Thus, it may indirectly affect retirees' life satisfaction through its effect on their social and leisure participation (Markides and Martin 1979).

Because of their relatively low incomes, female retirees must be considered a potential risk group in regard to retirement adjustment. Women may require special preretirement information in regard to their postretirement income situation and will also need education in money management to deal effectively with loss of income after retirement. Also, programs developed for female retirees will have to be cheap in order to attract low-income women.

Health. Another factor that has been found consistently to affect retirement adjustment is individuals' physical well-being. Health problems often force a person to retire before she or he is prepared for this life transition, and they preclude participation in a variety of social and leisure activities. In the case of women, failing health of a family member, particularly the husband, also plays an important role in the decision to retire and may thus force a hasty and unplanned transition; and care for ill family members can seriously restrict a woman's ability to engage in outside activities.

There is some evidence that health problems in fact hinder women's life satisfaction and morale (Jaslow 1976; J.H. Fox 1977). However, women may be more able than men to overcome the negative effects even of serious health problems. In her comparative study of healthy and chronically ill retirees, Levy (1980) found even chronically ill women to adjust relatively well to retirement provided their attitude toward this life transition was positive. This was not the case for chronically ill men. Based on these results, Levy (1980, p. 109) concludes:

> [The woman's] needs are radically distinct from [the] aging male's. . . . The aging woman seems to be especially vulnerable to a social isolation which has come about as a consequence of differential social expectations and training. Her distinct need lies in the area of social construction.

Since health problems constitute perhaps the primary reasons for retirement among persons otherwise unwilling to leave the labor force, and since negative retirement attitudes seem to have profound and lasting effects on women, female retirees with health problems constitute another target group for social programs. These women may learn to deal with their physical handicaps, but they may never fully adjust to their forced retirement. Women who are known to retire because of illness may benefit particularly from preretirement programs designed to reduce negative retirement attitudes.

Attitude toward Retirement. Levy's (1980) results already suggest a clear relationship between retirement attitudes and postretirement morale. Other studies also show that both men and women who approach retirement with a negative attitude experience problems in adjusting to retirement and score lower on diverse satisfaction and morale measures than individuals with positive attitudes (Sheldon, McEwan, and Ryser, 1975; Atchley 1976a). If, as Levy (1980) indicates, negative retirement attitudes have more-lasting effects on women than on men, then this could also explain why women tend to take longer to adjust to retirement than men (Atchley 1976b, 1976c; Streib and Schneider 1971).

In evaluating the relationship between retirement attitudes and adjustment, it is important to keep in mind that negative attitudes may be prompted by or reflect the anticipation of difficult and unsatisfactory life circumstances upon retirement. Negative retirement attitudes could thus represent a relatively valid, global indicator of future retirement problems and, in this capacity, provide another means to identify potential risk groups. This approach would be particularly appropriate for women if future research supports the existing evidence in regard to a stronger persistence of the relationship between retirement attitudes and adjustment for this population group.

Social and Leisure Activities. Meaningful social and leisure activities seem to represent a prerequisite for successful adaptation to retirement. While there is some indication that retirement results in a loss of social contacts with former work colleagues (see previous discussion), the effect of women's retirement on their social contacts with other persons remains unclear. Atchley (1976b; 1976c) reports differential effects for divergent occupational groups: A decline in social contacts occurred primarily among female teachers but not among the telephone-company employees. J.H. Fox (1977) found smaller social networks among retired than among the employed women, but retirees had more close friends than the employees and engaged in more interactions with neighbors.

That social contacts have an important effect on women's retirement adjustment was demonstrated in several studies. For instance, J.H. Fox

(1977) found social contacts to be more-important predictors of the affect balance of retired than other groups of women, and lack of social contacts ranks among the most frequently mentioned concerns of female retirees (Sheldon, McEwan, and Ryser 1975; Szinovacz 1982a).

Obviously, retirement leads to an increase in free time. While some women view this change positively, allowing them more time for interesting activities and decreasing stress due to overload problems and the adherence to a rigid time schedule, others find it hard to develop a new routine, complain about wasting their time, and express feelings of boredom and uselessness (Szinovacz 1978; 1980). However, little is known about how retired women spend their leisure time. The Austrian data referred to earlier suggest a relatively high level of home-centered activities among female retirees (Szinovacz 1979); but this trend may not apply to other nations (Havighurst et al 1969). Some U.S. studies indicate an increase in diverse leisure activities among middle-aged women (Hendricks 1977), and it also has been suggested that retirement leads primarily to an extension of those activities performed prior to the retirement transition. For instance, Atchley (1976a) found his sample of retired teachers to be quite busy with the management of financial and social affairs. Overinvolvement in social roles can be used as a means to reduce role strain. Thus, on the one hand, working women can legitimize underperformance in some roles by their work commitments. Retired women, on the other hand, will find it much harder to excuse themselves from diverse social and other obligations by referring to role stress. This could lead to a sudden increase in role obligations and could explain why some women claim to be extremely busy after retirement. Thus, those women who were not involved in a variety of leisure activities before retirement may find it difficult to develop new interests and hobbies.

Overall, most retired women seem able to occupy their time in a meaningful and satisfactory way unless health problems or low income prevent their participation in social and leisure activities (Sheldon, McEwan, and Ryser 1975; Barfield and Morgan 1978b). Indeed, among 115 recently retired women, retirement was perceived to lead to positive changes in the use of free time. Only one-fifth of these women indicated a decrease in satisfaction with the way they spend their time after retirement. For this sample, the most frequent leisure pursuits included church-related activities and volunteer work; but many women also indicated some interest in charity and educational programs, trips, and art-and-craft groups (Szinovacz 1982a). The organization of such activities for retired women may constitute an important task for agencies serving the aging population. It is also obvious from these results that increased efforts to involve retired women in volunteer and charity programs may benefit both the women and the agencies.

Marital Relations after Retirement. Interest in the effects of male retirement led to a fair number of studies investigating reactions of wives to their
husbands' retirement. Research on husbands' or couples' adjustment to
the wife's retirement is, however, practically nonexistent (for some new
evidence, see Szinovacz 1982b). Even critics of the neglect of female retirement in past research failed to propose an integrative approach that considers the employment status and retirement of both spouses (Beeson 1975;
Kline 1975; Lehr 1977). It is likely that earlier studies on wives reactions to
their husbands' retirement are biased owing to this restricted perspective.
For instance, frequent complaints about husband's interference with household tasks may be typical for housewives but not for retired wives (Darnley
1975; Fengler 1975).

While some studies indicate little involvement of wives in their husbands' retirement (Kerckhoff 1964; 1966), others do suggest concern with the
husband's retirement on the part of the wife (Fengler 1975). The one consistent finding on aging couples is that companionship, mutual understanding,
and expressive orientations are necessary conditions for marital satisfaction
at this life stage (Cavan 1962; Roberts and Roberts 1980; Lipman 1960;
1961; Darnley 1975). After the husband's retirement, both spouses need to
develop a more-expressive rather than instrumental orientation in order to
adapt successfully as a couple to this life transition (Lipman 1960; 1961). If
such support by the husband is lacking, women may find retirement particularly stressful.

Major problems experienced by couples with retired husbands center
around his involvement in household tasks. Particularly, lower-class wives
tend to view their husbands' increased participation in household activities
as interference in their domain, are dissatisfied with his performance of
household roles, and complain about having the husband underfoot.
Among middle-class couples and couples with retired wives, conversely, the
household participation of the husband is more accepted although spouses
may disagree on how tasks are to be performed (Kerckhoff 1966; Heyman
and Jeffers 1968; Maas and Kuypers 1974; Keating and Cole 1980; Szinovacz 1980).

The importance of retirement of either spouse for the marital relationship can be seen in the fact that during their working lives, spouses spend a
good part of their time and activities outside the home. After retirement,
they are reunited at home and may have to learn to adapt to each other's
presence and previously unnoticed habits (Foote 1956). Data from a small
study of female retirees and their spouses suggest that retirement adjustment of couples may be furthered by joint retirement. These couples planned
not only for joint retirement timing but also for joint retirement activities
that clearly reduced the stress of this life transition for both spouses. One of
the most commonly noted positive consequences of the wife's retirement

was the reduction in time stress experienced by many dual-work couples and the spouses' increased ability to engage in mutually satisfactory and joint activities. In contrast to previous findings, these wives did not object to their husbands' involvement in household tasks and only rarely perceived the husband's continuous presence at home in a negative way. Improvement in marital relations after the wife's retirement was also particularly pronounced among those couples in which the husband objected to his wife's working and/or held traditional attitudes regarding marital role-allocation patterns. However, if the wife experienced significant retirement-adjustment problems and attempted to rely solely on her husband for emotional support, serious problems in the marriage did occur (Szinovacz 1978; 1980).

One of the most common assumptions in regard to wives' retirement is that they will reassume their full-time household roles after retirement and that the division of tasks between spouses will become more sex segregated. Research evidence suggests, however, that this is only rarely the case. The assumption is contingent on the husband's remaining in the labor force after the wife's retirement or on traditional sex-role attitudes on the part of the husband. Also, the division of household tasks among aging couples seems to remain relatively sex segregated even if the wife works, thus necessitating little change after her retirement. Particularly if both spouses retire together, there is little reason for them to alter their previously established division of labor in the home. Both spouses may spend more time with these activities and may improve their performance of household roles (for example, the wife cooks fancier meals), but the overall distribution of tasks is not altered drastically. Indeed, some women complained that they find it particularly difficult to settle down to household tasks after their retirement (Szinovacz 1978; 1980).

Future research will have to consider both spouses' retirement patterns in order to arrive at a fuller understanding of retirement effects on married persons. Also, the marital-adjustment processes necessitated by retirement are seldom considered in retirement-preparation programs. Couples probably should be made aware of potential effects of retirement for the couple, and such programs ought to include both spouses.

Needs of Female Retirees. The limited literature on female retirement has not as yet provided us with sufficient information as to the specific needs of female retirees. Findings reported in this section suggest that an adequate income, meaningful social and leisure activities, and in the case of married women, mutual adaptation processes on the part of both spouses constitute important prerequisites for successful coping with this life event.

Compared to men, women seem somewhat disadvantaged in retirement because of their relatively low income and also because they often lack socialization for leisure activities and depend more on social contacts than men. Indeed, in her study of 115 retired women, Szinovacz (1982a) found "difficulties in meeting new people" among the most frequently mentioned problems. Another major area of concern indicated in this study was house maintenance and heavy household work. Even though these women had few health problems and were quite able to lead an independent life, they found it increasingly difficult to deal with heavy household work and home repairs. Given, particularly, nonmarried women's limited economic resources, they also cannot afford to hire outside help.

What seems evident is that women's retirement needs are distinct from those experienced by men because of their divergent socioeconomic position as well as their specific responsibilities and interests. These differences in the life situation of retired men and women may account for the sex differences in retirement adjustment shown in previous research. There can be little doubt that preretirement and other programs designed for retirees will have to take these differences into account.

Summary and Conclusion

Female retirement has received little attention from researchers because work was not considered a central or important role for women and because women were assumed to become full-time housewives again after they retire. The few studies that have been conducted so far lend little support to these assumptions. Indeed, women seemed to experience more retirement problems than men and to take somewhat longer in adapting to retirement.

Ironically, it may be precisely the factors referred to in these myths about women's retirement that render their adjustment to this life transition rather difficult. In their later years, women work outside the home either for financial reasons or because work offers them other rewards such as interesting activities, social contacts, and feelings of usefulness and accomplishments that are left unfulfilled by their household and familial responsibilities at home. Because they have chosen to work rather than to remain full-time housewives, retiring women may experience withdrawal symptoms when they retire and may find it particularly hard to adjust to the household routine they tried to escape in the first place (Atchley and Corbett 1977). Also, their interrupted work histories leave women quite frequently with low retirement incomes, and particularly late re-entry into the labor force after the launching of children can prevent many women from achieving their career goals (Atchley and Corbett 1977). Owing to their low incomes, retired women may be unable to engage in a variety of retirement activities, a condition that has been shown to render retirement adjustment difficult. Also, nonfulfillment of career goals can result in so-called goal frustration and negative retirement attitudes, particularly if retirement occurred for nonvoluntary reasons or was not planned (Atchley and Corbett 1977; Levy 1980). Finally, recent evidence also refutes the assumption that retirees happily return to the hearth and find fulfillment in the housewife role. Among married couples who retired together, the division of labor between the spouses seems not to be changed drastically after retirement, and even those women who become more involved in household activities are not necessarily fulfilled by these responsibilities. Their preferred roles include volunteer work and other leisure or social activities.

The evidence presented in this chapter leaves us clearly with more questions than answers. Not only are many of the existing studies on female retirement based on unrepresentative and/or small samples, some of the results are also contradictory. However, these investigations demonstrate beyond doubt that retirement constitutes an important life event for women that deserves careful study. Existing evidence also suggests that women's retirement needs differ from those of men. Preretirement programs and agencies dealing with retirees will have to take these differences into consideration. Specifically, female retirees require financial information and would profit from programs offering social contacts and leisure activities. The development of adequate retirement programs for women depends upon our understanding of this increasingly widespread social phenom enon; to acquire such understanding we need additional longitudinal and large-scale research on women's retirement.

References

Anderson, K.; C. Higgins; E. Newman; and S.R. Sherman. "Differences in Attitudes toward Retirement among Male and Female Faculty Members and Other University Professionals." *Journal of Minority Aging,* 1978, pp. 5–13.

Anderson, K.; R.L. Clark; T. Johnson. "Retirement in Dual-Career Families." In *Retirement Policy in an Aging Society,* edited by Clark, pp. 109–127. Durham, N.C.: Duke University Press, 1980.

Atchley, R.C. *The Social Forces in Later Life.* Belmont, Calif.: Wadsworth, 1980.

———. *The Sociology of Retirement.* New York: Halsted Press, 1976a.

———. "Orientation toward the Job and Retirement Adjustment among Women." *Time, Roles, and Self in Old Age,* edited by J.F. Gubrium, pp. 199–208. New York: Behavioral Publications, 1976b.

———. "Selected Social and Psychological Differences between Men and Women in Later Life." *Journal of Gerontology* 31 (1976c):204–211.

————. "Retirement and Work Orientation." *The Gerontologist* 11 (1971):29–32.

Atchley, R.C., and S.L. Corbett. "Older Women and Jobs." In *Looking Ahead. A Woman's Guide to the Problems and Joys of Growing Older,* edited by L.E. Troll, J. Israel, and K. Israel, pp. 121–125. Englewood Cliffs, N.J.: Prentice-Hall, 1977.

Back, K.W. "Transition to Aging and the Self-Image." In *Normal Aging II,* edited by E. Palmore, pp. 207–215. Duke University Press, 1974.

Bailyn, L. "Career and Family Orientations of Husbands and Wives in Relation to Marital Happiness." *Human Relations* 23 (1970):97–113.

Barfield, R.E., and J.N. Morgan. "Trends in Planned Early Retirement." *The Gerontologist* 18 (1978a):13–18.

————. "Trends in Satisfaction with Retirement." *The Gerontologist* 18 (1978b):19–23.

Barnett, R.C., and G.K. Baruch. *The Competent Woman.* New York: Halsted Press, 1978.

Beeson, D. "Women in Studies of Aging: A Critique and Suggestion." *Social Problems* 23 (1975):52–59.

Bell, B.D. "Role Set Orientations and Life Satisfaction: A New Look at an Old Theory." In *Time, Self, and Roles in Old Age,* edited by J.F. Gubrium, pp. 148–164. New York: Behavioral Publications, 1976.

Beller, D.J. "Coverage Patterns of Full-time Employees under Private Retirement Plans." *Social Security Bulletin* 44 (1980):3–10.

Bengtson, V.L. *The Social Psychology of Aging.* Indianapolis: Bobbs-Merrill, 1973.

Beuther, G., and A. Cryns. "Retirement: Differences in Attitudes, Preparatory Behavior, and Needs Perception among Male and Female University Employees." Paper presented at the Annual Meeting of the Gerontological Society, Washington, D.C., 1979.

Blau, Z.S. *Old Age in a Changing Society.* New York: Franklin Watts, 1973.

Block, M.R.; J.L. Davidson; J.D. Grambs; and K.E. Serock. *Unchartered Territory: Issues and Concerns of Women over 40.* College Park, Md.: Center on Aging, University of Maryland, 1978.

Campbell, A.; P.E. Converse; and W.L. Rodgers. *The Quality of American Life.* New York: Russell Sage, 1976.

Candy, S. "What Do Women Use Friends For?" In *Looking Ahead, A Woman's Guide to the Problems and Joys of Growing Older,* edited by L.E. Troll, J. Israel, and K. Israel, pp. 106–111. Englewood Cliffs, N.J.: Prentice Hall, 1977.

Cavan, R.S. "Self and Role in Adjustment during Old Age." In *Human Behavior and Social Process,* edited by A.M. Rose, pp. 526–536. Boston, Houghton Mifflin, 1962.

Clark, R.L., and J.J. Spengler. *The Economics of Individual and Population Aging.* Cambridge: Cambridge University Press, 1980.

Clark, R.L.; T. Johnson; and A.A. McGermed. "Allocation of Time and Resources by Married Couples Approaching Retirement." *Social Security Bulletin* 43 (1980):3–17.

Cumming, E., and W.E. Henry. *Growing Old: The Process of Disengagement.* New York: Basic Books, 1961.

Darnley, F. "Adjustment to Retirement: Integrity or Despair." *Family Life Coordinator* 24 (1975):217–225.

Dubin, R. "Industrial Workers' World: A Study of the Central Life Interests of Industrial Workers." *Social Problems* 3 (1956):131–142.

Duvall, E.M. *Marriage and Family Development.* Philadelphia: Lippincott, 1977.

Epstein, C.F. *Woman's Place: Options and Limits in Professional Careers.* Berkeley: University of California Press, 1970.

Eshleman, J.R. *The Family. An Introduction.* Boston: Allyn and Bacon, 1981.

Fengler, A.P. "Attitudinal Orientations of Wives toward Their Husbands' Retirement." *International Journal of Aging and Human Dvelopment* 6 (1975):139–152.

Fogarty, M.P.; R.H. Rapoport; and R.N. Rapoport. *Sex, Career, and Family.* Beverly Hills: Sage, 1971.

Foner, A., and K. Schwab. *Aging and Retirement.* Monterey, Calif.: Brooks/Cole, 1981.

Foote, N.N. "Matching of Husband and Wife in Phases of Development," Repr. no. 7. Chicago: Family Study Center, University of Chicago, 1956.

Fox, A. "Findings from the Retirement History Study." *Social Security Bulletin* 42 (1979):17–40.

Fox, G.L. "Nice Girl: Social Control of Women through a Value Construct." *Signs* 2 (1977):805–817.

Fox, A. "Effects of Retirement and Former Work Life on Women's Adaptation in Old Age." *Journal of Gerontology* 32 (1977):196–202.

Friedman, E.A., and H.L. Orbach. "Adjustment to Retirement." In *American Handbook of Psychiatry,* vol. 1, edited by S. Arieti. New York: Basic Books, 1974:609–645.

Friedman, J., and J. Sjogren. "Assets of the Elderly as They Retire." *Social Security Bulletin* 44 (1981):16–31.

George, L.K., and G.L. Maddox. "Subjective Adaptation to Loss of the Work Role: A Longitudinal Study." *Journal of Gerontology* 32 (1977): 456–462.

Haller, M., and L. Rosenmayr. "The Pluridimensionality of Work Commitment." *Human Relations,* 1971.

Harris, L., and Associates. *The Myth and Reality of Aging in America.*
Washington, D.C.: National Council on Aging, 1975.

Havighurst, R.J.; J.M.A. Munnichs; B.L. Neugarten; and H. Thomae.
Adjustment to Retirement: A Cross National Study. Assen: Van Gor-
kum, 1969.

Hendricks, J.A. "Women and Leisure." In *Looking Ahead. A Woman's
Guide to the Problems and Joys of Growing Older,* edited by L.E.
Troll, J. Israel, and K. Israel, pp. 114–120. Englewood Cliffs, N.J.
Prentice-Hall, 1977.

Henretta, J.C., and A.M. O'Rand. "Labor-Force Participation of Older
Married Women." *Social Security Bulletin* 43 (1980):10–15.

Hess, B.B., and E.W. Markson. *Aging and Old Age.* New York: Macmillan, 1980.

Hesse, S.J. "Women Working: Historical Trends." In *Working Women
and Families,* edited by K.W. Feinstein, pp. 35–62. Beverly Hills:
Sage, 1979.

Heyman, D.K. and F.C. Jeffers. "Wives and Retirement: A Pilot Study."
Journal of Gerontology 23 (1968):488–496.

Hoffman, L.W., and F.I. Nye. *Working Mothers.* San Francisco: Jossey-
Bass, 1974.

Holmstrom, L.L. *The Two-Career Family.* Cambridge, Mass.: Schenkman,
1972.

Huston-Stein, A., and A. Higgins-Trenk. "Development of Females from
Childhood to Adulthood: Career and Feminine Role Orientations." In
Life-span Development and Behavior, edited by P.B. Baltes, pp. 258–
297. New York: Academic Press, 1978.

Jacobson, C.J. "Rejection of the Retiree Role: A Study of Female Industrial Workers in Their 50's. *Human Relations* 27 (1974):477–492.

Jaslow, P. "Employment, Retirement, and Morale among Older Women."
Journal of Gerontology 31 (1976):212–218.

Kahana, E., and A. Kiyak. "The Nitty-Gritty of Survival." In *Looking
Ahead. A Woman's Guide to the Problems and Joys of Growing
Older,* edited by L.E. Troll, J. Israel, and K. Israel, pp. 172–177.
Englewood Cliffs, N.J.: Prentice-Hall, 1977.

Keating, N.C., and P. Cole. "What Do I Do with Him 24 Hours a Day?
Changes in the Housewife Role after Retirement." *The Gerontologist*
20 (February 1980):84–89.

Kerckhoff, A.C. "Husband-Wife Expectations and Reactions to Retirement." *Journal of Gerontology* 19 (1964):510–516.

———. 'Family Patterns and Morale in Retirement." In *Social Aspects
of Aging,* edited by I.M. Simpson and J.C. McKinney, pp. 173–192.
Durham, N.C.: Duke University Press, 1966.

Kimmel, D.C.; K.F. Price; and J.W. Walker. "Retirement Choice and
Retirement Satisfaction." *Journal of Gerontology* 33 (1978):575–585.

Kline, C. "The Socialization Process of Women." *The Gerontologist* 15 (1975):486–492.

Larson, R. "Thirty Years of Research on the Subjective Well-Being of Older Americans." *Journal of Gerontology* 33 (1978):109–125.

Laurence, M.W. "Sources of Satisfaction in the Lives of Working Women." *Journal of Gerontology* 16 (1961):163–167.

Lehr, U. *Psychologie des Alterns.* Heidelberg: Quelle and Meyer, 1977.

———. "Die Situation der Aelteren Frau: Psychologische und Soziale Aspekte." *Zeitschrift fuer Gerontologie* 11 (1978):6–26.

Levy, S.M. "The Adjustment of the Older Woman: Effects of Chronic Ill Health and Attitudes toward Retirement." *International Journal of Aging and Human Development* 12 (1980):93–110.

Lindenstein, Walshok M. "Occupational Values and Family Roles. Women in Blue-Collar and Service Occupations." In *Working Women and Families,* edited by K.W. Feinstein, pp. 63–84. Beverly Hills: Sage, 1979.

Lipman, A. "Marital Roles of the Retired Aged." *Merrill Palmer Quarterly* 6 (1960):192–195.

Lipman, A. "Role Conceptions and Morale of Couples in Retirement." *Journal of Gerontology* 16 (1961):267–271.

Little, V.C. "Retirement Roles of Women: Use of Time and Self." Paper presented at the International Congress of Sociology, Hamburg, 1981.

Livson, F.B. "Patterns of Personality Development in Middle-Aged Women: A Longitudinal Study." *International Journal of Aging and Human Development* 7 (1976):107–115.

———. "Coming Out of the Closet: Marriage and Other Crises of Middle Age." In *Looking Ahead. A Woman's Guide to the Problems and Joys of Growing Older,* edited by L.E. Troll, J. Israel, and K. Israel, pp. 81–92. Englewood Cliffs, N.J.: Prentice-Hall, 1977.

Lopata, H.Z., and K.F. Norr. "Changing Commitments of American Women to Work and Family Roles." *Social Security Bulletin* 43 (1980): 3–13.

Lowenthal, M.F., and C. Haven. "Interaction and Adaptation: Intimacy as a Critical Variable." In *Middle Age and Aging,* edited by B.L. Neugarten, pp. 390–400. Chicago: University of Chicago Press, 1968.

Maas, S., and J. Kuypers. *From Thirty to Seventy: A Forty-Year Longitudinal Study of Adult Life Styles and Personality.* San Francisco: Jossey-Bass, 1974.

Maddox, G.L. "Persistence of Life Style among the Elderly: A Longitudinal Study of Patterns of Social Activity in Relation to Life Satisfaction." International Congress of Gerontology: *Proceedings of the Seventh International Congress of Gerontology, Vienna, 1966.*

Mallan, L.B. "Women Born in the Early 1900's. Employment, Earning, and Benefit Levels." *Social Security Bulletin* 37 (1974):3–24.

Markides, K.S., and H.W. Martin. "A Causal Model of Life Satisfaction among the Elderly." *Journal of Gerontology* 34 (1979):86–93.

Matthews, S.H. *The Social World of Old Women.* Beverly Hills: Sage, 1979.

Morgan, L.A. "Toward a Formal Theory of Life Course Continuity and Change." Paper presented at the Annual Meeting of the Gerontological Society, San Francisco, 1977.

Muller, C.F. "Economic Roles and the Status of the Elderly." In *Aging and Society,* edited by E.F. Borgatta and N.G. McCluskey, pp. 17–41. Beverly Hills, Sage, 1980.

Neugarten, B.L. "Personality and Aging." In *Handbook of the Psychology of Aging,* edited by J.E. Birren and K.W. Schaie, pp. 626–649. New York: Van Nostrand Reinhold, 1977.

Older Women: The Economics of Aging. Washington, D.C.: Women's Studies Program and Policy Center, George Washington University, 1980.

Palmore, E.B. "Differences in the Retirement Patterns of Men and Women." *The Gerontologist* 5 (1965):4–8.

Palmore, E.B., and V.R. Kivett. "Change in Life-Satisfaction. A Longitudinal Study of Persons Aged 46–70." *Journal of Gerontology* 13 (1977):311–316.

Pampel, F.C. *Social Change and the Aged.* Lexington, Mass.: Lexington Books, D.C. Heath and Company, 1981.

Parnes, H.A. et al. *Dual Careers: A Longitudinal Analysis of the Labor Market Experience of Women.* Columbus: Ohio State University Press, 1976.

Pepitone-Rockwell, F. *Dual-Career Couples.* Beverly Hills: Sage, 1980.

Powers, E.A., and G.L. Bultena. "Sex Differences in Intimate Friendships in Old Age." *Journal of Marriage and the Family* 38 (1976):739–747.

Prentis, R.S. "White-Collar Working Women's Perception of Retirement." *The Gerontologist* 20 (February 1980):90–95.

Roberts, W.L. and A.E. Roberts. "Significant Elements in the Relationship of Long-Married Couples." *International Journal of Aging and Human Development* 10 (1980):265.

Rosenfeld, R.A. "Women's Occupational Careers." *Sociology of Work and Occupations* 6 (1974):283–311.

Rosenkaimer, D.; A. Saperstein; B. Ishizaki; and S.M. MacBride. "Coping with Old Age—Sex Differences." Paper presented at the Annual Meeting of the Gerontologist Society, New York: 1976.

Rosow, I. *Socialization to Old Age.* Berkeley: University of California Press, 1974.

Rubin, L.B. *Women of a Certain Age. The Midlife Search for Self.* New York: Harper & Row, 1979.

Schwab, K., and L.M. Irelan. "The Social Security Administration's Retirement History Study." In *Aging and Retirement: Prospects, Planning, and Policy,* edited by N.G. McCluskey and E.F. Borgatta, pp. 15–30. Beverly Hills: Sage, 1981.

Seltzer, M.M. "Suggestions for the Examination of Time-Disordered Relationships." In *Time, Roles, and Self in Old Age,* edited by J.F. Gubrium, pp. 111–125. New York: Behavioral Publications, 1976.

Sheldon, A.; P.J.M. McEwan; and C.P. Ryser. "Retirement, Patterns and Predictions," DHEW Publication no. (ADM) 74–79. Washington, D.C.: NIMH, 1975.

Sheppard, H.L. "Work and Retirement." In *Handbook of Aging and the Social Sciences,* edited by R.H. Binstock and E. Shanas, pp. 286–309. New York: Van Nostrand Reinhold, 1976.

Sherman, S.R. "Labor-Force Status of Nonmarried Women on the Threshold of Retirement." *Social Security Bulletin* 37 (1974):3–13.

Streib, G.F., and C.J. Schneider. *Retirement in American Society.* Ithaca, N.Y. Cornell University Press, 1971.

Simpson, I.H.; K.W. Back; and J.C. McKinney. "Orientations toward Work and Retirement, and Self-Evaluation in Retirement." In *Social Aspects of Aging,* edited by Simpson and McKinney, pp. 75–89. Durham, N.C.: Duke University Press, 1966.

Sobol, MG. "Commitment to Work." In *Working Mothers,* edited by L.W. Hoffman and I.F. Nye, pp. 63–80. San Francisco: Jossey-Bass, 1974.

Sommers, T. *Aging in America: Implications for Women.* Oakland, Calif.: NCOA, 1976.

Spence, D., and T. Lonner, "The 'Empty Nest': A Transition within Motherhood." *Family Coordinator* 20 (1971):369–375.

Stueve, A., and C.S. Fischer, "Social Networks and Older Women." Working Paper no. 292. Berkeley: Institute of Urban and Regional Development, University of California, 1978.

Sussman, M.B. "An Analytical Model for the Sociological Study of Retirement." In *Retirement,* edited by F.M. Carp, pp. 29–74. New York: Behavioral Publications, 1972.

Sweet, J.A. *Women in the Labor Force.* New York: Seminar Press, 1973.

Szalai, A. et al. (eds.) *The Use of Time.* The Hague: Mouton, 1972.

Szinovacz, M. "Female Retirement: Personal and Marital Consequences. A Case Study." Paper presented at the Annual Meeting of the Gerontological Society, Dallas, 1978.

———. *The Situation of Women in Austria. Economic and Family Issues.* Vienna: Federal Ministry of Social Affairs, 1979.

———. Female Retirement: Effects on Spousal Roles and Marital Adjustment." *Journal of Family Issues* 1 (1980):423–440.

————. "Women's Adjustment to Retirement. Preliminary Results." Report to the NRTA-AARP Andrus Foundation. Florida State University, 1982a.

————. ed. *Women's Retirement. Policy Implications of Recent Research.* Beverly Hills: Sage, 1982b.

Taylor, C. "Developmental Conceptions and the Retirement Process." In *Retirement,* edited by F.M. Carp, pp. 75–116. New York: Behavioral Publications, 1972.

Thompson, G.B. "Work Experience and Income of the Population Aged 60 and Older, 1971." *Social Security Bulletin* 37 (1974):3–16.

Troll, L.E. "The Family of Later Life: A Decade Review." In *A Decade of Family Research and Action,* edited by C.B. Broderick, pp. 187–214.

Troll, L.E.; J. Israel; and K. Israel. *Looking Ahead. A Woman's Guide to the Problems and Joys of Growing Older.* Englewood Cliffs, N.J.: Prentice-Hall, 1977.

Troll, L.E.; S.J. Miller; and R.C. Atchley. *Families in Later Life.* Belmont, Calif.: Wadsworth, 1979.

U.S. Bureau of the Census. *Census of the Population. 1970: General Social and Economic Characteristics.* Final Report PC(1)-C1, United States Summary. Washington, D.C.: U.S. Government Printing Office, 1978a.

————. *Demographic Aspects of Aging and the Older Population in the United States.* Current Population Reports, Series P-23, no. 59. Washington, D.C.: U.S. Government Printing Office, 1978b.

U.S. Department of Labor. *Employment and Training Report of the President.* Washington, D.C.: U.S. Government Printing Office, 1980.

Walker, J.W., and K.F. Price. "Retirement Choice and Retirement Satisfaction." Paper presented at the Annual Meeting of the Gerontological Society, 1975.

Walker, K.E., and M.E. Woods. *Time Use: A Measure of Household Production of Family Goods and Services.* Washington, D.C.: American Home Economics Association, 1976.

Labor Markets and Old Ladies' Homes

Brian Gratton

"I did sewing. I mean I was a dressmaker. I mean I worked in a factory."
—Claudia Wright (Pseud.), Boston, 1978

The meticulous records of the Home for Aged Women (HAW), founded in Boston, Massachusetts, in 1849, provide their reader two lessons—the first, that history reveals the deeper functions in institutions and, the second, that sex makes all the difference in the world. In this home's institutional archives we witness the development of philanthropy for the aged and comprehend such charity's potential and its limitations. The HAW was at once liberated by its sympathy for the dependent woman and constrained by ethnic and class biases. In its detailed case records, we glimpse the life of a character often lost in history's masculine accounts—namely, the woman who worked outside the home. By examining her occupational and familial characteristics, we observe the dramatic consequences of the sexual division of labor.

Institutional Charity

The HAW was the first charity for the aged established by a compact group of nativist, elite reformers who sought to reorder the administration of welfare in antebellum Boston. The HAW's illustrious fathers (a word used advisedly) were members of the Association of Delegates from the Benevolent Societies of Boston, organized in 1833–1834 by the Unitarian minister Joseph Tuckerman.[1]

This association set down the frame upon which nineteenth-century urban benevolence was to be stretched: curtailment of relief to thwart the ogre of pauperism, rigorous investigation of the "character and circumstances" of applicants, and cooperation of charitable agencies to enforce these principles and eliminate fraud.[2] By the late 1840s, the attention of these reformers had begun to center on the immigrant Irish poor; the reformer's violent reaction to the aliens among them was the source of the

The author is grateful for financial support given preliminary work on this subject by the Administration on Aging, grant no. 90-A-797.

HAW. In 1849, the association successfully petitioned for land from the city to benefit a class of poor "whose situation entitles them to peculiar sympathy," many of whom were "our own countrywomen—'Hebrews of the Hebrews'," who without such a charity, might drop "to the level of almshouse inmates and paupers." For the "City Almshouse" these women had a "natural repugnance which we cannot but respect in the poor of our own people—a repugnance to be herded with paupers of every character, condition and clime."³ (Among the appellants were the directors of the city's public almshouse.)

If there remained any doubts as to the reasons an asylum was needed, they were laid to rest upon the opening of the home on Charles Street on 1 May 1850. President Henry B. Rogers detailed the Christian character and breadth of New England charity and the disruption of that benevolence by the influx of "great masses . . . from other states and countries," strangers "foreign to our modes of thought—to our habits of industry and thrift—and to that self-education and discipline" that forestalled poverty. Foreigners had "taken possession of the public charities." It was impossible to assist the native and foreign populations in "homogeneous institutions" for "they form two distinct classes which are so entirely separated by education, temperament, and mental and religious prejudices, that they refuse to be associated together indiscriminately."⁴

By 1851, the HAW had established the rules that were to govern the institution. The central requirement was that charity be confined to Yankee women, and the blatant nativism of this home was to continue well into the twentieth century. In early 1851, the first foreigner was "rejected on acct. of her Foreign birth: Mrs. Wright, a very worthy & deserving woman, personally." Such instances often were reported in the records. Intolerance remained rife in the 1920s when the correspondence of the committee on admissions reveals the emphasis on U.S. and New England stock, though correspondents were advised privately that English parentage would not be damning.⁵

Catholics, though not officially barred, really were subject to the same restriction: Of 219 applications from the period 1900–1950 (when Catholics with native-born parents technically were eligible), only three were Catholic. Of these three, two cases were rejected (laid on the table) and one, without a decision recorded, was probably rejected. In the 1850s, a Protestant woman was rejected because of her husband's qualities: "Ireland, & a Catholic." In 1940 the social worker indicated her approval of Harriet Dolan: "Very anxious to enter—½ Protestant!"⁶

Although the home required testimonials to the "respectability" and "propriety of . . . conduct" of applicants, the occasional pretension of the managers that the HAW was a last resting place for those who had seen "better days," except as that meant Yankee birth, is undermined by a survey of the inmates' "laborious and useful occupations." A random survey of occupation among twenty-nine clients in the 1850s reveals the truth of that description. Twelve of the women were domestics, often referred to the HAW by the prominent families in which they had worked. Five were nurses and seven were seamstresses. Of eighteen fathers' occupations recorded, one was low blue collar and three were farmers, eleven were skilled blue collar, and three were from white-collar backgrounds. This is not a group of ladies but of women whose husbands and fathers were blue collar and whose own occupations provided no security for old age. This pattern continues across the remainder of the nineteenth century. For cxample, of twenty four cases selected randomly from records between 1861 and 1890, seventeen of the women had low blue-collar occupations, and the majority of their fathers and husbands were from skilled blue-collar occupations.[7]

The admissions policy of the home boiled down to age, Boston residence, and respectability by reason of native birth and some contact with the elite through work or church. The managers fully accepted the inability of women without families to provide for their old age, and it was for these wage-earning women—a very small group in the nineteenth century—that the charity provided. The rampant xenophobia of the managers shows that the primary goal of the HAW was to provide an alternative welfare system for poor Yankees. Such a welfare system violated the very rules the managers sought to impose on public welfare. There was a good measure of guilt in the decision to give assistance; many of the first recipients of HAW aid were domestics who had labored "for many years in respectable families." Nancy White had been "General Assistant in family of the late Mayor Wightman since eight years of age." Other worthy women were nurses, whose selfless service, it was said, prevented them from preparing for old age, and spinsters, who deserved (if Yankees) "'a shelter from the world's dread laugh'."[8]

The managers indeed were driven to explain their charity, and finally, when the fire and smoke of nativism cleared away, it was urban change and moral responsibility that justified their philanthropy: "The tie, which in former days had bound the rich and poor so closely together in our churches, had been loosened" by wealth, luxury, and the dramatic increases in population and immigration. The "simple and homogeneous society" was gone; the president of the HAW admitted that competition among workers was so fierce as to "reduce the chances of obtaining a comfortable subsistence," a "decent maintenance." Conscious of these changes, and driven by a profound nativism that blinded them to the violation of their own welfare precepts, the founders came to grips with the difficulties of the aged in an urban, commercial environment: "Society is *morally bound* to protect and take care of its aged members, who have worn out their best years in its service." What ironic cruelty that these were the same men who imposed upon the mass of poor (and their old fathers and mothers) the first U.S. system of punitive welfare.[9]

Yet the provision of special charitable service was, in the long run, perhaps not as important as another service of the HAW—namely, to provide for the financial and cultural needs of a social class, the Brahmins. After a brief struggle to exist on annual contributions, the HAW began to reap great bequests upon which Yankee charities were built. By 1878 assets were valued at $351,254.29. The remaining years of the nineteenth century were extremely lucrative; in 1910 the home reported assets at $1,117,824.82.[10]

Investment of this great capital followed the conventional pattern of safety and Brahmin interest. Investment was made primarily in bank stock and railroad stocks and bonds, a traditional conservative Boston investment pattern. In many cases these investments were in Brahmin-controlled enterprises. At times, HAW funds were available for direct lending to individuals or to other Brahmin financial institutions.[11]

In general, the HAW served the same economic function as other Brahmin charities. It gathered large amounts of capital together from eastern New England for the use of Boston capitalists and financiers, many of whom were members of its board of managers. The officers of the home were, almost without exception, Harvard-educated lawyers located in the State Street business area, specializing in investment and trust work and affiliated with numerous corporations. These men provided careful, honest, and sometimes gratuitous service for the home, although their law offices, banks, and brokerage firms benefited by processing the funds. However, the great profit in handling the bequests lay elsewhere. These funds underwrote the capitalization of the Brahmin business community, providing the foundation for those enterprises that ensured the powers of this caste and class. In this the Brahmins "did well by doing good."[12]

The utilization of the income produced by this capital was questionable. By 1900 the HAW had about $900,000 in assets. The charity was housing about 90 women and giving outside aid to another 120. Outside beneficiaries received an average of $105 per year; total expenditure on outside aid was about $12,000 per year at this time. The home, however, was absorbing an extraordinary amount of income for fewer beneficiaries— between $30,000 and $40,000 per year during the first decade of the twentieth century, despite the fact that medical costs were contained by denying admission to infirm or sick women.[13]

The ethnic bias and class function of this private institution had most immediate effects on the quality of its charity. If the welfare needs of Boston's aged had been the overriding concern of the HAW, outside aid would have been expanded and home care restricted to special cases; if $800,000 in assets had been placed at conservative interest, the managers would have had between $31,000 and $38,000 in funds per year, enough to double their outside-aid work and still to provide special care.[14]

Yet, in 1913, when it was proposed to consider "building a small home largely fitted up as a hospital; and of thereafter granting a large part of our aid on outside relief," the proposal was rejected and never reconsidered. The home also resisted the development of social work with its outside beneficiaries, except as such expertise would improve the efficiency of selection and reduce fraud.[15]

In their efforts to preserve the home and in their summary rejection of the early opportunity to use their funds more efficiently in outside aid, the HAW managers revealed the cultural functions of brick and stone. The heavy fixed costs of the home plant drained the income of the endowment. In 1863, President Rogers responded to the objection that charitable dollars were ill spent on the imposing new building in which his audience sat by arguing that such edifices kept charities in the public eye; but the great endowment soon made public notice, approval, and support largely irrelevant. The income of this "capital . . . held sacred" ensured the edifice would stand and relieved the managers of the trial of annual appeals for funds; the managers need only please themselves and others of their caste—the great building, as monument to them, their families, and Brahmin money, pleased them. There is little evidence that the idea of improving the lot of aging women in Boston was alive among them after the 1860s. The managers, along with their fellow Brahmins, turned increasingly inward, finding in their ethnic institutions a retreat from the polyglot clamor of late nineteenth-century Boston.[16] In this regard there is a decided sense of group self-congratulation running through the pages of managers' minutes and annual reports. Within these records is a perfect expression of the cultural significance of the home as Brahmin monument: Each year the dead are memorialized in black-bordered pages—however, the dead are not the poor women for whom the charity is intended but the managers, whose Harvard education, business acumen, and selfless benevolence here receive just tribute.

The treatment of the women who were aided corresponds with the historical functions of the institution. Strict rules governed the residents of the home, and disciplinary concerns fill the records. Invariably, the inmates are found guilty and the matron faultless. With due allowance for the difficulties of governing such an institution, there is no question that the life-contract system (the resident surrendered all assets in return for care until death) allowed the managers to exercise a dictatorial benevolence as fit their view of charitable work with beneficiaries thought of as being in their second childhood. Disquiet in the family was inevitable with one hundred residents, some of whom sufferered from dementia and depression, but these problems were exacerbated because the life-contract system put the clients at the mercy of the managers, because there was greater and greater distance between the managers and the residents as the charity took on more-symbolic and less-interpersonal importance, and because the managers assumed that beneficiaries of charity had no rights, having surrendered them to their benefactors by reason of their dependency. These circumstances suggest the significance of New Deal governmental welfare programs, a significance not lost on older people in the 1930s and 1940s who knew that the old-age pension could liberate them and that private, voluntaristic welfare could impose a form of bondage over them. Thus, in 1939, Carrie Stetson was reluctant to accept the home's assistance: "The OAA [old-age assistance] would give me more liberty and some spending money. At the [HAW] it seems to me I would have less freedom and practically no money to use."[17]

The privatistic nature of the HAW severely constrained the charitable impulse to help dependent women. By examining the history of this private charity, we have discovered how distant some of its functions were from those implied by its name and how well philanthropy sometimes serves the benefactors. However, in the lives of the beneficiaries another story is told, no less instructive and perhaps even less understood.

The Aged Women

The origins, purposes, and prejudices of the HAW mirrored a brother institution in Boston, the Home for Aged Men (HAM), but in terms of the people whom the HAW served, dissimilarities were as marked as similarities. The following analysis rests on 225 case records taken for three cohorts, and all surviving applications were taken in consecutive order from date of decision: (1) 1900s cohort, from January 1906 to January 1910 ($N = 67$); 1920s cohort, from April 1925 to April 1929 ($N = 43$); and 1940s cohort, from August 1944 to October 1949 ($N = 115$).[18]

Principal analysis deals with 180 approved applications (154 admissions and 26 outside aid) distributed in the cohorts as follows: $N = 67$, $N = 36$, $N = 77$. These case records provide date of birth, place of birth, marital history, residential history, occupational history, means of support, property, family histories, and for ever-married women, detailed information on husbands. From the case records we may reconstruct the nativity and origins of these women, their occupational experience, and the family structure of which they were a part.

Nativity

The overwhelmingly Yankee origins of the clients of the HAW is shown in table 7-1, which gives place of birth for each cohort and for 1900–1950. As

Table 7-1

Percentage Distribution of HAW Clients, by Birthplace, Cohort, and Demicentury

Birthplace	1900s Cohort		1920s Cohort		1940s Cohort		1900–1950 Demicentury	
Boston	16	⎫	36	⎫	32	⎫	27	⎫
Massachusetts[a]	27	97% New England	17	81% New England	20	67% New England	22	81% New England
Maine	. 27		17		7		16	
Other New England	27	⎭	11	⎭	9	⎭	16	⎭
Other United States	0		6		14		7	
Foreign	3		14		18		12	
Total	100 (N = 67)		100 (N = 36)		100 (N = 76)		100 (N = 179)	

Source: Sample of 179 clients of the Home for Aged Women, Boston.

Note: In this and subsequent tables, columns may not actually sum to 100 percent because of rounding.

[a]Outside Boston.

we have seen, the home was openly nativist. As late as the 1940s, 67 percent of the clients were New England born and, in the 1900s, 97 percent. At the turn of the century, 42 percent came from the two states of Maine and New Hampshire; the singular role of Maine highlights the rural, upper-New England background of the early beneficiaries of this Brahmin charity. Women from these states and rural Massachusetts reflect the great in-migration of rural Yankees to Boston in the nineteenth century: "the great numbers from our rural districts."[19] Only as this migration slowed did Boston become the most important birthplace. The HAW served its ethnic function in providing for these country cousins. After 1876, information regarding parental nativity was also required, and these data reaffirm the ethnic quality of the charity. In the 1900s, about 10 percent of clients' parents were born in Boston (the percentage of Boston-born parents never exceeds 18 percent in any cohort), over 30 percent elsewhere in Massa-chusetts, 25 percent in Maine, and nearly 20 percent in New Hampshire; New England accounted for 89 percent of the fathers and 96 percent of the mothers. In the 1920s, New England was the birthplace of 83 percent of the fathers and 78 percent of the mothers. In the 1940s, these proportions drop to 62 percent for mothers and fathers. By this time, foreign birth accounts for a significant percentage, but it is foreign birth of a particular kind. Of twenty-one mothers born abroad, seventeen were born in Maritime Canada, Scotland, or England. Of twenty-four foreign-born fathers, sixteen were born in these areas.

Foreign birth among the clients was exceedingly rare, and of the twenty-one foreign-born women admitted, aided, or approved between 1900 and 1950, nineteen were from the Maritime Provinces or England. Thus, until the 1940s at least, the home maintained its nativist stance. The residential living patterns of these women also demonstrate the ethnic character of the home. The aged women were usually residents of neighborhoods that were once Yankee but into which immigrants had since moved; these living circumstances correspond with the contemporary circumstances of many urban aged. The residential histories also provide some forewarning of the significance of gender: The occupations of the men aided by the HAM were significantly related to their residential areas—that is, residential areas were partly determined by class. No such association exists for women's occupations. However, there is a significant relationship between a woman's residence and her spouse's occupation.[20]

Occupation

The HAW required the applicant to list principal occupation in life as well as occupation currently held. In analyzing these occupations, five basic categories were used: none, low blue-collar, skilled blue-collar, low white-collar, and middle white-collar. The great majority of women listed five occupations: none, housewife, domestic servant (of various types), nurse, and seamstress. All seamstresses have been placed in low blue collar. Domestics of any kind (housekeepers, charwomen) were listed as low blue collar. Housewives were listed as having no occupation, or none. Nurses were listed as skilled blue collar; this classification overestimates the level of skill required in practical nursing. Table 7–2 shows the occupational distribution of the clients of the charity by cohorts and for the demicentury. Comparison with the data secured from the HAW's brother institution, the HAM, show the much greater significance of low blue-collar occupations among women (42 to 13 percent).

The old women left sound testimony to their "laborious and useful occupations," and what their records reveal is a grim account of toil, quite in keeping with the opportunities available to women in the U.S. labor market. There is an intriguing irony to the HAW's efforts to aid these working women, the largest group of whom were in the most menial occupations. The home was founded—and no accident this—at the very moment when the impropriety of women's engaging in useful work first captured the imagination of the ascendant U.S. bourgeoisie. The records examined here begin at the turn of the century, at the instant of a crisis in that imaginative view when some women demanded their rights and, among these, the right to work.[21]

Table 7-2

Percentage Distribution of HAW Clients, by Principal Occupation, Cohort, and Demicentury

Occupation	1900s Cohort	1920s Cohort	1940s Cohort	1900–1950 Demicentury
None	10	8	26	17
Low blue collar	63	44	22	42
Skilled blue collar	6	22	20	15
Low white collar	21	25	29	25
Middle white collar	0	0	4	2
Total	100 (N = 67)	100 (N = 36)	100 (N = 77)	100 (N = 180)

Source: Sample of clients of the Home for Aged Women, Boston.

The managers no doubt viewed their clients quite differently: Their beneficiaries had the misfortune to have to work in a time when proper women did not and when a working woman's chances were slim indeed.[22] However, no criticism of the women as working women emerges in the managers' reports though some single women undoubtedly chose this route. On several occasions a woman was rejected because of "her life long employment as a domestic," but it is unlikely this was the real cause.[23] The facts are too plain. If the HAM is a clerk's home, by the same token the HAW is, in 1900, the houseworker's last refuge. In sum, this most respectable of charitable homes was filled with housekeepers, laundresses, seamstresses, charwomen, and attendants; no effort was made to fill it with older widows who had never worked.

For the managers, the women were first and foremost ethnic sisters. Some had worked in Brahmin homes. They were without men (in some instances by choice) and thereby compelled to work, and they were honored for their efforts. Women were not ordinarily expected to work; in old age, after years of toil, they were natural objects of charity. Their husbands' and fathers' occupations sometimes helped them to achieve the respectability that could not be gained by their own work. Primarily from rural native backgrounds and emerging from a nineteenth-century economic structure, these women would be much more likely to work and to work at menial occupations than Yankee girls from Boston.[24]

Since the fundamental reading of the work experience of these relatively advantaged Yankee women will be an account of their degradation, we should first review how the tabulation in table 7-2 corresponds with the general circumstances of Boston's female population and female labor force.[25] A comparison may be summarized in three major points:

1. The HAW women did work, which makes them odd. Since any occupa-
    tional background, at any time, is recorded in HAW records, we cannot
    consider these proportions equivalent to the low percentages of women
    65 and over working when taken at a single census year, but the differ-
    ence (about 10 percent among all older women to about 80 percent
    here) is too great to be explained solely by differences in the type of
    data.

2. From census data, we know that almost no older women can be found
    in low white-collar occupations in 1900 and few in 1920. The women
    from the HAW, despite large numbers in low blue-collar work, are
    extraordinarily concentrated in white-collar work. These Yankee
    women were privileged by comparison to their aged sisters in the
    Boston labor force.

3. The cohort effect is visible in the work records of the HAW. The de-
    cline in low blue-collar work across the twentieth century (63 to 22 per-
    cent) reflects the fact that Yankee women working in domestic service
    were an aging group at the turn of the century. After this period, few
    such women would enter domestic service. Some older women, espe-
    cially widows, remained in this category (and their fate is discussed in
    detail later) using their ill-rewarded domestic skills. As Yankees, how-
    ever, HAW women escaped some of the worst effects of the twentieth-
    century labor market for women.

Reviewing the cohorts in table 7–2 shows the gradual upgrading of
occupational status for Yankee women during the first fifty years of the
century. That 21 percent of the women achieved white-collar status in the
1900s cohort—securing their positions during the nineteenth century—is
testimony to the advantages these Yankee women enjoyed; as late as 1910,
less than 20 percent of the female labor force was white collar and much less
of the aged female labor force.[26] The largest category of the HAW remained
low blue collar into the 1920s cohort. The belated opportunity for white-
collar work for the majority of these women underlines the fact that the
heralded expansion of the female clerical work force at the turn of the
century worked its initial effects on young women.[27] Older women were ill
equipped to move into this field and, one suspects, not only by reason of
lack of training but also for reasons of appearance, culture, and age itself.
Middle white-collar employment remained closed even to these paragons of
respectability.

Instead, women parlayed what they learned at the hearth—namely, the
domestic skills of sewing, cleaning, cooking, and nursing. These were
among the most poorly paid of all talents.[28] Domestic work accounted for
about one-fourth of all female workers aged 65 and over in Boston in 1890.

Laboring at jobs increasingly filled by immigrant women, these aged Yankees showed the customary occupational backwardness of older cohorts.[29] Few of their young Yankee sisters would enter domestic work. The records of the HAW show that older working women were compelled to accept one of a limited and unattractive group of alternatives: to labor as a servant in another person's home, to do piece work at home (primarily sewing), or to do light factory work, especially sewing in the shops in the garment district, mixing with immigrant women in an unpleasant and unremunerative approximation of factory life. Much of the history of women's work as domestic labor and of the ambiguity evoked by the transition from the hearth to the factory is given in a comment by a woman (not connected to the HAW) who worked in Boston's garment district: "I did sewing. I mean I was a dressmaker. I mean I worked in a factory."[30]

Perhaps the only advantage to this type of work was that it could be continued in old age, but continued at great cost—age was a ferocious combatant. Carrie Burnham found herself, in her sixties, "sewing at starvation prices" in a belt factory; she remarked that often she could not "get on my boots my feet are so swollen." The nurses who approached the home for assistance saw age as a great liability: Eva Webster noted that there was little "employment [given] to nurses passed 60 years," and Alice Piper, at 69, saw her own future: "I get very tired and it is to be expected that I'll not be able to continue work much longer."[31]

Only one alternative to work existed for these women, and its growth can be seen in the expansion in the proportion of those women who have never held an occupation: from 10 percent in the 1900s to 26 percent in the 1940s. Early in the century the HAW was not accepting many housewives whose husbands had suddenly died or single women whose inheritances had become thin but aided women who had worked to support themselves. The sudden increase in the 1940s is a direct consequence of nonworking women's benefits under government welfare; neither old-age assistance nor social-security survivor's benefits required a personal work history.

However, the continued dependence of women on work for their support is illustrated graphically in table 7-3, which shows the means of support that applicants to the HAW reported for each cohort. In comparison with male clients at the HAM, HAW women depend less on work in the 1900s and more in the 1940s. In fact, the women became more self-reliant than the men who applied to the HAM. Combining work, savings, and pensions as categories of independence, as opposed to those categories that demonstrate economic dependence, differences between the men and women over time are marked. In the 1900s cohort, 44 percent of the men reported work, savings, or pensions as a means of support, compared to only 28 percent of the women. By the 1940s, only 24 percent of the men reported independent income, while more than 60 percent of the women did so. Inso-

Table 7–3
Percentage Distribution of HAW Applicants, by Means of
Support and Cohort

Means of Support	1900s Cohort	1920s Cohort	1940s Cohort
Work	25	33	34
Savings	3	2	26
Pensions	0	5	12[a]
Relatives/friends	12	5	6
Public relief	3	2	11
Other relief[b]	34	40	8
None	23	14	3
Total	100 (N = 65)	100 (N = 43)	100 (N = 115)

Source: Sample of 179 clients of the Home for Aged Women, Boston.
[a]Includes social security (Old-Age insurance).
[b]Includes private relief, private and public relief, and work and relief.

much as this is not a reflection of differing policy, the reversal is a function of a substantial shift in work roles; after the New Deal men lost the center of independence, their work lives, but women maintained command of low blue-collar jobs and expanded their role as white-collar workers. Perhaps they managed their savings better. By the 1940s their work (and savings from it) permitted them greater independence than at the turn of the century and substantially greater independence than their male counterparts.

For all women, marital status played a key role in their work experience. A principal source of misery was the failure to marry—which consigned single women to the work place. Barbara Berg was not off the mark when she stated that "fear of a life of pauperism drove some women into marriages."[32] Other women failed to keep their husbands alive, and this was an even more-grievous error. Of all clients, 38 percent were single and 53 percent were widows. Widows, who had on average lost their husbands twenty years before application, were left with minimal savings or resources; 69 percent report that their husbands left them nothing. Mrs. Clementine Wales was able to live on her husband's property until her sixties. Then she found herself forced to work as a seamstress in a rug works, losing that, to do washing, and lacking the strength for that, to return to sewing: "At 72 years of age, I find myself unable to compete with the younger persons who do the sewing and sometimes [I] have little to eat." Mrs Dora Dearing was left a widow at thirty-three with three children; now eighty, she entreated the admissions committee not to deny her because she was old and feeble: "Brought up my children without any help never weighed 100 lb. do you

think I have worked years enough."[33] These woeful stories do not issue
from women whose husbands were failures. On the whole, their spouses
were men of middling occupations not unlike clients of the HAM, though
more concentrated in skilled blue-collar occupations. Across the period
1900–1950, only 5 percent of the spouses of HAW clients were in low blue-
collar occupations. About half were skilled blue collar, falling from 77 percent in the 1900s cohort to 33 percent in the 1940s. Over 40 percent were
white collar; in the 1940s, 33 percent were low white collar, and 24 percent
were middle white collar.

These occupational records imply the inability of the middling
classes—the skilled blue-collar and low white-collar groups—to provide
sufficient financial resources for the maintenance of their long-lived
members. However, data from an institution that aids dependents do not
provide a reliable test of the contemporary and recent argument that the
early twentieth century witnessed a new problem, the inability of the middle
classes to support their aged.[34] Still, the fact that the HAW served women
who were more likely than most to have white-collar jobs and husbands and
families of higher status does prove that such status was not a guarantee
against dependency.

A much better predictor of dependency than occupational status is
available. As is discussed in greater detail later, the families of these women
were ill equipped to protect them in old age, not because they had squan-
dered funds providing for children but rather the reverse—they had failed
to procreate enough sons and daughters to ensure support in old age.

Such family structure was particularly threatening for women because
the market reserved its greatest terrors for those women (primarily widows)
compelled to enter it late in life. Table 7–4 shows the distribution of women
in a cross tabulation of principal occupation and marital status. Row percentages show what proportions of an occupational category is single,
widowed, or married-separated-divorced; column percentages indicate what
proportions of a marital category are low blue collar, skilled blue collar,
and so on. Thus, 33 percent of the women who were in skilled blue-collar
occupations were widows, and 9 percent of all widows were in skilled blue
collar occupations.

Widows dominate the none, or no principal occupation, category; they
make up 87 percent of those women who have not had a principal occupation, yet they are but 54 percent of the population of women. Largely
widows have the luxury of not working. Single women make up but 3 percent of this category, though they are 38 percent of women as a whole.
Obviously, single women suffer one penalty from their marital status: they
must work. The widows' advantage is hardly universal, however. Those
who have not held a principal job, though a majority of that category, are
only 27 percent of all widows. The remaining 73 percent labor under a par-

Table 7–4
Percentage Distribution of HAW Clients, by Principal Occupation and Marital Status, 1900–1950

Principal Occupation	Marital Status						Row Totals	
	Single		Widowed		Married, Separated, Divorced			
	Row Percent	Column Percent	Row Percent	Column Percent	Row Percent	Column Percent		
None	3	1	87	27	10	19	17	(N = 30)
Low blue collar	31	34	54	46	11	50	42	(N = 75)
Skilled blue collar	59	24	33	9	7	12	15	(N = 27)
Low white collar	58	38	36	17	7	19	25	(N = 45)
Middle white collar	67	3	33	1	0	0	2	(N = 3)
Column percent	38		53		9		100	
	(N = 68)		(N = 96)		(N = 16)			(N = 180)

Source: Sample of clients of Home for the Aged Women, Boston.

Note: X^2 significant at .05. Data were not drawn from a probability sample.

ticular disability: These widowed women must work, and they are more likely than other women to be relegated to low blue-collar jobs. They make up 46 percent of all such workers, and if we were to exclude none as a category contradictory to work, the working widows' chances are miserable indeed—that is, 63 percent will end up in low blue-collar jobs, compared to 34 percent of single women.

Conversely, in the low white collar in which one-fourth of the women are found, the advantages of the single women are apparent. Thirty-eight percent of all single women enter this occupational category, while only 17 percent of the widows do so (23 percent if we exclude none). Here is a most significant difference in experience based on marital status. Single women worked most of their lives and, under that necessity, were more likely to prepare themselves for a career and to have more years to climb what few job ladders existed for women.[35] In addition, they were able to maintain work in new employment areas for women entered in youth, while married women returned to the traditional skills of the housewife, skills that could only translate into low blue-collar work in old age. Living on a deceased husband's savings was not a reasonable alternative for these women, whose average age was 51 at the time of the husband's death. The chronic shortage of servants and the similarity of menial tasks to those of their housework pointed the way for widows[36]: Among twenty-six who reported they never held a principal occupation (most widowed late in life), nine had just taken up work, all but one in a low blue-collar occupation. The experience was not a pleasant one, as Emma Webster reported: "Have disposed of all jewelry, ornaments, and clothing by piece . . . to get money to live on."[37] Put simply, it was misfortune piled on misfortune for a widowed middle-aged women to find herself compelled to seek work.

The study of HAW clients reveals a significant minority group among working women at the beginning of the century—namely widows bound into the lowest occupational categories. Widows and (a few) divorced women constituted about 15 percent of the female work force in 1890 and constitute (with a larger proportion divorced) about the same percentage today.[38]

The most important change in the female labor force has been the great increase in the number of married, older women (between 1940 and 1960 especially), which reduced the proportional influence of widows. Valerie Oppenheimer's thesis that the demand for female labor outstripped the supply of single, young women speaks to this point[39]; in view of the uses to which their labor was put, it might be added that the secondary supply of widows was also shrinking as widowhood became rarer, occurred later in life, and was sheltered by government welfare. The drama of the movement of married women into the labor force has obscured the fact that a proportion of them are the same women (figuratively speaking) as the widows and that all of them bear a striking resemblance in certain characteristics. The current (but flattening) double-peaked curve in female labor-participation rates (high in the early twenties, sharply declining in the childbearing years, and high again in the 40–55 age group) was foreshadowed in the early part of the century by the gradual return of widowed women to the labor force. In fact, a cohort born between 1876–1885 would peak in participation at ages 14–24 and then begin a steady decline until age 45–54 (in 1930), when participation would increase, as in recent times, but in this case because of higher incidence of widowhood.[40]

In qualitative if not quantitative terms, the widow of the past and the married working woman of the present are quite alike. They are middle-aged, often have children, and enter the labor market relatively untrained and without work experience since their early twenties. In certain important respects they are the same women. Thus, by way of conjecture, it can be argued that another similarity obtains between these historical groups. Women work (then and now) in a secondary labor market, characterized by marginal businesses, low wages, part-time employment, high turnover, and minimal advancement.[41] In the early twentieth century, HAW records show the particular proclivity of widows for such jobs.

Debate continues over whether this segmentation is a consequence of deliberate discriminatory practices at the firm level. Those who criticize the claim that women are consciously discriminated against point to older women's lower human capital, discontinuous work histories, and greater age as legitimate reasons for their segregation in inferior occupational sectors.[42] Certainly the widows of the HAW brought poor credentials when they applied for a job. They had little investment in market training conducive to success.[43] One father, "believing that he would always be able to take care of his daughters, did not train them to any useful occupation."[44] Ill prepared to enter the paid work force, these women fared poorly in it.

There are no empirical grounds in these case records for a test of the question of deliberate discriminatory practices, although a historian finds it difficult to believe that the hiring officer of the nineteenth-century firm did not practice at work what he surely preached at home. However, there is manifest evidence that the sexual division of labor—the sexist preparation that everyone agrees distorts women's occupational success—had profound implications for women's work life and hence, as these dismal records show, for the quality of their lives. The women did get training; there was investment in their future: they learned to clean, sew, cook, and attend to children and the sick. Their work career was not discontinuous—it was monotonously continuous—but the training, the career, the skills presented were those of the wife and cheaply bought at that.

The occupational experience of the clients of the HAW between 1900 and 1950 paints a dark picture for the older working woman in this period.

These women, especially the widows, must work in the labor market not-able for its deficiency of opportunity. The chief occupational category —low blue collar—had as its main virtues that it was natural to women's skills and that it could be retained in old age. A bleak work life followed directly from the training in nonmarket activities guaranteed these women because of their sex. Schooled in family work, their chief liability was lack of a family in which to ply their trade. In an important sense, women had no reasonable alternative to reliance on husband and family. Without these familial resources, work was onerous, poorly paid, and bereft of old-age security. Considering the manifold advantages of Yankee women and the varied occupational backgrounds of their husbands, it is reasonable to assume that work was but a temporary solution and that overt dependency in old age was automatic for any woman who survived to old age without a family or an inheritance.

Family

In familial terms, these women are astonishingly isolated, having yet fewer children and relatives than the quite isolated men from the HAM. They were, as one applicant said of herself, "lonely," and their isolation explains their public dependency.[45] The women, unlike their normal sisters, have remained single or their marriages have been broken by death. These two categories account for 38 percent and 53 percent of HAW clients. Adding to these the few separated and divorced women gives percentages for women unattached to men for each cohort: 1900s, 96 percent; 1920s, 92 percent; 1940s, 100 percent.[46] Those women who had lost their husbands had endured long widowhood: An average of twenty years at an average appli-cation age of 72 meant that they had begun a new life in their early fifties; as has been shown in the review of their occupations, this was not a propitious moment. Their marriages also had not provided them with the primary bulwark against overt dependency in old age: numerous children. Table 7–5 reveals the extraordinary childlessness of clients for the period 1900–1950. Single women and women with no surviving children made up 78 percent of those aided. It is obvious that these women are unusual in respect to the number of children they report.

Bereft of the possibility of support from children, these women were also short of other relatives to turn to. Table 7–5 shows how few relatives of any kind (including children) lived in Massachusetts. The average figure is about one relative per woman (men claimed about 1.4), with about 40 per-cent claiming no relative within the state.[47] These patterns of abbreviated family structure exhibit some changes over time, but the consistent fact is that the women have no effective kinship network. It is quite clear, then,

Table 7-5
Distribution of HAW Clients, by Number of Children and Number
of Massachusetts Relatives, 1900-1950

Number of Children or Relatives	Percent by Children	Percent by Massachusetts Relatives
Single	39	NA[a]
0	39	39
1	15	36
2	2	19
3 or more	5	6
	(N = 176)	(N = 171)

Source: Sample of clients at Home for Aged Women, Boston.

Note: For HAW clients, mean number of children is 0.369; excluding single women, mean is 0.602. Mean figures for HAM were 0.912 and 1.51 without single men. For HAW clients, the mean number of relatives is 0.988.

[a]Not applicable.

that this is the population at risk: old women without family who are single, widowed, divorced, or separated.

It is obvious that some old women with families require charity, but if this institution is any guide, these must be very few or immediately rejected on the grounds that their families must support them. The work of D.S. Smith and his colleagues suggests how strong were the pressures for intra-family support.[48] A reasonable speculation is that in families with surviving children, widows were usually forced into dependency on their children. Where this meant joint living arrangements, the widow could well become a domestic within the household—jobs assumed within the family were hardly distinct from those for women without families: cleaning, sewing, cooking, and attending to children and the sick. It has been argued that women do not suffer the trauma of retirement because their work role is not terminated but continues into old age. While this is obviously true, it celebrates the obvious rather than considers the low pay (whether in cash or kind) that attends these quite laborious and tedious tasks. Only in the 1940s could widows exploit an alternative in old-age assistance or survivor's benefits, which allowed them to subsist without working or depending upon their children.

Conversely, some women without families have provided for themselves in old age and do not become dependent. However, these too must make up a select group. The different occupations and varying marital histories of the women of the HAW underscore the fragility of independence for any women below the middle white-collar level (a level few women could achieve). The conditions for public or overt dependency— gathered as they are from but one home for aged women—lead straight to general conclusions about the covert dependency that must have been the lot of the great majority of older women. Their unenviable position was to be compelled to seek help from children or relatives. Historians of the family recently have advanced two distinct theories that obscure this historical experience. One theory celebrates the resiliency and supportiveness of the family as a welfare mechanism. The other, in opposition, recasts the traditional lament of family decline (as bureaucratic social-welfare services expand) in even more-sorrowful tones.[49] Both ignore this considerable body of women who had no family to turn to. Both ignore the malign consequences of dependency within the family. We cannot imagine that all old women found it comforting to be received into their children's homes as charity cases, to work if the children demanded it, and to have no choice, no reasonable alternative.

Unless these Yankee women are to be imagined as possessing some peculiar flaw (and does not this singularly high-minded home guard against that error?), they are representative of the single and childless women who faced old age without relatives and, in an indirect way, representative of women with families as well. Nothing in their ethnic background (except smaller families) suggests a particular disadvantage, rather the opposite. Their occupational histories fit the possibilities for women. What they lacked was a family.

Review of the lives of HAW clients has shown the intimate relationship between a woman's family life and her work life. If she was without husband, without family, she was condemned to earn her keep at certain of society's most arduous and unrewarding tasks: cleaning, cooking, sewing, tending the sick. If she is with a husband, with family, she is condemned to precisely the same duties. Indeed, the division between paid and unpaid female work is an artificial one; the rise of feminist scholarship will bring the old socialist argument that housework is work into the mainstream of academic discussion.[50]

For the aged woman, the significance of the family is patent. Without it, she is compelled to public drudgery followed by public dependency. However, in celebrating the family that used to be for sheltering the old mother, we have ignored the plain affinity between women's work inside and outside the home. The moral imperative of caring for the old folks is often cited when the family is remembered in a golden past, but attention needs to be paid to the value of the old person in an exchange of aid; attention needs to be directed to the use the family made of its old ones. Exchanges could be made amicably and to the satisfaction and pride of both parties; working for the family may have been superior to working for strangers.[51] However, it is questionable whether or not old women always relished the prospect of dependency in a child's home. It is unquestionable that grandmother paid part of her way in the very labors that we find so disconcerting when viewed as gainful employment.

Conclusion

Policymakers, politicians, and ordinary people are well aware that the older woman is a problematic figure in U.S. society. She represents an aging female labor force and a level of dependency so alarming that we are advised to remake social security, the penultimate governmental program. These two images found their historical expression in the HAW. Its case records have demonstrated the consequences of the sexual division of labor, consequences that hardly could have been confined to the women without families who were the home's clients. The HAW's institutional records provide a different lesson because they show the hidden functions in private philanthropy that constrain charity. Social security has given women who work in market and nonmarket activities a measure of independence that their work experience cannot supply. Without such a system they must resort to private charity or to family, sanctuaries that may be less benevolent than they appear.

Notes

1. Sources for this account of the nineteenth-century HAW are given in detail in Brian Gratton, "Boston's Elderly, 1890–1950: Work, Family, and Dependency," (Ph.D. dissertation, Boston University, 1980), chapter 6. Unpublished records of the home can be found at its location in Boston, and at the Schlesinger Library, Cambridge, Mass. For more-detailed discussion of the origins of antebellum welfare and the association, see Gratton, "The Boston Almshouse: 'A Reverence for God, the Hope of Heaven, and the Fear of the poorhouse'" (Paper presented at the Annual Meeting of the American Historical Association, Washington, D.C., 1980); and Daniel McColgan, *Joseph Tuckerman: Pioneer in American Social Work* (Washington, D.C.: National Association of Social Workers, 1940), pp. 244–255.

The HAW was never a women's association, although women participated in its founding and it was required that at least a minority of its managers be women.

2. McColgan, *Tuckerman,* p. 428.

3. HAW, *30th Annual Report* (Boston, 1880), pp. 5–6; A. Bigelow, et al., "Memorial to the City Government," 26 April 1849, inserted in HAW,

Minutes of the Meetings of the Board of Managers, Meeting of 6 December 1849, Cambridge, Mass., Schlesinger Library, and HAW Collection; and *Documents of the City of Boston, 1849,* no. 19. Cambridge Mass., Schlesinger Library.

4. Henry B. Rogers, *Remarks before the Association for Aged Indigent Females at the Opening of Their Home* (Boston, 1850), pp. 7–8.

5. The 1851 rejection can be found in HAW, *Records of Inmates, 1850–1858,* "Chiefly, cases not approved in Com^ee, or, rejected by the Board; or Names withdrawn;" Cambridge, Mass., Schlesinger Library, HAW Collection. For the 1920s, G. Glover Crocker to Miss Addie Sears, 21 June 1921 and 2 November 1922, and Correspondence of the Committee on Admissions, Boston, HAW Archives. For English birth, see G. Glover Crocker to Mr. Edward B. Richardson, 18 June 1924, Correspondence of the Committee on Admissions.

6. Selection of the sample from 1900–1950 is described in the text. The 1850s case can be found in HAW, *Records of Inmates, 1850–1858,* "Chiefly, cases not approved. . . ." The 1940 instance is from the social worker's comments on application no. 914 in the 1940s cohort of the 1900–1950 sample.

7. HAW, *Minutes of the Meetings of the Board of Managers,* Meeting of 18 July 1850, Cambridge, Mass., Schlesinger Library, HAW Collection; Rogers, *Remarks,* pp. 8–9; HAW, *11th Annual Report* (Boston, 1861), p. 7. The sample of twenty-nine was taken, selecting every third case from 1850 to 1858, from HAW, *Records of Inmates, 1850–1901,* Cambridge, Mass., Schlesinger Library, HAW Collection, Box 11. This blue-collar pattern continues in the twentieth century.

8. Henry B. Rogers, *Address Delivered at the Opening of the New Home for Aged Indigent Females* (Boston, 1863), p. 7; for the White case, see HAW, *Records of Inmates, 1858–1901.* The last quotation is from the will of Mary Townsend, who belonged to this sisterhood and provided the HAW a handsome bequest ($80,000) for the support of single women [as reprinted in HAW, *12 Annual Report* (Boston, 1862), p. 33]. This will is an extraordinary commentary on the life of the single woman in the nineteenth-century United States.

9. Rogers, *Address,* p. 7; and Rogers, *Remarks,* pp. 7–8. The moral responsibility of society is recorded in HAW, *3rd Annual Report* (Boston, 1853), p. 19, and is set in the context of extreme nativism.

The punitive welfare system that these same men designed for the immigrant and feckless poor sprang from a welfare theory that required that the poor fear an impoverished old age so that they would work and save. Without such fear, the working class would anticipate alms and diminish their labors in their youth. This thesis can be found in the English debate over the poor law, in which aid is denounced as stripping "that essential prop to industry, 'the terror of starving in old age'," as well as in U.S. sources such as late nineteenth-century criticism of Boston's welfare officers for aiding two old paupers and thus failing to impress upon the young "the necessity of providing for their old age." Keith Thomas, "Age and Authority in Early Modern England," *Proceedings of the British Academy* 62 (1976): 241; and Nathan I. Huggins, *Protestants against Poverty, 1870–1900* (Westport, Conn.: Greenwood, 1971), p. 67. As shown in Gratton, "Boston Almshouse," the association that created the HAW brought this theory to bear in antebellum Boston; hence, the confusion of the HAW managers when confronted by dependency among the Yankee old.

10. The 1878 assets are presented in HAW, *Minutes of the Meetings of the Board of Managers,* Meeting of 10 January 1878, Cambridge, Mass.: Schlesinger Library, HAW Collection. Those for 1910 recorded in HAW, 61st Annual Report (Boston, 1911), pp. 34–35. All figures are given in current, not real, dollars.

11. Investment is discussed in detail in Gratton, "Boston's Elderly," pp. 277–281.

12. I am indebted to Peter Dobkin Hall, "Family Structure and Class Consolidation among the Boston Brahmins" (Ph.D. dissertation, State University of New York at Stonybrook, 1975), for the interpretive framework of Brahmin use of charitable funds.

13. For the financial operation of the charity in the early twentieth century, see HAW, *50th and 60th Annual Reports* (Boston, 1900–1910).

14. Return on investment was figured by yield on U.S. railroad bonds between 1890 and 1910. U.S. Department of Commerce, *Historical Statistics of the United States: Colonial Times to 1957* (Washington, D.C., 1960), p. 656.

15. HAW, *Minutes of the Meetings of the Board of Managers,* Meeting of 27 February 1913; Cambridge, Mass., Schlesinger Library, HAW Collection; and Gratton, "Boston's Elderly," pp. 287–292.

16. Rogers, *Address,* pp. 18–19; and HAW, *12th Annual Report* (Boston, 1862), p. 6. Discussion of the role of charities in the fin de siècle retreat of the Brahmins can be found in Gratton, "Boston's Elderly," chapter 4. See, especially, the standard account in Barbara Miller Solomon, *Ancestors and Immigrants: A Changing New England Tradition* (Chicago, University of Chicago Press, 1956), pp. 43–58, 60, 82–102.

17. HAW, *Minutes of the Meetings of the Board of Managers,* Meeting of 16 April 1885; Cambridge, Mass., Schlesinger Library, HAW Collection; and Gratton, "Boston's Elderly," pp. 288–289. Stetson (pseud.) is case no. 875, 1940s cohort.

18. The HAM is discussed in Gratton, "Boston's Elderly," chapters 4 and 5. Data from this home's case records are used here for comparative purposes.

The first cohort for the HAW can be examined in HAW, *Records of Inmates, 1901–1916,* Cambridge, Mass., Schlesinger Library, HAW Collection; the remaining application forms remain in the HAW Archives. Applications were numbered irregularly. Most of the case records of women admitted have been preserved, but outside-aid cases and rejected applications are incomplete.

19. The managers remarked upon this migratory phenomenon in HAW, *52nd Annual Report* (Boston, 1902), p. 8.

20. The chi square of the last relationship is significant at .05 ($N =$ 108). The reader should note that probability samples were not used for the HAW and HAM data. The residence of the women is examined in detail in Gratton, "Boston's Elderly," pp. 297–302. In substance, their residential histories reflect what Stephan Golant and other social gerontologists call *cumulative inertia*—that is, persistence in the same neighborhood despite changes of address. Some, but less, evidence is found for movement from a customary neighborhood to a central-city district where transportation and other services were more readily available. See Golant, *The Residential Location and Spatial Behavior of the Elderly* (Chicago, University of Chicago, Department of Geography, 1972).

21. The domestic ideal for women was first developed in the antebellum period. See Barbara Welter, "The Cult of True Womanhood: 1820–1860," *American Quarterly* 18 (Summer 1966):151–174; Gerda Lerner, "The Lady and the Mill Girl: Changes in the Status of Women in the Age of Jackson," *American Studies Journal* 10 (Spring 1969):5–15; and Barbara J. Berg, *The Remembered Gate: Origins of American Feminism: The Woman and the City, 1800–1860* (New York 1978), especially pp. 113, 116, 121, 130, 137. The fin de siècle crisis is reviewed in detail by Peter Filene, *Him/Her/Self: Sex Roles in Modern America* (New York, New American Library, 1974), part I.

22. Though they would have stoutly denied it, the female managers were subtle defalcators of the reserves of the domestic myth: Their volunteer work was the middle- and upper-class woman's substitute for useful occupation. On this point, see Hilda Kahne (with Andrew I. Kohen), "Economic Perspectives on the Roles of Women in the American Economy," *Journal of Economic Literature* 13 (December 1975):1277.

23. HAW, *Minutes of the Meetings of the Committee on Admissions,* Meetings of 17 May 1893 and 19 April 1906, Cambridge, Mass., Schlesinger Library, HAW Collection.

24. See Robert W. Smuts, *Women and Work in America* (New York: Schocken, 1971), p. 38, for native women from rural areas in the labor force.

25. Data on Boston's older female population and labor force are presented in detail in Gratton, "Boston's Elderly," chapters 2 and 3.

26. Smuts, *Women,* pp. 21–22, on the advantages of native women of native-born parents in securing white-collar work. For 1910 figures, see Filene, *Him/Her/Self,* p. 29.

27. Expansion of female white-collar work is explored in Margery Davies, "Woman's Place Is at the Typewriter: The Feminization of the Clerical Labor Force, 1870–1930," *Radical America* 8 (July–August 1974): 1–28. Also see Elyce J. Rotella, "Women's Labor Force Participation and The Growth of Clerical Employment in the United States, 1870–1930" (Ph.D. dissertation, University of Pennsylvania, 1977). Rotella finds native birth and educational attainment (characteristics of younger age cohorts in 1900) were chief features of the female clerical labor force. The failure of older women to participate in this shift is discussed in Gratton, "Boston's Elderly," chapter 3.

28. On pay scales, see Ross M. Robertson, *History of the American Economy,* 3rd ed. (New York: Harcourt Brace Jovanovich, 1973), p. 382.

29. See Gratton, "Boston's Elderly," chapter 3, for cohort backwardness. David M. Katzman, *Seven Days a Week: Women and Domestic Service in Industrializing America* (New York: Oxford Press, 1978), pp. 65–66, 71–72, comments on the preponderance by 1900 of immigrant women in domestic service in cities like Boston.

30. The quotation is from an interview I conducted with Claudia Wright, (pseud.), Boston, 17 April 1978. There seemed to be some objection among the philanthropic Brahmins to mill work (on the floor, that is, not in the counting room), but a number of HAW clients worked in light industries, especially in garment sweatshops. Smuts (*Women,* pp. 15, 92–93) notes that sewing was the second most important area of paid home work for women after boarding and housekeeping. He provides a chilling account of a widowed seamstress of 65 supporting herself and helping another family on $2.70 per week. Sensational as it is, the story is not far from the facts of life for the HAW beneficiaries.

31. No case number, 1900s cohort; case no. 903, 1940s cohort; case no. 934, 1940s cohort. As early as 1901 the managers commented on the difficulty older nurses had in obtaining employment. HAW, *51st Annual Report* (Boston, 1901), p. 10. Cambridge, Mass.: Schlesinger Library Collection.

32. Berg, *Remembered Gate,* p. 131.

33. Reported assets at spouse's death probably ignored equity in a home. Quoted remarks (pseud.) are from 1900s cohort (no case number) and case no. 855A, 1940s cohort.

34. For a recent argument to this effect, see Caroline Hoppe and Judith Treas, "The Deserving Aged: A Los Angeles Retirement Home, 1896–1930" (Unpublished manuscript, 1980).

35. Investment (in human capital like training) suggests an intention to remain single, which may or may not have obtained for these women. J.

Gwartney and R. Stroup report that married women who decide to work fall behind their single coevals on the basis of such investment ["Measurement of Employment Discrimination According to Sex," *Southern Economic Journal* 39 (April 1973):575–587]. However, there is at present little difference between wages paid married women and those paid single women, according to Elizabeth M. Almquist, "Women in the Labor Force," *Signs* 2 (Summer 1977):851. Almquist does not indicate whether age controls were utilized for studying these marital groups.

36. Katzman, *Seven Days,* pp. 223–265, reviews the shortage of servants.

37. Case no. 61, 1920s cohort.

38. Smuts, *Women,* p. 23; and National Manpower Council, *Womanpower* (New York: National Manpower Council, 1957), p. 134. Figures for widowed women alone are difficult to find.

39. Valerie Oppenheimer, *The Female Labor Force in the United States* (Berkeley, CA, University of California Press, 1970); See Kahne, "Economic Perspectives," pp. 1250–1253.

40. On the double peak, see Kahne, "Economic Perspectives," p. 1554; and Smuts, Introduction, *Women,* pp. vii–viii. On the 1876–1885 cohort experience, see National Manpower Council, *Womanpower,* figure 3 and p. 127. For an excellent graphic presentation of the curves of participation for 1890, 1940, and 1956, see *Womanpower,* figure 2.

41. An extensive literature has developed around the secondary, or dual, labor-market thesis. An introduction to this concept for the female labor force can be found in Alice Kessler-Harris, "Women's Wage Work as Myth and History: Review Essay," *Labor History* 19 (Spring 1978):287–307; F. Weisskoff (Blau), "'Women's Place' in the Labor Market," *American Economic Review* 62 (May 1972):161–166.

42. For example, see Solomon William Polachek, "A Supply Side Approach to Occupational Segregation" (Paper presented at the Annual Meeting of the American Sociological Association, Toronto, 1981).

43. On such investment, see Kahne and Kohen "Economic Perspectives on the Roles of Women," *Journal of Economic Literature* 13 (December 1973), p. 1257.

44. Case no. 63, 1920s cohort.

45. Case no. 846, 1940s cohort.

46. The proportion of single women aided rises from 30 percent in the 1900s to 40 percent in the 1940s, while the proportion widowed declines from 61 percent to 53 percent. This is in line with changes in the marital status of women in general and native-born women in particular. See Gratton, "Boston's Elderly," chapter 2; and Peter R. Uhlenberg, "A Study of Cohort Life Cycles: Cohorts of Native Born Massachusetts Women, 1830–1920," *Population Studies* 23 (November 1969):407–420.

47. Hoppe and Treas find the residents of an early twentieth-century

Los Angeles retirement home short of kin, as does the literature for residents of institutions in our time. Hoppe and Treas, "Deserving Aged"; and Peter Townsend, "The Effects of Family Structure on the Likelihood of Admission to an Institution in Old Age: The Application of a General Theory," in *Social Structure and the Family: Generational Relations,* eds. Ethel Shanas and Gordon F. Streib (Englewood Cliffs, N.J.:Prentice-Hall, 1965).

48. D.S. Smith, "Life Course, Norms, and the Family System of Older Americans in 1900," *Journal of Family History* 4 (Fall 1979):285–298.

49. The first school is best represented by Tamara Hareven in her numerous works and as editor of the *Journal of Family History;* the second viewpoint by Christopher Lasch, especially in *Haven in a Heartless World: The Family Besieged* (New York: Basic Books, 1977).

50. The similarity of women's work inside and outside the home is remarked on by Smuts, *Women,* pp. 17–19; and Rosalyn Baxandall, Linda Gordon, and Susan Reverby, eds., *America's Working Women* (New York, Random House, 1976), p. xv. Kahne, "Economic Perspectives," p. 1263, notes that Juanita Kreps has maintained that, if so valued, housework would be equal to at least 25 percent of the GNP. Baxandall, Gordon, and Reverby, *America's Working Women,* p. 354, make the interesting suggestion that "welfare could be the salary women receive for raising children." The socialist argument can be found in Theresa Malkiel, "The Lowest Paid Workers," *Socialist Woman* 3 (September 1908):210–211. Charlotte Perkins Gilman anticipated this socialist position in *The Home* (New York, 1903). For recent work, see Wally Secombe, "The Housewife and Her Labour under Capitalism," *New Left Review,* no. 83 (January–February 1974), pp. 3–24; and Jean Gardiner, "Women's Domestic Labour," *New Left Review,* no. 89 (January–February 1975), pp. 47–58. See also Anne Oakley, *Women's Work* (New York: Pantheon, 1974); Susan J. Kleinberg, "Technology and Women's Work: The Lives of Working Class Women in Pittsburgh, 1870-1900," *Labor History* 17 (Winter 1976):57–72; and Bettina E. Berch, "Industrialization and Working Women in the Nineteenth Century: England, France, and the United States" (Ph.D. dissertation, University of Wisconsin, 1976).

51. On the idea of exchange of services, see Michael Anderson, "The Impact on the Family Relationships of the Elderly of Changes Since Victorian Times in Governmental Income-Maintenance Provision," in *Family, Bureaucracy, and the Elderly,* eds. Ethel Shanas and Marvin B. Sussman (Durham, N.C.: Duke University Press, 1977), pp. 50–51. The chapter offers perceptive comments on the negative aspects of family support of the aged. Interviews I conducted with older Bostonians in 1978 suggest an ideal of familial support as well as the exchange of services. Compare the discussion of these interviews in Gratton, "Boston's Elderly," chapter 2.

Bibliography

Almquist, Elizabeth M. "Women in the Labor Force." *Signs* 2 (Summer 1977).

Anderson, Michael. "The Impact on the Family Relationships of the Elderly of Changes since Victorian Times in Governmental Income-Maintenance Provision." In *Family, Bureaucracy, and the Elderly,* edited by Ethel Shanas and Marvin B. Sussman. Durham, N.C.: Duke University Press, 1977.

Baxandall, Rosalyn; Linda Gordon; and Susan Reverby, eds. *America's Working Women.* New York: Random House, 1976.

Berch, Bettina E. "Industrialization and Working Women in the Nineteenth Century: England, France, and the United States." Ph.D. dissertation, University of Wisconsin, 1976.

Berg, Barbara J. *The Remembered Gate: Origins of American Feminism: The Woman and the City, 1800–1860.* New York: Oxford University Press, 1978.

Cambridge, Mass. Schlesinger Library. Home for Aged Women collection.

Davies, Margery. "Woman's Place Is at the Typewriter: The Feminization of the Clerical Labor Force, 1870–1930." *Radical America* 8 (July–August 1974):1–28.

Documents of the City of Boston. 1849. Cambridge, Mass.: Schlesinger Library.

Filene, Peter. *Him/Her/Self: Sex Roles in Modern America.* New York: New American Library, 1974.

Gardiner, Jean. "Women's Domestic Labour." *New Left Review,* no. 89 (January–February 1975):47–58.

Gilman, Charlotte Perkins. *The Home.* New York: 1903.

Golant, Stephan M. *The Residential Location and Spatial Behavior of the Elderly.* Chicago: University of Chicago, Department of Geography, 1972.

Gratton, Brian. "The Boston Almshouse: 'A Reverence for God, the Hope of Heaven, and the Fear of the Poorhouse.'" Paper presented at the Annual Meeting of the American Historical Association, Washington, D.C., 1980a.

———. "Boston's Elderly, 1890–1950: Work, Family, and Dependency." Ph.D. dissertation, Boston University, 1980b.

Gwartney, J., and R. Stroup. "Measurement of Employment Discrimination According to Sex." *Southern Economic Journal* 39 (April 1973): 575–587.

Hall, Peter Dobkin. "Family Structure and Class Consolidation among the Boston Brahmins." Ph.D. dissertation, State University of New York at Stonybrook, 1975.

Home for Aged Women. *Annual Reports.* Boston, 1851 to 1933.

————. *Archives.* Jamaica Plain, Boston, MA.

Hoppe, Caroline, and Judith Treas. "The Deserving Aged: A Los Angeles Retirement Home, 1896–1930." Unpublished manuscript, 1980.

Huggins, Nathan I. *Protestants against Poverty.* Westport, Conn.: Greenwood, 1971.

Interviews. Conducted with twenty persons 60 to 70 years of age who had lived in Boston for the major part of their lives, Boston, February–May 1978.

Kahne, Hilda, with Andrew I. Kohen. "Economic Perspectives on the Roles of Women in the American Economy." *Journal of Economic Literature* 13 (December 1975):1249–1292.

Katzman, David M. *Seven Days a Week: Women and Domestic Service in Industrializing America.* New York: Oxford University Press, 1978.

Kessler-Harris, Alice. "Women's Wage Work as Myth and History: Review Essay." *Labor History* 19 (Spring 1978):287–307.

Kleinberg, Susan. "Technology and Women's Work: The Lives of Working Class Women in Pittsburg, 1870–1900." *Labor History* 17 (Winter 1976):57–72.

Lasch, Christopher. *Haven in a Heartless World: The Family Besieged.* New York: Basic Books, Inc. 1977.

Lerner, Gerda. "The Lady and the Mill Girl: Changes in the Status of Women in the Age of Jackson." *American Studies Journal* 10 (Spring 1969):5–15.

Malkiel, Theresa. "The Lowest Paid Workers." *Socialist Women* 3 (September 1908):210–211.

McColgan, Daniel T. *Joseph Tuckerman: Pioneer in American Social Work.* Washington, D.C.: National Association of Social Work, 1940.

National Manpower Council. *Womanpower.* New York, 1957.

Oakley, Anne. *Women's Work.* New York, 1974.

Oppenheimer, Valerie K. *The Female Labor Force in the United States: Demographic and Economic Factors Governing Its Growth and Changing Composition.* Berkely, Calif.: Greenwood, 1970.

Polachek, Solomon William. "A Supply Side Approach to Occupational Segregation." Paper presented at the Annual Meeting of the American Sociological Association, Toronto, 1981.

Robertson, Ross M. *History of the American Economy,* 3rd ed. New York, Harcourt Brace Jovanovich, Inc., 1973.

Rogers, Henry, B. Remarks before the Association for Aged Indigent Females at the Opening of Their Home. Boston, 1850.

————. Address delivered at the Opening of the New Home for Aged Indigent Females. Boston, 1863.

Rotella, Elyce J. "Women's Labor Force Participation and the Growth of Clerical Employment in the United States, 1870–1930." Ph.D. dissertation, University of Pennsylvania, 1977.

Secombe, Wally. "The Housewife and Her Labor under Capitalism." *New Left Review,* no. 83 (January–February 1974):3–24.

Smith, Daniel S. "Life Course, Norms, and the Family System of Older Americans in 1900." *Journal of Family History* 4 (Fall 1979).

Smuts, Robert W. *Women and Work in America.* New York, Schocken, 1971.

Solomon, Barbara Miller. *Ancestors and Immigrants: A Changing New England Tradition.* Chicago, University of Chicago Press, 1956.

Thomas, Keith. "Age and Authority in Early Modern England." *Proceedings of the British Academy* 62 (1976):241.

Townsend, Peter. "The Effects of Family Structure on the Likelihood of Admission to an Institution in Old Age: The Application of a General Theory." In *Social Structure and the Family: Generational Relations,* edited by Ethel Shanas and Gordon F. Streib. Englewood Cliffs, N.J.: Prentice-Hall, 1965.

Uhlenberg, Peter R. "A Study of Cohort Life Cycles: Cohorts of Native Born Massachusetts Women, 1830–1920." *Population Studies* 23 (November 1969):407–420.

U.S. Department of Commerce. Bureau of the Census. *Historical Statistics of the United States: Colonial Times to 1957.* Washington, D.C., 1960.

Weisskoff (Blau), F. "'Women's Place' in the Labor Market." *American Economic Review* 62 (May 1972):161–166.

Welter, Barbara. "The Cult of True Womanhood: 1820–1860." *American Quarterly* 18 (Summer 1966):151–174.

Part III:
Without and Within
the Family

There are marked variations among women in later life with respect to marital status, living arrangements, and life-styles. The chances that women will live alone in old age are much greater than for men. Among people 65 and over, 37 percent of women as compared to 75 percent of men live with a spouse. The proportion of older women living alone has increased dramatically within the last two decades, from 24 percent in 1960 to 41 percent in 1979. The shorter life expectancy of men, coupled with the fact that most men marry women younger than themselves, ensures women's greater probability of widowhood. Once widowed or divorced, older women are also less likely to remarry. There is only one bride for every nine bridegrooms 65 and over inasmuch as eligible same-age men not only are in short supply but also are much more likely to choose a younger wife. Widows thus account for about four in ten women between the ages of 65 and 74 and seven in ten women 75 and older.[1] Relatively little attention, however, has been paid to the variety of life-styles of older women and to the impact that transition out of marriage has upon their lives. Part III addresses some of these variations.

A fiction persists that the majority of elderly women live with their families in nonmetropolitan areas or in retirement communities. However, 64 percent of all women 65 and over lived in metropolitan areas in the United States in 1978, and about half of these resided within the central city rather than the urban fringe. Minority older women are most likely to be concentrated in urban areas; almost two out of three black and nearly nine out of ten Hispanic women live in urban areas, predominantly in the inner city.[2] While a few old women are rich widows living in elegant condominiums, half of all persons of all ages living in subsidized housing are elderly women living alone.[3] Some solitary women in urban centers have no fixed abode and carry their possessions in a shopping bag.

Jennifer Hand, in chapter 8, presents an analysis of the life-styles of this often-ignored segment of the urban aging-female population. The way of life of shopping-bag women is, she suggests, "both an affirmation of socially approved values and femininity and a rejection of established social arrangements." "A particular category of urbanite: solitary, homeless, economic outsiders, female, poor, whose sign is the bag," shopping-bag women come from diverse social backgrounds. Their common concerns are limited to their needs for shelter and the contents of their bags.

In sharp distinction to urban shopping-bag women are the equally diverse suburban older women described by Elizabeth S. Johnson in chapter
9. Johnson draws special attention to an emerging but little-described phenomenon, the graying of suburbia, in which women have grown old with
their suburbs. Using a case-history method, she explores the relationship
between components of life satisfaction among diverse suburban older
women to suggest that their old age is quite similar to their earlier years.

In chapter 10, Rita Braito and Donna Anderson turn our attention to
another, often overlooked, social category. Despite the old song suggesting
that the worst thing in the universe is a woman without a man, Braito and
Anderson note that ever-single women are more likely to be well educated
and to earn more than their male counterparts and that they are also more
likely to be well adjusted than the divorced or widowed aged. Braito and
Anderson also raise the question: Where do we go from here? on research
on ever-single elderly women, and they propose areas of inquiry.

Beth B. Hess and Joan Waring, in chapter 11, examine the potential
dimensions and familial sources of old-age dependency among women. Emphasizing that family relationships may become the salient women's issue in
the years ahead, Hess and Waring place the needs of female caregivers and
caretakers within the context of trends in public policies affecting the family
in the United States.

Victor W. Marshall, Carolyn J. Rosenthal, and Jane Synge elaborate
upon family relationships in later life in chapter 12. In an analysis of new
empirical Canadian data, they delineate the socially patterned bonds between adult parents and their children. The importance of age and sex of
parents and children as a factor in concern about parental health is also
examined.

The last chapter in this part, by Kay O'Laughlin, deals with facing
death. She reviews the impact of widowhood, attitudes toward death, and
morass of inconsistent findings that dominate most investigations of these
two aspects of death among the elderly. O'Laughlin presents results from
her research as well as that of others to highlight the impact of death and
ways of handling its presence among elderly women.

Notes

1. See Federal Council on the Aging, *The Need for Long Term Care:
Information and Issues,* DHHS Pub. no. OHDS81-20704 (Washington,
D.C.: U.S. Department of Health and Human Services, 1981) for these data
and additional information on demographic characteristics of the population aged 65 and over.

2. For further details on urban older women, see Elizabeth W. Markson and Beth B. Hess, "Old Women in the City," *Signs* 5 (Spring 1980): S127–S141.

3. Women's Equity Action League, *Budget Cuts Hurt Older Women* (Washington, D.C., April 1980), p. 1.

Shopping-Bag Women: Aging Deviants in the City

Jennifer Hand

A shopping-bag woman is a homeless vagrant who lives in urban public places and who carries her household with her in shopping bags. In New York City, a shopping-bag woman may be a solitary woman, frequently found by Carnegie Hall, bent over and clutching a handbag to her chest. She may be seen in the subway with a leg in plaster or waiting for an air-conditioned train in summer. She may pace the street, gesticulating occasionally, or she may be a quiet, genteel type seen sitting near the public library with a suitcase. She may sit neatly in a waiting room or she may stand aggressively beside a wheeled cart piled high and haphazardly with goods, boxes, bags, and clothing. Often, the number of bags, boxes, and piles becomes so great that it resembles an archaeologist's mound or a midden, the remains of habitation rather than the stuff of an ongoing life-style. Shopping bag women stand or sit with their bags on the street, in doorways, on the leeward angles of buildings, at corners, at subway entrances, at bus stations, in the lobbies of banks and corporations, in ladies' powder rooms of department stores, and in the entrance to apartment buildings. They wait in hospital clinic waiting rooms, and in the offices of doctors, lawyers, and priests. They are seen standing, seemingly poised uncertainly on a corner, sometimes crossing or recrossing streets aimlessly, and at other times marching purposefully along. They may show up at the same spot at the same time every day for, say, ten days and then disappear. On hot summer nights they go with the crowd to parks and to church steps. They follow parades. In freezing weather, they walk into parking buildings, hospitals, subways, apartment buildings, offices, basements, and schools, and stay. The life of such a woman resembles that of homeless and displaced refugees with whom we are familiar in other times and places as they travel, carrying things and valuables with them. However, shopping-bag women are not traveling to some different or safer place; they are at home where they are. We present here some findings from a study of these women undertaken from 1973 to 1978 in New York City.

Estimate of Numbers

The term *shopping-bag woman* or *shopping-bag lady* refers here only to women who have been homeless for at least one year and who have devel-

155

oped a stable life-style in that situation. I estimate that between 400 and 500 women of this type are living in Manhattan. This estimate of the number of shopping-bag women is based on a census made by me in 1976. It includes women whose appearance is unremarkable and who deny that they are homeless as well as the obvious and disreputable shopping-bag ladies who make no attempt to maintain a respectable front and have been the focus of media attention. It excludes women who are periodically homeless and women like the elderly tenant who looks for food in garbage with whom shopping-bag women are easily confused on the visual level. As the estimate does not include all homeless women, it does not provide the basis for calculating the need for shelter services in New York City. A recent estimate of this need puts the number of persons who require public-shelter services at 30,000 men and 6,000–6,500 women.[1]

There is now, in response to structural changes in the city—most particularly, the reduction of low-cost rental housing and the inadequacy of pensions in combination with health and social-services systems that seem designed to deter clients rather than to provide aid—a large and, I suspect, growing population of homeless persons. Some of these become shopping-bag women. Shopping-bag women are those women who, finding themselves for one reason or another alone, socially unattached and homeless, walked out into the streets and made a place for themselves there. Despite their poverty, powerlessness, and frequent misery, they discover resources and assert rights to space, property, independence, and status even as they act outside the institutions that ordinarily distribute these goods. Shopping-bag women have in common homelessness, poverty, femaleness, and the manner of their adaptation to the city. They are a category, not a group. Their sign is the bag they all carry.

Solitariness

Typically, when one comes upon a shopping-bag woman, she is alone. She may be in an area full of people, but if so, she will be off to one side in a private niche clearly separate from the crowd. This is most obvious in the case of the shopping-bag lady whose appearance, combined with more luggage than one would expect an ordinary traveler to have with her, helps to mark her out from the crowd. For example, a woman sitting on blankets under an escalator busy with commuters is clearly apart from that group, although she is in contiguous space. She is a solitary figure.

In their solitariness, avoidance of intimacy, lack of peer support, and expressed desire to be left alone, shopping-bag women are quite similar to people living in hotels for whom actual or self-proclaimed isolation is an adaptation to the conditions of hotel life. Sokolovsky and Cohen, for example, note that the dependent aged in hotels attempt to create the kind of support systems that diminish control of their lives by social systems. They report that "the ideal self-image of these aged persons emphasizing self-sufficiency and independence generates personal networks organized to limit the penetration of societal institutions into their lives."[2] Similarly, Stephens notes of women living alone in hotels that their loneliness is "a price they are prepared to pay to maintain their independence."[3]

The problems of balancing needs for social support with maintenance of self-respect and social status are even more difficult for homeless people. Solitariness is one mode of adaptation to this situation. In the case of the shopping-bag women, solitariness is taken to an extreme and is reinforced by the fact that she finds ways to support herself outside social networks. In addition, her strategies often require her to present herself as other than she is and to avoid notice and social interaction. Furthermore, the difficulties of reaffiliation via the bureaucracies credited with this function require such extraordinary efforts that homeless women are deterred from using these services.[4]

Disaffiliation among Shopping-Bag Women

The fact that shopping-bag women are solitary now implies neither anything about their previous existences nor that they are psychologically incapable of sociability or of participation in social networks. There are many and varied reasons why shopping-bag women found themselves in the situation of being alone, poor, unconnected, and without shelter or income. Life-history data are not available for all the shopping-bag women of New York and not complete and not verified for those I have interviewed. Therefore, it is not possible to say whether the characteristic orientation toward solitariness of the shopping-bag women observed and their lack of social affiliations are the continuation of life-long patterns, the result of recent trauma, or a recent adaptation to the conditions of life they meet on the street, one aspect of a viable modus operandi.

For this study, the Manhattan Police Department Sixth Precinct was chosen for systematic observation. This precinct coincides with the area of Greenwich Village. All the shopping-bag women of that area were observed. In addition, women were located and observed in other locations in Manhattan. The shopping-bag women observed at that time were quite varied in age, race, life experience, and appearance. In Greenwich Village, shopping-bag women were white, black, Hispanic, Catholic, Protestant, and Jewish, and ranged in age from 35 to 70, with a median age of 55. Citywide, they appeared to be predominantly white and over the age of 50. However, as no claim of completeness is made except for the one area, and as some homeless women go to great lengths to disguise their situation and are not easily recognizable, it is not possible now to make definitive statements about the social, religious, and ethnic background of women who are full-fledged shopping-bag women or about the growing population of homeless women in the city. What has emerged from the sketchy histories gathered by me and from those known to other people familiar with one or with large numbers of shopping-bag women is that the women now homeless come from a variety of ethnic-class backgrounds and that most, at some point in their adult lives, were affiliated to major social institutions—they worked, they married, they supported families, they had children. For some women now on the street, their present predicament is the end result of the attenuation of social bonds over many years through deaths, desertion, loss of family, illness, or unemployment until the final catastrophe—loss of a room or a check—seemed less an event than the natural culmination of a steady process of disaffiliation that had been eroding their personal social margin for years. Some had lived for years in a situation of narrow social margin.[5] Some had been recently completely dependent on an institution that had met every subsistence need. For others, their present situation of social isolation and physical aloneness was not something they previously had experienced or expected. They had had families, friends, homes and jobs and then, rather rapidly, were bereft of them.

Fay, for example, had been the only child of elderly middle-class parents. As a child and young adult she had associated chiefly with her parents. She never trained for an occupation. After their deaths, she continued to live in their apartment. She had a nervous breakdown and spent three years in a state mental institution in upstate New York. She was discharged and worked for awhile as a typist, not making any friends there. Following another admission to the hospital she was, in the terminology of the Department of Mental Hygiene, "repatriated" to New York City and supported there by welfare checks. A check did not come, and she was evicted from the hotel where she had been living. She put her suitcase in storage at Grand Central and took to sleeping there and, when it became warmer, in Bryant Park and, still later, in the Greenwich Village Sixth Precinct area. The only people she had ever had to call on were her parents, who were now dead. Welfare had cut her off, and after two attempts she gave up trying to be reinstated. The bureaucracies—state mental hygiene and city welfare—with which she had been involved now refused to know her. The welfare check had been her only affiliating link. With that link broken and lacking any other form of connectedness, she was totally outcast.

A similar process of loss of social connectedness had occurred in the lives of women much older than she for whom age alone had brought loss of family, including children, and friends through death as well as exclusion from the job market. Valerie, a woman of 79, already isolated by the loss of her family through death and her occupation through retirement, lost her cheap apartment and her entire neighborhood to urban development.

For others, though their present situation of social isolation and physical aloneness was not something to which they were accustomed, experience of isolation within the family or work situation can be inferred. For example, Mary had been a maid who lived with a family for at least fifteen years but who nevertheless never became an integral member of that family. She never had a family of her own, developed a network of friends, or had any kind of social life independent of her employers. She, like the married woman who simply just left, had no web of affiliations outside the family she was living with and was essentially isolated within that group. Three women I spoke with had been clerical workers. One had been a skilled bookkeeper and, the other, the personal secretary of a bank executive. The bookkeeper quit because "they were giving me too much to do. They just took advantage of me." The secretary says her boss was moved and she did not know where else to go for work. Two women, to my knowledge arrived in New York from out-of-state psychiatric hospitals. Another made a rapid transition from a New York State psychiatric center to the welfare office to the street. She never actually received welfare.

Social Attachments and Social Power

Even those shopping-bag women who at one point in their lives had a fairly broad range of social affiliations—job, family, friends, a neighborhood—were vulnerable to being disaffiliated permanently. In order to participate in a stable overtime system of personal connectedness, one must be not only affiliated but also hold powerful positions within that system at least to the extent that one is missed if one leaves and that the groups with whom one is connected are powerful enough to sustain themselves against the erosive powers of other groups. For example, an old person somewhat alienated from suburbanite upwardly mobile children, residing in an old neighborhood where she knows everyone, may become isolated rapidly if her area is subject to renewal. The shopping-bag women, in common with many others, lacked control over their social lives, even though they were, objectively, affiliated. Both those who had social ties and those whose social ties were negligible found themselves equally uprooted.

Howard Bahr writes that "power derives from affiliations. The powerless are the disaffiliated."[6] The types of affiliations normally available to women are, however, not those that bring lasting social power.[7] Women have been embedded primarily in two systems—the family and the neighborhood. Women, particularly older women,[8] have been affiliated in situations where their own position in the system was weak vis-a-vis other members (for example, maid, secretary, girlfriend, even wife) and where they have had to bargain for care and status through their husbands or children, holding no resources in their own name. Other ties in which they invested, neighboring, for instance, lacked the capacity to sustain them in times of crisis and were themselves weak in relation to competing organizations. As the history and present existence of shopping-bag women demonstrate, the number of affiliations or degree of isolation is not an accurate measure of power or of continued control over one's life and over one's resources built up over time. Rather, the type of affiliation, the quality rather than the quantity of an individual's links to social networks, is a better indication of an individual's power in a system and ability and willingness to maintain his or her place within it.

It seems that the previous affiliation of shopping-bag women to friends, family, and organizations afforded them little satisfaction. While they express the pains of loss—of family, of friends, of work—and talk about getting some help, an apartment, a boyfriend, a marriage, or starting a business, they also talk about the man they had to run away from, the boss who cheated them, the welfare worker who hates them, and the home they left, walked out on. This low level of prior satisfaction in combination with memories of helplessness against forces controlling or disrupting their social worlds results in a lack of enthusiasm among the group of shopping-bag women as a whole for renewal of ties to family or public sources of aid ranging from procrastination ("I think I'll call my sister next week," or "I'm going back to welfare next year") to outright revulsion and fear for some.[9] In order to protect themselves, they believe, they must stay alone. In order to avoid being locked up and put away, they must avoid people. In any case, they feel that they are better off alone. While they do complain of loneliness, of no one to talk to, and of being afraid because they are alone, they also fear being enclosed and being tied up with a lot of people. They may not like being as isolated as they are, but they prefer it to what they have known or expect from affiliations—loss of privacy, invasions of self, and constraints upon their movements. All these women, from the fully affiliated and socially integrated to lifelong loners and those totally dependent on health and welfare organizations, are now alone and show little willingness to reattach themselves. They appear to see solitariness and avoidance of both institutional aid and personal intimacy as a means of continued control over their own lives.

Peer Support among Shopping-Bag Women

Although they live in a similar style, shopping-bag women are not a social group. Even women who spontaneously describe themselves as shopping-bag women do not regard this common name as signifying common grounds for association and sociability. Solitariness is an integral part of the life-style and is supported by all, including those who do present themselves as members of a group with a common name.

Shopping-bag women in contiguous space with other shopping-bag women and women in a similar position act as a set of aggregated individuals rather than as a number of people with interests in common. Margaret, for example, knows two women she calls carton ladies because they sleep in cardboard boxes. She sees them at her spot, a hydrant. She has never spoken to them. There are three indoor places in Manhattan where numbers of shopping-bag women gather: Penn Station, Grand Central, and the Port Authority Bus Terminal. Observation in these facilities shows that contiguity does not make for sociability or the forging of common ties of interest. In a setting like the Penn Station ladies' room after 11:00 P.M., when the attendant goes off duty, women gather to wash, to rinse out clothing, to use the hand dryers, and to sleep in the stalls. About half these women are shopping-bag women, homeless for at least a year. The others are transients —women recently homeless; prostitutes; women whose social security has been spent, a regular monthly occurrence; and old women from hotels nearby who come from time to time for the greater sense of safety they find there. Only a minority of these women speak to each other. Most either completely ignore the others or leave if anyone speaks to them. Far from recognizing a common situation, the shopping-bag women simply turn their backs on each other and go to sleep.

Similarly, women who use the daily breadline at St. Francis's Church on 31st Street evidence very little interest in each other. Typically, the women come and go in silence. Women stand in line in the early morning waiting for the breadline to begin serving sandwiches and coffee at 6:45 A.M. The shopping-bag women are noticeable for their reluctance to stand around and chat with other women there. They tend to stand apart, to join the line only when it is moving, and then to scatter. One woman crosses the avenue only when the line has begun to move and always moves hurriedly away. Occasionally, one may hear encouraging comments on the breadline. Those who speak are not shopping-bag women but poor old women who arrange to supplement their food by standing on the breadline, teenage runaways, and junkies. The older women may take an almost parental interest in the younger ones and encourage them, for example, saying, "Never mind. Don't feel bad. Everyone has a bit of bad luck sometimes." The younger ones swap information or relive the experiences of the night before. Unlike these other women on the breadline, shopping-bag women apparently do not consider being together in some place for the same reasons sufficient grounds for friendly interaction. Even the sharing of a stressful event does not result in the formation of a network of support. For instance, four shopping-bag women were taken to the basement of the Port Authority Bus Terminal building at 42nd Street and locked in for several hours together before being taken to court. They knew each other by sight, being regular habitués of the facility. Their shared predicament encouraged them to talk together for the duration of their arrest. Immediately after they were released, however, they went their separate ways and never met again. Mutual recognition existed as before without any other interaction, as before.

It is surprising that these people in an objectively similar position— particularly a position so extreme—share so few concerns and very rarely share anything, including space, with each other. We might expect, for example, that people lacking a regular source of food shelter, as has been reported in tales of Skid Row,[10] would communicate with each other about matters such as where to go for food, for safe, good places of sleeping, and so on. However, the only common concern expressed by shopping-bag women is for their bags and for shelter for themselves. They do not share daily rhythms of eating, sleeping, and walking and rarely share information relating to these activities.

Peer Support among Men on Skid Row

It is interesting here to contrast this low level of community feeling and mutual aid with that reported for Skid Row men and Bowery bums, another disreputable and poor category and one with whom shopping-bag women often are associated. Before Nels Anderson published his pioneering study of the hobo,[11] the derelict population of Skid Row areas was considered to be a collection of isolated anomic individuals. His work stressed the existence of communal links among these men and so helped to establish the notion that life on Skid Row could be studied sociologically as a subculture. Wallace, for example, defines Skid Row as "an isolated and deviant subcultural community expressing the features of a distinct and recognizable way of life" and goes on to say that "skid row is a community which although deviant, contains many of the basic features of any community."[12]

However, all the studies that have found a subculture that includes sociability among homeless men also have been studies of Skid Row areas. Men in these areas live in an ecologically distinct area and are serviced by a complex of specialized institutions there. This contiguity and the importance of sociable drinking, or sharing the bottle, help to account for the kind of developed subculture that has been observed among the homeless, nomadic, alcoholic, disaffiliated, or lost men on Skid Row and says little about the social situation of homeless men (and women) living in other areas. The cohesiveness of the Skid Row community has serious limitations, and

Anderson in later work insists that he feels he overstated the degree of community cohesiveness among the hobos he observed in his original study. He also comments that "it was a way of life extinct as soon as it was written about."[13] Wallace, too, points out that Skid Row men do not want to claim membership in that community.[14] There may be, then, some elemental community among Skid Row alcoholics who are concentrated in one area and have at least one interest—drinking—in common. It is not the kind of community, however, that offers much in the way of mutual help and reliance or pride in belonging.

Making a Living

While they are members of the class of persons who live with a narrow social margin and though they lack both income and relationships with people who might support them, shopping-bag women do not look for public support in the form of welfare payments or institutional living. Other economically marginal or destitute people depend upon aid from the welfare bureaucracies or, as Richard Elman has shown,[15] upon other poor people. The shopping-bag women does not. She bypasses both the market system of distribution and the safety net of public assistance. In effect, she creates her own system of private welfare.

Subsistence

Shopping-bag women live, sleep, and eat in the city. Somehow, without participating in the normal social arrangements through which most citizens are provided with food, shelter, clothing, and other facilities, shopping-bag women eat, find shelter, collect large amounts of property, and survive for years. How do they do this?

They subsist by eating other people's leftovers found in garbage cans or still on the plates of self-service cafeterias, by begging for food money, or by accepting gifts of food. Obviously, they eat poorly. They eat very little and are usually hungry. They find the garbage to be an inexhaustible source of food and/or goods. They find shelter and places to be in spaces open to the public.

Concern with what is called the basic necessities of life is not a matter of continuous calculation among the women studied. They do, of course, need to eat, to drink, to be clothed and sheltered, to eliminate wastes, to receive medical care, and to sleep. Attempts to meet these needs, however, often are subordinated to other interests or to competing needs. The need for shelter, for example, appears to compete very successfully with the need for food. A woman may, for example, prefer to stay warm and dry in a church than cross the street in bad weather to stand in the breadline, even though she may then go without food until the next day's breadline. Hungry women will refuse food if the context in which it can be obtained violates or infringes upon a particular sense of identity. For example, shopping-bag women refuse to sit down with disreputable men at the traditional Thanksgiving meals provided by charitable institutions. They will also refuse food from individuals if they feel that acceptance places them in an unwelcome client role.[16] Lack of food alone cannot make one woman beg, another be seen in the breadline, another pick garbage, or another interrupt activities that are at the moment more important to her.

Acquisition of Goods

Shopping-bag women have no income or credit. Consequently, the manner in which they acquire goods is not the market one of payment/money exchange. She does not steal things. Rather, the shopping-bag woman discovers things, finding clothing, other small objects, goods she is or was accustomed to, things new to her, things in which her history inheres, objects of fantasy and reminiscence, as well as all the stuff imaginably useful for maintaining a social front or for constructing new ones. When she finds these things they are garbage. She goes shopping in garbage. She sorts and chooses. She collects and builds, or she selects and keeps a constant volume of property. In this process of discovery and use, value is given to discarded waste. Garbage is transformed into property. As the shopping-bag woman gathers and selects garbage, it becomes carefully selected clothing, objects of sentimental value, the wherewithal to set up house, or even commodities to be sold. It is easy for a shopping-bag woman in New York to do this because of the sheer abundance of goods discarded there and because in most sections of the city garbage is left lying on the street accessible to passersby. The volume of waste is too large for the public-sanitation and garbage-disposal services to deal with expeditiously. Because of general affluence and accelerated consumption, some goods, once having a dollar value on the market, are discarded rather rapidly and reappear as garbage. The kind of modern urban waste that appears in front of private homes and apartment buildings is the fruit of overproduction and consists largely of goods that have lost their commodity characteristics (their value on the market) but that have often retained a use value for others.[17] She gathers stuff like shoppers who find themselves suddenly with free access to stores full of goods. A shopping-bag woman may start out with nothing more than what she is wearing. She then acquires first a bag, then another, puts them on a wheeled cart, attaches more bags to the cart, gets a bigger cart or more carts, and so on until eventually she has an unmovable mound. There appears to be no practical limit to the amount of stuff collected. In one case, the need for mobility combined with a desire for goods resulted in a caravan of eight wheeled carts tied together two by two. Carts become unmovable with weight, baby carriages end up on top of a post-office cart, a rag on the street becomes the foundation for a solid pile of stuff.

The contents of most bags are an odd assortment of objects found, claimed, and kept, often sorted and resorted, cleaned and wrapped.[18] The shopping-bag woman carries things that have a practical and personal significance to her that is not readily identifiable to others. For example, one bag taken from a cart contained only wiring for lamps and a broken radio. Another woman carries around with her a bag full of 1960s *National Geographic* magazines. Other contents include cosmetics; hairpins; curlers, each wrapped in tissue paper; old bottles and containers; umbrellas; pieces of leather and ribbon; fabrics in odd shapes and sizes; empty cigarette cartons; and newspapers. The great piles of goods consist mostly of newpapers and clothing indiscriminate by color, sex, size, climatic appropriateness, and wear. When questioned about the kind and amount of stuff they have gathered together, they will say that "it's good things" without further explanation. Like many collectors and like consumers in general, a shopping-bag woman may not know exactly what she has or why she has it. However, she keeps on working collecting and shopping and may amass a quite amazing amount of stuff. City space then becomes her storage place as she is forced to leave some things in one place in order to move around. A woman may leave one bag in order to go off to collect more. Some keep only one change of clothing with them and store things in the twenty-five cent lockers in subway stations. Women may be seen standing by lockers quietly changing coats and hats, for example, or taking out food or drink. The locker acts as a closet where the costume suitable for one occasion or temperature is stored while others are worn. The lockers also contain small items that a woman was not able to resist picking up. For example, a clock, a leather handbag, and a *National Geographic* magazine were the items most mourned by a shopping-bag-woman retender (with pretensions of respectability) when she found that her locker had been cleaned out.

While the shopping-bag woman's method of acquisition of goods is not that of ordinary consumers, her motives of acquisition and basis for choice of one object over another are assumed to be similar. She requires objects, goods, and clothing not only, or even primarily, for their practical usefulness or as the means of self-cultivation but also for their expressive and evidential qualities. Goods, as Veblen has shown, are evidence of social status.[19] They are testimonials. Clothing, for example, not only is a barrier between the body, or parts of it, and the environment but also indicates the sex, economic standing, and often even the political leanings and attitude

toward the immediate occasion of the wearer. Goods ranging from furnishings and style of dinnerware to clothing and personal accessories are
embellishments of the social front of social routines. Goods, as Goffman
once said, are items of "sign equipment" and are necessary if a person is to
express what he or she wants to convey about a position in the social
world.[20]

It is not correct, then, to assume that a woman going through garbage
cans on a street is engaged in the purely practical activity of finding the food
and clothing that she has to have for survival. Rather, it is closer to her own
conception of her activity to say that she is shopping, a universal activity—
looking at and finding objects, sorting and selecting, adding to a collection.
This is, as described by the women, a practical activity as it means the
accumulation of a household, of things like pots that might be needed or
that might be preferable to things already owned. However, it is not an
immediately practical activity undertaken to meet a specific and urgent
need. Acquisition of this kind is largely for future use and present assertion
of status.

Loss of Property and Status

Ironically, the more objects, goods, and property a shopping-bag woman
has, the more likely she is to be treated like a nonperson—that is, the greater
potential she gathers for asserting status, expressing her individuality, reviv-
ing memory, linking herself to other groups, or presenting herself as she
wants to be (or used to be), the greater jeopardy she puts herself in of being
recognized as a vagrant. For example, the woman who gathers things like
pots, pans, curtains, lamps, a picture, a kettle—the makings of a household
she hopes to have or remembers having—is expressing a belief in the value
of having a home and kitchen. This claim is usually, but not automatically,
granted by passersby who, observing the pile of junk growing or seeing a
woman laden with such items, may identify her as a bum who by definition
lacks respect for normal social values. While most passersby are willing to
respect the belongings of a shopping-bag woman and have no motivation to
harass her, some people, out of curiosity, desire to find out what is in the
bags or, believing in the myth of bags full of money, do remove her stuff.

For example, in summer 1976, Lena was living in and around the lower
end of Sixth Avenue. She had had a household at Herald Square in a large
post-office dumpster that had been reclaimed by the post office, and she
arrived in the Greenwich Village area carrying one empty bag. Within a
month she had a broken baby carriage piled with stuff. She collected and
sorted daily, usually around dusk and after most residents had gone home.
One evening as she was sitting on the steps of a church with her latest

sewing in her hand, she heard the sanitation truck. Her cart was parked down by the trash can on the corner. Before she could move, the men had thrown it into the truck. She followed them, yelling and complaining. Later she simply said, "Believe it or not, the sanitation men lift it [the cart] up bodily and throw it in their cart. They are always stealing it. . . . Well, it's just a matter of me running away faster than they can!"

Her concern was well founded. She accumulated in the next two weeks a larger cart of things. This cart was attacked by neighborhood kids who scattered everything but who apparently did not find what they were looking for. She collected everything again and went to have coffee. In her absence, the children (in their mid-teens or young adults) had returned and set fire to her stuff. She shrieked and screamed but could not get close enough to extinguish the flames. After this, she left the neighborhood and moved to Third Avenue. Her home had been burned down deliberately.

Although the things Lena had lost were objects found rather than bought, they had become her private property; she owned them. Her distress was caused by loss of property and intensified by the realization that none of the normal protections against theft was available or extended to her and that the perpetrators were sometimes city officials doing their job. What she considered private property was treated as garbage. Her household was regarded by city employees as ownerless junk, an insulting and humiliating experience, and a signal that she would not regularly be accorded the rights of citizenship or civil rights. Thus, she suffers a double loss—loss of possessions and the self-feelings invested in them and tacit denial of the right to own property. She is a nobody, with no sign to say who she is. She has been disidentified.

Police Practice

Normally, police do not intervene on such occasions even if they happen to be on the spot. For example, Dolores was mugged one evening while an officer stood by. She was standing beside her cart on the south corner of Minetta Lane where it meets Sixth Avenue. Two boys came up and started pushing her cart, running up and trying to pull one of the loose bags off the cart. Dolores moved forward and took the bag off, holding it in one hand and meanwhile clutching another bag to her chest. They started darting up to her and brushing by her. She began to yell at them. They rushed at her together, pushed her, and grabbed the bag from her hand. It ripped. They scooped it up and ran off to the next corner (West Third) where they opened it, scattered things, and in the space of five minutes, threw the things down beside the garbage can. This scene was observed by passersby and by an officer who stood banging his stick on the ground by the curb on the block between Minetta and West Third Street. It was dusk and difficult to see clearly. However, there was no way that the officer could not have seen what was happening. He did not intervene. Moreover, the young robbers did not hesitate to run by him, laughing, putting him between Dolores and themselves. They seemed to be using him as a protection for them, and it is possible that if he had not been there Dolores might have left her cart and pursued them. She evidently felt that he would provide her with no protection and that he might even side with her attackers.

It is possible that this officer's sense of the area is such that he did think the shopping-bag woman was out of place there and that the community, using the children as surrogates, had a right to harass her and make her move away.[21] Another issue here is the belief that a type like the shopping-bag woman cannot own anything. If one does not own property, then one is not being robbed when others take something from near you or even from out of your hand. It is not, then, that the patrolman who thinks this way, faced with a situation like this one, enforces the law selectively according to the type of persons involved but rather that he takes the attitude that no law has been broken. On this occasion, it is not really accurate to say that the officer refused to protect the shopping-bag woman's property but rather that he sees her as not having any property to protect.

While the shopping-bag woman is demonstrating adherence to socially creditable values—home, property, and concern about her status and repute—she is simultaneously a parody of the institutions she is upholding. While parody is not her intention, her efforts can produce a ridiculous effect, unsettling to the originals, the normal people who pass by, and adding to the difficulty they have in coming to terms with the existence and presence of shopping-bag women. This difficulty and the claim that the stuff collected is just junk result in unsanctioned attacks on her property. Ironically, her attempts to participate expose her to ridicule, destruction of her belongings, and refusal of the full protection of the law as regards property.

A Place to Be

Unlike most of the urban population, the time and mobility of vagrant women are not routinely organized by occupational, family, or sociable interests or by the location of a fixed residence. Consequently, the places where they are found are accessible public places chosen in accordance with individual interests and concerns or in response to the demands of fatigue and boredom. Shopping-bag women are found in many distinct areas of the city—for example, on Park Avenue as well as on the Lower East Side, in the midtown shopping center, and in the financial center around Wall Street. They are found in high- and in low-rent residential districts. Clearly, they have found urban spaces receptive to their presence.

Shelter and Protection

Shelter and a safe place to sleep are a concern of all the women. They want a place that is clean and where they will not be troubled by other people or by vermin. Fear prevents some women from sleeping at night and interrupts the sleep of most others. Their immediate concern is with shelter that functions as a safe sitting or sleeping place. Comfort and keeping warm and dry are of secondary concern. They are drawn to places that they believe to be safe and well protected. They refuse to inhabit areas that are obviously disorganized like the Bowery.[22] The areas they choose to be in are respectable and well frequented. They appear to believe in the safety of crowds and the orderliness of people in aggregate situations.

Shopping-bag women in the Village area choose doorways that are sheltered from the weather, protected from behind, but open to easy scrutiny. For example, Ann slept for one winter among the cartons piled in a doorway that people lining up for a movie had to pass. She relies on the presence of a crowd to protect her. She had moved from a park because of harassment by residents. Places that they believe will receive special police protection if needed, and so discourage violence in their vicinity, are also chosen as places in which to sit or sleep. Banks are the best example of this protection. As one woman says, "Well, you know, if you sleep right here—well, they have all kinds of alarms and the police have to come running." The woman does not ask or expect that her person or she as an individual will be given police protection but that the place will be. By putting herself there she draws upon, and takes advantage of, the order that she believes to be inherent in the place. Women may also be found sleeping on park benches during the day and at night on hot vents by schools and hospitals, in locked toilets, in hotel lobbies, under the stairs of tenements, and even hidden in cartons in parks. Sally says that she slept every night for two years in a phone booth at the Hilton Hotel.

Chosen Settings

As shopping-bag women have no private place to which to withdraw, they have to perform acts in public that normally are performed only in private space or in special settings. Women change their clothing, wash themselves, and do their housekeeping in public places. For example, Lena likes to sew and, lacking the appropriate facility, sets up a sewing area on a street corner. She goes to work there, cutting, measuring, and putting together her piecework and calculating how much she could sell it for. Such a transformation of public space into what is essentially a private store or private room is a use compatible with the functions of the street.[23] The shopping-bag woman, here, can take her place alongside that of legitimate stores

where merchandise is also allowed to spill onto the sidewalk and beside mobile vendors who may or may not be licensed to sell. Other activities like
sorting goods, putting on makeup, reading, and sleeping are less compatible
with the functions of the street but, like Lena's sewing, one usually dis-
attended by passersby.

A woman like Lena gets access to space and continues to follow her
interests by relying on the lack of interest and civil inattention of passersby
and other users of public space. Public space is preeminently the domain
where a variety of persons and styles are expected and where individuals
tend to experience themselves as single atoms rather than as members of a
group. Consequently, such spaces are areas of low group egoism,[24] and they
are extremely vulnerable to interstitial use that does not disturb existing
order as well as to outright territorial invasion that aims to establish new
rules of ownership and use.[25] To the average urbanite, public space, the
street in particular, is an open area full of strangers, a moving mass, rich in
alternatives, in various ways of doing things, of getting from place to place,
anonymous. It is not an area to be invested in as an individual. There is little
motivation to protect the series of settings passed through.[26] Numbers of
people in such places form aggregates rather than groups, evidence a basic
indifference to what goes on there, expect a diversity of people, and do not
expect to enforce norms of behavior there. In this context, tolerance of odd
behavior and of activities like sewing, which is odd only because performed
out of place, is to be expected.

Nevertheless, there is regulation of behavior in public places, and the
shopping-bag woman may find herself restricted by police ("surrogate role-
reciprocals for the general public"[27]) or by groups and individuals with
competing or discrepant interests. As Lyman and Scott point out, public
space, while supposedly freely open to all persons, is in fact an area where
activities and persons may be restricted. They write:

> Certain images and expectations of appropriate behavior and of the
> categories of individuals who are normally perceived as using these terri-
> tories modify freedom.[28]

One result of these modifications of freedom is the exclusion of some
members of the public from certain public areas and restrictions on activities in other areas. Some public spaces are even made into private places
whose territorial boundaries are defended by the group that has made, for
example, a corner, a park, or a section of a building[29] into their "home
territory"[30] and successfully established new rules of ownership or use
there.[31] The design of a building and placement of doorways may perform
the same function, filtering out persons who are not favored users of the
space.[32]

Shopping-bag women avoid these restrictions by avoiding spaces that have been territorialized, by avoiding persons like the police who might take an interest in regulating their behavior and movements, and by fitting themselves into settings where they cannot easily be distinguished from the legitimate users, those whose actual identity qualifies them as favored or intended users.

For example, some women choose a particular facility to be in constantly and would probably spend twenty-four hours a day there if buildings did not close. It is appropriate that they are called by the name of the place they frequent. They are known as library ladies, church ladies, ladies'-room ladies, and hospital ladies. They subordinate themselves to the requirements of the place and make no imprint on it. Most of these women do not identify themselves in this way. Some do, having developed a close identification with the place and/or pride in their prowess there. Margaret, for example, is proud to describe herself as a bank lady. The bank, for her, is "the safest place, if you have money." She has no money but clearly felt at ease and even excited when she was in a bank. She was not attached to any one particular bank. All had the qualities she admired and enjoyed.

It is interesting here to note that though she was familiar with the setting of the bank, she had developed this familiarity in a role quite different from the one she now played. Now aged 66, she had been a live-in nursemaid. She had envied her employers their money and had been impressed by their manner while talking to bank officials. She remembered taking the rich children to meet the people at the bank. These memories and two other skills she had learned enabled her successfully to be a bank lady. First, as a nursemaid for children of other people who, as she put it, "didn't expect you to have a life of your own," she could, after a lifetime of such service, be in a group without her presence being felt, and second, she was practiced at concealing personal items and feelings. This woman, who has spent her life in other people's houses—"Of course, you soon learn to keep out of the way"—always feeling somewhat out of place, was able by her unobtrusive manner and sense of ease and security in the bank setting regularly to occupy a place there without anyone bothering her.

A priest at one church described some of the church ladies as "very devotional—they really enjoy being there. It's a good place for them." Pamela, a black woman, a singer, describes herself as a church lady. She has a professional interest in churches and is not concerned with their denomination. She is not devotional. She says that she "used to sing gospel in all the finest churches." She is regularly found on the steps of several different churches or waiting in their lobbies. In the one church that accepted her as a member of the congregation—a gay Catholic church—she would sing in the choir every Sunday and entertain afterward with poetry reading and gospel singing. She would leave at an appropriate time, saying she had to "go uptown now to sing." In the setting of the church and in her status as guest singer, she was at ease and happy.

Other women are attracted to the waiting rooms of hospital clinics and doctors' offices. They dress for the occasion and always carry a large hand-bag containing a few personal things and something to read. For this occasion, they usually check their bags in at a locker. They wait in doctors' offices that have a group practice or clinics where people are standing and sitting about in some line or another. A woman who comes in, passes as an unexceptional person, and takes a seat may remain undisturbed for hours in a doctor's waiting room and for full days in hospital clinics where the official sense of how long people wait is extremely tolerant of or callous about long waits. Unexceptional appearance is required. Over time, after weeks perhaps of going to a particular setting and being comfortable there, a few women lose the nervous edge of their awareness that they cannot, if challenged, justify their presence. Nancy, for example, has taken on the role, if not of patient in the hospital clinic at least of prepatient. "I know that if anything were to happen to me, I am in the right place. . . ," she said. Meanwhile, she lives out the status she anticipates. She went on to add, "I'm not really ill yet." After a year, she still is not ill but still is waiting in place for the event that will, one day, occur. While Nancy attained, in her own mind, the status of honorary patient, Olga moved from feeling great sympathy for all the sick people, "especially the little ones," she sat with all day, to giving assistance, giving information about procedures and things like the location of the telephone to genuine patients, and to acting as an intermediary between the staff and clients unfamiliar with how things are run. She has attained the status of hostess in the clinic waiting room.[33] The staff refer to her as the volunteer.

The Unintended Use of Public Facilities

Shopping-bag women are not alone in regarding public places as potentially private areas and in their readiness to transform public space and facilities into settings appropriate to private needs. People do, for example, sleep on subways.[34] Others act as though they are residents, hosts, or mayors of waiting rooms and outdoor plazas.[35] In addition, waiting rooms, parks, libraries, department-store facilities, and other large public buildings come to be used intensively as areas for socializing, entertainment, sleeping, and the transaction of personal business. In short, they are used as private living rooms in the manner described so well by Chase and in contradiction to their intended function in the urban infrastructural system.[36] These people have taken advantage of facilities designed for one purpose and have made them fit another personal, private need.

In this manner, unintended users participate in the competition for space, land, and buildings. The built environment is, as Pahl puts it:

> [T]he result of conflicts taking place in the past and in the present between those with different degrees of power in society—landowners, planners, developers, estate agents, local authorities, pressure groups of all kinds, insurance companies and so on. As the balance of power between these elements changes and as ideologies in society rise and fall, so the built environment is affected. It is a continuing situation.[37]

The public interest appears to play a minor role in this balance of power. For example, we find in New York City evidence of tremendous productive capacity and willingness to transform built form and spatial arrangements. However, such changes do not reflect attention to the everyday needs of the urban population, and we also observe an evident inability to provide adequate public services and to involve large sections of the population in the division of labor and rewards. The activity of unintended users in taking advantage of public facilities demonstrates the possibility that groups may assert their right to resources like shelter by appropriating facilities that appear in the public domain. In this case, ownership results from discovery rather than market exchange or politically influenced allocation, and rights of use are justified by either careful attention to existing custom or a why-not attitude in the face of affluence.

Place and Women's Status

It appears that the values of mainstream life in the United States have not been ignored by these women who live outside the networks of normal social relations and facilities.[38] Even those women, the shopping-bag ladies, who do not attempt to maintain a normal front and who appear unkempt and dirty, draw consciously on their past experiences, including those of mother, daughter, sister, or wife, and spend much of their time in typically feminine activities. They enact domestic roles. They sew, make up their faces, shop, and sort and clean their households. Much time is spent in housekeeping. The bag itself is a feminine badge, and these homeless women, living in a most unconventional way, repeat in their day-to-day lives the activities typical of the female sex-role stereotype.

While it is possible in theory for women who are prepared to disregard custom in their use of space also to develop new and odd uses and activities there, this does not in fact happen often. Rather, the activities in which they engage are mundane and ordinary and arouse curiosity only because they are performed out of place. The shopping-bag women tend to repeat the habits and rituals they learned in previous life situations and to engage in conventional activities even though they no longer are living in the style for which these activities originally made sense. Thus, they transfer habits, rituals, and styles developed in one setting to another quite different setting and enter restricted settings camouflaged as the individuals normally expected to use these areas.[39]

It is notable that women leading such an outcast existence nevertheless express so clear an attachment to major cultural symbols. Women all over the city are attracted to sleeping places in or near major cultural buildings or places of common cultural significance that they see as places with special protective qualities. Lena, for example, sits on the church steps not only because they are wide and afford a high vantage point from which to watch the street but also because "they are good people here, religious." Other women regularly visit locations that once meant home to them. Betty, for example, lost her apartment to redevelopment and still goes and stands outside the slick skyscraper where her building once stood. Vivian, a former secretary on Wall Street, visits lower Broadway. Carol, a library lady, sleeps on the steps of the public library by the monumental sculptured lions. She has no bags—instead, she uses a suitcase, carefully maintained. She opens it at night, spreads out her rugs, and sleeps in the shelter of the lions. She invests the area around the library with a proper, bookish, scholarly non-violent ambiance (quite contrary, incidentally, to what goes on in the park behind the library). She has aligned herself with the library. Another feels safe in a particular doorway and takes comfort in the sight of the spire of St. Patrick's Cathedral. While some shopping-bag women align themselves with these symbols of orderly social life, such as churches, library, theatre, and areas like Lincoln Center that represent peaceful social order or social integration, their fellow citizens are likely to look askance if they recognize them as shopping-bag women and to perceive them as spoiling or profaning rather than supporting the buildings' identity of high cultural value—as human litter, for example, rather than genuine worshippers or joint proprietors of what the community has created. It is the case that such places are well policed, provide comfortable indoor space, and are characterized by a quietly modulated social order, often with safe toilets. However, the pleasure a woman takes in this environment has to do, I think, not only with these practical aspects but also through being there to participate in this interstitial manner at the heart of social life.

Conclusion

Shopping-bag women exist in many U.S. cities and in London, Amsterdam, Paris, and Sydney. They maintain themselves on the streets and in the public buildings and facilities of these cities by taking advantage of the food, goods, and shelter they discover there. In the context of their values, the alternatives they are aware of, and the possibilities they perceive, this route is the one they elect. Shopping-bag women appropriate the wastes, the throwaways of the consumer market. In addition, they use public facilities for private purposes, for shelter, and as places to be, in contradiction to their intended purpose in the urban infrastructural system. Though her activity is directed toward socially approved ends like the acquisition of goods, property, and a home; oriented by conventional values of self-reliance, femininity, and privacy; and supportive of existing order, her way of life marks her as a person outside normal society, lacking respect for established social arrangements. These women have extended their social margin by taking an artifactual attitude toward the material culture of the city, by drawing upon public resources, and by using public facilities. They inhabit public space. They are a particular category of urbanite: solitary, homeless, economic outsiders, female, and poor, whose sign is the bag.

Notes

1. E. Baxter and K. Hopper, *Private Lives/Public Spaces: Homeless Adults on the Streets of New York City* (New York: Community Service Society of New York, 1981), p. 9.

2. J. Sokolovsky and C. Cohen, "The Cultural Meaning of Personal Networks for the Inner-City Elderly," *Urban Anthropology* 7 (1978):338.

3. J. Stephens, *Loners, Losers, and Lovers: Elderly Tenants in a Slum Hotel* (Seattle and London: University of Washington Press, 1976).

4. See Frances Fox Piven and Richard Cloward, *Regulating the Poor* (New York: Vintage Press, 1971).

5. See the discussion of narrow social margin in Jacqueline P. Wiseman, *Stations of the Lost* (Englewood Cliffs, N.J.: Prentice-Hall, 1970).

6. H. Bahr, *Skid Row: An Introduction to Disaffiliation* (New York: Oxford University Press, 1973), p. 30.

7. J. Bernard, *The Female World* (New York: Free Press, 1981), pp. 178–185, discusses the status differentials between men and women and calls attention to the "status charade" (p. 185) in which inferior status is compensated for by ritual signs of according superior status.

8. B. Hess and E. Markson, *Aging and Old Age* (New York: Macmillan, 1980).

9. An illuminating discussion of these issues is provided by Stephanie Golden in "The Transforming Tree: Finding Our Roots in the Homeless Women," *Conditions* 4 (Winter 1979):82–95.

10. See Nels Anderson, *The Hobo* (Chicago: University of Chicago Press, 1923); Samuel Wallace, *Skid Row as a Way of Life* (Totowa, New

Jersey: Bedminster Press, 1966); Bahr, *Skid Row;* Jacqueline Wiseman, *Stations of the Lost* (Englewood Cliffs, N.J.: Prentice-Hall, 1970; and James Spradley, *You Owe Yourself a Drink—An Ethnography of Urban Nomads* (Boston: Little, Brown, 1970).

11. Anderson, *The Hobo.*

12. Wallace, *Skid Row as a Way of Life.*

13. Nels Anderson, *Men on the Move* (Chicago: University of Chicago Press, 1940).

14. Wallace, *Skid Row as a Way of Life,* p. 77.

15. R. Elman, *The Poorhouse State* (New York: Pantheon, 1966).

16. This reluctance to accept aid is well illustrated in P. Townsend, *The Family of Older People* (London: Routledge & Kegan Paul, 1957); and Elizabeth Moen, "The Reluctance of the Elderly to Accept Help," *Social Problems* 25 (1978):295.

17. As Bensman and Vidich have pointed out, productivity is "not a problem for American society; the problem lies in taking the productivity off the market." See Joseph Bensman and Arthur J. Vidich, *The New American Society* (Chicago: Quadrangle Books, 1971), p. ix.

18. Alix Kates Shulman, in a recent novel, has provided a fascinating description of the contents and categorization of one shopping-bag woman's bags. See Alix Kates Shulman, *On the Stroll* (New York: Knopf, 1981).

19. T. Veblen, *The Theory of the Leisure Class* (New York: New American Library, Mentor Edition, 1953).

20. E. Goffman, *The Presentation of Self in Everyday Life* (New York: Doubleday Anchor, 1959).

21. See Egon Bittner in "The Police in Skid Row: A Study of Peace Keeping," *American Sociological Review* 32 (1967):699–715; and Jonathan Rubenstein, *City Police* (New York: Farrar, Straus, and Giroux, 1973). Both authors point out that working policemen develop particular views of the social order that vary from district to district and setting to setting and that they exercise discretionary powers that have no clear legal mandate. The jurisdiction of the patrolman and his attentiveness to illegal activities vary by place as well as by his assigned jurisdictional powers.

22. D. Ball, "The Problematics of Respectability," in *Deviance and Respectability,* ed. Jack Douglas (New York: Basic Books, 1973).

23. See Lyn Lofland, *A World of Strangers* (New York: Basic Books, 1973).

24. G. Simmel, *The Sociology of Georg Simmel,* ed. Kurt Wolff (New York: Free Press, 1950).

25. S. Lyman and M. Scott, "Territoriality: A Neglected Sociological Dimension," in *A Sociology of the Absurd,* ed. S. Lyman and M. Scott (Pacific Palisades, Calif.: Goodyear, 1970).

26. O. Newman, *Defensible Space* (London: Architectural Press, 1975).

27. S. Greer, *The Emerging City* (New York: Free Press, 1962), p. 60.

28. Lyman and Scott, "Territoriality."

29. N. Linday, "Drawing Socioeconomic Lines in Central Park: An Analysis of New York's Cultural Clusters," *Landscape Architecture* (November 1977):54–59.

30. Lyman and Scott, "Territoriality."

31. S. Stephens, "The Market as Citicorp: At the Core of the Apple," *Progressive Architecture* (December 1978):54–58.

32. William Whyte, in *The Social Life of Small Urban Spaces* (Washington, D.C.: The Conservation Foundation, 1980), discusses the filtering effect of buildings with public indoor space and writes, "The cross section of the public that uses the space within is somewhat skewed—with more higher income people, fewer lower income people and, presumably, fewer undesirables" (p. 79).

33. See Whyte, *Social Life;* and Lofland, *World of Strangers* for discussion of this phenomenon of unofficial hosting.

34. E. Love, *Subways Are for Sleeping* (New York: Signet, 1956).

35. Whyte, *Social Life,* notes that "it is characteristic of well-used places to have a 'mayor'. He may be a building guard, a newstand operator, or a food vendor" (p. 44). Mayors or hosts may be anyone who takes an interest in the place and who is willing to act as a communication center.

36. Analysis of the phenomenon of unintended use and of processes of community formation in public spaces and facilities is found most notably in the work of Glean Chase. His observations of community formation among unintended users of the Port Authority in New York who transform the waiting rooms into community spaces appear in "A Study of Unintended Users in Public Facilities" (Master's thesis, New School for Social Research, 1973).

37. R. Pahl, *Patterns of Urban Life* (London: Longmans, 1970), p. 60.

38. Gerard D. Suttles's "Urban Ethnography: Situational and Normative Accounts," *Annual Review* (1976), p. 16, discusses the distinction between macrocultural values and stereotypes, the variable responses to each and the implications for urban research. He writes, "in our major cities, center and periphery stand in a precarious balance that is easily unsettled" (p. 16).

39. E. Goffman, *Stigma* (Englewood Cliffs, N.J.: Prentice-Hall, 1968). He writes that social settings establish the categories of persons likely to be encountered there.

Suburban Older Women

Elizabeth S. Johnson

During the 1950s, young couples with an eye on the future moved to the developing suburbs. The possibilities seemed limitless. Today, however, those suburban neighborhoods have become increasingly populated by persons who have grown old with their communities. Researchers have yet to explore the life-styles of those older persons—particularly older women—who continue to inhabit the suburbs, often without the aid of spouses or children or ties to particular agencies or institutions. What is it like to be an older woman living in the suburbs today?

Thirty-nine women, 65 years or older and residents of Longwood (pseudonym), a small community that is part of a larger, northeastern metropolitan center, provided information about their lives in the suburbs. The women discussed their personal histories and past and present relationships with others. This chapter provides an overview of their lives.

The Women

The women had diverse backgrounds. They ranged upward to 90 years of age and were neither extremely wealthy nor desperately poor. They resided in elderly housing, private apartments or condominiums, or own their homes. They lived alone, with their husbands, adult sons, daughters, or boarders. They represented all three major religious denominations; some also said they were agnostic. Several had never married; others had been widowed twice. Not all had children. Many were in good or excellent health; a few were homebound. Although several were employed, many had not held jobs since they were married. While some thought the women's movement was wonderful, many did not.

There were some differences between those women under 75 and those over that age, but the differences were almost imperceptible. For example, one 90-year-old, Mrs. Sevitz, still participates in community life; 73-year-old Mrs. Lord, meanwhile, has difficulty walking and has withdrawn from active participation outside the home.

The women held several common traits. The interviewees lived in the same community (Longwood) but did not belong to specific organizations

The research reported herein was performed as part of a larger project, "Older Women and their Social Networks," supported by a National Institute of Mental Health postdoctoral fellowship at the Department of Sociology, Boston University.

179

and did not receive services from particular agencies. At the time of the interviews, they were not connected with any one individual. Also, some of the women believed they were inappropriate as interviewees because they had no problems.

The women's names were obtained, for the most part, from community census lists. Those names, along with certain details about their lives, were changed to protect their anonymity.

Background Information

The process of growing older is accompanied by changes not only in social relationships but also in role and perspective. The main task for women in their twenties is often to master the challenges and responsibilities of marriage, family-life, and career. At that pivotal point in her life when a woman begins to build the foundations for the rest of her adult years, the roles of wife, mother, and/or employee become increasingly complex. The building process continues well into her middle years, when there is a continual expansion of family and friendship networks.

There are strong indications that attitudes formed during these years (or earlier) are retained throughout life. As the middle years approach, however, the woman's main task is to let go of her maturing children. The women may be forced to adjust also to the loss of a husband, friend, or family member as divorce, relocation, and death take their toll.

In order to place this research in perspective, it is worth noting Fischer's analysis of life in the suburbs.[1] Fischer noted that the primary psychosocial difference between urban and suburban groups reflects self-selection—that is, characteristics of the individuals who want to and do move there—rather than ecological characteristics such as density or distance. He pointed out, however, that modest differences, unexplained by self-selection, do exist— particularly, the localization of social life and the relative absence of unconventionality in suburbia.

Unlike previous decades that saw the suburbs populated largely by households that included children under 18, the current decade sees suburban communities populated by older persons who (having moved to the area after World War II) witnessed their children's moving out. Quite often, these older persons are now widowed women.

An Overview of the Women

This section presents capsule descriptions of the women and is organized by their marital status. Because the number of widowed interviewees was so large (thirty out of thirty-nine), they are grouped by living arrangement—that is, whether or not they lived alone.

Widows Who Live Alone

Mrs. Chirillo, a 70-year-old bundle of nervous energy, was the second child of Italian Catholic immigrants who named her in honor of the saint on whose birthday she was born. Forced to quit high school after the ninth grade, Mrs. Chirillo's aborted education is one of her biggest regrets. She married her next-door neighbor, a man fourteen years her senior who died twenty-four years ago. Three children out of eight pregnancies survived into adulthood. She worked in a factory to support her family after her husband became increasingly disabled from his war wounds.

Mrs. Cohen, a petite 84-year-old widow, feels her life has been a series of mistakes. She was separated from her husband when the children were young but never divorced. Her youngest son committed suicide twenty years ago. She blames herself for not being a "good mother."

Mrs. Crane, 77 years old and widowed for several years, is healthy both physically and mentally. Her desire always to be progressing gives her an openness that is very appealing. She is currently planning to reupholster her dining-room chairs and to wallpaper her bedroom. She serves informally as the neighborhood chauffeur.

Mrs. Eisen, age 66, is tall, slim, and vivacious. She has been widowed for three years, is "desperately lonely," and is actively recruiting a prospective husband. A talent for piano-playing has allowed her to be social and to augment her income throughout life. She has a natural daughter and a retarded adopted daughter who both appear (at last) to be in stable life situations. Her adopted daughter, particularly, has caused much grief over the years.

Mrs. Frank is a slender widow who looks younger than her 71 years. She lives in a two-family house in Longwood that is co-owned by her brother. Childless as a result of a hysterectomy to remove a tumor when she was only in her twenties, she was employed as an accountant all of her life and retired recently. Since her husband died twelve years ago, three men have asked her to marry them, but she has refused because of her fear that they will become disabled or die.

Mrs. Fraser, now 78, moved from Idaho to Longwood when her husband died several years ago to be near her only daughter. She has made a good adjustment with the help of two friends who are also widows. The three women shop and visit together often. Mrs. Fraser keeps in touch with other friends she reluctantly left behind in Idaho but enjoys the security of living only a few houses away from her daughter.

Mrs. Golden, age 74, is a dynamic widow who lives in a luxurious one-bedroom condominium that her sons bought for her soon after her husband died several years ago. Although quite active, she concentrates on her family, which includes two sons, their wives and children, and her six brothers and sisters.

Mrs. Harris, 83, is well to do but has been twice widowed and is unhappy. Her second husband, to whom she was married for almost twenty years, was a victim of Alzheimer's disease and was confined to a nursing home for the last few years of his life. The contrast between the regard in which he was held by his colleagues in engineering (where he was listed in *Who's Who*) and his later decline into senility was frightening and difficult for her. As a result, she suffered a slight stroke.

Mrs. Heming, a 69-year old widow, has gone from riches to rags and back again. The daughter of wealthy parents who were forced to give up their Cadillacs during the Depression, Mrs. Heming worked in a bank and advanced to an administrative position when, at the age of 40, she met and married her husband. The bank was about to demote her because of her marriage, so she quit. Although she never had any children, Mrs. Heming regards her husband's son from his first marriage (his wife died) as her son and his children as her grandchildren.

Mrs. Kaplan is a 65-year-old attractive, blond, self-employed typing specialist who has been widowed only a few years and is still adjusting to the loss of her husband. She has few friends in the traditional sense but is close to her two daughters and has ongoing relationships with regular clients. She talks on the telephone with each of her daughters two to six times a day with the aid of a special attachment that allows her to keep typing while she is talking.

Mrs. Lakowitz is a 75-year-old healthy widow whose entire life has revolved around her family. She emigrated with her Jewish parents from the USSR when she was six years old. For many years the Lakowitzes operated a small grocery store in a community not far from Longwood. They moved to Longwood after selling the business. Mrs. Lakowitz feels isolated and alone even though she has telephone contact daily with her sister and son and weekly with two daughters who live in other states. Her daughter's divorces remain disturbing to her; she feels unsettled due to their transition.

Mrs. Lord, at 73, is the youngest of the homebound women. She has been widowed for five years and is proud of her ability to maintain an independent life even though she has a great deal of difficulty moving around. Her two daughters live in other states but are important sources of support as are four sisters who all live in the area. The divorce of one daughter ten years ago remains an enigma to her. She has the financial resources to pay for the help she needs and has considerate neighbors who shovel snow and watch her house when she is away.

Mrs Rein is a 70-year-old physician's widow. Her primary task is the preservation of her husband's memory through a memorial fund she has established. She lives in a one-story brick house that she and her husband built thirty years ago. Her husband's study remains as he left it. Mrs. Rein never had any female friends but concentrated her energy in a number of civic organizations and also on her family. She does not regard herself as the typical senior citizen.

Mrs. Ricci, at 74, finds herself in an unexpected living situation as the resident of a housing complex for low-income elderly. She is angry that her daughter has not invited her to move in, an expectation that her cultural background fostered. She has been widowed for several years and now has a boyfriend. Until she was 15 she lived with wealthy relatives in Naples, then immigrated to the United States where she worked in a garment factory with her husband until she had her three children.

Mrs. Roberts, age 88, is bitter and depressed. She has had health problems in the past few years and is no longer able to move around easily. Twice widowed, she is estranged from her only son as a result of his marriage thirty years ago to a divorced woman, whom she refers to as "that tramp." She receives many services to help maintain her life in the community but wishes to be moved to a nursing home.

Mrs. Rosen, an attractive, well-groomed 84-year-old widow has lived alone for only the past three years. Although widowed thirty years ago, Mrs. Rosen lived with her daughter and son-in-law until they decided to move to a smaller house after their children were grown. Mrs. Rosen, who had thought that she, like the furniture, would move with them, was shocked to find herself setting up housekeeping at the age of 81. Three daughters are in daily contact both by telephone and in person. She fears that if she cannot continue to live independently with the help of her daughters, she will be forced into a nursing home. She wishes she had not used the opportunity to live with a daughter until her old age.

Mrs. Sallers, a 69-year-old widow, has severe arthritis and is in almost constant pain. She lives in her own home and has an apartment that she rents to a tenant with whom she is friendly. She would like to live in elderly housing near her best friend but cannot because adequate financial resources render her ineligible. She still drives but is afraid to unless accompanied by someone. She shows a great deal of courage and self-reliance in spite of the physical and personal losses she has experienced over the years.

Mrs. Scott is a delightful 83-year-old widow who has a throaty resonant voice. She loves bridge and has a number of groups with whom she plays. Her car, a treasure to her but to no one else, was demolished in a recent accident. Because cataract surgery is scheduled for the near future, she does not plan to replace the car and is anxious about the changes in life-style that will be created by the lack of a car.

Mrs. Sevitz, age 90, zips around in taxis to temple, to universities where her son and husband taught, and to the community center. Widowed for ten years, she described the period immediately following her husband's death as a "nightmare." She has remained in the single-family colonial-style home that she and her late husband purchased some sixty years ago and is in frequent contact with her daughter, son, and granddaughter who live in the area.

Mrs. Simpson, a 90-year-old widow, lives alone in the home that was built some sixty years ago for her sister and brother-in-law. After her sister died, Mrs. Simpson married her brother-in-law and helped to raise her nieces and nephews with whom she remains involved. She regards them as her children and their children as her grandchildren. Because she married late after experiencing life as an independent woman, she feels widowhood was somewhat easier for her. Loneliness occasionally gets her down, but she looks forward to living to 100.

Mrs. Vliet lives in elderly housing and across the hall from her best friend of twenty years. She has been widowed for many years and supported herself as a nurse until she retired. Afterward, she began a second career as a church outreach worker. Two of her children live in other states. She is in weekly telephone contact with her daughter, but is somewhat estranged from her son.

Mrs. Wright, a rather short and stocky gray-haired widow, looks younger than her 79 years. She immensely enjoys living in an elderly housing project. She is healthy and economically secure, if not financially advantaged. She feels her upbringing in a Christian home has been an important factor in her life. The placing of her father in a nursing home after he had lived with her for four years was one of the most traumatic events of her life. She has good relationships with two sons and their families and frequently accompanies one of her sons on outings in his sailboat. She is constantly involved in handiwork projects and has been an officer and member of many civic and private organizations.

Widows Who Live with Others

Mrs. Butler, a 77-year-old widow, was raised by missionary parents in China until she came to the United States to attend one of its best prep schools and then Radcliffe College on scholarship. She married the physician son of her parents' best missionary friends, had three children, and worked with her husband as a missionary in China until they were expelled by the Communists in 1950. Her late husband's sister lives with her in Longwood.

Mrs. Collins, an 85-year old widow, has rotated between the homes of her three children for twenty years. She walks with a limp, the result of an accident in which she fell out of a second-story window when two years old. An only child, her father and grandfather each drowned at sea in separate accidents.

Mrs. Frankel, a 74-year-old, sturdy-looking woman, has had her daughter and family live with her since her husband died nineteen years ago. Socially quite active, she enjoys a weekly game of Mah-Jongg with several couples with whom she and her late husband were friendly. Financial difficulties during the Depression forced the Frankels to live with his parents.

Mrs. Jones is an 83-year-old black woman who has lived her entire life in the same house in Longwood. After being widowed many years ago, she continued to work as a janitor until age 65. Although she was asked to continue beyond retirement age, she was ready to retire. Her only daughter lives in Washington, D.C., but her granddaughter lives in the house with Mrs. Jones. Although she is homebound, friends from the community, especially from her church, visit each day.

Mrs. Levy, age 73, emigrated from Ireland thirteen years ago to be near her only daughter shortly after her paternal grandfather, maternal grandmother and husband died within a three-year period. Only her daughter could bring her out of her depression. Mrs. Levy has become an active and valued participant at the Longwood Jewish Community Center.

Mrs. Murray is a 79-year-old lady of Irish Catholic heritage who has the perfect living situation. She and her unmarried son share an apartment in a house co-owned by her daughter, who lives on the first floor. Mrs. Murray worked as a secretary until she was 72 but retired because of a desire for the companionship of people her own age. She leads an active life as a volunteer and traveler.

Mrs. Owens is still employed as a librarian at the age of 78. She has been widowed for forty years and has developed a diverse network of friends and acquaintances from her work, church, and literary associations. A boarder has lived with her for many years, and the two women share dining and some interests but are not best friends. Her only daughter lives near by and is in frequent contact.

Mrs. Turner has lived an upstanding life all of her 69 years. Her family owned a farm while her father attended a seminary. Dancing and drinking were forbidden. She went to work as a church fundraiser and spent her young-adult years traveling from city to city, arranging shows and productions. Her dream was fulfilled when she married a minister. After that, much of her time was spent in the work expected of a minister's wife. Now that she is widowed, her income is limited but she manages by renting out several rooms to students whom she regards as friends. She has had several serious heart attacks and was aided during her recovery by her daughters and a sister.

Married Women

Mrs. Drake, a 65-year-old married woman, is still actively involved in her career as a specialist in aging. The only child in an upper-middle-class Protestant family, her father died of complications while being operated on six months prior to her birth. She was raised by grandparents, who were socialists. Her mother remarried when she was 15. When Mrs. Drake later married a Jewish man, her parents sent her an official letter that she had been disowned.

Mrs. Dudley is still employed at 72. She has switched careers from that of nurse to community-education specialist. Like Mrs. Drake, she is active in elderly affairs. She is a petite, gray-haired, energetic woman who recently cut her work schedule from seven days to five.

Mrs. Frost, a beautifully complexioned 69-year-old woman, lives with her husband and 40-year-old son. She grew up as the daughter of a physician who was a member of a highly regarded and social Boston family. Most of her female friends are widowed and live in Florida. Mrs. Frost's husband is several years older but still works in his own business and is reluctant to retire. As a result, Mrs. Frost is somewhat bored and gets only limited enjoyment from her life.

Mrs. Pedlino, age 67, has been married for forty-eight years. Since her retirement five years ago, she has gained thirty pounds. She expresses her vibrant personality through a heavy Italian accent. Her self-image is as a helper of others. One of ten children including three sets of twins-her twin is still alive—she came to the United States from Italy when she was 17.

Mrs. Raskin still teaches piano at age 68. Both Mrs. Raskin and her husband of forty-eight years take many classes and have an intimate and supportive relationship. Of her three children, two have been divorced (one is remarried). Mrs. Raskin is active in working with programs for senior citizens and also is involved with her grandchildren. Although she does not attend temple often, she finds solace in her religion. In addition, she has her piano, which she loves to play.

Mrs Travers, age 68, is deeply suntanned from playing golf and looks fit. Her husband was a bank officer and the Traverses are financially comfortable. Their home, a two-story colonial, is located in one of the nicer sections of Longwood. Two daughters live nearby and are in frequent contact. The younger daughter is easier to be around even though she is more of a concern to the Traverses due to her divorce. The Traverses would like to see the daughter settled because they "will not be around forever."

Single Women

Miss Pratt, at age 70, is the daughter of a 102-year-old mother who resides in a chronic-care hospital. Although her family was middle class, Miss

Pratt's father died when he was in his fifties, one year short of the employ-ment tenure needed to assure his wife a pension. Until her retirement, Miss Pratt was a recreation worker. She has used her savings to pay for her mother's stay in nursing homes during the past seven years. Miss Pratt is an insomniac who reads library books and forgets to return them. She has a distant relationship with her two married brothers but has no one to turn to in an emergency.

Miss Spence, a 65-year-old diminutive, energetic, and enthusiastic woman who never married, continues to work part time at her laboratory technician's job. She is a college graduate who wanted to become a veter-inarian but could not due to a lack of finances after her father's death. She remains an animal lover, especially of her cat. She lives in an apartment but would like to move to a farm where she could take care of the animals.

Miss Trent, a tall, 68-year-old woman with an aristocratic manner, has never been married. She attributes her excellent health to a strict schedule of daily exercise. She walks with a light limp as the result of a fall several years ago in which she broke several vertebrae. For many years she was seriously involved with a man who recently married someone else. Miss Trent contin-ues to live in the family home furnished with many antiques and spends much of her money for upkeep. Throughout childhood she competed with her brother for her parents' and grandparents' attention. She never suc-ceeded, at least to her satisfaction.

The Setting

Located near Boston, Longwood (population less than 100,000) is one of its oldest suburbs. A majority of its population is middle class, although the city is characterized by religious, ethnic (primarily Jewish, Italian, Irish, Yankee), and socioeconomic diversity within its largely white neighbor-hoods. In 1979, 13.1 percent of its population was 65 or older: 15.2 percent female, 10.8 percent male. The total number of residents in elderly housing is less than 500, although more units are under construction. There are several nutrition sites for the elderly as well as drop-in centers. Public transportation including bus, trolley, and commuter rail is available but not in all neighborhoods. Ironically, the better neighborhoods are more often without such transportation.

The Residences

The women live in Longwood in one-family homes, two-family homes that they own or rent, private apartments, condominiums, or elderly public housing. None of the women lives in a hotel, nursing home, or rest home.

Public Housing for the Elderly

Mrs. Wright lives in a well-maintained, federally subsidized elderly housing project and enjoys her living situation immensely. She prefers to pay rent (figured as a percentage of her annual income) so that she can remain unconcerned about maintenance or other details relevant to home ownership. Her small four-room apartment is on the ground floor of the two-story building that overlooks a major road and its intersection with another. Mrs. Wright enjoys the location as it gives her the chance "to see what's going on out there." Public transportation is also close by. The apartment is decorated with pictures of family, art prints, knick-knacks, and craft items.

In order to qualify for such housing, Mrs. Wright and several other eligible women—Mrs. Vliet, Mrs. Roberts, Mrs. Cohen, and Mrs. Ricci—had to have incomes that fell below a certain level and only a small amount of savings. They also could not have transferred property or money to someone else within a fixed number of years before they applied for the housing. There is a long waiting list for these apartments, and most applicants wait at least three years before being accepted.

Private Apartments

Mrs. Lakowitz continues to live in the same apartment that she and her late husband rented after they retired from their grocery store and moved to Longwood. The apartment is small and exceedingly neat and clean but somewhat gloomy due to the dark colors and heavy furniture, bric-a-brac, and pictures that crowd the available space. "It is very difficult to move a whole houseful of furniture into an apartment," Mrs. Lakowitz explains. She is not on very friendly terms with her neighbors.

Mrs. Chirillo also rents an apartment but has remained in the same neighborhood where she once owned a home. The apartment is one-half of a modern one-story duplex owned by a relative and shared by a niece. (Another woman, Miss Spence, is similar to Mrs. Chirillo in that she rents in the same area in which she grew up.)

Miss Pratt lives in an old Victorian house that has been converted into apartments. The building is not well maintained, and the hallways are dark and dirty. Miss Pratt pointed to bloodstains on the hall walls that were caused by an alcoholic who lives upstairs. Her complaints to the wife of the superintendent of a nearby apartment building have resulted in a vacant unit being held for her in that building. Miss Pratt was "caught off my guard" and accepted it. In spite of the poor quality of her present housing, Miss Pratt is ambivalent about moving because the present apartment offers a measure of privacy that she fears will be lost in the new building. She believes that many single older female tenants; "old biddies" as she calls them, will pry into her affairs. Also, there are no mailboxes in the new unit; instead, the superintendent's wife delivers the mail, and Miss Pratt is worried that everyone will know her business. In addition, the new apartment costs $9 more per month.

Private Homes

Women who live in one-family homes include Mrs. Crane, Mrs. Scott, Mrs. Levy, Mrs. Pedlino, Mrs. Owens, Mrs. Heming, Mrs. Kaplan, Mrs. Sevitz, Mrs. Simpson, Mrs. Raskin, Mrs. Frankel, Mrs. Butler, Mrs. Dudley, Miss Trent, Mrs. Turner, Mrs. Frost, Mrs. Jones, Mrs. Collins, Mrs. Drake, Mrs. Eisen, Mrs. Travers, Mrs. Lord, Mrs. Rein, and Mrs. Harris. Mrs. Lord's two-story Victorian, representative of so many of these women's homes, has eight rooms, dark woodwork, worn Oriental rugs, and many near antique pieces of furniture. Mrs. Crane, who also lives in a Victorian-style house, feels established in her neighborhood and would not want to give up her home for an apartment. A couple of friends rented an apartment only to find that when they closed the door they felt locked in. Mrs. Crane does not want that.

The main differences between the women who live in single-family homes and those like Mrs. Murray, Mrs. Frank, and Mrs. Sallers who occupy apartments in two-family homes, are that the latter have slightly less space but are closer to neighbors. Their furnishings and feelings about their apartments are not different from the other women's feelings about their homes. Mrs. Murray, for example, believes she has the best possible living situation. She originally lived with her husband on the first floor of the two-family home, while her married daughter lived on the upper floors. When Mr. Murray died, she and her daughter traded apartments and rearranged the finances of the house so that Mrs. Murray and her unmarried son could live in the smaller upstairs apartment and her daughter, who has a larger family, could have the downstairs one. The "intimacy at a distance" that she is still able to maintain with her daughter is very attractive. Her closest relationship remains with that daughter.

Mrs. Frank also lives in the second-floor apartment of a two-family home that she co-owns with a brother who lives downstairs. Although she is not as involved with him as Mrs. Murray is with her daughter, the security of having a family member nearby is appealing.

Several of the women live in luxurious condominiums in modern buildings. Both Mrs. Golden and Mrs. Rosen have condominiums purchased for them by their children. Mrs. Golden's is expensively furnished and has many pictures and some paintings done by her on the walls. There are also many plants in the living room. Mrs. Rosen's condominium is also taste-fully furnished but in a style inconsistent with her 84 years. Mrs. Rosen had to set up housekeeping three years ago when her daughter moved to a smaller home. Her daughter selected Mrs. Rosen's furniture, and the style reflects her taste.

Some of the women have furnishings that are quite luxurious, others have less-luxurious furniture that reflects the era in which most of them were making their purchases. Like Mrs. Rosen, Mrs. Collins's surroundings do not fit her age. Because she lives in her daughter's home, the furnishings reflect her daughter's style rather than her own.

Like Miss Trent, some of the women inherited their possessions and even their homes from their parents. Miss Trent's home has been in the family for generations. The pride she takes in it causes her to spend much of her money on repair and maintenance. The rooms are quite large and spa-cious. They are graciously furnished with antiques that have always been a part of the house. A single exotic plant decorates the living room. Miss Trent finds her furniture infinitely preferable to the ''cheaply constructed modern pieces that are available today.'' Some of her furniture, like that of other women who are forced to be thrifty, is a bit worn, but this does not detract from the warmth of the rooms.

The women have interesting stories to tell about their furniture. Mrs. Butler's home has many artifacts dating from her missionary days in China. Both Mrs. Eisen and Mrs. Rein have baby-grand pianos. Mrs. Eisen's dominates the living room; she has played professionally over the years. Because Mrs. Rein's late husband wanted children right after they were married, Mrs. Rein interruped a fledgling career as a bel canto opera singer to have babies. In exchange for her ''presents of grandbabies,'' Dr. Rein presented his wife with a baby-grand Steinway.

Whether the women have stories to tell as romantic as those of Mrs. Butler or Mrs. Rein, they all seem to enjoy every room of their homes, not only for their present style but also for the past they represent. One of 90-year-old Mrs. Simpson's greatest pleasures is to be able to remain in her home ''with all of its memories and mementos.''

Of all the women who own their own homes, Mrs. Sallers is the only one who would prefer to live elsewhere—in her case, she would like to live in elderly housing near her best friend ''because there is a lot going on there.''

Several other women from various types of housing were dissatisfied with their present living situations. Mrs. Ricci lives in elderly housing but is upset that her daughter does not invite her to move in with her. She remembers that back in Italy her grandparents came to live with her family and that caring for them was a sign of respect and gratitude.

Mrs. Rosen owns a luxury condominium but had never expected to be living by herself after spending so many years with her daughter who took the furniture—but not Mrs. Rosen—when she moved to a smaller home. Mrs. Lakowitz lives in the apartment she had rented with her husband. When he died, however, their son recommended that she remain in the apartment rather than move back to the community where she had been born and where her sister lived. Although she has a great deal of telephone contact with her son, she sees him only a few times a year and feels that she made a mistake staying in Longwood.

The women's dissatisfaction with their living situations seems to be related to unhappiness with their children rather than anything intrinsic about their residences or the suburb. Specifically, they feel that their expectations regarding their elderly living situations were not met adequately by their children.

Expectations

Three women stood out from the others in terms of the poor quality of their lives: Mrs. Lakowitz, Mrs. Roberts, and Miss Pratt. When comparing them, the following differences were observed: Mrs. Lakowitz was healthy, Mrs. Roberts was not, and Miss Pratt had some physical problems including recently diagnosed diabetes. Mrs. Lakowitz had an adequate financial situation; Mrs. Roberts and Miss Pratt did not. Mrs. Roberts had a poor relationship with her only son; Miss Pratt had little contact with her two brothers. Miss Pratt's 102-year-old mother lived in a chronic-care hospital, was blind and almost deaf, and was not able to be emotionally supportive of Miss Pratt. Mrs. Lakowitz had frequent telephone contact with her three children but saw them much less than she would have liked and thus felt somewhat abandoned.

These three women had unmet expectations regarding their lives. Mrs. Roberts expected to be cared for in her old age, but after her second husband died, there was virtually no possibility because of her advanced age of finding another husband who would allow her to feel that someone again cared. The health and social-service system had not neglected her—she lived in elderly subsidized housing, had meals on wheels delivered daily, and was visited by a social worker, friends, and a 90-year-old neighbor—but was still angry that her only son did not visit. Thirty years ago he left her to marry the divorced woman with two children. Mrs. Roberts and her son have been unable to resolve the differences between them. Mrs. Lakowitz also expected her son to play a larger role in her life than he has chosen to do; and she never expected her two daughters to become divorced. Miss Pratt was always something of a loner—she went unaccompanied to Europe several times and never married—but she never expected her mother to be alive at age 102 when she was 70 years old. She never expected that her best female friend would abandon her after many years of friendship.

Other women who were somewhat depressed also had strong unfulfilled expectations. In her old age, Mrs. Ricci expected, because of her cultural heritage, to live with her daughter. Her daughter has chosen not to ask, and Mrs. Ricci has lived by herself in elderly housing, a situation she finds humiliating. Mrs. Rosen lives in a fancy condominium but never expected to be setting up housekeeping at 81, after living as a widow with her married daughter for thirty years. Mrs. Frost did not expect to be the only one of her friends still married—her friends are all widowed and have relocated to Florida. Mrs. Cohen never expected her son to commit suicide many years ago, and she has never resolved her guilt over his death.

To a large extent, the ability of these women to rationalize their unmet expectations, or to adapt to the choices and decisions of significant others, has been directly related to their view of life. Mrs. Simpson, homebound and living alone at 93, has wished that family and friends would visit her more but also realized they were busy. Mrs. Lord, homebound and living alone at 73, has maintained low expectations and was therefore either not hurt or would not admit to any discrepancy between what she wanted and what she has.

Most of the women hedged their answers when they were asked if they would live with a child if they desperately needed assistance. Only those women who were totally secure in the belief that a child would provide care for them, no matter what, were willing to say they expected their child to take care of them if the need arose. Mrs. Murray was quite satisfied with her life at least partly because of a secure relationship with her daughter—Mrs. Murray does not doubt her daughter would be willing to care for her should she need help. Other women, whose children, particularly daughters, held life-style values different from theirs, faced the difficult position of wanting to be with that daughter (should the need arise) yet being reluctant to appear to condone an imperfect aspect of that child's life-style. Mrs. Kaplan provides a good example. Her older daughter was married to a man who was not a good provider; her younger daughter chose to live with a man who had not yet been divorced from his wife. Mrs. Kaplan thus found it difficult to consider the prospect of living in either household. Another woman, Mrs. Dudley, said she would live with a daughter with whom she has been the best of friends, depending on that daughter's life-style at the particular time.

The expectations these women had for their children turned into a source of concern when the expectations were not met. Mrs. Lord, Mrs. Lakowitz, Mrs. Jones, Mrs. Raskin, and Mrs. Eisen had experienced an adult son or daughter's decision to end a marriage by divorce. Their expectations for stability and happiness for their children and their own vicarious pleasure in their children's lives were shaken when the child divorced. Those mothers whose daughters or sons had remarried or whose sons had achieved a stable life-style were more at peace than those women whose children had not yet settled.

In summary, three basic areas contributed to the life satisfaction of the suburban older women: health, finances, and family relationships. If they had good family relationships—that is, relationships that met their expectations—they were better able to tolerate health difficulties and even reduced finances. However, if their expectations regarding family relationships were not met, then any problem with health or finances was intensified and the women were likely to feel depressed or even devastated. For those women without spouses or children, relationships with siblings and friends took on increased importance.

Conversely, if the women enjoyed good health and finances but had unmet expectations regarding family relationships, they were less likely to be able to appreciate their good fortune in these other areas. Mrs. Lakowitz was a good example of a woman who had sufficient income and health to do whatever she wanted. She wanted to do very little, however, because of her depression concerning her relationships with her son and daughters who had chosen not to relate to her in the way she expected they would.

Conclusion

There is a great deal of reassurance in the women's stories that old age is quite similar to the earlier years. If we liked the way we were in the earlier years, we will probably like the way we are in the later ones. If we were friendly and enjoyed others without imposing our expectations, we will probably continue to receive lifelong support from family and friends. Becoming widowed, having health problems, seeing one's financial position deteriorate, and being isolated in the suburbs certainly affect the lives of older women. However, the way we deal with those issues, the type of socialization, and the learning of interpersonal skills that we have experienced ultimately will be more important in the perceived quality of our old age than any demographic data; at least it was for the women who were interviewed for this study.

Note

1. Claude S. Fischer, *The Urban Experience* (New York: Harcourt, Brace, Jovanovich, 1976).

10 The Ever-Single Elderly Woman

Rita Braito and
Donna Anderson

This chapter identifies what is known about the ever-single elderly woman in our society. These women typically have made up a very small portion of the entire population, but there is evidence that their numbers may increase with time. The increasing trend toward marrying later and remaining never married, plus the fact that women outlive men, portends increases in the number of elderly never-married women as we move into the twenty-first century. As singlehood becomes a viable alternative to marriage, more and more women may choose to remain single over their lifetimes.

Although the concept of singlehood is on the rise, marriage and remarriage remain the norm. We have no knowledge of current ever-single elderly women to determine how they have coped with living in a deviant status. We have no baseline information upon which to gauge the changes that will occur over time as social norms change. We have little idea how they differ from married, widowed, or divorced elderly women. For example, do they share the common problems of the aged plus special, unique advantages or disadvantages because they have never married? Are they the lonely, socially isolated individuals who are overrepresented in institutions because of having no family or friends to care for them? Or can they better cope with the vagaries of being old by virtue of their independence and making do by themselves? Questions like these remain unanswered because of lack of research into this special population. Even less is known about minority ever-single women.

People in the ever-single marital status only recently have been studied as a separate research focus.[1] Most often they have been included in the single group that also includes the separated, divorced, and widowed. When they have been separated into a unique research category, more often than not, age has not been controlled. This fact is especially important because the ever-single group, theoretically, can include teenagers to centenarians. The majority of people in this group is usually under 30, and it is reasonable to assume that the majority will eventually marry. Our knowledge of the ever-single person over 30, who has moved out of the so-called appropriate age at which most men and women in the United States marry, is limited.

195

The state of our existing knowledge about the ever-single person, especially the ever-single elderly woman, is scanty at best.[2] At this stage of investigation, we can only pull together what information exists on this specific group and make inferences from other bodies of literature on ever single and the elderly. We would have liked to look at the various theoretical approaches applied to this group and to discuss, for example, from the perspective of role theory, who the role models are for elderly ever-single women; or we would like to consider these women from the standpoint of deviance—being nonmarried in a society in which most people are so committed to the idea of marriage that they remarry following a divorce or the death of a spouse (in the younger age groups). If the ever single are deviant, what other deviant groups are they like? From the framework of exchange theory,[3] what exchanges did they make—at what cost did they negotiate their singlehood? How have the exchanges changed with aging? From a social-network, or support, framework, in a society in which the lack of a support system is associated with early institutionalization, did that lack contribute to their having entered nursing homes earlier than their married counterparts? For those who remained independent, what facilitated such independence? What networks do they have now, and will these networks enable them to maintain greater flexibility in living arrangements as they age? The functional school has had little to say about this group except that some people can be released from childrearing where population growth and industrialization have made the production of children less important for the welfare of the general society. Conflict theory, which has had much to say about the family and its relationship to the means of production, also has not dealt with the ever single in either a macro- or microanalysis. Is there conflict among family members as it relates to provision of care for the elderly, and have unmarried daughters provided such care? For theory development and application, the need for investigating the implications of marital status, rather than controlling it, becomes important.

While the major purpose of this chapter is to consider what is known about ever-single elderly women, it should be clear that the most important research is yet to be done. This chapter discusses the literature available and identifies the major categories in which the elderly frequently have been investigated. Throughout the chapter, the term *ever single* is used interchangeably with the terms *never married* and *single,* but unless otherwise specified or clear by context, it refers explicitly to the ever single. Because studies have used different age groups to denote elderly, no consistent cut-off point for age has been used in this review. Usually, age 55 has been the lower age limit when denoting elderly.

Demographic Characteristics

Who are the ever-single elderly? At present, about 7 percent of the total population 65 and over is female and about 6 percent is male.[4] Examination of table 10–1 indicates that ever singles 55 and over are predominantly women and white. In general, ever-single women outnumber ever-single men, reflecting the pattern found in other marital-status groups. For the white ever-single elderly population, women outnumber men nearly two to one in every category. Surprisingly, however, for the black group, after age 65 men live longer than their female counterparts. In fact, after age 75, there are nearly three times as many men as women. Among Hispanics, men also outnumber women after age 75 (although to a far lesser degree than among the blacks). Explanations for such discrepancies are not readily available but certainly warrant investigation.

Education

From a variety of sources it appears that ever-single women, as a group, are well educated.[6] Howe's data on older women from the Aging Woman Project in Madison, Wisconsin, describe an ever-single population that has had 15.9 years of education as compared with 12.8 years for the marrieds, 11.8 years for the divorced, and 11.9 years for the widowed.[7] This same pattern is noted by Glenn, Ross, and Tully.[8] Ever-single women also have been reported as being more intelligent[9] and having higher-status origins,[10] which could contribute to their higher educational attainment.

It has been well documented that ever-single women have more years of formal education than their male counterparts. In fact, higher educational attainment has been used as an explanation of why some women never marry. Some writers claim the increased opportunity for a career and high income make singlehood an attractive option among well-educated women. Others claim that well-educated women simply are not chosen for marriage. that men traditionally marry less-well-educated women or that a well-educated woman could pose a threat to the supremacy of a man in the male/female relationship. In these days of two-paycheck families, the educational attainment of women might be seen as an asset rather than a liability.

Income

In general, ever-single people earn less money than those in any other marital-status group, and ever-single women earn more than ever-single men.[11]

Table 10–1
Number of Never Married, 55 and over, by Race and Ethnicity, 1978

Race and Ethnicity	Female	Male
All races		
55 and over	1,347	1,024
55 to 64	519	529
65 to 74	538	347
75 and over	290	148
White		
55 and over	1,246	903
55 to 64	962	474
65 to 74	500	298
75 and over	284	131
Black		
55 and over	97	106
55 to 64	54	50
65 to 74	37	39
75 and over	6	17
Spanish origin		
55 and over	32	21
55 to 64	11	9
65 to 74	17	7
75 and over	4	5

Source: Modified table from Women's Study Program and Policy Center at George Washington University in conjunction with the Women's Research and Education Institute of the Congress Women's Caucus, *Older Women: The Economics of Aging.*

As indicated in table 10–2, among ever singles 65 and over, women are more highly represented than men in every money income category except two. They also outnumber men at the highest income level and in the group that is without income. On the average, as shown in table 10–3, elderly ever-single women earned about $1,000 more than elderly ever-single men in 1977 ($4,716 for women; $3,689 for men). Comparing white men and women in comparable jobs, the women make less money; on the whole, however, the female ever single is better off than her ever-single male counterpart. This may reflect the fact that ever-single women are a more highly educated group than ever-single men. Higher income for ever-single women has also been noted by Havens.[12] Unfortunately, insufficient data preclude similar comparisons for black and Hispanic men and women.

A very different pattern for black and Hispanic ever-single appears (tables 10–4, 10–5, and 10–6). No black ever-single women are represented

Table 10–2
Money Income, by Sex, for U.S. Total Population and Ever Singles of All Races, 65 and over, 1977
(numbers in thousands)

Total Income	Single			All Marital Statuses	
	Total	*Men*	*Women*	*Men*	*Women*
Total	1,322	495	828	9,170	13,298
Without income	20	7	14	25	976
With income	1,302	488	814	9,145	12,322
$0 to $999	20	11	9	87	417
$1,000 to 1,499	52	14	38	173	1,062
$1,500 to 1,999	62	22	40	244	1,489
$2,000 to 2,499	166	67	99	591	1,686
$2,500 to 2,999	100	55	45	510	1,286
$3,000 to 3,499	129	60	70	706	1,252
$3,500 to 3,999	90	39	51	696	1,033
$4,000 to 4,999	136	58	78	1,066	1,139
$5,000 to 5,999	108	40	67	950	772
$6,000 to 6,999	50	11	40	793	515
$7,000 to 7,999	83	27	56	597	394
$8,000 to 8,999	61	8	53	431	275
$9,000 to 9,999	37	14	23	339	194
$10,000 to 11,999	49	13	36	518	245
$12,000 to 14,999	71	17	55	429	269
$15,000 to 19,999	51	16	35	450	165
$20,000 to 24,999	15	7	8	199	63
$25,000 and over	22	10	12	366	64

Source: U.S. Bureau of the Census, "Money Income in 1977 of Families and Persons in the United States," *Current Population Reports,* Series P-60, no. 118 (Washington: U.S. Government Printing Office, 1979), table 45.

in the income level of $7,000 and over, but incomes of ever-single black men range up to $10,000. Both ever-single black men and women are in the modal category of $2,000 to $2,499. The same modal income holds true for Hispanic ever single. However, among the Hispanic, a different pattern is present. Some ever-single Hispanic women are in the top four income categories, perhaps reflecting the presence of Cuban migrants who, compared with other Hispanic groups, often have upper-level incomes.[13] Interestingly, no Hispanic ever single is in either of the two lowest income categories. This fact may reflect problems associated with census on migratory workers and on low-income populations. We also can note that the white ever-single woman earns more than both black ever-single men and women.

Table 10–3
Median and Mean Incomes, by Sex, for Total U.S. Population and Ever Singles of all Races, 65 and over, 1977

Income in Dollars	Single			All Marital Statuses	
	Total Both Sexes	Men	Women	Men	Women
Median	$4,234	$3,689	$4,716	$5,526	$3,088
Standard error	164	175	226	62	27
Mean	6,173	5,641	6,492	8,035	4,234
Standard error	207	333	263	119	49

Source: U.S. Bureau of the Census, "Money Income in 1977 of Families and Persons in the United States," *Current Population Reports,* Series P-60, no. 118 (Washington: U.S. Government Printing Office, 1979), table 45.

Table 10–4
Money Income of White Ever Single, 65 and over, 1977
(numbers in thousands)

Money Income	Both Sexes	Men	Women
Total	1,213	428	784
Without income	14	3	11
With income	1,198	425	773
$1 to $999	19	9	9
$1,000 to 1,499	47	11	36
$1,500 to 1,999	57	22	34
$2,000 to 2,499	130	45	85
$2,500 to 2,999	88	45	43
$3,000 to 3,499	119	53	67
$3,500 to 3,999	83	35	48
$4,000 to 4,999	122	50	72
$5,000 to 5,999	102	40	62
$6,000 to 6,999	49	11	38
$7,000 to 7,999	78	22	56
$8,000 to 8,999	61	8	53
$9,000 to 9,999	36	13	23
$10,000 to 11,999	49	13	36
$12,000 to 14,999	71	17	55
$15,000 to 19,999	51	16	35
$20,000 to 24,999	15	7	8
$25,000 and over	22	10	12

Table 10–4 continued

Money Income	Both Sexes	Men	Women
Median income (dollars)	4,462	3,902	4,879
Standard error (dollars)	176	198	249
Mean income (dollars)	6,425	5,987	6,666
Standard error (dollars)	222	375	274

Source: U.S. Bureau of Census, "Money Income in 1977 of Families and Persons in the United States," *Current Population Reports,* Series P-60, no. 118 (Washington: U.S. Government Printing Office, 1979), table 45.

Table 10–5
Money Income of Spanish-Origin Ever Single, 65 and over, 1977
(numbers in thousands)

Money Income	Both Sexes	Men	Women
Total	33	12	21
Without income	1	—	1
With income[a]	32	12	20
$1 to $999	—	—	—
$1,000 to 1,499	—	—	—
$1,500 to 1,999	1		1
$2,000 to 2,499	9	3	7
$2,500 to 2,999	3	2	1
$3,000 to 3,499	3	2	1
$3,500 to 3,999	4	2	3
$4,000 to 4,999	3	1	2
$5,000 to 5,999	—	—	—
$6,000 to 6,999	—	—	—
$7,000 to 7,999	1	1	—
$8,000 to 8,999	—	—	—
$9,000 to 9,999	—	—	—
$10,000 to 11,999	1	1	—
$12,000 to 14,999	2	—	2
$15,000 to 19,999	2	—	2
$20,000 to 24,999	3	1	2
$25,000 and over	—	—	—

Source: U.S. Bureau of Census, "Money Income in 1977 of Families and Persons in the United States," *Current Population Reports,* Series P-60, no. 118 (Washington: U.S. Government Printing Office, 1979), p. 178, table 45.

[a]Data on median and mean income levels are omitted due to insufficient data to compute these figures.

Table 10-6
Money Income of Black Ever Single, 65 and over, 1977
(numbers in thousands)

Money Income	Both Sexes	Men	Women
Total	99	56	43
Without income	6	4	2
With income	93	52	41
$1 to $999	1	1	—
$1,000 to 1,499	5	4	2
$1,500 to 1,999	6	—	6
$2,000 to 2,499	31	17	14
$2,500 to 2,999	11	10	1
$3,000 to 3,499	9	6	3
$3,500 t0 3,999	5	2	3
$4,000 to 4,999	14	8	6
$5,000 to 5,999	6	—	6
$6,000 to 6,999	1	—	1
$7,000 to 7,999	3	3	—
$8,000 to 8,999	—	—	—
$9,000 to 9,999	1	1	—
$10,000 to 11,999	—	—	—
$12,000 to 14,999	—	—	—
$15,000 to 19,999	—	—	—
$20,000 to 24,999	—	—	—
$25,000 and over	—	—	—
Median income (dollars)	2,665	3,460	B[a]
Standard error (dollars)	228	100	B
Mean income (dollars)	3,190	4,313	B
Standard error (dollars)	193	141	B

Source: U.S. Bureau of Census, "Money Income in 1977 of Families and Persons in the United States," *Current Population Reports,* Series P-60, no. 118 (Washington: U.S. Government Printing Office, 1979), table 45.

[a]Refers to lack of sufficient baseline data to compute figure.

Attitudes about Being Single

Freedom is an important word to the ever-single woman. Howe's respondents identified the following advantages to being single: freedom to run their own lives, fewer financial worries, personal space, freedom from family responsibilities, and the freedom to pursue a career.[14] These factors were especially important to both the divorced and ever single who perceived them to be significantly more salient to themselves than did the widows in the study. Overall, ever-single and divorced women were more like each other than they were like the widowed. It is interesting that all groups ranked freedom to do particular things as more important than freedom from various conditions. "Freedom to run my life as I want" was cited by all groups as the most important element of being single, followed by "having my own personal space." Freedom to pursue a career was ranked third by the ever single, fourth by the divorced, and fifth by the widowed.

Howe's study also notes the attitudes of ever-single elderly women about the disadvantages of singlehood.[15] "Difficulty of the social situation" was seen as the greatest disadvantage followed by lack of companionship. Growing old, loneliness, and no one to talk to were rated third.

Although Tunstall reports that ever-single elderly women mention their regret in not having had children,[16] Howe's ever singles did not report the same sentiment.[17] Howe suggests that her findings may differ from Tunstall's because of class differences in the populations studied.

Keiffer, using a life-history analysis, studied ever-single academic women born between 1900 and 1920.[18] She found that from an early age, these older, successful academic women had a sense of their own intellect and had developed a self-confidence that led to successful careers. She also noted that never married was associated universally with a diffusion of affectivity, a need for affiliation, and a strong sense of the need to mature. An ever-expanding group of students whom they had advised and helped personally was particularly important to all the subjects of the study.

Physical and Mental Health

Howe indicates that ever-single women over 65 report having better health than separated or divorced women.[19]

Verbrugge, comparing marital-status groups and reports of chronic limitations and disability, identifies married people as the healthiest, followed by the ever single, the widowed, the separated, and the divorced, in that order.[20] With few exceptions, ever-single people of both sexes had the lowest rates of coronary heart disease, hypertension, hypertensive heart disease, rheumatoid arthritis, osteoarthritis, syphilis, and dental problems needing prompt attention. They also had the lowest glucose levels and highest blood hematocrit levels, perhaps indicating low levels of diabetes and anemia. The never married between ages 17 to 44 had more visual and hearing impairments and other organic or neurological conditions such as paralysis and lower-extremity and hip impairments. Such impairments may have developed before birth and may have reduced the likelihood of marriage. Single people had the lowest rates of short-term disability but differed little in that regard from the married. In relation to physician visits, the ever-single woman age 45 and over had patterns similar to married women age 45 and over.

In terms of acute conditions, the married, ever single, and widowed had very similar incidence patterns; the divorced and the separated, however, reported a higher incidence of disability.

When never-married women and men were compared, women reported having a higher incidence of acute conditions; within types of acute conditions, men reported having more injuries. In terms of sex, the ever single differed from those in other marital statuses only with respect to the number of infective and parasitic diseases (the difference between never-married men and women only 0.5 percent, with men reporting more such ailments). In other marital-status categories, women reported more illnesses than men, with differences ranging from 4.2 to 8.1 percent.

In age-standardized data related to work disability, married people have the lowest rates of disability, followed by the never married, the widowed, and the divorced, with the separated having the highest rates. The difference between the single, widowed, and divorced in this category is small—about 1 percent. Never-married people had their disabilities longer than those in any other marital status; this is true regardless of age. This fact could help to explain their earlier commitment to nursing homes. The young-elderly ever-single woman might move into a nursing home earlier than her married elderly female counterpart.

Using 1960 and 1970 data, Verbrugge reports that single people (all currently unmarried), have the highest institutionalization rates and enter nursing and personal-care homes at younger ages.[21] Although the ever single represent only 5 percent of community residents 65 and older, they comprise 14 percent of nursing-home populations.[22] She attributes the earlier entrance of single people (all currently unmarried) to the severity of their health problems, the lack of opportunity for outside care, and the low level of responsibility society takes for them. It might also be explained by marital-status changes after institutionalization—becoming divorced or widowed.

As a group, single people have higher rates of admission to mental hospitals than other marital groups. Bloom reports that the most important variable associated with inpatient status in a psychiatric facility is marital disruption; repeat admissions to a state hospital were more often associated with living alone than with other considerations.[23]

Gove found that the incidence of suicides in the never married was less than expected.[24] The suicide pattern for never-married women decreased in numbers from ages 25 to 59 and increased from 60 to 64. In an analysis of Swedish data, Gove found that never-married men had a higher suicide rate than never-married women but that each had a higher rate than the married.[25] The rates were also lower for ever-single women than for ever-single men in Swiss, Canadian, and New Zealand populations.[26]

Family and Friends

Perhaps one of the most distinctive characteristics of ever-single people is their lack of children; and being single and being childless have consequences for social interaction.

Although Bachrach did not include the never married in her analysis of childlessness and social isolation, she found that there is a "strong association between childlessness and the probability of social isolation of people in their old age as compared with people who have children."[27] The childless are more likely to be living alone; being alone they are also less likely to have had social contacts within the last day or two. Their relationships are influenced by the status of their health and by their occupational class. This is probably true for the ever-single as well as other marital-status categories.

Persons without children tend to resume closer relationships with brothers and sisters than those who are married and have children.[28] Persons without children tend to resume closer associations with siblings upon the death of spouse but, interestingly, not as close as single persons.

Atchley, Pignatiello, and Shaw found that never-married older teachers had more interactions with their relatives than those who were married but that never-married, older telephone workers had lower interaction rates with kin and more contact with nonrelated friends than similarly situated married women.[29]

Never-married older female telephone employees had lower interaction levels than married female employees; the never married saw their parents and siblings somewhat more than the currently married, and the widows saw parents and siblings the most frequently.

Willmott and Young, reporting on a 1943 population of twenty-five people of pension age who were single (not currently married) and without children, concluded that never-married people see their brothers and sisters much more often than those who are or have been married.[30] They stated that 65 percent of the never married below pension age and 43 percent of those above pension age had seen a sibling within the last twenty-four hours. An additional 17 percent below pension age and nineteen percent above pension age reported seeing siblings during the previous week. Between 62 percent and 68 percent of the never married, compared to 24 percent to 42 percent of their married counterparts, had seen siblings very recently. In this same study, Willmott and Young reported that out of their sample of twenty-five, three men and fourteen women were living with siblings (eleven of these women were spinsters).[31] They identified several types of living arrangements among the ever-single elderly living with siblings: living with extended family related to them through siblings, for example, nieces or nephews; living with siblings; and living with fictive families. *Fictive families* have been defined as people who live together as family (for example, sisters, cousins, friends) who provide some of the same support as a nuclear family. Married siblings provided links with other relatives—mainly, nephews and nieces or grandnephews and grandnieces— whom the elderly single treated as if they were their own children or grand-children. From the group not living with siblings, one was living with a niece, another one lived with a grandniece, and a third lived with a cousin. Five were living with female friends whom they treated much as they would a sister. Six single people lived alone. Those who had siblings saw a great deal of them. Contrary to the sample investigated by Willmott and Young, Braito and Anderson, using a snowball sample of ever single, report that all ever single aged 55 and over ($N = 26$) lived alone.[32] Such differences be-tween studies could be cultural: Willmott and Young had an English sam-ple,[33] and Braito and Anderson and Howe had a U.S. sample.[34] It is also possible that in the thirty-year span between the studies, an actual differ-ence had surfaced in the kinds of societies to which these persons belonged.

Babchuck is one of the few researchers to keep the ever single separate in his analysis.[35] Using a probability sample of 800 noninstitutionalized per-sons 45 and older, living in Nebraska, he relates the number of confidants to marital status and to the number of primary relatives.

Overall, the relationship between all marital statuses and primary and confidant friendship was not significant. Relatives were cited as confidants more often than friends: only thirty persons in his sample felt isolated from their kin. Never-married persons were more likely than those in any other marital status to have no confidants among their primary relatives or friends. In that, they resembled the divorced and the separated more than they resembled the married or widowed. They were also more likely than those in any other marital status to have two or three primary relatives and friends; thus, they represent a picture of being represented among both the socially isolated and the very sociable.

Some data suggest that after one year, widows and widowers have worked their way through their grief and that greater feelings of well-being emerge.[36] Even though the ever single do not have children who might help them work through their sorrow when they lose a close friend, they may have siblings who can help them in the same way. A recovery after a reason-able period of mourning might also be true for the ever single as it is for the widowed. Since women, in general, tend to have more confidants than men, it seems that they might be in a better position to develop new friends than their male counterparts.

As people get older, how do they meet new people, develop new friends? The process is not like making instant coffee; it takes time to develop trust and mutal interests, and persons in older age groups are often constricted in where they can go and what they can do.

The ages of 65 and 70 seem to be important turning points for the elderly in terms of friendship. In Babchuck's study, although there was no correspondence between age and the number of primary relationships, after the age of 70, more than one person in five was without a primary friend.[37] This reduction in the number of primary friends appeared to begin about age 65. We can draw no real conclusion about his findings for the never married because marital status was not controlled.

Babchuck emphasized that "kin are [not] necessarily a part of one's primary group, but the assumption that they are is frequently made by researchers."[38] This statement is especially important because many conclusions have been reached about the ever single based upon just such assumptions.

Housing Arrangements

The living arrangements of some ever single also have been discussed in the section of family and friends. No research has emphasized specifically where ever-single elderly women are likely to live, but it is possible to identify the types of housing they are likely to be in.

Sherman, in an interesting methodological study of retirement housing, drew a random sample of well elderly residents in different types of retirement housing: a retirement hotel, a village manor, a life-care home, retirement villages, and apartment towers (100 persons from each type of housing).[39] Control by sex was not reported, but the percentage of women occupying each site was. Since women are more numerous than men among the ever-single elderly, we may infer that women are the majority in every category identified. Because of numbers in the general population, we would expect that the majority of women in every site would be either married or widowed but that the next highest number would be the ever single.[40] In Sherman's investigation, the ever-single elderly were more likely to be in a retirement hotel or in a life-care center (this particular life-care center was a church-sponsored facility).[41] The village-manor arrangement cost the most money, the life-care home was the next most expensive, then the retirement hotel, the retirement villages, and the apartment towers, in that order. Some retirement hotels supplied two meals daily so the money put out each month is not strictly comparable to the other facilities represented. In the retirement hotel, 100 percent lived alone; in the life-care home, 76 percent lived alone. Those who lived in housing for the retired had higher incomes than their counterparts in a matched dispersed community sample.

In another study, conducted by Bild and Havighurst, in which controls were set up for marital status and sex, investigators found that most of the never married lived in residential hotels.[42] In one of these locations, the number of men and women was approximately the same, but in another, men outnumbered women three to one. Public housing was the next most frequent residence, followed by locational or ethnic housing. More ever-single women than ever-single men were homeowners. From these two studies, it appears that the ever single are more likely to be living in residential hotels or in life-care centers.

Braito and Anderson noted that in their ever-single sample of persons aged 50 and over, most lived alone.[43] The majority in every age group indicated that at retirement, they would prefer to live in a retirement home. However, where one lives is probably related to one's income, and since retirement homes cost more than other types of housing for singles, a large gap between what the retired ever single want and what they can afford may have implications for their life satisfactions.

We have already noted that the majority of the ever single live alone. Hughes and Gove report that "there is a slight tendency for living alone to be worse for the never married than for the widowed and worse for the widowed than for the divorced."[44] Yet, there is also evidence that living alone may be better than living with another adult. Families, Hughes and Gove suggest, are usually focused on parents and children and are not likely to be able to incorporate other unmarried adults.[45] Consequently, those who live alone may suffer less feeling of displacement than those who live with other adults. Hughes and Gove concluded that the benefits of living alone came close to outweighing the costs. Although the study was controlled for age, it is unlikely that their sample included a large population of the ever single elderly. We need to know if living alone rather than with other adults is better for the ever single. Would it be better for the frail ever-single elderly?

Work and Retirement

In our society, work is a major source of satisfaction and self-esteem. There is some speculation that it might be even more important for the never married who may use work as an arena for social contacts and for validating their self-image. Streib and Schneider, using a convenience sample and doing longitudinal research, reported on retirement data gathered in 1953.[46] They found that men are likely to retire at an earlier age than women; women who work into the later part of their lives may not differ markedly from men in their retirement patterns. Palmore came to the same conclusion.[47] Streib and Schneider note that most persons who have had administrative jobs retire around age 70 and that a larger percentage of men than women are willing to retire (37 percent as compared with 29 percent).[48] Women were more reluctant to retire (57 percent as compared with 49 percent of the men). Comparing those who want to retire, more women than men were willing to retire voluntarily. At the beginning of the longitudinal study, retirees who were reluctant, but who would retire voluntarily, were equal in number among the men and the women; during the fourth contact, the number of women who were reluctant to retire increased. Eventually, the number became equal for men and for women in this category. Based on other data, Streib and Schneider report that women who are reluctant to retire are likely to say that they want to continue working for the enjoyment it gives them.[49] Willingness to retire was related to the health of the person; people with good health preferred to work longer.

In Streib and Schneider's sample, women represented more professional categories than they do in the population at large.[50] Women who retired reported that they had sharp feelings of uselessness more often than men did. This work challenges the assumption that women can always return to their domestic roles and therefore will not experience the problems of adjusting that men do. Their data also show that the adjustment to retirement that women go through depends upon the relationship of the date of the interview to the date of retirement (see also chapters 5 and 6).

The only information specific to the elderly ever-single woman in the Streib and Schneider study was that both married and ever-single women were more likely to retire voluntarily than the widowed or the divorced.[51]

Atchley, in discussing never-married elderly telephone employees and teachers, reports that marital status, when high income is controlled for, affects work orientation; ever-single women have a higher work orientation.[52] Atchley's study, however, is inconclusive and could be occupationally specific. Much more detailed investigation needs to be undertaken. Future studies should control the data for income levels and keep the various marital statuses and the two genders separate.

Ward suggests that the role of work is very important to the never-married person.[53] His analysis of National Opinion Research Center (NORC) data indicates that while the ever single seem to want to retire, the loss of their role at work creates more problems for them than for the married person; they reported less happiness and sense of excitement about life. Unfortunately, Ward did not identify his results by the sex of the respondent. We do not know if retirement affects ever-single women and men differently. Since there is evidence in the literature that never-married women are better educated and have higher incomes than never-married men,[54] it is possible that work roles are more important to these women than they are to the never-married men and that their work gives them greater financial rewards. Ward reports that never-married women had the highest income of women in any marital status.[55] He notes, however, that income alone would not necessarily explain the lower ratings of a global happiness among never-married persons, especially among women; it seems reasonable that the reduction in social contacts and in a sense of accomplishment that comes to the ever-single woman when she retires from work could explain such a statistic.

If both are deviants in the social system, then work, as the place where they are likely to be accepted like others, is very important to both ever-single men and women. To study the effect of the loss of the work role on a person's happiness or satisfaction with life requires a different research method from most of those we have been citing here; the study must be longitudinal rather than cross sectional. Some evidence suggests that ever-single people under 50 (before retirement) lead less-contented but more-exciting lives than those over 50, but here again the results have not been controlled by sex, health, social contacts, or other variables that could affect the outcome as much as the fact of being ever single.[56] Excitement declines 21.4 percent between the 25–49 age group and the 50-plus age group. This statistic suggests that retirement may negatively influence perceived happiness. Ward and Fox both studied women and retirement and found that in reducing income, retirement is a blow to psychological well-being.[57]

Not only is longitudinal research into questions like these necessary, but also we need to know more about the meaning of work to people. Since older persons often must contend with failing health, any decrease in happiness might be attributed to this fact rather than a reluctance to retire.

Life Satisfaction

Differences in the findings on life satisfaction and marital status seem to depend on whether the study sample was conducted with a small, selective group or whether a larger sampling of the population was taken. Several studies illustrate the differences in conclusions. Gubrium, Townsend, Tunstall, Willmott and Young, and Kutner et al., utilizing small, less-representative samples, find that never-married women and men are as happy as or happier than married persons with their lives.[58] Research utilizing more-representative samples of never-married older people tends to find that the never married are less happy than the married and only slightly happier than the widowed and divorced.[59] While the results from national samples are more representative of the ever-single population, findings from the smaller, less-representative samples should not be ignored. They may have uncovered findings that are specific to a particular ever-single population that would not have been identified in the more-general types of analyses that have been done.

Conclusions from many of the extensively quoted studies that show no differences between marital status and happiness need to be viewed with caution. Many have collapsed the ever single with the separated, widowed, and divorced and compared them with the currently married.[60]

Gubrium, reporting on twenty-two mostly ever-single women aged 60 to 94, states that in terms of self-definitions, the never-married avoided locating themselves at any one period of life.[61] When asked about loneliness, they stated they preferred being alone or suggested such a question was inappropriate. They tended to value their independence and considered their status as normal. However, when queried regarding particular people for whom they felt lonely, they mentioned siblings, parents, or friends. Thus, although he indicates they typically say they have always been isolated, their interview responses suggest involvement with people. For example, they say they visit friends and talk on the telephone. If they are isolated as he suggests, perhaps his small sample represents the ever single without confidants whom Babchuck has identified.[62]

More research needs to be done on the subject of how people define life satisfaction and how it is related to other aspects of their life. For example, the importance of income to matters of happiness and life satisfaction cannot be ignored. Hutchinson, in his study of low-income and poverty-level elderly, reports that regardless of marital status, the lower the income, the lower the individual ranked his or her happiness and life satisfaction and the higher the reported incidence of loneliness and worry.[63] Furthermore, ever-single men and women may define life satisfaction differently. Glenn, for example, found that although married men and women indicate that they are happier than the never married, never-married women at every age report more frequently that they are happier than do their male counterparts.[64] Ever-single women from 40 on reported 10 to 16 percent more often that they were happier than their male single counterparts. Petrovsky,[70] comparing married and widowed men and women, found that women had more intimate friends and more-diverse social worlds as well as more intimate contacts outside the family.[43] It is possible that the ever-single woman, compared with her ever-single male counterpart, might be in the same position.

The data from Babchuck and even Gubrium could be interpreted to suggest the probability of there being two types of ever singles: the socially isolated and the socially active.[66] These two types of ever singles may experience life conditions that are very different and that affect their rating of life satisfaction.

Activity

Studying the activity of the ever single, Braito and Anderson report no relationship between age and activities-alone behavior and only a slightly negative relationship between age and activities with others.[67] They also report a negative correlation between age and total amount of activity. The standard deviations they reported were large, suggesting diversity within the group. On the one hand, they suggest that it would be inappropriate to characterize the ever single as social isolates. On the other hand, activity did decrease with age. Whether this decrease was due to poor health or to the declining number of friends or relatives with whom they interacted is not known. Such diminishment possibly could be traced to decreasing finances. However, such a finding of less activity as the ever single grows older does point out that there may be a problem in sustaining feelings of well-being for previously active ever single.

Sexuality

Little research has been done on the sexual behavior of the current ever-single elderly. An exception is the work of Christenson and Johnson who used the Kinsey et al. data collected during the 1940s and 1950s to research a sample of seventy-one never-married women aged 60 and over.[68] Like most samples of the older, never-married women, they were highly educated.

They found that nearly two-thirds of this group engaged in sexual activities very similar to those engaged in by the separated, widowed and divorced. This sexual involvement would have occurred at a time when sexual intimacy outside of marriage was much more restricted than it is now. One-third of the sample had had no overt sexual experience beyond simple petting, and this subsample reported a higher incidence of religious devoutness than the rest of the sample. Although the size of the sample decreased to fourteen as age increased, the never married showed no marked differences in patterns of sexual aging when compared with those who had been married. For both groups there were clear-cut decreases in incidence and frequency by age 55.

Some investigators have conjectured that lesbians may make up a substantial portion of the never-married population. Christenson and Johnson report that eight elderly women engaged in extensive homosexual activities but that none was exclusively homosexual in orientation.[69] Therefore, the incidence of homosexuality in the elderly ever-single population is similar to that reported in findings on the younger population. The data reported are limited to one study and are subject to all the criticism leveled at the early Kinsey et al. research. Later research, however, has confirmed many of Kinsey et al. earlier findings.[70]

One conclusion that might be drawn from this research is that although ever-single elderly women share the same marital category, there is a wide range of individual differences in the area of sexuality. Overall, they were not an asexual population, and those who seemed to be asexual were more likely to be religiously devout; this same pattern exists among younger people, according to more-recent data.

Rural Elderly and Ever Singles

Powers, Keith, and Goudy, in their extensive assessment of elderly rural family relationships and friendships, do not mention the never married.[71] Scott studied the dimension of life satisfaction among the rural elderly in a southern rural isolated county.[72] Her rural sample included thirty ever singles between the ages of 65 and 99. This number represented 7.2 percent of the random sample investigated during 1976–1977 and included eleven men and nineteen women. They were better educated than those in the total sample—8.4 years compared with 6.8 years.

In Scott's study, rural ever singles were not social isolates.[73] One-third lived alone, one-third lived with siblings, and one-third lived with other relatives. The mean number of siblings was 2.9. If siblings lived within the same town or neighborhood, the members of this sample saw them daily or weekly. Twenty-nine percent reported adequate incomes, and 57 percent had adequate incomes if they were careful. Most of the married and the widowed (89 percent and 90 percent respectively) had a confidant, while only 64 percent of the singles had one. Rural ever singles were intermediate between married and widowed in their expression of loneliness, while marital status was unrelated to the frequency of interaction with others and to reported unhappiness.

The sample size in this study precluded any discussion of sex differences among the rural elderly ever single. If we want to know more about the ever single, we will have to use sampling techniques involving stratification to get a sufficient number of participants. However, this study is one of the few that did not collapse the ever single with the others currently unmarried, and differences among these groups emerge. This research on the rural population, which separates the ever single from others currently married, depicts the rural ever single as being comparable to nonrural female ever singles in terms of being better educated, having adequate incomes, and being diverse in terms of having or not having confidants.

The Ever-Single Black Elderly

The tables presented earlier in this chapter show that the ever single black men aged 55 and over outnumber the black ever-single women in the population. The difference is more dramatic when one compares the 65–74 age

group with the 75-and-over age group. A reversal also occurs for those of
Spanish origin in these last two age groups. These findings contrast strongly
with the profiles of white women, who outnumber men almost two to one in
every age category 55 and over. There is no ready explanation for the differences between these groups. Ever-single elderly women are overrepresented
in nursing homes, and it may be that this finding is also true for Hispanic
and black ever-single women, particularly as they move into the age groups
where there is a greater incidence of frailty. It seems unlikely that this population (of black and Spanish-origin women) suddenly marries. Both black
Hispanic elderly do not live as long as whites, and the family-support
systems of these groups are also likely to be strong. However, they would be
overrepresented in lower-income populations, and given the lack of support
from the larger society, such populations would be more likely to be institutionalized. Why women and not men are institutionalized is speculative;
data on nursing homes would have to be scrutinized closely.

Higgenbotham, using census data in discussing marital options of
educated black women, presents data indicating that 5.9 percent of black
women were unmarried at ages 40 to 44, as compared to 4.5 percent of
white women at the same ages; at ages 55 to 64, 4.6 percent of black women
and 4.7 percent of white women were unmarried.[74] This would suggest that
a slightly higher percentage of black women marries later. When one compares the percentage differences at younger ages, the contrast is even
greater—ages 35 to 39, 13.3 percent black, 4.2 percent white; ages 32 to 34,
14 percent black, 5.9 percent white; ages 25 to 29; 26.3 percent black, 14.9
percent white; and ages 20 to 24, 60.5 percent black, 42.9 percent white. Not
only do black women marry at a later age, there is also a larger percentage
of black ever-single women at most ages.

Staples, using 1960 census data, reports that between the ages of 35 and
44, 8 percent of black women as compared with 7 percent of black men and
7 percent of black women in the North and West and 12 percent of black
men and 9 percent of black women in the South were never married.[75] Men
usually marry women with lower education than themselves. Black men are
no exception. However, there is no question but that black elderly women
of all marital statuses are overrepresented among the poor, as are blacks in
general. The data on discrimination suggest that being elderly adds one
more burden to the minority person and that being female adds one more.

The black ever-single woman, like the white ever-single woman, tends
to be better educated than her male counterpart. Women with five or more
years of college education were more likely to be ever single; given the differential in education and sex ratio, a larger population of never-married
black elderly women may remain single since there are not enough well-
educated black men to marry. Similar data are not available or have not
come to the attention of the authors on Hispanic and other minority populations. It may be that better-educated women, of whatever population

group, have more options in deciding whether to marry or stay single. It is also possible in our male-dominated society that the better-educated woman is seen as a less-desirable marriage partner since she is more likely to be independent in nature and self-reliant.[76]

Summary

Ever-single elderly women comprise a diverse population. It has been suggested that perhaps they can be cast as two distinct types—those who are socially isolated and those who are socially connected (maintain confidants). However, we can make several generalizations about the elderly ever-single woman. She tends to be better educated than her male counterpart. Although generally healthy, she is overrepresented in nursing homes or other health-care institutions. She is less likely to commit suicide than her ever-single male counterpart. The ever-single elderly woman is likely to have a positive relationship with family, and siblings are often a source of integration with other members of the extended family. Living and housing arrangements of elderly ever-single women are diverse. They may live with siblings, members of the extended family, friends, or alone. They are more likely than ever-single men to be homeowners. They seem to be highly committed to work and are more likely to be involuntarily retired and to suffer from the effects of the diminished income after they retire. They seem to have less excitement in life as they grow older. The data on work motivation based on telephone employees and teachers suggest that when income variables are controlled, they have a higher work orientation.

Where Do We Go from Here?

Much of the data suggest that ever-single elderly women represent diverse populations, with about 25 percent being isolated and another 25 percent having many social contacts. There is no reason to assume that the problems affecting older women, as discussed by Markson and Hess, are different for the ever single except, and perhaps this is an important exception, that most elderly rely on their children for support.[77] On whom do the ever single rely? What are the kinship, friendship, or institutional ties from which they can obtain support? Is it possible that earlier institutionalization into nursing homes might be reduced if more or different support groups were available in the community? If such a support system could reduce the incidence of institutionalization among the ever single, might that finding also hold true for other elderlies living alone—for example, those who have lost both spouse and children?

In the future, given the high incidence of teenagers keeping their children and yet remaining single and the greater social acceptance for ever singles to have children, the composition of the ever-single population and the subsequent problems they experience may be different from what they are now. Demographers tell us that people will have fewer siblings in the future as family size decreases. What can we learn from the current elderly whose parents had fewer children because of the Depression? On whom are they relying—friends, fictive families, children of siblings, or public-welfare programs?

We end this chapter with some of the same questions we asked in the beginning. Answers are still lacking, but perhaps we have indicated areas in which information should be collected. Obviously, more research is needed, not only on the ever-single elderly women but also on subpopulations within the ever single—Hispanic, black, Asian, and native-American.

As the pioneers of being ever single in a society in which marriage is the norm, current never marrieds can inform us of the factors associated with being able to survive when the normative marriage net is circumvented. Problems associated with being an ever-single woman and elderly may be widespread or insignificant; we do not know. Longitudinal research is needed as well as direct inquiry into lifestyles if policy relevant to this growing population is to be developed. As of now, they are still the relatively unseen elderly and may be the ones falling through society's safety net because of lack of family assistance, death of confidants, and marching into the frail-elderly category.

Notes

1. Rita Braito and Donna Anderson, "Aging and the Never-Married" (Paper presented at the Annual Meeting of the American Sociological Association, Boston, August 1979); Elizabeth Howe, "Growing Old Single" (Paper presented at the National Gerontological Society Meeting, Washington, D.C., 1979); Elmer Spreitzer and Lawrence E. Riley, "Factors Associated with Singlehood," *Journal of Marriage and the Family* 36 (1974): 533–542; and Russell Ward, "The Never Married in Later Life," *Journal of Gerontology* 34 (1979):861–869.

2. Donna Anderson and Rita Braito, "The Mental Health of the Never-Married: Social Protection, Social Reaction, and Social Selection Models," *Alternative Life Styles* 4 (1981):108–124; Nicholas Babchuck, "Aging and Primary Relations," *International Journal of Aging and Human Development* 9 (1978–1979):137–151; Braito and Anderson, "Aging and the Never-Married; and Ward, "The Never Married in Later Life."

3. James J. Dowd, *Stratification among the Aged* (Monterey, Calif.: Brooks/Cole, 1980).

4. U.S. Bureau of the Census, "Social and Economic Characteristics of the Older Population," *Current Population Reports,* Series P-23, no. 85 (Washington, D.C.: U.S. Government Printing Office, 1978).

5. Women's Studies Program and Policy Center at George Washington University and the Women's Research and Education Institute of the Congresswomen's Caucus, *Older Women: The Economics of Aging* (Washington, D.C.: George Washington University, 1980).

6. Jessie Bernard, *The Future of Marriage* (New York: World, 1972); and Spreitzer and Riley, "Factors Associated with Singlehood," p. 536.

7. Howe, "Growing Old Single."

8. N.D. Glenn, A.A. Ross, and J.C. Tully, "Patterns of Intergenerational Mobility of Females through Marriage," *American Social Review* 39 (October 1974):683–699.

9. Spreitzer and Riley, "Factors Associated with Singlehood," p. 536.

10. Glenn, Ross, and Tully, "Patterns of Intergenerational Mobility," p. 693.

11. U.S. Bureau of the Census, "Money Income in 1977 of Families and Persons in the U.S.," *Current Population Reports,* Series P-60, no. 118 (Washington, D.C.: U.S. Government Printing Office, 1979).

12. E.M. Havens, "Women, Work and Wedlock: A Note on Female Marital Patterns in the United States," *American Journal of Sociology* 78 (1973):980.

13. Jon Hendricks and C. Davis Hendricks, *Aging in Mass Society* (Cambridge, Mass.: Winthrop Publishers, 1977).

14. Howe, "Growing Old Single."

15. Ibid.

16. J. Tunstall, *Old and Alone: A Sociological Study of Old People* (London: Routledge & Kegan Paul, 1966).

17. Howe, "Growing Old Single."

18. Carolynne Keiffer, "The Never-Married Mature Academic Woman: A Life History Analysis" (Ph.D. dissertation, University of Missouri, Columbia, 1979).

19. Howe, "Growing Old Single."

20. Lois M. Verbrugge, "Marital Status and Health," *Journal of Marriage and the Family* 41 (May 1979):267–285.

21. Ibid.

22. "Chartbook on Aging in America: The 1981 White House Conference on Aging (Washington, D.C.: U.S. Government Printing Office, 1981).

23. Bernard L. Bloom, *Changing Patterns of Psychiatric Care* (New York: Human Science Press, 1977).

24. Walter R. Gove, "Sex, Marital Status and Suicide," *Journal of Health and Social Behavior* 13 (1972):204–211.

25. Ibid.

26. Ibid.

27. Christine A. Bachrach, "Childlessness and Social Isolation," *Journal of Marriage and the Family* 42 (August 1980):627–636.

28. Lillian E. Troll, Sheila J. Miller, and Robert C. Atchley, *Families in Later Life* (Belmont, Calif.: Wadsworth, 1979).

29. Robert C. Atchley, Linda Pignatiello, and Ellen Shaw, "The Effects of Marital Status on Social Interaction Patterns of Older Women," *Aging Research* 1 (March 1979):83–96.

30. Peter Willmott and Michael Young, *Family and Class in a London Suburb* (London: Routledge & Kegan Paul, 1960), pp. 53–54.

31. Ibid.

32. Braito and Anderson, "Aging and the Never-Married;" and Willmott and Young, *Family and Class in a London Suburb*.

33. Willmott and Young, *Family and Class in a London Suburb*.

34. Braito and Anderson, "Aging and the Never-Married"; and Howe, "Growing Old Single."

35. Babchuck, "Aging and Primary Relations."

36. Rudy Fenwick and Charles M. Burresi, "Health Consequences of Marital Status Change among the Elderly: A Comparison of Cross-Sectional and Longitudinal Analysis," *Journal of Health and Social Behavior* 22 (June 1981):106–116.

37. Babchuck, "Aging and Primary Relations."

38. Ibid., p. 150.

39. Susan R. Sherman, "Methodology in a Study of Residents Retirement Housing," *Journal of Gerontology* 28 (July 1973):351–358.

40. U.S. Bureau of the Census, "Money Income in 1977."

41. Sherman, "Methodology in a Study of Residents Retirement Housing."

42. B.R. Bild and R.J. Havighurst, "Senior Citizens in Great Cities: The Case of Chicago," *The Gerontologist* 16 (1976):5–88.

43. Braito and Anderson, "Aging and the Never-Married."

44. Michael Hughes and Walter Gove, "Living Alone, Social Integration, and Mental Health," *American Journal of Sociology* 87 (1981):64.

45. Ibid.

46. Streib and Schneider, *Retirement in American Society: Impact and Process* (Ithaca, N.Y.: Cornell University Press, 1971).

47. E.B. Palmore, "Differences in the Retirement Pattern of Men and Women," *The Gerontologist* 5 (1965):4–8.

48. Streib and Schneider, *Retirement in American Society,* p. 68.

49. Ibid.

50. Ibid.

51. Ibid.

52. Robert C. Atchley, "Orientation toward the Job and Retirement Adjustment among Women," In *Time, Roles, and Self in Old Age,* ed. Jaber F. Gubrium (New York: Human Sciences Press, 1976), pp. 199–208.

53. Ward, "The Never Married in Later Life."

54. Ibid.

55. Ibid., p. 864.

56. Ward, "The Never Married in Later Life."

57. Judith Huff Fox, "Effects of Retirement and Former Work Life on Women's Adaptation in Old Age," *Journal of Gerontology* 32 (March 1977):196–202; and Ward, "The Never Married in Later Life."

58. Gubrium, "Marital Dislocation and the Evaluation of Everyday Life in Old Age"; and Gubrium, "Being Single in Old Age," *International Journal of Aging and Human Development* 6 (1975):29–40; B. Kutner et al., *Five Hundred over Sixty* (New York: Russell Sage, 1956); P. Townsend, *The Family Life of Old People* (London: Routledge & Kegan Paul, 1957); Tunstall, *Old and Alone;* and Wilmott and Young, *Family and Class in a London Suburb.*

59. Angus A. Campbell, "The American Way of Mating: Marriage, Children, Maybe." *Psychology Today* 8 (1975):37–43; Norval Glenn, "The Contribution of Marriage to the Well-Being of Males and Females," *Journal of Marriage and the Family* 37 (August 1975):594; Ward, "The Never-Married in Later Life," p. 861; and Jan D. Yoeder and Robert C. Nichols, "Life Pespective Comparison of Married and Divorced Persons," *Journal of Marriage and the Family* 42 (May 1980):413–419.

60. John N. Edwards and David L. Klemmack, "Correlates of Life Satisfaction: A Reexamination," *Journal of Gerontology* 28 (October 1973):497–502.

61. Gubrium, "Being Single in Old Age."

62. Babchuck, "Aging and Primary Relations."

63. I.W. Hutchinson, "The Significance of Marital Status for Morale, and Life Satisfaction among Low Income Elderly," *Journal of Marriage and the Family* 37 (May 1975):287–293.

64. Glenn, "Contribution of Marriage."

65. Mare Petrovsky, "Marital Status, Sex, and Social Networks of the Elderly," *Journal of Marriage and the Family* 38 (1976):749–756.

66. Babchuck, "Aging and Primary Relations" and Gubrium, "Being Single in Old Age."

67. Braito and Anderson, "Aging and the Never-Married."

68. Cornelia V. Christenson and A.B. Johnson, "Sexual Patterns in a Group of Never-Married Women," *Journal of Gerontology* 20 (1973): 351–356; and A.C. Kinsey et al., *Sexual Behavior in the Human Male* (Philadelphia: W.B. Saunders, 1953).

69. Christenson and Johnson, "Sexual Patterns in a Group of Never-Married Women."

70. Kinsey et al., *Sexual Behavior in the Human Male.*

71. Edward Powers, Patricia Keith, and Willis Goudy "Family Relationships and Friendships," in *Rural Environments and Aging,* eds. R.C.

Atchley and T.O. Byerts (Washington, D.C.: Gerontological Society, 1975.

72. Scott, "Dimensions of Life Satisfaction among Single Rural Elders Compared to Their Married and Widowed Contemporaries," *Alternative Life Styles* (1979), pp. 359–378.

73. Ibid.

74. Elizabeth Higgenbotham, "Is Marriage a Priority: Class Differences in Marital Options of Educated Black Women," in *Single Life: Unmarried Adults in Social Context,* ed. Peter J. Stein (New York: St. Martins Press, 1981).

75. Robert Staples "Black Singles in America," in *Single Life: Unmarried Adults in Social Context,* ed. Peter J. Stein (New York: St. Martins Press, 1981).

76. Bernard, "Note on Changing Life Styles."

77. Elizabeth Markson and Beth B. Hess, "Older Women in the City," *Signs: Journal of Women in Culture and Society* 5 (1980):S127–S141.

Bibliography

Anderson, Donna, and Rita Braito. "The Mental Health of the Never Married: Social Protection, Social Reaction, and Social Selection Models." *Alternative Life Styles* 1 (1978):108–124.

Atchley, Robert C. "Orientation toward the Job and Retirement Adjustment among Women." In *Time, Roles, and Self in Old Age,* edited by Jaber F. Gubrium. New York: Human Sciences Press, 1976.

Atchley, Robert C., and Sheila J. Miller. "Older People and Their Families." *Annual Review of Gerontology and Geriatrics* 1 (1980): 337–369.

Atchley, Robert C.; Linda Pignatiello; and Ellen Shaw. "Interactions with Family and Friends: Marital Status and Occupational Differences among Older Women." *Research on Aging* 1 (1979):83–89.

Babchuck, Nicholas, "Aging and Primary Relations." *International Journal of Aging and Human Development* 9 (1978–1979):137–151.

Bachrach, Christine A. "Childlessness and Social Isolation." *Journal of Marriage and the Family* 42 (1980):627–636.

Baker, Luther G., Jr. "The Personal and Social Adjustment of the Never-Married Woman." *Journal of Marriage and the Family* 30 (1968): 473–479.

Bell, Bill D. "Life Satisfaction and Occupational Retirement: Beyond the Impact Year." *International Journal of Aging and Human Development* 9 (1978–1979):31–47.

Bellin, Seymour S., and Robert H. Hardt. "Marital Status and Mental

Disorders among the Aged." *American Sociological Review* 23 (1958): 155–162.

Bequaert, L.H. *Single Women: Alone and Together.* Boston: Beacon Press, 1976.

Bernard, Jessie. *The Future of Marriage.* New York: Bantam Books, 1972.

———. "Note on Changing Life Styles: 1970–1974." *Journal of Marriage and the Family* 37 (1975):582–593.

Bild, B.R., and R.J. Havighurst. "Senior Citizens in Great Cities: The Case of Chicago." *The Gerontologist* 16 (1976):5–88.

Blau, Zena. "Structural Constraints on Friendships in Old Age." *American Sociological Review* 26 (1961):429–439.

Bloom, Bernard L. *Changing Patterns of Psychiatric Care.* New York: Human Sciences Press, 1977.

Bloom, Bernard L.; Shirley J. Asher; and Stephan W. White. "Marital Disruption as a Stressor." *Psychological Bulletin* 85 (1978):867–894.

Booth, Alan, and Elain Hess. "Cross-Sex Friendship." *Journal of Marriage and the Family* 36 (1974):38–47.

Braito, Rita, and Donna Anderson. "Aging and the Never Married." Paper presented at the American Sociological Association, Boston, August 1979.

Bultena, Gordon L. "Rural-Urban Differences in the Familial Interaction of the Aged." *Rural Sociology* 34 (1969):5–15.

Campbell, Angus A. "The American Way of Mating: Marriage Is Children, Maybe." *Psychology Today* 8 (1975):37–43.

Chartbook on Aging in America: The 1981 White House Conference on Aging. Washington, D.C.: U.S. Government Printing Office, 1981.

Christenson, Cornelia V., and A.B. Johnson. "Sexual Patterns in a Group of Older Never-Married Women." *Journal of Gerontology* 20 (1973): 351–356.

Clark, Margaret, and Barbara G. Anderson. *Culture and Aging.* Springfield, Ill.: Charles C Thomas, 1967.

DeJong-Gierveld, Jenny. "Social Isolation and the Image of the Unmarried." *Sociologia Neerlandica* 7 (1971):1–14.

Dilic, Edhem. "Psychological Adjustment to Growing Old in the Village." *Sociologija Sela* 15 (1977):48–61.

Dowd, James J. *Stratification among the Aged.* Monterey, Calif.: Brooks/Cole Publishing Company, 1980.

Edwards, John N., and David L. Klemmack. "Correlates of Life Satisfaction: A Re-Examination." *Journal of Gerontology* 28 (1973):497–502.

Fenwick, Rudy, and Charles M. Burresi. "Health Consequences of Marital Status Change among the Elderly: A Comparison of Cross-Sectional and Longitudinal Analyses." *Journal of Health and Social Behavior* 22 (1981):106–116.

Fox, Judith Huff. "Effects of Retirement and Former Work Life on Women's Adaptation in Old Age." *Journal of Gerontology* 32 (1977): 196–202.

George, Linda K., and George L. Maddox. "Subjective Adaptation to Loss of the Work Role: A Longitudinal Study." *Journal of Gerontology* 32 (1977):456–462.

Glenn, Norval. "The Contribution of Marriage to the Psychological Well-Being of Males and Females." *Journal of Marriage and the Family* 37 (1975):594.

Glenn, N.D.; A.A. Ross; and J.C. Tully. "Patterns of Intergenerational Mobility of Females through Marriage." *American Sociological Review* 39 (1974):683–699.

Gove, Walter R. "Sex, Marital Status, and Suicide." *Journal of Health and Social Behavior* 13 (1972):204–211.

Gove, Walter R., and Michael Hughes. "Possible Causes of the Apparent Sex Differences in Physical Health." *American Sociological Review* 44 (1979):126–146.

Gubrium, J.F. "Marital Desolation and the Evaluation of Everyday Life in Old Age," *Journal of Marriage and the Family* 36 (1974):107.

———. "Being Single in Old Age." *International Journal of Aging and Human Development.* 6 (1975):29–40.

Havens, E.M. "Women, Work, and Wedlock: A Note on Female Marital Patterns in the United States." *American Journal of Sociology* 78 (1973):975–981.

Health Resources Administration. "Measures of Chronic Illness among Residents of Nursing and Personal Care Homes." *Vital and Health Statistics* 12 (1974):1–65.

Health Service Administration. "Persons Hospitalized, by Number of Hospital Episodes and Days in a Year, United States, 1968." *Vital and Health Statistics* 10 (1971):56.

Hendricks, Jon, and C. Davis. *Aging in Mass Society.* Cambridge, Mass.: Winthrop Publishers, 1977.

Hess, Beth B., and Elizabeth W. Markson. *Aging and Old Age.* New York: Macmillan, 1980.

Higginbotham, Elizabeth. "Is Marriage a Priority: Class Differences in Marital Options of Educated Black Women," pp. 259–267. In *Single Life: Unmarried Adults in Social Context,* edited by Peter J. Stein. New York: St. Martin's Press, 1981.

Howe, Elizabeth. "Growing Old Single." Paper presented at the Annual Meeting of the Gerontological Society of America, Washington, D.C., November 1979.

Hughes, Michael, and Walter Gove. "Living Alone, Social Integration, and Mental Health." *American Journal of Sociology* 87 (1981):48–74.

Hutchinson, I.W. "The Significance of Marital Status for Morale and Life

Satisfaction among Lower Income Elderly." *Journal of Marriage and the Family* 37 (1975):287–293.

Jackson, James S.; John D. Bacon; and John Peterson. "Life Satisfaction among Black Elderly." *International Journal of Aging and Human Development* 8 (1977–1978):169–179.

Keiffer, Carolynne. "The Never-Married Mature Academic Woman: A Life History Analysis." Ph.D. dissertation, University of Missouri, 1979.

Kinsey, A.C.; W.B. Pomeroy; C.E. Martin; and P.H. Gebhard. *Sexual Behavior in the Human Male.* Philadelphia: W.B. Saunders, 1953.

Kivett, Vira R., and Max Learner. "Perspectives on the Childless Rural Elderly: A Comparative Analysis." *The Gerontologist* 20 (1980): 708–716.

Knox, David. *Marriage: Who? When? Why?* Englewood Cliffs, N.J. Prentice-Hall, 1975.

Knupfer, Genevieve; Walter Clark; and Robin Room. "The Mental Health of the Unmarried." *American Journal of Psychiatry* 122 (1966): 841–850.

Kutner, B.; D. Fanshel; A. Togo; and T. Langner. *Five Hundred over Sixty.* New York: Russell Sage Foundation, 1972.

Larson, Reed. "Thirty Years of Research on the Subjective Well-Being of Older Americans." *Journal of Gerontology* 33 (1978):109–125.

Laslett, Barbara. "Family Membership, Past and Present." *Social Problems* 25 (1978):476.

Lee, Gary R., and Marilyn Ihinger-Tallman. "Sibling Interaction and Morale: The Effects of Family Relations on Older People." *Research on Aging* 2 (1980):367–391.

Lowenthal, M.F., and C. Haven. "Introduction and Adaptation: Intimacy as a Critical Variable." *American Sociological Review* 33 (1968): 120–123.

Markson, Elizabeth W., and Gretchen R. Batra. *Public Policies for an Aging Population.* Lexington, Mass.: Lexington Books, D.C. Heath, 1980.

Markson, Elizabeth W., and Beth B. Hess. "Older Women in the City." *Signs: Journal of Women in Culture and Society* 5 (1980):S127–S141.

Martin, Walter T. "Status Integration, Social Stress, and Mental Illness: Accounting for Marital Status Variation in Mental Hospitalization Rates." *Journal of Health and Social Behavior* 1 (1976):280–294.

Overall, John E. "Associations between Marital History and the Nature of Manifest Psychopathology." *Journal of Abnormal Psychology* 78 (1971):213–221.

Palmore, E.B. "Differences in the Retirement Pattern of Men and Women." *The Gerontologist* 5 (1965):4–8.

Palmore, Erdman, and Vira Kivett. "Change in Life Satisfaction: A Longitudinal Study of Persons Aged 46–70." *Journal of Gerontology* 32 (1977):311–316.

Pearlin, Leonard I., and Joyce S. Johnson. "Marital Status, Life-Strains, and Depression." *American Sociological Review* 42 (1977):704–715.

Petrowsky, Mare. "Marital Status, Sex, and Social Networks of the Elderly." *Journal of Marriage and the Family* 38 (1976):749–756.

Powers, Edward A., and Gordon L. Bultena. "Sex Differences in Intimate Friendships of Old Age." *Journal of Marriage and the Family* 38 (1970):739–747.

Powers, Edward; Patricia Keith; and Willis Goudy. "Family Relationships and Friendships." In *Rural Environments and Aging,* edited by R.C. Atchley and T.O. Byerts. Washington, D.C.: Gerontological Society, 1975.

Scott, J.P. "Dimensions of Life Satisfaction among Single Rural Elders Compared to Their Married and Widowed Contemporaries." *Alternative Life Styles* 2 (1979):359–378.

Shanas, Ethel. *Old People in Three Industrial Societies.* New York: Atherton Press, 1968.

———. "The Family as a Social Support System in Old Age." *The Gerontologist* 19 (1979):169–174.

Sherman, Susan R. "Methodology in a Study of Residents Retirement Housing." *Journal of Gerontology* 28 (1973):351–358.

Spreitzer, Elmer, and Lawrence E. Riley. "Factors Associated with Singlehood." *Journal of Marriage and the Family* 36 (1974):533–542.

Spreitzer, Elmer, and Eldon, E. Snyder. "Correlates of Life Satisfaction." *Journal of Gerontology* 29 (1974):454–458.

Staples, Robert. "Black Singles in America." In *Single Life: Unmarried Adults in Social Contest,* edited by Peter J. Stein, pp. 40–51. New York: St. Martin's Press, 1981.

Stein, Peter. "Being Single: Bucking the Cultural Imperative." Paper presented at Annual Meeting of the American Sociological Assoication, New York, September 1976.

———. "Single Adulthood." Paper presented at the Annual Meeting of the American Sociological Association, Toronto, 24–28 August 1981.

Streib, Gordon, and C. Schneider. *Retirement in American Society: Impact and Process.* Ithaca, N.Y.: Cornell University Press, 1971.

Streib, Gordon, and Rubye Wilkerson. "Older Families: A Decade of Review." *Journal of Marriage and the Family* 42 (1980):937–956.

Townsend, P. *The Family Life of Old People.* London: Routledge & Kegan Paul, 1957.

Troll, Lillian E.; Sheila J. Miller; and Robert C. Atchley. *Families in Later Life.* Belmont, Calif.: Wadsworth, 1979.

Trunstall, J. *Old and Alone: A Sociological Study of Old People.* London: Routledge & Kegan Paul, 1966.

Turner, R. Jay, and John W. Gartell. "Social Factors in Psychiatric Out-
come: Toward the Resolution of Interpretive Controversies." *American Sociological Review* 3 (1978):368–382.

U.S. Bureau of the Census. "Money Income in 1977 of Families and Persons in the United States." *Current Population Reports.* Series P-60,
no. 118. Washington, D.C.: U.S. Government Printing Office, 1979.

U.S. Department of Commerce. Bureau of the Census. "Social and Economic Characteristics of the Older Population: 1978." Series P-23,
no. 85. Washington, D.C.: U.S. Government Printing Office, 1979.

Verbrugge, Lois M. "Females and Illness: Recent Trends in Sex Differences
in the United States." *Journal of Health and Social Behavior* 17 (1976):
387–403.

————. "Marital Status and Health." *Journal of Marriage and the Family*
41 (1979):267–285.

Ward, Russell. "The Never-Married in Later Life." *Journal of Gerontology* 34 (1979):861–869.

Warheit, George J.; Charles E. Holzer, III; Roger A. Bell; and Sandra A.
Arey. "Sex, Marital Status and Mental Health: A Reappraisal." *Social Forces* 55 (1976):459–470.

Willmott, Peter, and Michael Young. *Family and class in a London Suburb.* London: Routledge & Kegan Paul, 1960.

Women's Studies Program and Policy Center and the Women's Research
and Education Institute of the Congress Women's Caucus. *Older Women: The Economics of Aging.* Washington, D.C.: George Washington University, 1980.

Wood, Vivian. "Aging Women: Social Connectedness in Later Life."
Paper presented at the Thirty-second Annual Meeting of the Gerontological Society of America, Washington, D.C., 1979a.

————. "The Older Women Alone." Paper presented at California State
University at Fresno, as part of a weekly public forum on aging, 22
March, 1979b.

————. "Older Women and Education." Paper presented at the 1980
Annual Meeting of the American Educational Research Association,
Boston, 1980.

Yoeder, Jan D., and Robert C. Nichols. "Life Perspective Comparison of
Married and Divorced Persons." *Journal of Marriage and the Family*
42 (1980):413–419.

11

Family Relationships of Older Women: A Women's Issue

Beth B. Hess and
Joan Waring

Family relationships in old age may well become the preeminent women's issue in the years ahead. Much depends on the kind of political consensus that is reached on ways to maintain a conscionable, if not entirely satisfactory, quality of life for the elderly in the United States—especially the very old. Whatever the measures decided upon, the lives of women—as daughters, mothers, citizens, and old persons—will be touched powerfully.

For women, old age has a double edge. Women are the primary users of those public policies and family practices that affect how old people are treated and cared for. Not only do women constitute the large majority of old people, but also they spend many years at being old and becoming very old before their lives come to an end. By all attributes of status, the very frail old woman is among the most powerless of persons, vulnerable to all the indignities of age, poor health, the lower social status accorded females, and uselessness. In many ways, she exemplifies the ultimate in actual as well as symbolic annihilation of women (Tuchman 1978). Therefore, the condition of very old women and their lack of personal and social power must become central to the consciousness of all women and, particularly, to those who set the agenda of the women's movement.

There is another sense in which the care of the elderly is of crucial concern to women and the women's movement. In the United States, as in most societies, nurturance of dependent kin and care of the ill still fall within the realm of women's work. Many women in the United States, especially those in middle age have been socialized to assume responsibility for the preservation of family bonds and, with varying degrees of willingness, make efforts to fulfill their kinship obligations. However, the social context is changing, as are the lives and work and work places of women. Herein lies the emergent women's issue: how to provide humane care for the elderly while respecting the autonomy of both generations of women.

Shaping the Consensus

Several powerful forces are at work to reshape a national consensus on ways to provide for the elderly—especially the very old. This consensus will need to reconcile the humanitarian aspirations of the U.S. people with the self-interest of individuals. The tension between these forces is a recurrent theme in our cultural history—the urge to do good deeds yet foster self-reliance. This dialectic is exemplified in the current debate over community-based versus family-based care for the elderly.

One of the forces creating the need for a reassessment of policy is the secular trend toward increased life expectancy. Recent declines in age-specific death rates for middle and ever-older ages make it imperative that the potential magnitude of adult dependency—and the resources it will require—be taken into account by both those responsible for the common-weal and those who allocate resources within the family.

In terms of its family implications, improvement in life expectancy has dramatically increased the likelihood of middle-aged or even young-old couples having a living parent. Today, over 80 percent of middle-aged couples have at least one living parent, compared to fewer than half at the beginning of the century. Rather, 47 percent have more than one living parent, compared to only 10 percent in 1900 (Uhlenberg 1980). Thus, even if norms of filial obligation have not changed much over the years, the probability of having to act on these responsibilities has increased.

Extended life expectancy also has increased vastly what might be called the grandparent ratio. Where only one child in four in 1900 had all four grandparents alive at its birth, six out of ten do today (Uhlenberg 1981). Moreover, most of these grandparents can be expected to survive the child's youth, giving some children greater opportunities than ever to form and develop relationships with members of the oldest generation in the family. However, these very opportunities could, in time, become obligations.

Another long-term trend is the expectation that the government should be caretaker of early resort in matters relating to old-age dependency. Since 1937, minimum levels of income for the elderly population have been secured by extensions of the social-security program. Medical care, although largely hospital based, is now available through Medicare and Medicaid. A wide array of programs from subsidized meals to special tax relief is provided through state and local governments as well as the federal bureaucracy. Support for welfare-state solutions to the problems of aging to ameliorate the insults of poverty and ill health remains strong among most segments of the population (NCOA 1981) despite antiwelfarism ideology. In comparison to other needy persons, the elderly tend to be perceived as deserving poor.

Another secular trend that will shape decisions affecting the well-being of the elderly is the decline in nuclear-family size. Throughout this century, with the exception of the aberrant period following World War II, fertility rates have moved downward and now border on replacement levels. This means that there will be relatively few family caretakers for the old, so that the burdens of family-based care cannot be shared by large numbers of siblings and necessarily will be concentrated on the few surviving children—particularly daughters and daughters-in-law. It seems doubtful, though not impossible, that dramatic shifts away from public provision of care in old age will affect fertility decisions—that is, it is unlikely women will bear more children as a form of social insurance in old age.

A recent, related trend that must be an essential consideration in emerging policy is the entrance of women into the work force in virtually revolutionary proportions over the past two decades. Commitment to the work force makes the honoring of caretaking obligations to elderly parents problematic, especially if still-younger family members require attention. It is likely that many women will resist withdrawing from the labor force and relinquishing the rewards of paid work in order to minister to decrepit family members (see chapters 6 and 7). However, an absence of affordable alternatives, particularly government-sponsored programs, may raise the opportunity cost of labor-force participation to the point where the material and psychic rewards it affords cannot compensate for tensions generated by a needy or untended elderly patient. For working daughters, the question of humane alternatives becomes crucial.

However, still other trends in the social environment will complicate reaching consensus. Among these are a change in the political climate and a concomitant softening of support for federal provision to care for the elderly. Not only are there new directions in public policy, but also the sheer numbers of old individuals combined with the rising costs of public programs for income maintenance, health care, housing, and social services for an aging population are leading gradually to a major reassessment of family-support systems. Indeed, the family-support system is in the process of being rehabilitated from charges of abandoning the elderly and other failings. Moreover, this rediscovery of family strength is taking place precisely at the moment when the family network can be perceived as the most efficient and inexpensive channel for the provision of services to the elderly.

Given these current political and economic realities, there may be a push for the household, as a matter of morality as well as necessity, to become the locus of care for the old; but the issue is whose household? That of the older person(s) or that of adult offspring? The impersonal intergenerational transfers that encouraged older persons to remain independent (that is, social security, Medicare, and the like) may not be the models for the future. Rather, intrafamily caretaking, supported by tax incentives, could be preferred to community-based programs. This scenario places the issue of the family relationships of older women into the framework of women's concerns in general. When examined in this context, the central question becomes how the interests of both generations of women can be reconciled. Will care of the elderly be the new responsibility tying women once more to the sphere of the home, reinforcing her traditional nurturant role? Conversely, will the very old and frail elderly remain able to determine the place and conditions of their final years?

In this chapter, we discuss the potential magnitude of the need for care-takers for the old, review the family situation of elderly women, and point to dilemmas of caretaking and possible resolutions.

Old-Age Dependency: The Potential Dimensions

The combination of increased life expectancy and low birth rates means that the proportion of old people in our society will increase dramatically in the next century—perhaps close to 20 percent in 2030. The most rapid rates of increase today are at the oldest age levels. For example, over the next twenty years it is expected that 60 percent of the increase in the population aged 65 and over will be accounted for by the growth in the size of the 75-and-older age group (Price 1982). In 1980, there were 1.5 million women aged 85 and older and 680,000 men compared to 918,000 and 490,000 respectively in 1970 (Bureau of the Census 1980a).

Life expectancy of women at birth is now 78 years and that of men, slightly over 70. Women who reach age 65 can expect to live almost nineteen additional years and men another fourteen or so (Bureau of the Census 1980a). The sex differential in longevity is expected to persist for the fore-seeable future—even if the gap is somewhat narrowed by more-salubrious health behaviors on the part of men (Verbrugge 1979) or as a result of increasingly less-sex-stereotyped socialization and social roles (Siegel 1980).

Old age, especially advanced old age, carries with it high risks of health conditions that compromise physical mobility and interfere with the exer-cise of self-care. Of the 22 million persons 65 and older not in institutions in 1979, over 45 percent reported some limitation of activity, including 17 per-cent unable to perform usual activities, 22 percent limited in only selected areas, and 7 percent experiencing curtailment of activities other than those directly needed for self-care (FCOA 1981). While most old people—even if partially disabled or chronically ill—do manage to cope with the essential tasks of daily living, some are heavily dependent on others. Slightly over 2 percent of those 65 and older living in the community are bedfast, an addi-tional 2.6 percent require help in their homes, while 6 percent need assis-tance in getting around their neighborhoods. It is noteworthy that twice as many bedfast and homebound elderly are receiving care in their own homes as those in institutions, indicating the extent of caretaking efforts already being made on behalf of old people. Of course, the very old are the most constrained by health considerations and need the most help. The differ-ences are quite sharp. Whereas fewer than 5 percent of those 65 to 74 have difficulty in moving beyond their neighborhoods, over 30 percent of those 85 and older do.

When all the numbers are added up, roughly 4 million older persons have physical limitations sufficient to require some help at home or in being enabled to leave their homes and neighborhood. These 4 million, however, are not representative of the population of old people as a whole. In one major study (Shanas 1979a), while 14 percent of the total sample were bedfast, housebound, or in need of assistance in moving outside their homes, these conditions characterized 25 percent of elderly black women. In general, women of both races reported more limitations in capacity for self-care than did men and blacks more than whites. At the very oldest ages, however, the racial differential narrows considerably, probably reflecting the highly selective survival of blacks that is manifest also in the racial crossover in mortality rates after age 75.

In addition to physical disabilities, mental illness can restrict the capacity for self-care for a small proportion of elderly. The Federal Council on Aging (1981) estimates that between 15 and 25 percent of the noninstitutionalized elderly may have "significant symptoms" of mental illness. About 5 percent suffer from senile dementia, and 10 percent are severely depressed. In many cases, these psychological impairments occur in conjunction with physical decrements, but it seems likely that an additional 4 million elderly might require help in daily living because of their mental or emotional states.

To this rough estimate of at least 8 million in need of assistance, we must add the hundreds of thousands of elderly who pass through episodes of acute illness and thus are temporarily dependent on others. The vast majority of those in need of care will be women over the age of 75—because there are more of them than men, because they are less likely to have a healthy spouse, and because women's morbidity rates are higher at all adult ages.

Despite the numbers at risk, the vast majority of old people lives in the community, not in institutions. The proportion of the elderly population living in institutions has not risen appreciably since the advent of Medicare/Medicaid and the nursing-home construction subsidies of the late 1960s. For the past two decades, between 4 and 5 percent of the population 65 and over has been in nursing homes on any one day (FCOA 1981). However, the number of elderly patients in institutions has risen dramatically, increasing 17 percent in just the period between 1973 and 1977. The increase is especially evident among women and the very old. Recent government figures indicate that approximately one in four women age 85 and over are in nursing homes (FCOA 1981; U.S. Senate 1981).

As for the 95 percent of elderly who live in the community, the great majority of men lives in families, primarily as heads of households; even at age 75 and older, almost two-thirds live in their own residence with spouse.

In contrast, only one-third of older women age 65 and older live with their husband, and four in ten live alone. Fewer than 20 percent reside in the home of an adult child (U.S. Senate 1981). Since 1965 the major demographic change in older women's living arrangements has been the increase in those who are able to maintain an independent residence as widows, largely as a result of liberalization of social-security benefits and the availability of health insurance. Typically, the elderly prefer their independence and "intimacy at a distance" (Rosenmayr and Kockeis 1962)—that is, to live near but not with their children. This goal is achieved for close to eight in ten older persons, and 75 percent live within one-half hour's travel from one of their offspring. They see and speak with their children regularly, and they engage in a continuous exchange of goods and services. This pattern has not changed in the two decades since Rosenmayr and Kockeis's research, despite continued geographic mobility of offspring (Shanas 1979b). Living arrangements in old age are determined basically by the same factors as in earlier life-course stages: income, marital status, health, and orientation toward extended kinship bonds.

This, then, is the demographic reality of the aging woman: outliving her husband, maintaining an independent residence, remaining in contact with offspring and other kin, and surviving through her eighth decade. As she grows old, the possibility of increased frailty, depletion of personal financial resources, and scarcity of suitable safe accommodations will render problematic her continued ability to function independently.

Resources

Just as the problems of old age are not evenly distributed among all subpopulations of the elderly, neither are the resources required to cope successfully. Indeed, there is an inverse relationship between the two: Those with the gravest problems are typically those with the fewest personal and social resources. The very old and frail, the never-married or widowed women, and minority aged are found disproportionately among the poverty population, the homeless, the ill, and those in public institutions. It is not that extreme old age suddenly places these individuals into such conditions; rather, the situation for some is merely the last stage in a history of deprivation. Subpopulations without much power or social value at earlier life stages can hardly be expected to command these resources in old age.

Marriage and Nonmarriage

There are essentially two familial resources for older persons: one's spouse and one's offspring. With respect to the former, we have already noted the high probability that older women will not have a living spouse, while the great majority—almost four in five—of elderly men will be sharing a household with their wives. Fewer than half of all women aged 65–74 are in the census category of "married, spouse present," a proportion that dips to roughly one-fifth of those 75 and over. An additional small percentage of white women, but almost 15 percent of black elderly women, will be listed as "married, spouse absent." Among those now in old age, approximately 5–6 percent will have never married, and a smaller percentage are divorced and not remarried (Bureau of the Census, 1980a).

It is expected that in the years ahead that the category of divorced and *not* remarried will increase with the general rise in divorce rates among younger persons. If age-specific remarriage rates remain much the same as at present, then the older the woman at the time of divorce, the less likely to be remarried. Therefore, although equal numbers of men and women divorce, not all remain in that status and not for equal periods of time: men remarry sooner and at higher rates than do women. Even at age 65 and over, remarriage rates were 17 per 1,000 unmarried men compared to 2 per 1,000 unmarried women. There is little reason to expect these ratios to change. By the year 2000, it is estimated that 22 percent of all adults will have been divorced (including perhaps half of all those who marry this year) but that most will also have contracted a second, if not third, marriage. Nonetheless, the proportion of divorced but not remarried women who reach old age should increase considerably in the decades ahead.

Largely because there are so few divorced persons today, very little research has been conducted on the interaction between their unique marital status and the realities of aging. General survey data, however, have documented the comparatively poorer health (Verbrugge 1979), financial destitution (Espanshade 1979), higher mortality risks (Gove 1973), and lower levels of life satisfaction (Wilson and DeShane 1980) of divorced men and women at all ages, especially for women in old age. Compared to age peers who are widowed, much less still married, the financial, health, and emotional status of divorced older women is extremely precarious. Despite all recent efforts to achieve fair divorce settlements, the economic impact remains much more devastating for women than for men. Not only are alimony and child-support payments rarely honored in full, but also less than half of currently divorced women received any property settlement (Bureau of the Census 1981c). Moreover, custody of children both increases the income needs of the household while reducing the ability of the mother to pursue full-time employment. By old age, these disadvantages have accumulated to reduce her capacity for autonomy and self-sufficiency. The elderly divorcee, thus, has a strong claim on feminist concern, representing the extreme case of the same variables that affect the lives of older women in general.

Widowhood. The most common condition for older women, however, will remain widowhood. While life expectancy has increased for both men and women, the incidence of widowhood will not decline but simply will occur at later ages. Also, widowhood possibly will extend over a longer period of time than at present since the disparity between male and female life expectancies continues to increase. What we can expect in the future is rising proportions of widows aged 75 and over. For example, there are approximately 13 million widowed older persons of both sexes today, but in the year 2050, if current age-specific death rates continue, there will be close to that number of widows aged 75 and over alone (Evers 1980). This projection, however, could be wide of the mark if remarriages characterized by wide age discrepancies increase—that is, marriages contracted in mid-life tend to involve brides much younger than their husbands compared to first marriages. We lack sufficient data on this point to make firm predictions of its impact on the onset of widowhood.

What is the full impact of widowhood? There is, first of all, the considerable loss of household income. Elderly households headed by women receive roughly 60 percent of the median income recorded for male-headed households. In addition, while 15.7 percent of all elderly had incomes below the poverty level in 1980, this was true for almost 28 percent of old women with no husband present, the greater proportion of whom would be widows (Bureau of the Census 1981b)

Income loss is perhaps the most pervasive effect of widowhood, affecting standard of living, the likelihood of maintaining independent residence, and the degree of dependence upon both public and private sources of support. However, many other consequences of not being married have differential impact by gender.

Life Satisfaction. Being married appears to have different consequences for men and women. On the one hand, Gove (1973) emphasizes the preservative effect that marriage has for men, lowering dramatically the probability that they will commit suicide, be victims of homicides or fatal accidents, contract lung cancer or cirrhosis of the liver, and so forth through a long list of sociogenic physical and mental disorders. In contrast, differences between married and nonmarried women on these same variables are less extreme. On the other hand, Glenn (1975) produces strong evidence from a variety of national samples that marriage is usually a more-important component of life satisfaction for women in comparison to men; and so it may be through the greater part of the family life course. In old age, however, data suggest that being married is more critical to well-being and life expectancy of men than of women (Ward 1981). With respect to health status, however, widowed women are no better off than widowed men (Verbrugge 1979).

Adjustment to Widowhood. Since husbands and wives both derive important, albeit different, benefits from being married, it might be expected that both would experience comparable difficulties in adjusting to the loss of a spouse. Indeed, evidence from a number of limited studies finds little difference by gender in adjustment to bereavement (for example, Kunkel 1979). The most consistent finding has been a more-pronounced reduction in social interaction for widowed men compared to continued high levels of sociability among women. Yet the finding of similar levels of difficulty in adjustment may obscure two very different causal factors, as Arens (1979) concludes from a reanalysis of data from the 1974 Harris survey: The lowered social participation for men and the lowered income of widowed women both serve to depress measures of well-being. Also, racial differences appear to interact with gender to produce variations in the length of mourning. Wilkinson (1980) reports that among a national sample of widowed social-security beneficiaries ($N = 5,673$) white men grieved for the shortest period while nonwhite men grieved the longest, with no differences by race among female respondents.

Among widowed women, adjustment has been shown to be related to anticipatory socialization, instrumental skills, a sense of internal control, education, income, and urban experience (Lopata 1981; Rux 1979; Haas-Hawkins and Ziegler, 1980). These characteristics are, of course, associated with independence, and it is expected that future cohorts of women will enter old age with higher levels of education and more-extensive work experience, improving their ability to cope with bereavement and widowhood, including the economic aspects, more successfully than those now old. Yet these potential advantages could be erased by the greater burden of poverty faced by women who will become widowed at even later ages (Borker and Loughlin 1979). Encouraging widows to work in order to maintain adequate incomes will be of little avail since most widows under age 64 are already employed while those 65 and older have few skills in great demand by employers (Morgan 1980).

In dealing with bereavement, it might seem that women with surviving offspring would have an advantage over those whose adult children were not available for so-called grief work. Yet several studies have found that the role of offspring is not as great as commonly assumed. For example, Bankoff (1978) found that support from children was less crucial to adjustment than that of friends, especially other widowed women. Possibly, suggests Bankoff, open displays of desolation before one's children may damage self-esteem whereas the same expressions of loss evoke empathy and solidarity among peers. Nonetheless, whatever support could be tendered by offspring was considerably greater than that proffered by the helping professionals, whose ministrations were found by most of the Chicago-area widows to be less than adequate.

The Still Married. From the foregoing, it is obvious that having a surviving spouse is associated with well-being, emotional and financial, in later life, and it is the case that increasing proportions of women will enter old age still married. At age 70 and over, in one recent national survey, respondents with a marriage partner were far more likely than those without to describe their quality of life as excellent or very good (Flanagan 1979). This finding, however, should be qualified by data from another national sample in which the crucial intervening variable between marital status and morale was similarity of physical functioning (Research and Forecasts 1980). This finding suggests that demoralization occurs when one spouse's physical condition deteriorates to the extent that customary companionship can no longer be sustained and when care of the less-capable spouse can be perceived as a burden.

In general, however, marriages that survive to old age are noted for high levels of expressed satisfaction (Rollins and Cannon 1974; Glenn 1975; Spanier, Lewis, and Cole 1975). Presumably, most unhappy marriages will have been dissolved by divorce, desertion, or death by this time. Also, the high level of marital satisfaction may be due in part to the opportunities for growth and change provided by childrearing and time to couples flexible enough to allow their relationships to develop and change. Further, the absence of children in the home, at either end of the family cycle, is associated with greater sharing and companionship between husband and wife (Miller 1976). Last, strong cognitive forces probably reduce dissonance and rationalize a marriage that encompasses two-thirds of one's life. For whatever reasons, later-life marriages are characterized by high levels of positive affect, even though the last task of the wife will be to manage after her husbands' death (Lopata 1979; Shanas 1979a).

Family Resources: The Importance of Children

The second major familial resource for older persons is their offspring. Although the importance of children to the well-being of elderly parents may seem self-evident, a considerable debate enlivens the gerontological literature. The emphasis on women in this debate is both intentional and necessary—intentional because the focus of this chapter is older women but also necessary because almost no research has been done on the importance of children to the well-being of older fathers. Most men, as noted, have their needs met by a wife. Moreover, the cultural assumption of mothers' overwhelming stake in childrearing tends to minimize the role of fathers and the potential importance of continuing ties to their children.

Women without Children. Not only do many women reach their later years having survived their husbands, but also about one in five will either have been childless throughout her life or have survived her offspring. An unknown additional number will have lost contact with any adult children, perhaps through divorce, desertion, or as the result of intrafamily conflict. What are the effects of being without the potential support of offspring? Most clearly, childless women have a higher probability of ending their life in a long-term facility, due largely to the absence of residential alternatives. They also, not unexpectedly, are likely to score lower on measures of family satisfaction than those with offspring (Singh and Williams 1981). On other measures of well-being, however, the evidence is considerably less clear.

In fact, the presence of children does not necessarily add to the psychological well-being of parents of any age. The high level of marital happiness of newlyweds and empty-nest couples is due in no small part to the absence of children. Studies of morale, life satisfaction, and so forth of older persons, reviewed in Hess and Waring (1978), indicate a minimal contribution of offspring to parental well-being, particularly when the parents are both alive and/or enjoy extensive friendship interaction. An analysis of data from six recent national surveys, by Glenn and McLanahan (1981), found that the effect of offspring on the global happiness of older adults is either negligible or negative, especially in the case of highly educated white men. These researchers concluded that, "overall, there is little evidence that important psychic rewards are derived from the later stages of parenthood" (Glenn and McLanahan 1981, p. 409).

The effects of offspring may, however, vary by economic status and ethnicity. Minority groups often retain traditional expectations of offspring so that the elderly derive satisfaction from the existence of dutiful children (Kim and Belcher, 1980); in other cases, financial exigencies mandate household sharing (see Gelfand and Kutzik 1979 for a collection of essays on ethnicity and aging). Yet, in other instances like the general impoverishment still endured by Appalachian elderly, the presence or absence of offspring makes little difference in measures of well-being (Lerner and Kivett, 1980; Lee, 1979; Kivett and Lerner 1980a; 1980b).

In contrast, among elderly women in retirement communities, the availability of offspring, even one child, appeared to be more important than the presence of a husband in accounting for the higher levels of emotional support experienced by married compared to nonmarried respondents (Lipman and Longino 1981; Longino and Lipman 1981). In this population, the husband's role was perceived primarily as instrumental, while the children were sources of emotional support.

For those women (and men) who never had children, the lack of pervasive negative effects in old age is probably linked to the same process that accounts for the high levels of satisfaction also found among the never married: By the time one reaches old age, adaptations and alternative support systems already have been constructed (see chapter 10). Since the incidence of childlessness is highest among the well educated, it seems likely that these women have other important survival resources. One recent study of married and unmarried older women, both without children, illustrates this point (Johnson and Catalano 1980). The researchers followed a sample of women after discharge from an acute-care facility. The married women displayed symptoms of social regression—that is, withdrawal from all contacts outside the marriage during convalescence—while the nonmarried called upon the accumulated resources of friends, other relatives, and formal services to cope with emergencies and to retain their independence.

This tendency to utilize the extended-kin network is characteristic of those who are not currently part of a nuclear family (Shanas 1979b). Siblings, particularly those who are close age peers, often assume increased importance in the social-life space of older persons without spouse or offspring. Nieces, nephews, and cousins are the least frequently mobilized family resource, although in families characterized by a strong sense of solidarity and who have developed a master theme of kinship obligation, even distant relatives will respond to the needs of older family members. Moreover, a relative without children may have given special attention to certain nieces and nephews over the years, thus earning the right to invoke the rule of reciprocity in much the same manner as parents. Considerations of inheritance cannot be ignored either, since there is evidence that some older persons make bequests to those who have been of recent assistance to them, regardless of blood ties (Rosenfeld 1979).

The more-typical situation, however, is for an aged parent to have at least one child with whom she or he is in frequent contact. About 80 percent of those with surviving offspring live within a few hours' drive from one of their children and exchange visits, phone calls, and letters on at least a monthly basis. Let us, then, look more closely at these ties.

Parent/Child Bonds. While having offspring is not essential to well-being in old age, generational linkages within families remain strong (Troll and Bengtson 1978). In this regard, it may be useful to employ a distinction made by Bengtson and Black (1973) between ties of sentiment and those of solidarity. The former refers to feelings of affection and concern directed toward specific family members; the latter refers to a generalized sense of obligation to the lineage as a whole. Given this sense of solidarity, it is not necessary, for example, to be fond of one's parents, or to be without rancor, in order to feel deeply responsible for their well-being. Indeed, most older persons feel that their offspring will be a dependable resource when needed.

Yet this generalization about filial responsibility obscures many important variations—by age and gender of the parent and offspring as well as by race, ethnicity, and socioeconomic status. We have already mentioned the expectations for care embedded in certain ethnic subcultures, although the actual provision of services by children will depend on many other factors. In addition, when families are at extreme economic disadvantage, primary dependence may fall upon public agencies, with government perceived as the legitimate provider of care (Bengtson and Burton 1980; NCOA 1981). For example, one large-scale study of social-service recipients in a southwestern state found that the majority of the poor depended upon non-family assistance even when the recipient had a living spouse and offspring (Dunckley and Lutes 1979). Where poverty is not linked to minority status, as in Hawaii, ethnic differences in expectations and provision of services remain strong (Rose, Izutzu and Kagan 1980).

In general, however, ethnic traditions of filial piety tend to weaken wherever a system of public-welfare services is established. In the United States, attitudes regarding the role of family members in providing help varied systematically by immigrant generation, progressively weakening as family members become more assimilated into the dominant culture (Weeks and Cuellar 1981). Yet, research in this area is somewhat unreliable. Most studies are small scale and geographically idiosyncratic, respondents are often asked who should provide care rather than who does, and responses characteristically are generalized and idealized. About the only clear conclusion is that norms of filial responsibility are far from uniform and appear to be undergoing historial change.

In an earlier essay (Hess and Waring 1978), we argued that such a shift is now occurring in the United States (and other modern social-welfare states) from norms of obligation to those of voluntary intergenerational relationships in later life—that is, as income maintenance and health care are assumed as a public responsibility, older parents and their adult children may base their continued exchanges of services and support on bonds of affection and friendship. Daniel Yankelovich (1981) interprets recent survey data to suggest the full dimensions of this change: Just as parents now sacrifice less for their children than in the immediate past, so also do they expect less from their children in the future than their own parents currently expect of them. In answer to questions regarding the responsibility of offspring to provide for their parents' care in old age, close to 77 percent of persons now in the childrearing phase indicate that they have minimal expectations of their own children. Concomitantly, compared to their own parents, these younger mothers and fathers are not as willing to defer their own gratification in order to provide for offspring.

Since the majority of elderly survivors will be women, and since the female members of the family will be expected to assume caretaking responsibilities, this transition period in societal norms can serve as a paradigm of the dilemma proposed at the outset of this chapter: how to reconcile the needs of both generations. The aged woman must balance her ideal

wishes against more-realistic hopes, while members of the younger generation must resolve conflicts between felt obligation and the constraints imposed by their own life situation, family resources, and modern values of
self-fulfillment.

In a recent survey of attitudes toward the aged (NCOA 1981), only one-
third of respondents aged 65 and over and just under one-half of the general
public under age 65 say that children should assume more responsibility for
their elderly parents. These attitudes, several data sets suggest, are more
broad than deep. When presented with specific examples of situations
requiring intervention, for example, the proportions endorsing familial
responsibility tend to decline along with the numbers of offspring engaged
in parental caretaking (Sussman 1979). Similarly, national sample data
analyzed by Waring (1979) indicate that although almost all respondents
felt that the family should assume some responsibility for elderly parents,
less than half intended this to mean "a great deal," and these percentages
varied greatly across domains of responsibility. For example, 29 percent
thought that families had a great deal of responsibility to elderly parents for
ensuring adequate income, 40 percent with respect to adequate housing, 47
percent for making sure that the parent was not lonely, and 50 percent for
assuring, though not providing, proper health care. As is often the case, the
youngest group of adults, those aged 18–24, was most likely to endorse
strong filial-responsibility norms, being least at risk of having to follow
through on their attitudes. Respondents over 65, particularly those with the
least faith in the social-security system, were the next highest endorsers of
responsibility norms. The lowest level of endorsement was found among
high-income respondents, precisely those most able to support their elderly
relatives, but then, their parents may not need financial assistance, while
they themselves can prepare for their own income security in old age.

Waring's data also provide further support for the thesis that filial
attention today is more focused on expressive rather than instrumental domains—that is, to see that one's parent is not lonely rather than to provide
income support and to monitor health care rather than ensure adequate
housing. Nonetheless, when the situation requires, the elderly normally can
rely on the active intervention of offspring. However, intervention does not
necessarily mean the direct provision of care, the issue that has entered the
public-policy debate and whose outcome is so consequential to both generations of women.

Caregivers to the Elderly. Disabled elderly who live in the community
obviously are restricted in their living arrangements. For those still married,
it is possible to remain in their own homes, assisted by their spouses. It is
more likely that an older disabled man will be tended by his wife than that
the wife will receive care from her husband. For the disabled wife, however,

the husband still may be in the labor force and unable to render constant care. Under these circumstances, secondary caregivers, typically an unmarried daughter or other female relative are called upon (Shanas 1979b; Myllyluoma and Soldo 1980). In her study of old people discharged from an acute-care hospital, Johnson (1979) found that while offspring's motivation to provide support was high, situational impediments intervened (their own children, jobs, marital relationships, and so on) so that spouse or siblings became primary caregivers, many of whom were not in the best of health themselves. Johnson concluded that the high value placed on independence often impeded the search for nonfamily alternatives.

Some widowed, divorced, or never-married old persons, however, are able to maintain an independent residence when severely disabled, if they live in a community that provides in-home care services or if they are wealthy enough to afford full-time trained caretakers. Younger family members, particularly those in the labor force, are often more willing—and able—to purchase rather than to provide care (Soldo and Myllyluoma 1980). Other old people, especially those with adult offspring living nearby, can remain in their residences with only surveillance during the day. A few may take advantage of new technologies permitting instant communication with a hot line (Dibner, Markson, and Batra 1981). However, if one cannot negotiate the basic activities of daily living over a long period of time, the ultimate recourse is to move into the home of a family member—a move that is rarely taken without misgivings on the part of both the disabled person and the caregiver. For those without adult offspring, the choice is limited by the willingness of other relatives or friends; often, institutionalization is necessary simply to secure basic care.

Whether one remains at home or moves to the household of another, the primary caregiver in all likelihood will be a woman (Shanas 1979b; Myllyluoma and Soldo 1980; Horowitz and Shindelman 1980). Of course, the probability also is that the disabled old person will be a woman—typically a widow who is over age 80 and suffering from at least one disabling condition. Thus, although sons and daughters appear to be concerned equally about their elderly parents in studies of attitudes and, in some ethnic traditions, are equally expected to be primary caregivers, the task typically falls to daughters and daughters-in-law—women who themselves may be approaching old age or in the young-old age category. Many recently will have embarked on new lives of their own as students, workers, volunteers, and community activists. Varying proportions will still have offspring at home; in one community survey, Bremer (1980) found that even at ages 45 and older, over 60 percent of Mexican-American women had several children at home, as did 18 percent of black mothers and 25 percent of white mothers.

In 1979, labor-force-participation rates for women at mid-life were 58 percent of those 45 to 54 and 41 percent for women 55 to 64, higher for divorced and never-married than for the currently married, and higher for those with no children under age 18 than for those with dependent off-spring. However, when the middle-aged woman is also primary caretaker of an elderly relative, labor-force participation is considerably lower: Only 25 percent of female caregivers under age 65 were in the labor force compared to half their male counterparts in a large national survey of over 3,000 units representing 1.5 million households in which disabled elderly relatives were cared for by other family members (Soldo and Myllyluoma 1980). Clearly, caregiving inhibits labor-force participation for both men and women but particularly for women. The higher the caregiver's income, the more likely he or she is to remain in the labor force since the opportunity costs of leav-ing are commensurately higher. Given the type of employment held by most women, opportunity costs probably operate to encourage withdrawal from employment. In general, Soldo and Myllyluoma found that younger caregivers (those under age 65) tended the needs of less-disabled elderly, presumably because of lower thresholds of tolerance for caretaking demands, while older persons took care of the more disabled, either because they were a spouse or had fewer competing demands on their time and ener-gies.

Such caregiving—whether one is 45 or 64—is not without stress. We know of no study that has not documented the burdens imposed by daily care of an infirm patient. Regardless of past relationships between mother and daughter, the immediate demands of the situation seem to be the most important predictors of caregivers' emotional well-being (Cicirelli 1979; 1980). The arrangement whereby the disabled older person is cared for in the household of kin often represents an effort to avoid institutionalization and one that is sustained until the inconvenience outweighs the sense of obligation. Despite family traditions associated with ethnicity, and even the availability of alternative caretakers that is the advantage of a large family, the perceived burden of care determined the decision to institutionalize the relative living in the household (Teresi et al. 1980).

The older relatives are touched certainly by their situation. Grams and Fengler (1980) found that older persons residing in the home of an adult child and grandchildren had lower morale and satisfaction scores than the elderly in other arrangements, although much of their dissatisfaction could stem from the disabling conditions that made joint living necessary. Hughes and Gove (1981) suggest that living with other people can compromise men-tal health when the costs of sharing a household outweigh the benefits, as may well be the case of many elderly in the home of offspring, particularly when a third generation is also present.

While it is often assumed that dependency will be harder for older men to bear than for women, a mother is not necessarily any less affected by her loss of autonomy, often an independence only established at mid-life. The loss of income and health that forces her to forfeit her freedom can be doubly galling on that account. Moreover, sharing a household could be harder for women than men since the home traditionally has been considered a woman's world and since there will be many more points of potential conflict between members of the two generations. Yet despite such difficulties, most middle-aged and young-old daughters manage to care for their elderly mothers and mothers-in-law until some crisis upsets the balance between resources and demands—either a severe decrement in the older person's mental and physical health or a major change in the daughter's houschold—that necessitates institutionalization.

Family Caregiving in the Future. How likely is it that more families in the future will become primary caregivers to needy relatives? For one thing, elderly parents of the future will have fewer offspring than those currently old. Population growth at replacement levels—about 2.1 children per married woman aged 15 to 44—appears to have stabilized over the past decade, and most demographers expect a continuation of low fertility rates on the basis of women's reported desires for small family size (Bureau of the Census 1981c). Other population analysts (for example, Easterlin, Wacherster, and Wacher 1978), however, foresee a rise in fertility desires and behavior once the small birth cohorts of today reach adulthood and find that their standards of living are rising, precisely because there are relatively so few of them in relation to the high-level jobs available. For persons now in their childbearing years, however, the future will be one in which they can call upon the help of only one or two adult offspring.

Another factor of great importance is the higher educational and employment levels of adult women today and in the future. Will they be as willing as women in the past to remain at home caring for the ill and needy? Or will they even be able to afford to, given the higher proportions who will be divorced and living on limited incomes? At the level of public policy, will the perceived need to balance the budget by reducing social-welfare expenditures continue to dominate the political economy of the United States, so that families will be pressed into providing services previously defined as public responsibilities, rationalized by appeals to traditional virtues of intergenerational bonds?

The history of family-support legislation offers some instructive insights (Newman 1980). In her extensive examination of filial-support legislation and its effects, Newman notes that such laws are still in effect in twenty-five states and can be invoked to deny public assistance to old people whose children can be shown to be able economically to support their parent(s). Seven states do have family-responsibility provisions incorporated in their Supplemental Security Income (SSI) statutes—that is, an older person can be declared ineligible for SSI on grounds that relatives can assume her support. Newman concludes that:

> [A]vailable evidence provides a convincing case that these laws are, at best, an irritant and, at worst, damaging to whatever family ties do exist, however weak. . . . Being forced to live together by law rather than by choice cannot have very salutory effects on family cohesion. (p. 4]

Legislation is seldom neutral in its effects on family, however benignly intended or worded, and while it may be possible to strengthen family ties through law, amicable relationships cannot be legislated into existence.

Some interesting legislative initiatives are aimed at easing the financial burden of family caregivers—for example, providing tax credits, deductions, or flat grants. Again, unless the task is assumed willingly, potential difficulties are many. What is to prevent a family from taking in an older relative simply to increase family income but with small intention to provide care? If supervision is called for, another layer of intrusion into family life may be created. As it is, abuse of elderly family members already occurs (Block and Sinnott 1979; Hickey and Douglass 1981), sometimes inadvertently, as when caregivers use excessive restraints lest the old person hurt herself, but also sometimes intentional, in order to have social-security checks or other property endorsed over to the caregiver. Few abused older women are either willing or able to complain about their treatment because of embarrassment at having raised such children, fear of retaliation, and absence of alternative arrangements to inhibit resistance to abusive behavior.

How could families be encouraged to assume the burden of care willingly? Sussman (1977; 1979) has conducted a series of studies designed to discover what types of incentives might increase the likelihood of family caretaking. Given lists of both economic and service incentives, respondents tended to prefer the financial assistance provided by a monthly check. Among those who were caring for an older relative, however, the preference was for services, particularly health-care assistance. In a replication of the Sussman study, Horowitz and Shindelman (1980) found that with respect to financial incentives, the overwhelming preference was for direct supplements such as cash grants or food stamps rather than deferred benefits through tax credits or deductions. In the service category, again, the felt need was for immediate relief from daily responsibilities through, for example, homemaking and health-care assistance. Overall, responding caretakers (80 percent were women) overwhelmingly preferred service to economic supports; indeed, many did not bother to fill out the section on financial incentives. Further, the more services already utilized by the caregivers, the more ready to prefer additional services, leading to the conclusion that experience with public-service systems had been largely positive.

Female caregivers in the near future, however, may be operating under conditions of reduced community-based services, making the other alternatives institutionalization of the mother or continued caregiving under increasingly difficult circumstances. They will find themselves at risk of so-called family burnout, defined as the physical, emotional, and spiritual exhaustion that often strikes providers of direct care to an older relative. Burned-out families lose their ability to cope with the stress of the situation, but it is likely the primary caregiver also will have to bear the brunt of other family members' exhaustion and stress. While male children may contribute monetary support to satisfy their obligations, female kin often are expected to sacrifice their own goals and to render personal care to the ill and dependent members of their family, of any generation.

And herein lies the rub: how to reconcile the needs of both generations of women. There is much evidence of a mellowing of relationships between mothers and daughters when both have completed essential childrearing tasks and when many immediate causes of intergenerational tensions are removed from their common sphere. Baruch and Barnett (1981) go so far as to describe an "era of good feelings" when the daughter is in her middle years and her mother enters old age. Differences in values and life-styles will have been adjusted to or reconciled. They can meet as women who have shared the vicissitudes of marriage and parenthood and who have managed to carry on the family line.

Since most elderly women are not destitute or disabled—at least to age 80—they can control the timing and pace of intergenerational contacts, precisely to avoid strain. Moreover, any relationship that has endured five decades or more has real or perceived benefits. As with marriages, the unsatisfying or destructive relationships have been allowed to lapse, although one cannot become an ex-child or -parent; but ties can become attenuated and perfunctory.

In recognition of the problematic aspects of care of frail and ancient parents, the trend in public policy over the past five decades in most industrialized nations and, to a lesser extent, in the United States has been toward the provision of publicly funded entitlements to income, housing, transportation, and health care for older persons no longer in the labor force. However, conservative political forces now seek to curtail federal support for such programs out of a genuine ideological commitment to dismantling entitlement programs in favor of private enterprise and/or the natural support system of family and friends. Both of these latter alternatives are proposed as more in keeping with traditional U.S. values than the impersonal, bureaucratic interventions of government programs. It remains to be seen whether this view of public policy will prevail over the long term. Many elderly, and their adult offspring, have a stake in the maintenance of present programs; and as we have pointed out before (Hess and Waring 1978), removing such issues from the interpersonal realm of family relationships may actually increase goodwill among family members; that is, once care of the aged is defined as a general obligation of members of modern socities—in recognition of their past contributions to societal well-being—then questions of priorities in the allocation of familial resources no longer inhibit personal relationships among kin.

Women, in particular, have much to lose if this policy changes. Both older and younger women will be less able to control their own fate—the older to remain independent with the aid of a full array of entitlements and the younger to choose not to devote the rest of their lives to the care of ill or disabled and impoverished relatives. The next few years promise to be crucial in determining the conditions under which the elderly in general will live out their last decades and in which women's choices will expand or contract.

References

Arens, Diana Antos. "Well-Being and Widowhood: Interpreting Sex Differences." Paper presented at the Thirty-second Annual Scientific Meeting of the Gerontological Society, Washington, D.C., November 1979.

Bankoff, E. "Support from Family and Friends: What Helps the Widow." Paper presented at the Thirty-first Annual Scientific Meeting of the Gerontological Society, Dallas, November 1978.

Baruch, G., and R. Barnett. "Women in the Middle Years: Correlates of Well Being." Paper presented at the Thirty-fourth Annual Scientific Meeting of the Gerontological Society of America, Toronto, November 1981.

Bengtson, V.L., and D. Black, "Intergenerational Relations and Continuities in Socialization." In *Life-Span Developmental Psychology: Personality and Socialization,* edited by P. Baltes and K.W. Schaie. New York: Academic Press, 1973:207–234.

Bengtson, V., and L. Burton. "Families and Support Systems among Three Ethnic Groups." Paper presented at the Thirty-third Annual Scientific Meeting of the Gerontological Society of America, San Diego, November 1980.

Block, M.R., and F. Sinnott. *The Battered Elder Syndrome.* University Park: University of Maryland Center on Aging, 1979.

Borker, S.R., and J. Loughlin. "Implications of the Present Economic Position of Middle Aged Divorced and Widowed Women: Another Generation of the Elderly in Poverty." Paper presented at the Annual Meeting of the Americn Sociological Society, Boston, Mass. 1979.

Bremer, T.H. "Diversity in the Empty Nest." Paper presented at the Thirty-third Annual Scientific Meeting of the Gerontological Society of America, San Diego, November 1980.

Cicirelli, V.G. "Kin Relationships of Childless and One-Child Elderly in Relation to Social Services." Paper presented at the Thirty-second Annual Scientific Meeting of the Gerontological Society, Washington, D.C., November 1979.

————. *Personal Strains and Negative Feelings in Adult Children's Relationships with Elderly Parents.* Lafayette, In. Purdue University, Department of Psychology, 1980.

Dibner, A.; F. Markson; and G. Batra. "Linking the Aged to Human Services." Paper presented at the Annual Meeting of the American Psychological Association, Los Angeles, August 1981.

Dunckley, R.; and C. Lutes. "Confidante Relationships among the Aged Poor as a Function of Age, Sex, and Race." Paper presented at the Thirty-second Annual Scientific Meeting of the Gerontological Society, Washington, D.C., November 1979.

Easterlin, R.; M. Wacherster; and S. Wacher. "Demographic Influences on Economic Stability: The U.S. Experience." *Population and Development Review* 4 (1978):1–22.

Espanshade, T.J. "The Economic Consequences of Divorce." *Journal of Marriage and the Family* 43 (1979):615–625.

Evers, M. "The Demographic Basis of Future Widowhood." Paper presented at the Thirty-third Annual Scientific Meeting of the Gerontological Society of America, San Diego, November 1980.

Federal Council on the Aging. *The Need for Long Term Care: Information and Issues,* DHHS Publication Number OHDS81-20704. Washington, D.C.: U.S. Department of Health and Human Services, 1981.

Flanagan, John. *The Quality of Life of Older Americans.* Palo Alto, Calif.: American Institute of Research, 1979.

Gelfand, Donald E., and Alfred J. Kutzik, eds. *Ethnicity and Aging: Theory, Research, and Policy.* New York: Springer, 1979.

Glenn, N.D. "The Contribution of Marriage to Psychological Well-Being of Males and Females." *Journal of Marriage and the Family* 37 (1975): 594–600.

Glenn, N.D., and Sara McLanahan. "The Effects of Offspring on the Psychological Well-Being of Older Adults." *Journal of Marriage and the Family* 43 (1981):409–422.

Gove, Walter R. "Sex and Marital Status and Mortality." *American Journal of Sociology* 79 (1973):45–67.

Grams, A., and A.F. Fengler, "The Older Parent in the Extended Family." Paper presented at the Thirty-third Annual Scientific Meeting of the Gerontological Society of America, San Diego, November 1980.

Haas-Hawkings, G., and M. Ziegler. "An Exploratory Study of Adjustment to Widowhood." Paper presented at the Thirty-third Annual Scientific Meeting of the Gerontological Society of America, San Diego, November 1980.

Hess, B., and J. Waring. "Parent and Child in Later Life: Rethinking the Relationship." In *Child Influences on Marital and Family Interaction,* edited by R.M. Lerner and A.B. Spanier. New York: Academic Press, 1978:241–268.

Hickey, T., and R.L. Douglass. "Mistreatment of the Elderly in a Domestic Setting: An Exploratory Study." *American Journal of Public Health* 71 (1981):500–507.

Horowitz, A., and L.W. Shindelman. "Social and Economic Incentives for Family Caregivers." Paper presented at the Thirty-third Annual Scientific Meeting of the Gerontological Society of America, San Diego, November 1980.

Hughes, M., and W.R. Gove. "Living Alone, Social Integration, and Mental Health." *American Journal of Sociology* 87 (1981):48–74.

Johnson, C. "Impediments to Family Supports to Dependent Elderly." Paper presented at the Thirty-second Annual Scientific Meeting of the Gerontological Society, Washington, D.C., November 1979.

Johnson, C., and D.J. Catalano. "Childless Elderly and Their Family Supports." Paper presented at the Thirty-third Annual Scientific Meeting of the Gerontological Society of America, San Diego, November 1980.

Kim, M.S., and J.C. Belcher. "Family Support Systems for the Aged in the Dominican Republic." Paper presented at the Thirty-third Annual Scientific Meeting of the Gerontological Society of America, San Diego, November 1980.

Kivett, V., and R.M. Lerner. "Perspectives of the Childless Rural Elderly: A Comparative Analysis." *The Gerontologist* 20 (1980a):708–716.

————. "Situational Influences on the Morale of Older Rural Parents in Child-Shared Households." Paper presented at the Thirty-third Annual Scientific Meeting of the Gerontological Society of America, San Diego, November 1980.

Kunkel, S. "Sex Differences in Adjustment to Widowhood." Paper presented at the Thirty-second Annual Scientific Meeting of the Gerontological Society, Washington, D.C., November 1979.

Lerner, R.M., and V.R. Kivett. "Older Adults and Their In-Laws: An Assessment of Attitudes and the Quality of Relationships." Paper presented at the Thirty-third Annual Scientific Meeting of the Gerontological Society of America, San Diego, November 1980.

Lee, Gary R. "Children and the Elderly: Interaction and Morale." *Research on Aging* (1979):335–360.

Lipman, A., and C.F. Longino. "The Wife, the Widow, and the Old Maid: Support Network Differentials of Older Women." Paper presented at the Thirty-third Annual Scientific Meeting of the Gerontological Society of America, San Diego, November 1980.

Longino, C.F., Jr., and A. Lipman. "Married and Spouseless Men and Women in Planned Retirement Communities: Support Network Differentials." *Journal of Marriage and the Family* 43 (1981):169–177.

Lopata, H.Z. *Women as Widows: Support Systems.* New York: Elsevier, 1979.

———. "Widowhood and Husband Sanctification." *Journal of Marriage and the Family* 43 (1981):439–450.

Lopata, H.Z., and H.P. Brehm. "Public and Family Contributions to the Economic Supports of Widows." Paper presented at the Thirty-third Annual Scientific Meeting of the Gerontological Society of America, San Diego, November 1980.

Miller, B.C. "A Multivariate Developmental Model of Marital Satisfaction." *Journal of Marriage and the Family* 38 (1976):643–657.

Morgan, L.A. "Work in Widowhood: A Viable Option? *The Gerontologist* 20 (1980):581–587.

Myllyluoma, Jaana, B.J. Soldo. "Family Caregivers to the Elderly: Who Are They?" Paper presented at the Thirty-third Annual Scientific Meeting of the Gerontological Society of America, San Diego, November 1980.

National Council on Aging. *Aging in the Eighties: America in Transition.* New York: Louis Harris and Associates, 1981.

Newman, S. "Government Policy and the Relationship between Adult Children and Their Aging Parents: Filial Support, Medicare, and Medicaid." Paper presented at the Thirty-third Annual Scientific Meeting of the Gerontological Society of America, San Diego, November 1980.

Price, B. *Datatrack 9: Older Americans and their Economic Status.* Washington, D.C.: American Council on Life Insurance, forthcoming.

Research and Forecasts. *Aging in America: Trials and Triumphs.* New York: Rudder and Finn, 1980.

Rollins, B.C., and K.L. Cannon. "Marital Satisfaction over the Family Life Cycle: A Re-evaluation." *Journal of Marriage and the Family* 36 (1974):271–282.

Rose, C.L.; S. Izutsu; and M. Kagan. "Familial Supports and Well-Being in Hawaiian Elders: A Japanese-Caucasian Comparison." Paper presented at the Thirty-third Annual Scientific Meeting of the Gerontological Society of America, San Diego, November 1980.

Rosenfeld, J.P. *The Legacy of Aging.* Norwood, N.J.: Ablex, 1979.

Rosenmayr, L., and E. Kockeis. "Family Relations and Social Contacts of the Aged in Vienna." In *Social and Psychological Aspects of Aging,* edited by C. Tibbitts and W. Donahue. New York: Columbia University Press 1962:492–500.

Rux, Julia. "Instrumental Adaptation to Widowhood." Paper presented at the Thirty-second Annual Scientific Meeting of the Gerontological Society, Washington, D.C., November 1979.

Shanas, E. "The Family as a Social Support System in Old Age." *The Gerontologist* 19 (1979a):169–174.

———. "Social Myth as Hypothesis: The Case of the Family Relations of Old People." *The Gerontologist* 19 (1979b):218–227.

Siegel, J. "On the Demography of Aging." *Demography* 17 (1980):345.

Singh, B.K., and J.S. Williams. "Childlessness and Family Satisfaction." *Research on Aging* 3 (1981):218–227.

Soldo, B.J., and Myllyluoma, J. "Caregivers Who Live with Dependent Elderly." Unpublished article, 1982.

Spanier, G.B.; R.A. Lewis; and C.L. Cole. "Marital Adjustment over the Family Life Cycle: The Issue of Curvilinearity." *Journal of Marriage and the Family* 37 (1975):263–275.

Sussman, M.B. "Incentives and Family Environments for the Family." Report to the Administration on Aging. Washington, D.C., 1977.

———. "Social and Economic Supports and Family Environments for the Elderly." Report to the Administration on Aging. Washington, D.C., 1979.

Teresi, J.A.; J.A. Toner; R.G. Bennett; and D.E. Wilder. "Factors Related to Family Attitude toward Institutionalizing Older Relatives." Paper presented at the Thirty-third Annual Scientific Meeting of the Gerontological Society of America, San Diego, November 1980.

Troll, L., and V. Bengtson. "Generations in the Family." In *Handbook of Contemporary Family Therapy,* edited by W. Burr, R. Hill, I. Reiss, and I. Nye. New York: Free Press, 1978.

Tuchman, G. "Introduction." In *Hearth and Home: Images of Women in the Mass Media,* edited by G. Tuchman, A.K. Daniels, and J. Benet. New York: Oxford University Press, 1978.

Uhlenberg, P. "Older Women: The Growing Challenge to Design Constructive Roles." *The Gerontologist* 19 (1979):236–241.

———. "Death and the Family." *Journal of Family History* 5 (1980): 313–320.

U.S. Bureau of the Census. "A Statistical Portrait of Women in the United States." *Current Population Reports: Special Studies.* Series P-23, no. 100. Washington, D.C., February 1980a.

U.S. Bureau of the Census. "Fertility of American Women: June, 1979." *Current Population Reports.* Series P-20, no. 358. Washington, D.C.: December 1980b.

U.S. Bureau of the Census. "Fertility of American Women: June, 1980." *Current Population Reports.* Series P-20, no. 364. Washington, D.C., August 1981a, advance data.

U.S. Bureau of the Census. "Money Income and Poverty Status of Families and Persons in the United States: 1980." Advance data from the March 1981 *Current Population Survey, Current Population Report,* Series P-60, no. 127, Washington, D.C., August 1981b.

U.S. Bureau of the Census. "Child Support and Alimony: 1978" *Current Population Reports,* Special Studies, Series P-23, no. 127, Washington, D.C., September 1981c.

U.S. Senate. Special Committee on Aging. *Developments on Aging 1980. Part 1.* Washington, D.C.: U.S. Government Printing Office, 1981.

Verbrugge, L.M. "Marriage Status and Health." *Journal of Marriage and the Family* 41 (1979):267–285.

Ward, R.A. "Sex Differences in the Impact of Widowhood: Social Support and Life Satisfaction." Paper presented at the Annual Meeting of the Society for the Study of Social Problems, Toronto, August 1981.

Waring, J. "Intergenerational Responsibilities: A Current View." Paper presented at the Thirty-second Annual Scientific Meeting of the Gerontological Society, Washington, D.C., November 1979.

Weeks, J.R., and J.B. Cuellar. "The Role of Family Members in the Helping Networks of Older People." *The Gerontologist* 21 (1981):388–394.

Wilkinson, A.M. "Factors Associated with Duration of Bereavement." Paper presented at the Thirty-third Annual Scientific Meeting of the Gerontological Society of America, San Diego, November 1980.

Wilson, K., and M. DeShane. "Divorced Elderly: A Group at Risk." Paper presented at the Thirty-third Annual Scientific Meeting of the Gerontological Society of America, San Diego, November 1980.

Yankelovich, Daniel. *New Rules.* New York: Random House, 1981.

12 Concerns about Parental Health

Victor W. Marshall,
Carolyn J. Rosenthal, and
Jane Synge

The family is, and probably has to be, the major provider of health care to its members, perhaps especially if the members are children or very old (Rakowski and Hickey 1980, p. 290; Shanas 1981; Tobin and Kulys 1980; Treas 1977). This fact, as Pratt (1976, p. 2) has observed, has been neglected or obscured by the emphasis in the sociology of the family on the loss of functions that has been held to accompany an alleged move to the nuclear family and by an emphasis in medical sociology on the professional health-care system. Important demographic changes in the past century have altered both the structure of the family and the organization of behavior within it. While families always have played a significant part in ensuring the health of their members, the requirements for such familial support assume new dimensions as more people live to be old or very old. Accompanying increased longevity is the growing likelihood that a family will have one or more members who requires some form of assistance for health reasons, either in crisis situations or for protracted periods of time.

This chapter focuses on the need for assistance from children and the awareness of such need by the children. Need for assistance varies by both age and sex of the parent. Women typically outlive their husbands. Their own health tends to remain better until somewhat later in life than that of men. While men can obtain considerable assistance from their spouse, this possibility is curtailed for women by widowhood. At the same time, in our society, the caregiver role frequently is cast upon women. Recognition by children and especially by daughters, of filial responsibilities for the provision of health care to parents leads to a structuring of concerned watchfulness, a monitoring of parental health, and for most adult children, a readiness to provide care.

Attention has focused recently on the intermediary function that adult children assume between aged parents and the health-care system (Sussman 1977), where children may serve as sources of information and informal referral or as advocates for their parents. It is also becoming widely recognized that children provide a very large amount of direct health and social-service assistance to their parents, accounting for upward of 75 percent of such assistance to the community-dwelling elderly (Brody 1978, p. 18;

Comptroller General 1977; 1979; Shanas 1968, pp. 428–429; Tobin and Kulys 1980). However, in this chapter we are interested specifically in the concerns of the adult-child generation that emanate from and in turn strengthen the caregiving function.[1]

Data and Methodology

In the Generational Relations and Succession Project (GRASP), we interviewed (for 1.5 hours) a stratified random sample of men and women aged 40 and older, living in Hamilton and Stoney Creek, Ontario, considered a representative Canadian middle-sized urban area. One-third of respondents were aged 70 and over, another third aged 55–69. Of those interviewed, 10 percent said they had never raised any children. Thirty-three percent have no grandchildren. Seventy-one percent were currently married or in a common-law union, 17 percent were widowed, 6 percent were single, and 5 percent were separated or divorced. From these interview respondents, we obtained the names and addresses of their adult (age 18 and over) children, to whom we mailed questionnaires. Parents furnished names for about three-fourths of their children, and about three-fourths of these returned the questionnaire, giving us data for 49 percent of the adult children eligible for the study.

In this chapter, when discussing children, we draw on data from 506 adult children of the 263 parents from whom we received back at least one mailed child's questionnaire. In some of the analyses, some of the parents are counted twice or more, depending on whether we have data from one, two, or more of their children. This allows us to maximize the case base to include each child and to avoid having to construct ratio or other averaging measures for the child data. We do not regard this factor as seriously skewing the analysis, given the moderately large sample size and the fact that children sampled in this way, while not technically selected independently of one another, can be thought of as drawn into a sample in a manner analogous to a two-stage cluster sample.

When not specifically describing the parent-child relationship (like when describing the health status of our interview respondents), we employ the total interview sample including those without children and those with children not included in the study. This is done so as to maximize our available information and to enable us to address the family-structure reality that many older persons have no living children or no relationship with a child. Readers should, however, beware of the shifting case base in various sections of the chapter.

When moving from this specific analysis to generalization, an additional caution, concerning sampling, is in order. Streib (1980) recently has called attention to the "excluded 20 percent" of the aged, particularly the very old, who are not interviewed in community studies of the aged. Although we drew our stratified random sample from current property-assessment rolls (which are used to bill citizens for property taxes each year), for various reasons we underrepresent the institutionalized and the very ill elderly.

After excluding respondents found to be deceased or not locatable, we lost 12 percent of eligible respondents aged 40 or older due to their lack of facility in the English language and 12 percent due to their own serious illness, to bereavement, or because they were preoccupied with providing health care to another family member. Proxies were not used, and we deleted from this analysis the five cases interviewed in nursing homes or homes for the aged.[2] This study therefore represents English-speaking community-dwelling persons who, even if many are quite old, tend to be in reasonably good health. The social-class spread is indicated by the fact that 25 percent earned $8,000 or less annually, while 22 percent earned $25,000 or more. More than half the respondents listed British as their main ancestry through either the maternal or paternal line, or both—other ethnic backgrounds included Irish, Italian, and German respondents, but not in large numbers. The area has a very small nonwhite population.

Health Status of the Parental Generation

Taking all 464 initial interview respondents (including those not considered in relation to their children later in this chapter), a number of indicators suggest that the health of most is quite good until the seventies or even the eighties. Self-rated health as excellent or good has been found to be related inversely to age in most studies (Riley and Foner 1968, p. 292; but see Shanas 1968, p. 51 for contrary data), and we found a strong relationship for both men and women (men, Tau C = .212, sign. = .0001; women, Tau C = .106, sign. = .001). This relationship occurred despite the fact that the highest proportions assessing their health as only fair or poor were just 50 percent for men in their eighties and 42 percent for women in their eighties. Moreover, when asked to compare their present health to their health three years ago, men were as likely to say their health was better now as that it was worse now until the decade of the seventies, and women until the decade of the eighties. In their seventies, however, almost a third saw their health as turning for the worse, and one-half of men in their eighties did so. Just under one-half of women in their eighties compared their present health unfavorably to that of three years previously. For further details, see table 12–1.

Table 12-1
Selected Health Indicators, by Age and Sex, of Initial Interview
Respondents (Parents)

		Age Group (Percent Falling in Response Category)					
Health Indicators	Sex	40–49	50–59	60–69	70–79	80 and over	All Ages
See health as fair or poor	Male	10	27	32	36	50	29
	Female	17	26	42	37	42	32
Present health worse than three years ago	Male	15	20	16	30	50	23
	Female	22	27	22	20	46	25
Current physical condition or illness	Male	38	52	63	63	64	55
	Female	44	62	67	75	85	65
Health problem stands in way a great deal	Male	5	15	18	36	29	20
	Female	9	13	20	18	42	18
Health problem stands in way not at all	Male	75	61	50	41	21	54
	Female	70	57	49	47	27	53
Five or more days spent in hospital in past year	Male	5	14	13	16	29	14
	Female	0	6	4	19	23	10
Needs help over long period due to illness	Male	0	5	3	9	36	7
	Female	0	6	9	4	19	6
Number of men		40	66	38	56	14	214
Number of women		46	68	45	57	26	242

Note: Within each sex, increasing age is significantly related to lowered health status, at the .05 level or usually well beyond, using Tau C. The data are not fully cleaned as yet, accounting for the missing observations on eight individuals.

Such global questions reflect more than physical health and may be influenced by optimism (Maddox and Douglas 1973) or a great willingness to accept such limitation on the part of older people (Riley and Foner 1968, pp. 292–294); yet they are quite meaningful within a broad definition of health as a social reality (Maddox and Douglas 1973). Some additional questions, sometimes misleadingly labeled as measures of objective health status, may be less susceptible to mood or morale than these more-global assessments. Thus, we asked: Is there any physical condition, illness, or health problem that bothers you now? Fully 55 percent of men and 65 percent of women reported such a condition, and well over 90 percent of the conditions reported were coded as chronic. Reporting such a condition was directly related to age, and the relationship was particularly strong for women. Women were more likely than men in any of our age groups to report such a condition, and fully 85 percent of women in their eighties reported one.

The proportion who said that health problems cause no interference with the attainment of their goals falls regularly with increased age from about three-quarters to about one-half of men and women, while the proportion who said that health problems interfere a great deal rises to three of ten men in their eighties and four of ten women.

The experience of hospitalization increases regularly by age for both men and women, such that 19 percent of women and 16 percent of men in their seventies report having spent five or more days in a hospital during the previous year, with 23 percent of women and 29 percent of men in their eighties having done so.

These data point to situations during which a parent might have benefited by health care provided by another family member, perhaps a child, for acute or chronic illnesses. We also asked a specific question about the need for care of a chronic nature: Are you yourself currently in a position where you usually need help over a long period of time because of your health? None of our respondents in their forties reported the need for such help, and less than one in ten below the age of 80 did so. However, 20 percent of women and fully 36 percent of men in their eighties reported the need for such help on a continuing basis.

Considered together, these data suggest a quite healthy sample of people, with modestly declining health beyond the decade of the forties but greater decline apparent during the seventies and over the age of 80. While the proportion of respondents with severe health problems is not high until the seventies or eighties, the proportion who may be said to be in robust health begins to fall more quickly in the decades after the forties. This is evident, for example, in the consistent decline in the proportion of men or women saying their health problems cause no interference with their desired activities.

People, therefore, can reasonably come to be more concerned with the reality or the possibility of their own declining health as they grow older through and beyond the fourth decade. At the same time, people in their forties, fifties, and sixties are quite likely to have parents twenty to thirty or more years older than themselves for whom health difficulties are more a reality than a possibility. Health, then, is very much a family concern for people in the second half of life.

The Structure of Concern in Families:
Age and Sex Differences

In Canada, as in the United States, about one in five persons over age 65 is now over age 80 (for Canada, Denton and Spencer 1980, p. 20; for the United States, Shanas 1980, p. 279). As people are more likely to remain reasonably healthy until their seventies or even their eighties, their children in their forties and fifties may come to be increasingly concerned with monitoring their parents' health status, providing care as needed.

One measure of the concern children might have about the health of their parents was the question: How much do you worry about problems that might arise in the future should your parent become seriously ill or unable to look after himself or herself? Would you say . . . not at all, only a little, or a great deal? Seventeen percent of the children of our initial interview respondents said they worried not at all, but 36 percent said they worried a great deal.

Daughters were only somewhat more likely than sons to worry a great deal should a parent become ill (39 versus 30 percent). The increasing age of the child is associated with greater expressed concern but significantly so only for women. Sixty percent of daughters who are in their fifties or older claim to worry a great deal should one of their parents become ill in the future. Further details are presented in table 12-2.

Age of child, of course, bears some relationship to age of parent, and the older the parent, in general the more likely were children to worry about their future health. However, the relationship remained significant only for concerns about fathers, and much of the variability is due to concerns about very old parents—namely, fathers in their seventies or older and mothers in their eighties. There is just not a great deal of serious concern about the future health of mothers until the mothers reach their eighties, whereas concern about the fathers deepens as the fathers enter their seventies.

The nature of these concerns can be understood by drawing upon responses to a follow-up question to the previous one that asked the respondents to describe which problems they worried about and an additional question that asked: What is your main concern about your parent(s) now? These questions were answered in writing by the children of our initial interview respondents and in an interview situation by our respondents with reference to their own parents. The two data-gathering approaches yielded information suggesting similar concerns, as would be expected given the wide and overlapping age range of our parent sample and the derivative child sample.

Younger respondents tended to voice concerns that the parents' present good health might not last or that the parent was not adequately guarding his or her helath, as the following excerpts illustrate:

Table 12-2

Concerns about Parent's Future Health, by Age and Sex of Child and of Parent

Age	Not at All		Only a Little		A Great Deal		Row Ns	
	Son	Daughter	Son	Daughter	Son	Daughter	Son	Daughter
Age of Child[a]								
50 and older	15.8	25	36.8	14.3	47.4	60.7	19	28
40–49	15.2	18	39.4	46	45.5	36	33	50
30–39	29.5	6.8	50.8	53.4	19.7	39.7	61	73
Younger than 30	21.3	14.2	51.7	49.3	27	36.5	89	148
Column Ns	45	42	97	139	60	118	202	299
Age of Parent[b]	Mother	Father	Mother	Father	Mother	Father	Mother	Father
80 and older	30	16.7	20	33.3	50	50	30	18
70–79	18.2	8.8	47.7	43.9	34.1	47.4	44	57
60 69	22.7	10.5	42.4	68.4	34.8	21.1	66	38
50–59	21.2	12.9	45.2	54.5	33.7	32.7	104	101
40–49	16.7	27.3	50	54.5	33.3	18.2	36	11
N	60	28	120	118	100	79	280	225

[a]The relationship without controlling for sex shows significant age differences (X^2 = 14.52, df = 6, sign. = .03), and a trend toward greater concern expressed by older children (Tau C = .055, sign. = .077, with N = 501). Controlling for sex, a significant age difference persists for daughters only, but there is a trend for daughters and sons for increased age to be associated with increased concern. For sons, X^2 = 10.98, df = 6, sign. = .09, gamma = .138, Tau C = .090, sign. = .07. For daughters, X^2 = 16.59, df = 6, sign. = .01, gamma = .066, Tau C = .040, sign. = .207.

[b]Without controlling for sex, X^2 = .03. For fathers, raw X^2 = 13.72, df = 8, sign. = .09, gamma = .198, Tau C = .122, sign. = .02. For mothers, X^2 = 8.09, df = 6, sign. = .43, gamma = .02, Tau C = .018, sign. = .367.

She works too hard for her age. She should slow down a bit.

My mother is stubborn and doesn't take her medication until the last minute. I've tried to tell her to take nitro when she feels any pain.

Overwork, emotional strain of his occupation, the effect of his illness would have on my mother. I don't know what I'd do without him.

She is quite heavy which is not good for her heart or back. She should lose weight.

Some children expressed the wish that their parent would seek retirement or semiretirement or the hope that the parent would remain healthy enough to enjoy retirement or be able to shift from a very active life to one geared to declining health.

With increased age of the adult child, and correspondingly of the parent, specific incidents accentuate these concerns or may engender them. It might be ventured that children do not become overly concerned until a triggering event in the form of a health crisis is experienced by one of their parents. Our data support this, but with qualification. There is no relationship between a child's degree of concern and his or her parent's claim to have helped in a health crisis by a child (Tau C = .006, sign = .44). However, the more-direct test in this case is the relationship between perceived health crisis and degree of concern as both are defined by the child.

Based on the reports of the children, concerns about future problems if the parent should become seriously ill were related significantly to their own report of having helped one of their parents in a health crisis during the past year. (The question, unfortunately, did not distinguish between the parents. See table 12-3.)

The questionnaires returned by adult children of our interview respondents did not contain a direct question as to what might have stimulated such concern, but the interview respondents were asked this question with respect to their own parents, and their responses truly reflect the vicissitudes of age. Their concern was heightened, they reported, by observing memory loss and dizzy spells in their parents, by strokes, heart attacks, illnesses, hospitalizations, and ultimately, the death of one of their parents, leaving increased concern for the survivor, usually a widowed mother.

In the absence of a dramatic stimulus for concern, small events can build up a sense of anxiousness for the parent, as observed by a 57-year-old woman discussing her mother:

> [My main concern is] her health and the problems that come with old age, like forgetfulness and confusion. She complains a great deal. Just today for the first time she put something on high on the stove to heat, and then went to lie down. My son came in a while later and the house had started to fill with smoke. . . . I suppose I must consider these kinds of things in the future.

Consideration of such things, of course, is not a future but a present concern for this daughter. In fact, this consideration of age differences rests on a more-basic finding in which we find agreement with Neugarten (1979, p. 260) that concern for one's parents is found at all ages.

Data gathered through survey methods cannot capture the phenomenology of concern, but we have enough evidence to suggest a progressive

Table 12-3
Concerns about Parents' Future Health, by Provision of Health-Crisis
Help as Reported by Child and by Parent

Provision of Help		Not at All	Only A Little	A Great Deal	All	Row Ns
Child says provided	Men	16.3	32.6	46.7	33.3	66
health-crisis help	Women	31.7	46.8	56	48.3	143
to parent[a]	All	23.8	41	52.8	42.3	209
Parent says received health-crisis help from child[b]		81.8	76.9	79.3	78.6	505

[a]With 494 observations, Kendall's Tau C = −.206, sign. = .0000. For sons, N = 198, Tau C = −.230, sign. = .0007; for daughters, N = 296, Tau C = −.160, sign. = .005.
[b]With 505 observations based on child responses and multiple counting some parents, Kendall's Tau C = .006, sign. = .44.

increase, with aging of the parent and the child, in the degree of concern adult children feel for their parents, as well as changes in the definition of such concern. These definitional changes relate in many instances to issues of parental dependency or its threat and the ways in which this dependency can be affected by factors such as the geographical proximity of the child to the parent, the structural and social situation of the child, and the affection that may or may not link parents and children.

Continuing Independence as a Mutual Goal

Children in our study express a desire that their parents be able to remain independent. Independence usually is valued by all our interview respondents, of whom close to 90 percent in any age or sex group agree with the statement: I find it hard to have to depend on other people. However, that a parent might remain independent with increasing age has different and varied implications for the children. Children made many quite general statements expressing a worry or concern that their parents might lose their independence, as in the following:

I don't want her to lose her independence through illness.

I would not want her to get ill and have to live with someone. I would like to see her remain self-sufficient.

A child who said the degree of her worry about her mother fell in between our two coding categories of "only a little" and "a great deal" said:

> I worry that my mother could become ill, or fall, and be unable to contact anyone to get help, as she lives alone. Another concern is that she might attempt to manage on her own when she needs help, that she could be sick and alone.

It appears to be difficult to strike a balance between independence and dependence. While the preceding comment is from one child, a second child who says she worries a great deal puts the same concerns in a different interpretive framework. Her greatest worry, should her mother become ill in the future, is that:

> Loss of independence, especially physical, would devastate her. She would hate to feel a burden. I distrust institutions, but she would refuse to live with me.

The mother, in this child's view, is very independent and "appears to enjoy spending time alone, but I'm not so sure".

The interdependence of older parents and their children can be seen in the views of two daughters who see their parents as currently healthy. One, aged 45, said, "I'm the only daughter and I worry if she will need my help." Another, aged 53, said of her mother, "She's in better health than I am. There's only eighteen years between us. I worry that she'll be cared for if something happens to me". This respondent is not old, but she can see her own aging as occurring within the possible lifetime of her mother. With recent data, Shanas (1981) has noted that "for the majority of persons aged 80 and over and still living in the community a middle-aged child in the 50s and 60s or even older has assumed responsibility either for care in a joint household or for the provision of necessary services to nearby elderly parents that make life in the community possible for them." In such circumstances, worries about own health interact with concern about the health-related changes in need for assistance by the parent.

Distance Increases Concern

Some investigators distinguish between existing and functional kin. Cantor and McGloin (1977, cited in Tobin and Kulys 1980, p. 375) define a functional child or sibling "as one whom the elderly person sees at least once a month or with whom the elder is in phone contact weekly" (Tobin and

Kulys 1980, p. 375). Whereas they found 64 percent of an urban sample to have a living child, only 54 percent had a functional child. This distinction points to the importance of distance in affecting the extent to which children can provide a supportive system for parents experiencing health or other difficulties. We found that living at a distance from parents was a common source of increased concern among our respondents. One respondent's main concern is the following:

> I would prefer to live closer so that I would be available for assistance with transportation. Also, living so far away, I know nothing about medical facilities in [the parents'] area.

This adult child's main worry was:

> The primary problem of living at a distance and in another country. My parents would be unable to move to my home to be cared for. The necessity of long-distance travel to look after my parents, conflicting with my own responsibility with my family.

In many intergenerational studies, the members of different generations are entered into a sample only if they are proximate geographically, in order to reduce interviewing costs. Such studies might underestimate the importance of the familial bond at a greater distance. In our research, questionnaires were returned from Europe, Oceania, the United States, and all across Canada. The immigrant character of Canada, its expansiveness (several thousand miles from Atlantic to Pacific), and the nature of its economy that leads, in many cases and for many reasons, to geographical dispersion of families appear to have profound effects on intergenerational concern. Children are concerned that their parents might "become seriously ill when we live so far from them", and as a respondent put it:

> If one parent is left after the other's death. Living in England makes it difficult to be with them. Mother is an invalid so she couldn't come and live with me.

This sentiment was echoed by another child living in the United Kingdom who worries about "my parent dying and me (being the only unmarried daughter) being expected to give up home and job in England and return to Canada to care for my father."

Distance and the child's availability to provide care in other respects sometimes interact, as in the case of a respondent who worries a great deal about "who would look after her [mother] as I am a single parent 2,000 miles away."

Competing Obligations Increase Concern

As the previous examples illustrate, social characteristics such as being a woman or being single can increase the likelihood, in the eyes of the respondents, of being selected as caregiver, while characteristics such as being a single parent or being of an age or health status that is itself an at-risk characteristic can make the prospect of finding oneself in a caregiving role seem quite onerous. As Neugarten (1979, p. 263) argues, a child's relationship to an aging parent must always be considered in the context of others in the family unit. Thus, one 53-year-old woman whom we interviewed (4151) said she foresaw "no real problems really" because she felt either parent could look after herself or himself if the other died, but she also noted, "I have two sisters near them who can look after them."

The term *the caught generation* (Marcus 1978) describes the situation of middle-aged people, usually women, who find themselves torn between competing obligations toward aging parents and children, while frequently increasingly worried about the health of their spouses. As one adult child in this situation wrote on the questionnaire:

> My father has had several heart attacks and we live quite a distance from each other, and I worry that I can't be near him if anything should happen. And I have twins five years old and I can't leave easily to be with him.

The reality of the caught generation is also well illustrated in the words of one woman. Asked to describe what would worry her about her father should he become seriously ill, she said she would worry a great deal:

> Because my mother has always done all the shopping, housework, cooking, and general household chores. My father, who has been ill, is very dependent on her. Home care would be necessary to keep them both happy. I am not able to maintain two households.

Her main concern about her father at this time is the following:

> As an older arthritic wife with young children and an ailing husband, I am concerned that I will not be able to provide physical care for my aging parents. Hopefully their finances will allow paid help for their physical maintenance.

Note that these competing obligations do not imply a necessary diminution of concern for the parent but rather a conflict between such felt obligations. Returning to a consideration of table 12–2, we do find some evidence that some women, differently affected than men by age-related familial pressures, may decrease the amount of concern they express for their parents. This may reflect a deflection of concern to other generations. However, there are two reasons why we would not readily accept such an interpretation. The first is that our data do not allow a direct test, in that our data on felt obligations to or concern for family members other than the parent are not systematic. The second reason is that this logic implies that human beings possess a fixed and finite reservoir of concern. In this imagery of human emotion, concern can be siphoned out of the reservoir into other reservoirs, but a gain in the amount of concern stored in one place is matched by a loss in that stored in another. It seems ludicrous to us to treat concern, or other emotions like love, in zero-sum terms. Our data, in fact, suggest that concern grows in response to need without any arbitrary limits on the human capacity for such growth.

Concern for the health of a parent and the actual provision of care probably reinforce one another. At any rate, our cross-sectional data do not allow us to impute one-way causation. While it seems reasonable to suggest that a parental health crisis acts to indicate such concern or to reinforce existing concerns, the provision of health care, whether in a crisis situation or more routinely, probably is both response to and developer of such concern.

We also asked the children a question about general health care (which would include both crisis and routine care) provided to the specific parent we had interviewed. Children could signify whether or not they had provided personal care in illness to the parent during the previous year, and 28 percent said they had done so. Half of these were concerned a great deal about the future health of their parent, compared with just 30 percent of those who had not provided such help, and the relationship between concern and provision of help is both strong and significant (Tau C = −.163, sign = .0001, gamma = −.319).

Concern, Watchfulness, Interaction, and Perceived Closeness

The degree of concern about the future, should the parent become ill, was associated significantly with the chance that the child would describe the relationship with the parent as close or extremely close on a six-point scale of closeness (Tau C = .105, sign = .004) and with the frequency of contact with the parent in person or by telephone, as reported by the child. Of the 36 percent of our child respondents who claimed to worry a great deal about what would happen if a parent became ill, 48 percent claimed to have seen this parent "today or yesterday." Fully 60 percent said they usually saw the parent at least as often as once or twice a week, contrasted with just 43 percent of those who claimed not to be concerned about their parent in this way. Telephone contact was even more pervasive. Forty percent of our highly concerned children had spoken with their parent during the past two days and 70 percent within the past week.

Our overall data suggest close contact between most of our parents and the children from whom we gathered data, but even against the background of high contact, concern about the parent leads to even more contact, either for its own sake or, no doubt, because such contact is necessary in order for the child to be able to provide help in a general situation of need or in a time of crisis.

We think of this concern about the parent as a kind of watchfulness that develops in children as their parents grow older and begin to manifest signs that their health is no longer all that it used to be. Children come to monitor the health of their parents, and in many families, the children keep one another informed as to the health of the parents. We have shown that some family members are more directly involved in this watchfulness than others, depending upon age, sex, proximity, and other aspects of family structure. The analyses further suggest that such concern is structured in meaningful ways by age and sex of both the children and their parents.

As Neugarten has observed (1979, p. 261), while women still report more concern for their parents than men, the difference by sex is not strikingly large. We did find differences based on sex of the child and of the parent, but these interact with age. This interaction no doubt reflects in part the fact that women tend to remain healthier and to live longer than men. These differences also no doubt reflect the social dynamics of the family life course in a society in which women are still expected to be more involved in nurturance than men.

In our sociological interest with the basic demographics of age and sex, we should not, however, lose sight of the apparently strong and appropriate matching of care and watchful health monitoring to the needs of the parent. This leads, if you will, to a more-situational than structural interpretation of the dynamics of health care in the family.

Summary and Conclusion

While the health of most people remains quite good until they reach their seventies or eighties, advanced age is recognized as increasing the risks of illness and loss of independence. In response to and in anticipation of such changes, adult children often become increasingly concerned about their parents's health and about the ways in which their own lives will be affected by the needs of their parents. The stimulus for such concerns is affected by differential morbidity and mortality (or life expectancy) of women and men. The extent of such concern is affected by differential expectations for filial responsibility that are held for, and often by, women and men. In addition, other family-status variables such as single parenthood or number of siblings can act to increase or decrease the worries of the generation of adult children, while increased geographical distance and competing career or familial obligations will increase the degree of concern.

Few of the adult children of our interview respondents expressed no concern at all about a parent becoming seriously ill or unable to maintain self-care, while over a third said they worried a great deal. In general, daughters worry more than sons, and fathers are worried about more than mothers. Worrying, and also being worried about, in general increases with age of parent and adult child. The exceptions to these generalizations most likely result from pressures on women in their forties to be concerned for other family members such as the spouse and children who are struggling to establish their own families. However, having not accounted for these exceptions with data, for the present our central conclusion must be to note the general structuring of concern by age and sex of parent and child, leaving a detailed consideration of the reasons for this structuring to future analyses by ourselves and others. We have also shown a high degree of concern for parents regardless of the age and sex of the children. This is an important yet, we believe, largely neglected aspect of the experience of being a member of a family, against which the various patterns of heightened concern must be seen as variations on a theme.

Concern can build up as individually trifling incidents or characteristics are cumulatively noted by the children: A parent's forgetfulness, a mild illness, episodes of irritability or depression on the part of the parent, while in themselves not necessarily major, can become linked into a pattern that initiates or increases the worries of the child.

As worries for the sake of the parent increase, worries about the implications of progressive dependence of the parent for the child's life also increase. This works in two ways. A child can worry that her or his life will be disturbed or because features of that life, like living at a great distance from the parent, might make it difficult or impossible to provide needed care.

We found only a small amount of evidence of a reluctance or unwillingness to provide care. One respondent worried that having a widowed mother would lead to conflicts over childrearing practices and life-style, and there were some expressions, both with and without regret, that the respondent or a sibling felt alienated from the parent. As one said, "I have no concern about him, as he has chosen not to include me in his life." It is possible that greater lack of concern might have been identified by children whose addresses were not provided to us by their parent or who did not return the questionnaire.

In most instances, care will probably be provided, even if reluctantly. One would hesitate to moralize about the goodwill of the respondent who said: "I have looked after both parents for twenty-seven years and they have become very dependent on me. We are very tied down and I don't know how much more my nerves and health can stand."

As in many other studies, we found evidence of what has come to be called the caught generation of women (but also some men) who find themselves torn between competing obligations to parents, children, and spouses; and we also found evidence of people worried that the need to care for an ill parent might interfere with career fulfillment. However, we did not find evidence that such conflicts led to callousness on the part of adult children. Instead, concern about parents seems most directly related to perceived need of the parent for assistance. As often has been found in contemporary studies of intergenerational relations (for reviews, see Abu-Laban 1980; Brody 1978; Maddox 1975; Shanas 1979; Tobin and Kulys 1980), perceived closeness between the generations was found to be high in our sample, and interaction in the form of visits and telephone contact was also high; however, both closeness and interaction were heightened when the parent had been ill and in need of assistance. This runs counter to some claims that parents who pose a burden on their children may alienate them.

While we have focused on structural patterns of concern or worry about the health status of parents, the previous point suggests a more-situational interpretation of the genesis and course of concern for the parent. It may be that family life leads, in the normal case, to the development of a vast reserve of affection and obligation, which may never be mobilized but which is there if needed by the parent.

These conclusions must be judged in the context of several limitations of this analysis. Although this is not a constraint of the research project, in this preliminary analysis we have focused on dyadic relations. It would be desirable to examine the structuring of concern within the context of whole families—that is, within the broader context of family members (Maddox 1975, pp. 321–322). How is concern for the parent affected by variables such as birth order, number of siblings, patterns of geographical proximity, and the relationship of parental obligations to obligations toward the spouse's parents (Brody 1978, p. 17)? These are but some of the questions that would need to be answered before a clear understanding of concern for parents might be gained.

Another important limitation of the present analysis is our inattention to class and ethnic differences. We have restricted our analysis to developing a general picture of the adult child's concern for the parent, but future analyses will be based on the assumption that the degree and the nature of such concern will vary by class and ethnicity. Dowd and Bengtson (1978), with a U.S. comparison between whites, blacks and Mexican-Americans, found increasing age to be a leveler of ethnic differences in familial interaction. Reviewing the literature on class differences in kinship relations, Troll, Miller, and Atchley (1979, p. 101) conclude that class differences are not as large as sex differences. However, they focus almost exclusively on helping relationships, and in any case, were differences in concern less strong by class and ethnicity than by sex, this does not mean they should be disregarded.

Readers should also bear in mind that the methodology might well produce a bias against the reporting of conflict between the generations. Children were entered into the sample by parents, who for various reasons did not provide the addresses of one-fourth of their children; and one-fourth of those children to whom questionnaires were sent did not return them. At both stages, respondent loss may be weighted toward those children who do not maintain close relationships with or manifest high concern for their parents. Nonetheless, we do not see an easy way out of this methodological difficulty.

Finally, in this analysis we have focused exclusively on the real or perceived needs of the parental generation for help due to changes in health. We have thereby ignored the wider context of needs and assistance of which health is but one, albeit a major, example, and perhaps more important, we have not here considered assistance provided by the parental generation in response to the real or perceived needs of their children. In fact, our data reveal extensive, two-directional help on many dimensions, with parents, for example, providing more financial assistance to children than they receive from them, while children provide more assistance with activities of daily living and help in a health crisis to parents than they receive from them.

In one of the rare studies that explicitly deals with the child's concern about parents, Lieberman (1978) asked a number of questions about age-related changes in their parents and parents-in-law of a sample of 807 children between the ages of 20 and 70. Not only health changes but also financial difficulties and dependence on the child for advice and moral support, time, energy, and money were inquired about, and parent concern was evaluated on a scale measuring the extent to which these changes had bothered or preoccupied respondents. Health changes were reported with much greater frequency than financial changes, but analyses are reported for a combined measure. In addition, parents and parents-in-law were combined because there were no differences found in the relations of the children.

In the resulting analysis, no significant differences were found by age or sex in perception of the changes or the extent to which the respondent was bothered by such changes. These measures would be similar to our measures of concern for the parent. Age and sex did, however, discriminate respondents who relied on informal helping networks from those who went to professionals for help. Those who went to professionals were much more likely to be women and to be over 30 years old. Lieberman concludes that "concern about parental change is not, as often assumed, a specifically mid-life issue, but rather one which is at hand throughout the range of adult life for significant numbers of people" (Lieberman 1978, p. 496). This finding is consistent with our own, although we did find significant sex and age differences overlain on generally high levels of concern for the parent. Our findings are also consistent with the following conclusion by Lieberman (1978):

> The young adult is more likely to be one of several people to play a supportive role in meeting increasing needs of his parents; the major burden may well be taken by the other parent or an older relative. In contrast, in later life, the responsibility for direct care may rest entirely on the middle-aged or "young-old" child. [p. 496]

Our Canadian data are consistent with the findings of this somewhat broader analysis based on U.S. data. The fact that we found greater sex and age differences than Lieberman calls for further investigation, as does the difference between our focus on health concerns and her wider focus of parental concern. However, a detailed analysis of these broader contexts of concern is beyond the scope of this chapter (but see Rosenthal, Marshall, and Synge 1981a; 1981b).

Maddox (1975), also speaking of the United States, makes a point that is probably equally applicable to the Canadian context of our research:

> [E]ffective parents strive to make themselves dispensible to their children. Families, in essence, are programmed to self-destruct in the sense that children become emotionally detached from their parents. . . . But a decade of research has demonstrated that the characterization of detached generations has been considerably overdrawn. [p. 330]

Most of the research that has shown that the generations are not detached from one another has focused on interaction and exchange of goods and services. We have drawn attention here to another aspect of attachment between children and parents—namely, the concern they have for one another. Concern for the parent, with its concomitant stance of worried watchfulness, is a socially patterned and highly prevalent social bond between the generations.

Notes

1. This is a report of the Generational Relations and Succession Project (GRASP), funded by the Social Sciences and Humanities Research Council of Canada through grant number 492-79-0076-R1. Additional sup-

port has been provided by the National Health Research Development Program of Health and Welfare Canada through a National Health Scientist award to Victor Marshall and by the Office on Aging, McMaster University. Invaluable staff support has been provided by Brenda Nussey, Christine Davis, and Margaret Denton. We are particularly grateful to the many people who were interviewed or who completed questionnaires for the study.

2. To obtain 464 completions, we attempted to contact 1,081 persons, drawing new cases randomly as needed. We could not locate 117 persons, of whom 30 were known to be deceased and 68 known to have moved. This left 964 contacted persons, of whom 116, or 12 percent, could not speak or write English. Subtracting language ineligibles leaves a total of 848 eligible contacted persons, from which base we calculate the following rates: 12 percent excluded because their own health was too poor or they were preoccupied with the ill health or death of another family member; 33 percent refusal; 55 percent completion.

References

Abu-Laban, S.M. "The Family Life of Older Canadians." In *Aging in Canada: Social Perspectives,* edited by Victor W. Marshall, pp. 125–134. Toronto: Fitzhenry and Whiteside, 1980.

Brody, E.M. "The Aging of the Family." *Annals, American Association of Political and Social Science* 438 (1978):13–27.

Cantor, M.H., and J. McGloin. "Friends and Neighbors—An Overlooked Resource in the Informal Support Systems." Paper presented at the Thirtieth Annual Meeting of the Gerontological Society of America, San Francisco, 1977.

Comptroller General of the United States. *Report to the Congress: The Well-Being of Older People in Cleveland, Ohio.* Washington, D.C.: General Accounting Office, 1977.

Denton, F.T., and B.G. Spencer. "Canada's Population and Labor Force: Past, Present, and Future." In *Aging in Canada: Social Perspectives,* edited by Victor W. Marshall, pp. 10–26. Toronto: Fitzhenry and Whiteside, 1980.

Dowd, J.J., and V.L. Bengtson. "Aging in Minority Populations: An Examination of the Double Jeopardy Hypothesis." *Journal of Gerontology* 33 (1978):427–436.

Lieberman, G.L. "Children of the Elderly as Natural Helpers." *American Journal of Community Psychology* 6 (1978):489–498.

Maddox, G.L. "Families as Context and Resource in Chronic Illness." In *Long Term Care: A Handbook for Researchers, Planners and Pro-*

viders, edited by Sylvia Sherwood, pp. 317–347. New York: Spectrum Publications, 1975.

———. "Sociology of Later Life." *Annual Review of Sociology* 5 (1979): 113–135.

Maddox, G.L., and E.B. Douglas. "Self-Assessment of Health: A Longitudinal Study of Elderly Subjects." *Journal of Health and Social Behavior* 14 (1973):87–93.

Marcus, Lotte. "The Situation of the Elderly and Their Families: Problems and Solutions." Paper presented at the National Symposium on Aging, National Bureau on Aging, Ottawa, 1978.

Neugarten, B.L. "The Middle Generations." In *Aging Parents,* edited by Pauline K. Ragan, pp. 258–265. Los Angeles: University of Southern California Press, 1979.

Pratt, L. *Family Structure and Effective Health Behavior.* Boston, Houghton Mifflin, 1976.

Rakowski, W., and T. Hickey. "Late Life Health Behavior: Integrating Health Beliefs and Temporal Perspectives." *Research on Aging* 2 (1980):283–308.

Riley, M.W., and A. Foner, eds. *Aging and Society. Volume I: An Inventory of Research Findings.* New York: Russell Sage Foundation, 1968.

Rosenthal, C.J.; V.W. Marshall; and J. Synge. "The Head of the Family: Authority and Responsibility in the Lineage." Paper presented at the Tenth Annual Meeting of the Canadian Association on Gerontology in conjunction with the Thirty-fourth Annual Scientific Meeting of the Gerontological Society of America, Toronto, November 1981a.

———. "Maintaining Intergenerational Relations: Kinkeeping." Paper presented at the Tenth Annual Meeting of the Canadian Association on Gerontology in conjunction with the Thirty-fourth Annual Scientific Meeting of the Gerontological Society of America, Toronto, November 1981b.

Shanas, E. "The Psychology of Health." In *Old People in Three Industrial Societies,* edited by Ethel Shanas, P. Townsend, D. Wedderburn, H. Friis, P. Milhoj, and J. Stehouwer, pp. 49–70. New York: Atherton Press, 1968.

———. "Social Myth as Hypothesis: The Case of the Family Relations of Old People." *The Gerontologist* 19 (1979):3–9.

———. "Self-Assessment of Physical Function: White and Black Elderly in the United States." In *Second Conference on the Epidemiology of Aging,* edited by Suzanne G. Haynes et al., Bethesda, Md.: National Institute on Aging, 1980.

———. "Older Parents: Middle-Aged Children." Paper presented at meetings of International Association of Gerontology, Hamburg, 11–17 July 1981.

Streib, G.F. "The Aged, the Family, and Society: A Sociological View." Paper presented at the Thirty-third Annual Scientific Meeting of the Gerontological Society of America, San Diego, November 1980.

Sussman, M.B. "Family, Bureaucracy, and the Elderly Individual: An Organizational/Linkage Perspective." In *Family, Bureaucracy, and the Elderly,* edited by Ethel Shanas and Sussman, pp. 2–20. Durham, N.C.: Duke University Press, 1977.

Tobin, S.S., and R. Kulys. "The Family and Services." In *Annual Review of Gerontology and Geriatrics,* edited by Carl Eisdorfer, pp. 370–399. New York: Springer Publishing, 1980.

Treas, J. "Family Support Systems for the Aged: Some Social and Demographic Considerations." *The Gerontologist* 17 (1977):486–499.

Troll, L.E.; S.J. Miller; and R.C. Atchley. *Families in Later Life.* Belmont, Calif.: Wadsworth Publishing Co., 1979.

13 The Final Challenge: Facing Death

Kay O'Laughlin

I called up my sister and told her not to apply for elderly housing. It's too depressing. All you see is illness and death. Three people have died this month. You see the ambulance pull up and you wonder who it is this time.
—A retired woman who has lived in elderly housing for five years

Older women face a multitude of losses. Those who are married are likely to outlive their husbands and enter widowhood. As their children become grown, older women give up much of the active mothering role that has filled their time for many years. Career women face retirement and the loss of a work role valued by society. Many older women face the loss of health, mobility, and connectedness with other people. The older a woman lives to be, the more friends she loses to death. In the final challenge, she faces her own death. It is sad that these struggles receive little recognition or support from a society that has overvalued youth, that is just beginning to appreciate middle age, and that still recoils from old age.

Until a few generations ago, most people were born at home and died at home, and everyone lived more intimately with death. The problem of death was not relegated to old age. Young people died with almost as much frequency as old. Changing death patterns (reduced infant mortality and maternal childbirth mortality and longer life expectancies) have allowed us to consign the issue of death to old age. In present U.S. culture, death has been distanced and denied, often in a most sophisticated fashion. The distancing of death corresponds to societal patterns of devaluing the elderly, especially old women, and of depending on institutional care provided by hospitals and nursing homes.

Denial of death in the past half-century has been studied and documented.[1] With the recent exploration of this denial of death has come a realization of its profound and far-reaching consequences. Most people of either sex are ill prepared to cope with death personally or to aid family or friends in mourning. For women, the problem is particularly striking. While women today can expect to outlive their spouses as much as an average of 18.5 years, as many as two-thirds of all widows may never consider the possibility of widowhood prior to their husband's death.[2]

In a professional context, the denial of death impedes the ability of

275

caregivers to aid dying patients and their families. Perhaps the most extreme example of this is what has been called the abandonment of the dying patient by medical personnel.[3] Generalized denial of death has the profound effect of increasing the psychological isolation of the elderly, who are shunned by younger people for being reminders of the inevitability of aging and death.[4] The ability—or inability—of medical and social-service professionals to cope with death becomes more salient when one considers that more people now die in hospitals or nursing facilities than in their own homes.[5]

Mourning

Older women, by necessity, become mourners. Unfortunately, just as society tends to deny death, it tends to deny mourning. The dynamics of mourning have received relatively little attention in the psychological literature. That bereavement has been studied so little can be attributed more to inertia, taboo, and inherent methodological difficulties than to the obscurity of the problem. Theorists describe mourning as both an intrapsychic and a social process, though they have not agreed on whether mourning is a normal human process or a pathological one. Most describe a continuum with one end indicating normal grief and the other indicating pathological grief.[6] Gorer explored the current cultural links between denial of death and decline of mourning whereby mourning is treated as a weakness and a self-indulgence rather than as a psychological necessity.

The mourner, too, is viewed typically by others as a burden, for she or he is not cooperating with the so-called fun morality—that is, that everyone has an ethical duty to enjoy oneself as much as possible and to do nothing that diminishes the enjoyment of others. Gorer stressed the implications of these attitudes for society, saying that "if one can deny one's own grief, how much more easily can one deny the grief of others, and one possible outcome of the public denial of mourning is a great increase in public callousness."[7] Kreis and Pattie made similar observations: "We have fallen into a dangerous pattern of avoiding grief, of treating it as a necessary evil, of reacting mechanically. . . . Grief does not fit our way of life, therefore neither does the mourner except for a short period."[8]

However, mourning is necessary for mental and physical health. The dangers of failure to mourn have been well documented and include arrested personality development, physical and mental illness, and even suicide as oucomes both of failure to mourn and of the lack of social support for the bereaved.[9]

The extent of sex differences in the mourning process has not been documented thoroughly, but it is apparent the women face some special problems. For instance, among today's elderly, when a woman loses her husband, she also may lose much of her own identity and her place in a social network. The elderly widow receives mixed messages about her expected behavior. She is supposed to become reclusive and to identify herself as a widow (for example, by wearing mourning attire), and at the same time she is not to burden others with her pain.

Mourning is not a fixed, invariable process for all people. There is some evidence that among women the intensity of mourning varies according to age and the type of death the spouse experienced. For example, Ball found that young widows (under age 46) had stronger grief reactions than middle-aged and elderly widows. Ball explained that "for the young person sudden death creates a more threatening situation, while in the older person prolonged death puts more stress on the coping ability of the survivor and weakens the defenses, physically and mentally."[10] She noted that most of the widows in her study felt worse one month after their husband's death than at the time of death; the friends and relatives who had offered immediate support withdrew by the end of the month. Carey also found that there was a significant age factor in widows' adjustments; older widows were better adjusted. Carey suggested that this difference may be a reflection of younger widows' feeling cheated by their mate's short life span.[11]

Sheskin and Wallace, studying the ways that widows' bereavements differed according to cause of death (suicide, natural, and accidental death), found that anticipation was an important factor in a wife's ability to accept her husband's death and to make a healthy adjustment afterward. Unanticipated deaths were associated with the most difficult and severe bereavement reactions.[12] Apparently, the knowledge that death is approaching allows anticipatory grief work and forces the wife to begin to redefine her role and to imagine a changed life-style. Often, a woman caring for a dying husband assumes many new roles and responsibilities that may have a positive relationship to her adjustment after death. However, there is a negative side to the assumption of new responsibilities, as Sheskin and Wallace point out: The wife may become so preoccupied with her dying husband's needs that she isolates herself from friends and sources of support that she will need later.

Many widows encounter rigid social expectations of how they ought to feel and act, and those who stray from the stereotype risk censure. Sheskin and Wallace found that many widows whose husbands had suffered from a debilitating illness or who had committed suicide experienced a measure of relief after the death.[13] The relief was associated with release from intolerable stress. However, the emotion of relief often had to be disguised because it was not an acceptable component of bereavement. The widows of suicides especially were stigmatized and often blamed themselves or were blamed by others for their husband's demise. In general, they received less support from friends and caretakers and were the target of more questioning and criticism. Thus, it appears that the mourning and readjustment process for widows of suicides may be unusually difficult and prolonged.

Some research suggests sex differences in bereavement and mourning, but those differences have not been clearly defined. Carey, for example, found that adjustment was more difficult for widows than for widowers at all ages. He speculated that the widow's adjustment is more problematic because a woman tends to lose part of her identity when her husband dies and because men remarry much more easily (and thus move into a new support system). Furthermore, widows are likely to have problems with finances and decision making if those tasks had been part of the male role. Carey also found that anticipatory grief was an important factor in a widow's adjustment but not in a widower's. He suggested that women may need a longer grieving period than men or that women may have formed deeper emotional attachments.[14] Elaborating on this concept, it is also possible that men have been socialized to deny their grief more and to move more quickly in restructuring their lives. Obviously, remarriage is more feasible for older men than for older women; they have more potential mates within their age group and have much more freedom to select a mate from a younger age group. Health and mortality statistics, however, contradict the notion of easier adjustment for widowers. They are more prone to illnesses, emotional disturbances, and early death than widows of a matched group. Clearly, more research is needed on sex differences in bereavement and mourning, with an eye to interventions that will foster healthy adjustments.

Death Attitudes

In talking with elderly women about death, it is apparent that attitudes toward death are extremely complex. There is no single, unidimensional attitude, no one concept that can be measured easily. They have fears, anxieties, doubts, desires, and hopes. They have negative feelings, positive feelings, and ambivalent feelings. They may feel one way about the death of loved ones and very different about their own death. One of the most useful distinctions in viewing death attitudes came from Collett and Lester. They emphasized the need to separate attitudes in terms of death and dying and self and other. A person may have one attitude about death (the state of being dead) and a very different attitude about the experience and process of dying. Also, contemplating one's own death and dying may tap different emotions than contemplating the death or dying of other people.[15]

Research studies of attitudes toward death have explored only a small area of the total possible realm of investigation.[16] For example, most studies

have been done with college-student samples, and students' attitudes, obviously, are likely to be different from those of middle-aged or elderly people
who have experienced death and mourning time and time again and who are
closer to their own deaths.

For many years there has been a taboo on talking with old people about
death, perhaps based on an assumption that old people are afraid of death
and that talking about it would only increase their fears. A variety of
investigators, however, have challenged this premise. For example, Cole
found that older people tend to experience lower levels of death anxiety
than younger people,[17] Martin and Wrightsman reported a tendency for
older people to report less fear of death,[18] and Swenson concluded that
older people are noted for their fear of death and that those in poor health
may look forward to death.[19] Indeed, Spilka found a negative correlation
between fear of death and age.[20]

Throwing further doubt on the belief that death is a taboo topic among
the old, Wass and colleagues interviewed elderly people and found that they
were willing and even eager to discuss death-related themes. Not only was
the majority neither anxious nor upset by the topic, but also they indicated
that they would prefer to know the truth about terminal illness and would
want to die a natural death rather than to have life prolonged by artificial
means.[21] Bell found that in a geriatric sample, the health of a respondent's
spouse was more significantly related to the person's death attitudes than
was her or his own health. In situations where a spouse exhibited poor
health, respondents demonstrated greater fears related to their own death.[22]
Weisman and Hackett noted that for many people the fear of impairment is
greater than the fear of death.[23]

Elderly men and women do not view death with the same thoughts and
feelings, according to some surveys, although findings are inconsistent.
Some studies report men have higher death anxiety than women; some
report women have higher anxiety; some report no differences. Vernon has
summarized findings of numerous studies on this issue.[24] To review briefly,
three studies (Swenson, Christ, and Rhudick and Dibner) found no sex
difference in death anxiety.[25] Jeffers and colleagues noted that elderly men
had greater fear of death than elderly women.[26] Diggory and Rothman,
observing that women feared bodily dissolution more than men, also
reported that women expressed more fear about the pain of dying, while
men focused concern on care of dependents.[27] Spilka found sex differences
in three of nine dimensions he studied: Women showed greater belief that
death is related to pain, punishment, and failure.[28] McDonald found
women had higher levels of death anxiety than men did.[29] Blumenfield,
Levy, and Kaufman noted a significant sex difference in whether people
would want to be informed of a fatal illness: 92 percent of men and 87 percent of women said they would want to be informed.[30] As this brief recapit-

ulation of research on gender-linked differences in death anxiety indicates, the findings to date are far from conclusive, often contradictory, and reflect various methodological and sampling approaches to the study of this constellation of attitudes.

What, then, may one conclude from the morass of inconsistent findings? Regardless of which sex fears death more, older women, as noted earlier, face a series of deaths of important people. The most obvious loss is the death of a mate, which catapults a woman into widowhood. Death of friends, though less frequently addressed, also seems to have a strong emotional impact on an older woman's well-being. Finally, and least frequently discussed, is the older woman's process of facing her own mortality. In the following sections of this chapter, older women's reactions to widowhood, deaths of friends, and approaching their own deaths are discussed. I draw on research of other investigators, as well as my own, that has involved interviews and discussion groups conducted with elderly people, primarily women. My research investigated the attitudes toward death held by an urban, elderly population and tested a treatment model aimed at decreasing fear of death. The treatment consisted of a series of workshops in which participants discussed aging, loss, and death in relation to their values and philosophies. Results are discussed later in this chapter.

Widowhood

For most women, facing old age also means facing widowhood. One woman in six in the United States over the age of 21 is a widow.[31] While there are about 10 million widows in the United States, there are only about 2 million widowers. Women tend to be widowed before age 60 and to live into old age as widows.[32] Remarriage is the exception rather than the norm, since women greatly outnumber men in the upper age groups of the population.

As a group, widows are economically and educationally disadvantaged. They have the lowest income of any segment of our population.[33] The average widow lives on little more than $6,000 a year.[34] The stereotype of the U.S. widow as wife of a middle- or upper-class executive is fallacious; a disproportionate number of widows are from economically disadvantaged backgrounds.[35] The average number of years of education for widows is lower than the mean for all U.S. women. The picture for minority women is even bleaker than the average; they are likely to have the lowest incomes, least education, and are least likely to be able to live independently.[36]

The problems of widows have been largely ignored by the public and even by mental-health professionals. Certainly our neglect of widows is connected both to denial of death and to women's secondary status in society.

Several researchers have noted that when a woman's husband dies, she loses her status and even much of her identity.[37] This is most likely to be true for older or traditionally socialized women. Thus, the widow is faced with enormous tasks. Not only must she grieve for her husband and cope with her changing social and financial status, but also she must forge a new identity for herself with little help from others.

Of course, some widows are able to cope with changing times and to redefine personal roles and goals. These women are emotional survivors. An example of this type of widow is an outgoing woman of 80, whom I met in an interview study. In the past few years she completed undergraduate studies, earned a master's degree in philosophy, and continues to audit courses that interest her. She lives in elderly housing where she has numerous friends. She knows and uses community resources to help her with any problems of health, finances, and transportation.

Another group of widows who are survivors are those who still belong to a closely knit family or peer-group system and who find the parameters of their lives changed relatively little by the loss of a spouse. An illustration of this, again drawn from my interviews, is an active woman of 75 who lives in a senior-citizens' apartment building. She is in touch daily with two sisters who live in the area, and she has friends in her building. She paints, knits, and attends exercise classes and a discussion group. She says:

> My life did not change when my husband died. He used to sit in the living room all day and watch TV. I'd be in the other room, painting or writing, or I'd go out to visit my friends. I still do all those things. I think for a man it would be more difficult [to be a widower] because he'd have to learn to do new things like cooking for himself.

Widows like this woman, who belong to tightly knit family or peer systems, are not spared the grief work, but they do not have the concomitant burdens of finding new activities and developing new support systems.

Lopata pointed out that traditionally socialized widows often find themselves to be social isolates who are unable to function in a changed society that does not recognize their needs or give them meaningful roles. Lopata sees widows as increasing in number and in need of societal resources to improve the quality of their lives. The withdrawal of these women from mainstream society may be a reflection of helplessness and inability to keep up with a rapidly changing world rather than a voluntary disengagement.[38]

In my own research on poor, urban, elderly women, I have often met widows who fit the category of the social isolate. They are women caught between two worlds. For example, Mrs. D., a woman in her fifties, was widowed several years ago. Her husband died suddenly in a shocking accident, and she was notified of his death in an impersonal manner over the telephone. Mrs. D. has little contact with her family, who disapproved of the marriage in the first place, and no contact with her husband's family. She has several health problems that prohibit her from working steadily. With no savings and a meager income from SSI, she is forced to live in a run-down rooming house in a tough area. She says she has not cried for her husband and feels that she must be strong. However, she has had three heart attacks, each occurring on an anniversary of their marriage or of his death.

Mrs. A., a widow in her eighties, lived quietly, kept to herself, and escaped notice of her neighbors in a senior citizens' apartment building until she began to dress inappropriately, lose her keys, and had a small kitchen fire. Her building manager made a referral to a geriatric outreach worker. Whenever Mrs. A. mentions her husband, who died thirty years ago, her eyes fill with tears. She sometimes believes that he is still living with her and says things like "I saw him in that chair this morning . . . sitting there, smiling at me."

Both of these widows may be considered to have pathological grief reactions and other psychiatric problems (Mrs. A. was diagnosed as having an organic brain syndrome). However, it is apparent that neither woman had support from family, friends, or professionals at strategic points in the grieving and readjustment processes. As noted earlier, grieving is both an endopsychic and a social process. The willingness of others to aid the mourner may help the grieving process—and their unwillingness may impede it.

In interviews and group sessions I have conducted with the elderly, the death of a spouse typically was acknowledged as a trauma that people never get over (surpassed only by the painfulness of losing a child, which was described as the wrong order of things). Some comments from widows follow:

> Nothing is more traumatic. There's no end to the pain.

> When your loved one is taken away from you, when you're used to having a houseful and all of a sudden you're left alone—that's another downhill.

> I feel that I'm young enough at heart. . . . I want that companion of mine to be with me, to go here and there. This is holding me back; that I can't do the things I'd love to do if my husband was alive.

An elderly single woman stated emphatically:

> I'm glad now I never married. When I see people who lose a spouse . . . they are devastated.

Loneliness is a major problem for widows. The loneliness stems from many sources. A widow may lose friends who were primarily her husband's friends. She may be left out of social events comprised of couples. She may be perceived as a threat to other women since she is presumed stereotypically to be in search of another husband. The widow is also a painful reminder of the reality and immediacy of death. The decline of mourning rituals means that most people are uncertain about how to treat a widow. Friends may assume she prefers to be alone, or they may stay away, not knowing what to do or say. It is thus not surprising that widows frequently report that other widows are their best sources of support. Silverman, who pioneered the widow-to-widow program, lists various reasons that a new widow may accept help from another widow more readily than from professional caretakers. As she noted:

> With another widow it is not necessary to justify or clarify how she feels. She feels she is not alone; that someone else has gone through this. The perspective from talking to another widow helps her to understand and accept her feelings as normal and natural. A widow who helps others is a model for the future. Another widow is a teacher who can help her with concrete problems. She serves as a bridge to the widowed community and then to the community at large.[39]

Other writers have noted that another widow is likely to understand the urges to make major (and sometimes ill-advised) decisions or the temptations to turn to drugs or alcohol as a means of coping.[40] Lindsay described the upheaval and disorganization of the widow's life with the phrase *the first-year crazies,* another concept most readily understood by a widow who has lived through it.[41]

It may be that widow-to-widow programs are the most effective interventions for the newly bereaved woman. However, it is appalling that in our society widows have been left to help themselves and that few interventions have been offered or tested. Few professional agencies have programs specifically focused on the needs of the widowed. The Widows Consultation Center in New York opened in 1969 as the first professional social-work agency in the country devoted to the problems of widows.[42] The fact that this was the first such agency may be construed as an indicator of the intensity of death denial in this culture and also as an indicator of the low status ascribed to older women. Lindsay points out that even feminist women's groups have failed to address the problems of widows in any major way.[43]

Indeed, most research on widows is of a descriptive nature. Few studies have explored interventions to help widows cope with bereavement and adjustment to new life-styles and the myriad of associated pressures. One study involving widows documented the usefulness of therapy groups for bereaved women. In 1977, Barrett conducted a study of therapeutic interventions for widows.[44] Subjects were placed in three types of therapy groups: self-help, confidante (paired with another widow in a helping relationship), and women's consciousness raising. Subjects in all groups showed increased self-esteem and joy in womanhood. Subjects in the consciousness-raising group reported the most positive life changes. The fact that women in all three groups arranged to continue meeting after the research ended attest to the need of many widows for ongoing support.

Deaths of Friends

While the death of a husband is recognized as very traumatic, the impact of deaths of friends who form an elderly woman's support network has received very little attention. Most elderly people live in urban settings, and urban elderly women tend to be without families or isolated from them.[45] Hess and Markson report that the role of friend becomes especially salient in old age and that having contact with close friends correlates with satisfaction and with mental health.[46] Yet those women who develop friendships with other elderly are precisely those most likely to be affected seriously by deaths among their cohorts. Mason found that experience with deaths of others explained the most variance in measured fear of death in her study of elderly black women—that is, those who had experienced the deaths of many friends demonstrated the highest levels of death anxiety and had the most negative conceptualizations of death. It is interesting that the impact of deaths of relatives may be different from deaths of friends. On the one hand, in Mason's sample it appeared that those women who had experienced the deaths of many relatives had few negative thoughts about death, little fear of their own impending death, and few inconsistent thoughts about death. On the other hand, women who had experienced the deaths of many friends had many negative thoughts about death, suggesting that deaths of friends are more emotionally significant to the elderly than deaths of family members. Mason explained, "This emerges in light of the fact that an elderly person's family has, for the most part, been gradually whittled away by death over many years, whereas the deaths of friends are more recent and thereby more immediately painful and a reminder of the persons' own vulnerability.[47]

   Mason's findings seem relevant to the situation of many elderly women who are living in age-segregated apartment buildings, where they frequently observe illness and death among their friends and peers. This situation suggests the need for structured therapeutic interventions, and it has implications for housing policies. While congregate and age-segregated housing offers many benefits to the elderly, it also places them in direct contact with deaths of numerous peers. A recent review of the literature revealed no studies of the relationship between time in elderly housing and fear of death. Bell studied patterns of interaction and life satisfaction of elderly people in congregate housing and found a suggestion of decreasing satisfaction and interaction with time in the congregate setting. Bell concluded that "the data suggest the congregate setting to possess insufficient resources to offset the objective and subjective decrements of old age."[48]

In death-attitude research among the elderly, I have found a recurrent theme of strong emotional reactions to observing or hearing about the deaths of friends and neighbors. Perhaps the most numerous and emotion-laden comments concern the frequency and visibility of illness and deaths of neighbors. The thematic material implied a connection between seeing deaths of peers and increasing awareness of one's own mortality. A common reaction seemed to be withdrawal from intimacy and a negative stereotyping of other elderly people in the building. For example, these comments from elderly women:

> I'm all alone here. If I were sick or died in here, no one would know [with tears in her eyes]. No one cares. The old people here are so negative. They've given up living. They're stagnant, feel no excitement. I hate the gossip. I keep to myself and keep busy.

> Elderly housing is absolutely beyond description, beyond what was expected. People who have lived in a real neighborhood are not happy in elderly housing. People should be told: "You are starting a new type of life, altogether different, not a family life. You get what you give." I like my privacy. I keep to myself.

The impact of illness and death seems to be omnipresent. An often-suggested remedy is mixed-age housing. For example:

> I think there should be a mixture [of ages]. It cuts down on the morbid talk like "so-and-so died" or "Three people died last week." They can get very morbid talking to each other. And they can get very withdrawn. You never hear a child's laughter or see children playing. You never talk to a younger person who's going to a dance or dating or going to school.

> I'd rather see mixed ages. In the last three months there have been five deaths here. And there's always someone going to the hospital.

In the former comment the woman's use of the word *they* represents a common distancing technique. Many women talked about the way seeing death affected other people or people in general without expressing the feelings as their own. One woman attributed the feelings to her husband, though they also seemed to be her own:

> Before my husband died we visited an elderly housing building and my hus-
> band said, "I'm not ready for that." You see the regression, live and in
> color. You see people in walkers and wheelchairs, and that bothers people.

The next comment was from a lady who seemed resigned to the negative aspects of the situation:

> Eight people have died on my floor in seven years. People don't like to talk
> about it. They just say, "Oh, there's the ambulance. I wonder who it is?"
> I'm getting old. I don't need activities. I may die anytime.

A person who loses a close friend or relative to death may also experience the loss of an important role, especially if she had been caring for the ill or dying person. As one elderly woman explained it:

> It's really a double loss. It's the loss of a person and of your role in helping
> them . . . and the feeling that they need you in some way.

Thus, the death of others (which is experienced increasingly with age) may represent not only the loss of an important person but also a diminished sense of being needed, useful, and appreciated. This logically connects with decreased self-esteem. Several women described a circular process in which the death of friends leads one to be isolated and depressed, making it very difficult to make any new friends. With each loss of a friend, feelings of abandonment may intensify, as illustrated in this comment from a 70-year-old widow:

> I'm all alone in the world. I used to have a lot of friends and now I'm down
> to two. One is in a nursing home and won't last long.

Watching a friend deteriorate physically or mentally seems to stimulate death fears for many elderly people. In my interviews, I asked people how they would feel about visiting a senile friend (this is an item on the Collett-Lester Fear of Death Scale[49]). Avoidance of a painful situation was a typical response. For example:

> I'd go once, but I wouldn't make a habit of it.

> I'd try to be cheerful, but I don't know what good it would do to visit the
> person.

One woman expressed her dismay at seeing a good friend deteriorate due to dementia:

> It seems that the smartest and most intelligent people lose their abilities.
> The mediocre stay mediocre.

Dynamically, the reactions to seeing a friend deteriorate through dementia may be seen as a precursor to death fears—that is, when one becomes senile, death is not far behind.

I also asked women how they would feel about discussing death with a friend who is dying. The majority of women responded with the idea that they would not bring up the topic of death but would be willing to talk if a friend broached the matter first. For example:

Not unless they brought it up.

I'd be worried about the right thing to say, but I wouldn't shut them off.

I'd keep up my cheerful thoughts and words.

I've had to watch my words, pretend it wasn't so. I kept saying to a friend who died of cancer: "You know you're not going to get completely well, but you have to make the best of it." I tried to bring up her spirits, but it didn't work. It's human to want to encourage them.

Some women lamented the lack of communication and felt strongly that people should talk openly with dying friends and family members:

I had a brother-in-law who had cancer. It broke my heart to hear him say how the doctor could find nothing wrong with him. I'm all for telling. The person should be told. There may be some things they want to take care of; also, spiritual matters.

We should talk about it. I should have said goodbye. I had a friend who was dying. He knew it, I knew it, but we never talked about it. We should have talked. I should have said goodbye to him. [Her eyes filled with tears as she spoke.]

No one in my family could talk about death. I talk about death all the time. I like to know that when I go, they'll say mass and put me in a certain place. I tell my son what I want done.

A minority of women I interviewed felt strongly that it is best not to talk about dying with their friends at all:

That's for people who are trained—clergy.

You don't have to say anything at all.

I'd avoid talk about this. Talking about death would not help. I'd feel worse to talk. It's better to go in with a smile, say everything will be OK, and pray.

As several researchers have suggested, the death of a friend may be perceived as an alarming reminder of one's own mortality. Elderly people whom I have interviewed often made the point that reaction to a death depends upon the age of the deceased, that it is more difficult to accept the death of a younger person. The frame of reference seemed to be the subjects' age—that is, the death of someone at least several years older than oneself was more acceptable than the death of someone the same age or younger. Following this line of thought, the deaths of friends about one's own age are especially difficult to face.

Death of Self

Logically, it might seem that the deaths of spouses and friends would stimulate thoughts and feelings about one's own death. However, in my research I found that even women who talked openly about deaths of others were unlikely to initiate talk about their own death. This is consistent with theories that state that a certain amount of death denial is necessary for a person to be able to carry on with the business of daily life.

On an individual level, the denial of death is often linked to a fear of death and a desire for self-preservation. Zilboorg claimed that no one is free of the fear of death, and he described the fear as an expression of the instinct for self-preservation. To carry on with our daily lives, the affect of fear must be suppressed.[50] The result is what Becker called "an impossible paradox: the ever present fear of death in the normal biological functioning of our instinct of self-preservation, as well as our utter obliviousness to this fear in our conscious life."[51]

Not all theorists concur that fear of death is innate. Leming, for example, argued that fear of death is a socially learned phenomenon.[52] Weisman and Weisman and Hackett described some patients who apparently have no fear of death and even look forward to it with acceptance and serenity.[53]

Lieberman, in a longitudinal study lasting three to four years, followed eighty senior citizens (ages 65–91, mean age 80) and found that "those individuals who are approaching death, more than those of the same age not close to death, provide more statements about death. Death as a salient theme does not occur throughout old age with the frequency as when the aged person is actually close to his own death."[54]

In interviews, I asked elderly women whether they ever had thoughts about how old they would live to be and, if so, to state the age. In a group of thirty, about one-quarter of the respondents could not name an age. They said they had not thought about it, that it was an impossible question, or that only God could answer. Half of those who responded with an age added ten years to their present age (a nice, round figure: one more decade). Only two people said they expected to live less than five years. The oldest respondent, who was 88, said she expected to live to 100. A key for many people seemed to be how long their parents had lived; they expected to live as long or longer than their parents had.

Elderly participants in workshops where death was discussed made a clear distinction between the death and dying of others and one's own death and dying. It was far easier to discuss the death of others than to talk about personal death. For example, in one group that consisted of seven women and two men, there was an energetic discussion of near-death experiences and people's thoughts about life beyond death. At the start of the next session, one man commented, "Last week you were in a morbid place." Two women added that one group ought to be more upbeat and most members signaled agreement. Another woman noted that the previous week had been "heavy." When the leaders asked what had made the session heavy, several responses indicated that it was the personal nature of the discussion, that for the first time in the group people were contemplating their own death rather than talking about family or friends. For example, these comments came from women in the group:

> I don't think anybody is too anxious to find out. Like my father used to say, it's the old snake in the basket trick. You're kind of fascinated with it, but you don't want to get in the basket with the snake.

> Last week felt sadder.

> Yeah, and I think people were getting anxious or tense. Maybe resistance or something.

> Or it reminds you each one of us may have had experiences coming close to it [death] and it's not the happiest thing in the world. You want to back away from it.

Participant-observation and survey research offer some data on how elderly people think, feel, and plan about their deaths. For example, Hochschild, who studied a community of widows for a three-year period, described norms for dying agreed upon by the widows.[55] There was a good and a bad way to die. The good way meant remaining active to the end and being ready in both the practical and philosophical sense—having a will and burial plans and being on good terms with people. Essentially, the good way involved facing death rather than turning one's back on it. Talking about the deaths of others seemed to be a way of thinking about one's death and planning for it.

Religion, the traditional source of support in coping with death-related concerns, is apparently still a strong factor in the way people who are now elderly approach their deaths. In interviews with the elderly, Wass found that 45 percent of respondents rated religious upbringing as the factor that most influenced their present attitude toward death. Over 60 percent indicated a strong belief in afterlife, and over 70 percent wished that there is life after death.[56] In my interviews, elderly women frequently cited religion as their source of strength in coping with deaths of significant others and in anticipating their own death.

Perhaps new death rituals are developing within the context of new living situations for the elderly. Hochschild noted that the widows in her study attended funerals of even those people in the building whom they did not know well. She suggested that by going to the funerals of others, they were experimentally going to their own. Hochschild described another death-related ritual that may be a means of coping with death anxiety: The woman tried to guess how long a person had left to live and, after a death, tried to figure out whether the deceased had foretold her impending death.[57] Another modern ritual may be the ambulance watching that goes on in most senior citizen's apartment buildings. These rituals may function as anticipatory socialization and as a form of reassurance of one's own presence and grasp of life, even in the midst of death.

Interventions

In the light of evidence that fear of death increases among elderly women as they experience the deaths of friends, it seems urgent to develop models for supportive interventions. This has direct relevance to congregate housing for the elderly, where people witness or learn of the deaths of cohorts with great frequency. Women who develop friendships and support systems with other women are likely to be affected deeply by their deaths. A discussion and support-group model seems to hold much promise for helping older women cope with death. One example of an effective group intervention was noted earlier in the reference of Bennett's work with widows. In another study, Michaels explored the effects of discussing grief, loss, death, and dying on depression levels in a geriatric outpatient sample.[58] Subjects were placed in three groups: (1) a highly structured cathartic grief group, (2) a highly structured social and topical discussion group, and (3) a control group that did not meet. The study did not examine sex differences. The treatment group consisted of nine women and one man; the placebo group consisted of five women and five men; and the control group consisted of seven women and four men. Results showed that both the therapy and placebo groups improved, while the control group deteriorated. Findings indicated that the cathartic grief group was more effective than the discussion group in reducing depression levels. The effectiveness of the grief group, placed in the context of earlier evidence that the elderly want to talk about death, suggests that it is time to lift the taboo on discussing death themes with older people.

To test an intervention model for helping the elderly cope with death and loss, I conducted a series of discussion groups, called life-cycle workshops, which met weekly for five weeks. Elderly participants, primarily women, discussed aging, death, bereavement, life values, and philosophies. Death attitudes were measured in pre- and postinterviews using several scales and questionnaires. The experimental group indicated a decrease in fear of one's own dying, while the control group showed no attitude change. Qualitative analysis of the interviews and group sessions provided additional evidence that the elderly do want opportunities to discuss death and loss in open and supportive settings. In evaluating the value of the workshops, comments such as the following were typical:

> People were very easy with one another very soon. That surprised me. The subject matter [of death] didn't seem to bother them as much as I thought it would.

> When you talked about dying, it was such a controversy [laughs]! Then, too, because it wasn't morbid to talk about dying. We have to face reality. When you're well, that's the time to talk about it.

> What impressed me most was how casual and right most people accepted the topic of death.

The discussion of near-death experiences seemed to have a strong impact on several women's attitudes about the dying process, as indicated from postinterview comments like these:

> Now, after talking about the things we did, there are more facts than there were before. I wouldn't be surprised [to find dying an interesting experience].

> There's more after death . . . it's a whole different thing than I thought.

> It didn't bother me before [not to know what death is like]. That's part of the same question. . . . I'm more interested now . . . a possibility is there.

Most death-attitude research to date has focused on the negative aspects of death and dying. Certainly many positive attitudes exist and ought to be studied as extensively as the negative ones are. Many elderly women have faced cumulative losses and have become experts at dealing with death. Those who have developed an understanding or acceptance or philosophy of death may have much to teach us—if we will open the channels of communication.

The workshop or discussion-group model holds much promise as a therapeutic intervention. Attitude change may occur as a function of catharsis; open discussion of death relieves some anxieties. The establishment of supportive relationships with other group members may also diminish anxiety by reducing the isolation an individual feels. One of the best results of conducting workshops in senior citizens' housing is that some lonely and isolated individuals make connections with other people, and leaders can foster this process by addressing the topic of loneliness and ways to cope with it.

Summary

The denial of death and mourning in this society, which has been documented extensively in recent years, has far-reaching consequences for older women. Pervasive death denials has the profound effect of increasing the psychosocial isolation of elderly women and of leaving them with few supports or coping skills. In general, older women face painful cumulative losses. They may lose husband, family, and friends to death. They may give up roles of wife, mother, worker. They may lose health, mobility, independence, and social status. Many older women lose all sense of being loved, needed, wanted or appreciated.

Unfortunately, even the mental-health and social-service professions have neglected the needs of older women. There are few interventions to help them cope with this myriad of losses. Research indicates that older people do want to talk about death but they have few opportunities or outlets for doing so. In light of evidence that fear of death increases among elderly women as they experience death of friends, it seems urgent to develop models for supportive interventions. The direct relevance to the trend toward congregate housing for the elderly, where people witness or learn of death of peers with great frequency is clear. Discussion groups offer much promise as therapeutic modalities and have the advantage of helping socially isolated people to connect with others. The lack of professional attention to the needs of widows must be remedied. Widow-to-widow groups have demonstrated the need and efficiency of dealing with death in a direct manner. Perhaps a lesson to be found in the success of widow-to-widow outreaches is that caretakers must deal with their own death attitudes in order to help the bereaved.

Finally, we must expand our approach to old age and death to include an appreciation of the positive as well as negative aspects. In seeking out the knowledge, wisdom, and creativity of the elderly, we have much to gain. Sometimes, while confronting the immediacy of death, there is an unparalleled zest for life. As one lovely woman of 88 told me:

> I plan to live to be 100. Even then I won't have read all the poetry I want to read, tried all the recipes I collect, or spent enough time with those I love.

Notes

1. For example, E. Becker, *The Denial of Death* (New York: Macmillan, 1974).

2. J.A. Peterson and M.P. Briley, *Widows and Widowhood* (New York: Association Press, 1977).

3. A.H. Kutscher, "Practical Aspects of Bereavement," in *Loss and Grief: Psychological Management—Medical Practice,* eds. B. Schoenberg et al. (New York: Columbia University Press, 1970), pp. 280–297.

4. Avery Weisman, "Death, Dying, and Loss," (Presentation to the Boston University Summer Institute in Gerontology, 1980).

5. G. Gorer, *Death, Grief, and Mourning* (New York: Doubleday, 1965); and A.L. Strauss and B.G. Glaser, "Awareness of Dying," in *Loss and Grief: Psychological Management—Medical Practice,* eds. B. Schoenberg et al. (New York: Columbia University Press, 1970), pp. 298–304.

6. Sigmund Freud, "Mourning and Melancholia," in *Standard Edition of the Complete Psychological Works of Sigmund Freud* (London: Hogarth Press, 1917; Erich Lindemann, "Symptomatology Management of Acute Grief," *American Journal of Psychiatry* 101 (1944):141–148; J. Bowlby, "Grief and Mourning in Infancy and Early Childhood," *The Psychoanalytic Study of the Child* 15 (1960):481–498; Gorer, *Death, Grief, and Mourning;* and G.M. Vernon, *Sociology of Death* (New York: Ronald Press, 1970).

7. Gorer, *Death, Grief, and Mourning,* p. 131.

8. B. Kreis and A. Pattie, *Up from Grief* (New York: Seabury Press, 1969), p. 6.

9. Lindemann, "Symptomatology Management," pp. 141–148; Melanie Klein, "Mourning and Its Relation to Manic Depressive States," in *Contributions to Psychoanalysis, 1921–1945* (London: Hogarth Press, 1948, p. 311–338; H. Barry and E. Lindemann, "Critical Ages for Maternal Bereavement in Psychoneuroses," *Psychosomatic Medicine* 22 (1960): 166–181; Gorer, *Death, Grief, and Mourning;* Vernon, *Sociology of Death;* and R.J. Lifton and E. Olson, *Living and Dying* (New York: Bantam Books, 1974).

10. Justine Ball, "Widows' Grief: The Impact of Age and Mode of Death," *Omega* 7 (1976–1977):307–333.

11. Raymond Carey, "Weathering Widowhood: Problems and Adjustments of the Widowed during the First Year," *Omega* 10 (1979–1980): 163–174.

12. A. Sheskin and S.E. Wallace, "Differing Bereavements: Suicide, Natural and Accidental Death," *Omega* 7 (1976–1977):229.

13. Ibid.

14. Carey, "Weathering Widowhood."

15. L.J. Collett and D. Lester, "The Fear of Death and the Fear of Dying," *Journal of Psychology* 72 (1969):179–181.

16. B.D. Bell and C.D. Batterson, "The Death Attitudes of Older Adults: A Path Analytical Exploration," *Omega* 10 (1979–1980):59–76.

17. M.A. Cole, "Sex and Marital Status Differences in Death Anxiety," *Omega* 9 (1978–1979):139–147.

18. D. Martin and L.S. Wrightsman, "The Relationship between Religious Behavior and Concern about Death," *Journal of Social Psychology* 45 (1965):317–323.

19. W.M. Swenson, "Attitude toward Death in an Aged Population," *Journal of Gerontology* 16 (1961):49–52.

20. B. Spilka, "Death and Cultural Values: A Theory and A Research Program" (Paper presented to American Psychological Association, Washington, D.C., September 1967).

21. H. Wass et al., "Similarities and Dissimilarities in Attitudes toward Death—A Population of Older Persons," *Omega* 9 (1978–1979): 337–354.

22. B.D. Bell, "The Impact of Housing Relocation on the Elderly: an Alternative Methodological Approach," *International Journal of Aging and Human Development* 7 (1976):27–38.

23. Avery Weisman and Thomas Hackett, "Denial as a Social Act," in *Psychodynamic Studies on Aging,* eds. S. Levin and R. Kamaha (New York: International Universities Press, 1967).

24. Vernon, *Sociology of Death.*

25. W.M. Swenson, "Attitude toward Death in an Aged Population," *Journal of Gerontology* 16 (1961):49–52; A.E. Christ, "Attitudes toward Death of a Group of Acute Geriatric Psychiatric Patients," *Journal of Gerontology* 16 (1961):56–59; and P.J. Rhudick and A.S. Dibner, "Age, Personality, and Health Correlates of Death Concerns in Normal Aged Individuals," *Journal of Gerontology* 16 (1961):44–49.

26. F.E. Jeffers et al. "Attitudes of Older Persons toward Death: A Preliminary Study," *Journal of Gerontology* 16 (1961):53–56.

27. J.C. Diggory and D.Z. Rothman, "Values Destroyed by Death," *Journal of Abnormal and Social Psychology* 43 (1961):205–210.

28. Spilka, "Death and Cultural Values."

29. G.W. McDonald, "Sex, Religion, and Risk-Taking Behavior as Correlates of Death Anxiety," *Omega* 7 (1976):35–43.

30. M. Blumenfield, N. Levy, and D. Kaufman, "The Wish to Be Informed of a Fatal Illness," *Omega* 9 (1978–1979):323–326.

31. Lynn Caine, *Widow* (New York: Wm. Morrow and Co., 1974).

32. Phyllis Silverman, *If You Will Lift the Load, I Will Lift It Too* (Hackensack, N.J.: Gutterman-Musicant-Kreitzman, 1976); and Silver-

man, *Helping Each Other in Widowhood* (New York: Health Sciences Publishing Corp., 1975).

33. Peterson and Briley, *Widows and Widowhood.*

34. R. Lindsay, *Alone and Surviving* (New York: Walker and Co., 1977).

35. H.Z. Lopata, *Widowhood in an American City* (Cambridge, Mass.: Schenkman Publishing Co., 1973); and Lopata, *Women as Widows* (New York: Elsevier, 1979).

36. Lopata, *Women as Widows.*

37. Caine, *Widow;* Lopata, *Widowhood in an American City;* and Lopata, *Women as Widows.*

38. Lopata, *Women as Widows.*

39. Silverman, *If You Will Lift the Load.*

40. Caine, *Widow;* and Caine, *Lifelines* (New York: Doubleday, 1978).

41. Lindsay, *Alone and Surviving.*

42. S.R. Hiltz, *Creating Community Services for Widows* (Port Washington, N.Y.: Kennikal Press, 1977).

43. Lindsay, *Alone and Surviving.*

44. C.J. Barrett, cited in Peterson and Briley, *Widows and Widowhood* (New York: Association Press, 1977).

45. B. Hess and E. Markson, *Aging and Old Age* (New York: Macmillan, 1980); and E.F. Mason, "Fear of Death in Elderly Black Women" (Ph.D. dissertation, Boston University, 1979).

46. Hess and Markson, *Aging and Old Age.*

47. Mason, "Fear of Death," p. 114.

48. Bell, "The Impact of Housing Relocation."

49. Collett and Lester, "Fear of Death."

50. G. Zilboorg, "Fear of Death," *Psychoanalytic Quarterly* 12 (1943):465-475.

51. E. Becker, *The Denial of Death* (New York: Macmillan, 1974), p. 17.

52. M.R. Leming, "Religion and Death: A Test of Homan's Thesis," *Omega* 10 (1979-1980):347-364.

53. Avery Weisman, *On Dying and Denying* (New York: Behavioral Publications, 1972); and Weisman and Thomas Hackett, "Denial as a Social Act," in *Psychodynamic Studies on Aging,* eds. S. Levin and R. Kamaha (New York: International Universities Press, 1967).

54. Lieberman, reported in G.M. Vernon, *Sociology of Death* (New York: Ronald Press, 1970), p. 186.

55. H.R. Hochschild, *The Unexpected Community* (Englewood Cliffs, N.J.: Prentice-Hall, 1973.

56. Wass et al., "Similarities and Dissimilarities."

57. Hochschild, *The Unexpected Community*.

58. F. Michaels, "The Effects of Discussing Death, Grief, Loss, and Dying on Depression Levels in a Geriatric Outpatient Therapy Group" (Ph.D. dissertation, Auburn University, 1977).

Part IV:
Health Issues in
Later Life

Part IV examines selected health problems that are likely to occur among older women. While chronic diseases and disability increase among both sexes with advancing age, women have specific health concerns not shared by men. Menopause and increased likelihood of osteoporosis are two examples. Coronary heart disease, while lower among women than men at all ages, remains a leading cause of death for old women.

Lawrence J. Kerzner, in chapter 14, presents an extensive review of current medical literature on menopause, osteoporosis, fractures, falls, and coronary heart disease as they affect women. William B. Kannel and Frederick N. Brand elaborate upon coronary heart disease and hypertension in chapter 15. They draw upon data from a major longitudinal survey—the Framingham Epidemiological Heart Disease Study—to show that elevated blood pressure (hypertension) is one of the primary risk factors for death from cardiovascular diseases, including coronary heart disease. Both chapters include references that the interested reader may consult for further details on the topics discussed.

14 Physical Changes after Menopause

Lawrence J. Kerzner

This chapter addresses some of the physical and physiological changes that occur with aging that set women apart from men of the same age. Essential to this discussion is the decision at what point we distinguish youth from old age. While we commonly make reference to a person as a young child, an older child, a young adult, an older adult, or an old person, other than chronology there is no commonly accepted way of identifying aging. Considering that there is no chronological definition of the point at which a person is considered old and that a person's years may belie their physical, mental, social, and economic functioning, it is inaccurate to use chronology as the only parameter as a definition of aging. Formalized societal definitions of *old* may not take into account the uniqueness of every member of a population. As every person's physiologic and functional ability varies in youth, so it differs as one ages. Mandatory retirement at age 65 or 70 has not taken into account such variability, and many people functionally are not much different at age 65 from the way they were at 55.

Physiological changes of aging in the absence of disease are qualitative; there can be no true point at which a person is considered to enter old age. Gerontologists' division of old age into young-old (age 65–75) and old-old (75 and older) has a basis in physiology; increasing organ function declines and increased co-existence of disease in the older grouping lead to increased frailty, dependence, and requirement for supporting services.

For organ- and cell-related functions, age 30 represents a time of peak activity. For the kidneys, it is a time of peak ability to clear certain biologically active materials from the bloodstream, and for the respiratory system, it is a time of maximum ability to ventilate and oxygenate. For many organs there is a steady linear decline in these abilities, beginning at about age 30 and extending over the life of the person. The amount of extra organ function that is present above that necessary to sustain life represents a form of reserve the person could call upon should the body be stressed.

These changes in organ functional reserve and homeostatic capacity may not produce any limitation in life-style whatsoever except in persons who are dependent upon maximum organ function, like athletes engaged in competitive sports. In extreme old age, these declines may allow for increased susceptibility to disease. As a corollary, it is sometimes difficult to distinguish between changes that are due to normal aging and those that are due to disease. This chapter discusses the following issues that affect women as they age: menopause, cardiovascular disease, falls and fractures, osteoporosis (softening of bones), and the use of estrogen.

Menopause

While the capacity for reproduction absolutely ceases at menopause, before menopause there is a gradual decline in fertility that can be demonstrated to occur as early as age 30–35 (Federation CECOS 1982). Approximately 27 million women over the age of 50 in the United States have gone through menopause, after which they have an average life expectancy of 28 or more years. There is no equivalent to menopause among men because there is no specific time after puberty when they are infertile as a result of age.

Under physiological conditions, FSH (follicle-stimulating hormone) and LH (luteotropic hormone) stimulate ovarian production of estrogen from granulosa cells and progesterone from corpus luteum respectively. While there are other steroid hormones with estrogenic effect in premenopausal women the major estrogenic steroid is estradiol. As FSH levels vary throughout the menstrual cycle, so do estrogens, reaching a peak between ovulation and menstruation. In women undergoing normal menses, estradiol levels vary from 65.6 to 137.2 pg./ml. (Goldfarb 1979). At menopause the ovary becomes unresponsive to gonadotropic stimulation and undergoes involution, becoming small, pale, and more wrinkled, shrinking to one-third its preexisting size. Ovarian production of estrogen and progesterone virtually ceases. Due to release of negative feedback inhibition, FSH and LH increase markedly and do not display the cyclic variations that occur premenopausally. Clinically, constant high levels of FSH and LH are physiologic markers of primary ovarian failure either pre-or postmenopausally. There is, however, a suggestion that menopause many not be the result of primary ovarian failure since, while undeveloped ova diminish in number throughout life, substantial amounts remain after menopause. Also, animal studies have demonstrated that old ovaries transplanted to younger hosts cycle normally in response to the hormone gonadotropin (Aldin and Korenman 1980).

Comparison of ovarian venous blood with that of the systemic circulation indicates that the postmenopausal ovary secretes large amounts of testosterone, moderate amounts of androstenedione, and small amounts of estrogens (Judd et al. 1974). After menopause, variation in levels of estrogenic and progestational hormones is lost. In postmenopausal women aged 73–89 years, estradiol levels are approximately 6.5 pg./ml. (Goldfarb 1979). Estrone levels are approximately 25 percent of premenopausal levels.

Progesterone levels decline approximately 60 percent. These changes occur within a few years after menopause and remain that way throughout life.

While ovarian production of estrogens ceases at menopause, estrogens produced from other sites are present. Postmenopausally, almost all estrogens are derived from fat cell metabolism of the adrenally derived precursor, androstenedione. Metabolism of androstenedione proceeds in such a way as to produce estrone, which is the major postmenopausal estrogen.

In men, there is no such rapid hormonal decline at any one point in life. Testosterone production appears to be relatively constant from ages 20–50 and decreases slowly thereafter such that between ages 20 and 50 testosterone levels are approximately 600 mg./100 ml. of blood; whereas in men aged 80–90, testosterone levels are approximately 250 mg.

In general, hormones act as a messenger to specific body tissues to allow for their metabolism in such a way that they are kept in a well-developed and mature form. This allows for target organs to perform a specialized function. Estrogenic stimulation is necessary for the growth and maintenance of breast tissue and urogenital tissue and plays an important role in the maintenance of skin and subcutaneous tissue integrity as well as pelvic-supporting tissues. Metabolically, estrogens play an important although poorly defined role in the maintenance of calcium metabolism and, subsequently, bone strength; the regulation of plasma lipids; and the development of atherosclerotic vascular disease. There are certainly also many other as yet unspecified functions of estrogens in adult women. Diminished levels of hormone below the amount necessary for support of target-organ functions frequently allow for involution of those tissues with consequent decrease in size and function of the organ. This aspect of physiology obviously has great implication in the pathogenesis of health problems in older women as declines in estrogen-supported tissue activities occur after menopause and with advancing age.

After menopause the uterus begins to atrophy, diminishing to as small as 1 cm. from the nulliparous adult size of 8 x 4 x 2.2 cm. (Talbert 1977). Vaginal and urogenital epithelium becomes thinned, vaginal secretions diminish, and the mucosa becomes easily subject to abrasions with minimal trauma. Vaginal musculature may become shortened and noncompliant and may be an underlying cause of painful coitus. Atrophic changes in the distal urethra may produce painful urination, urinary incontinence, and recurrent urinary-tract infection. These findings represent the components of an atrophic urogenital syndrome that, when symptomatic, may be ameliorated by the local application of estrogenic creams. Such therapy can be beneficial when used judiciously with women experiencing moderate to severe symptoms.

Estrogens have been implicated as one factor in the maintenance of normal tone of the pelvic-support structures. A decline in estrogen levels, in conjunction with birth trauma and other nonspecific hereditary factors, may predispose women to pelvic laxity in allowing for prolapse of the bladder wall through the vagina or prolapse of the rectum through the weakened posterior vaginal wall. Local application of estrogens in such circumstances is not effective in alleviating the problem. In selected instances, surgical therapy for such problems may be indicated.

Estrogens are also important in the maintenance of subcutaneous fat distribution. Beginning around age 35, mammary glands become progressively replaced by fat. Decline in circulating estrogens allows for thinning and drying of skin with diminution of its luster and flexibility.

The rapid decline in circulating estrogens temporally is associated with a menopausal syndrome consisting of hot flashes due to vasomotor instability and psychiatric symptoms that are sometimes classified as depression. Such a symptom complex could be considered an estrogen-withdrawal syndrome as it may occur not only upon normal decline of natural hormone production at menopause or after surgical castration but also upon abrupt cessation of hormone therapy after menopause. Up to 85 percent of postmenopausal women experience hot flashes. They usually diminish in severity and frequency over two years. In patients with hot flashes, a reliable correlation between objective skin-temperature changes in patients' symptoms has been demonstrated, indicating underlying vasodilatation. The discovery of elevations of LH occurring at the time of each flash underscores the important role of the central nervous system in the development of flashes rather than the dilatation being a purely peripheral vascular phenomenon (Casper, Yen, and Wilkes 1979). When exogenous estrogens are administered, slow tapering may prevent the development of or decrease in the severity of hot flashes.

The existence of neuropsychiatric symptoms as part of an estrogen-withdrawal syndrome remains greatly debated (Alington-MacKinnon and Troll 1981). As the time of menopause or surgical castration in a person's life may be marked frequently by stressful life circumstances (for example, middle-age, surgery, or sterilizing drug therapy), psychiatric symptoms unrelated to loss of estrogen may become manifest because of stress alone. The development of depressive symptoms may be inversely proportional to a person's understanding of the physiology of menopause and the dissolution of surrounding myths. During menopause there is marked intercultural variation in the prevalence of psychiatric symptoms. Critical evaluation of the medical literature relating to hot flashes, vasomotor instability, and neuropsychiatric symptoms is crucial. Precisely what symptoms are inevitably associated with menopause remain unclear. The following sections describe conditions common to postmenopausal women and conclude with a discussion of the use of estrogen, its relationship to cancer, and therapeutic use in treating osteoporosis.

Cardiovascular Disease

At all ages, women have a lower risk of having atherosclerotic vascular disease compared to men in comparable high-risk groups. Factors placing a person of either sex at high risk include cigarette smoking, hypertension, and excessive cholesterol in the blood. Mortality from ischemic heart disease is less in women of all age groups. The HDL (high-density lipoprotein) cholesterol fraction—specifically, the HDL/LDL (low-density lipoprotein)—is thought to correlate inversely with the risk of vascular atherosclerosis. HDL functions to inhibit the deposition of cholesterol in vascular endothelium and hence decreases atherogenesis. Premenopausal women in general have higher HDL/LDL cholesterol ratios than men, possibly due to the presence of estrogens. On that basis alone they may be subject to less atherosclerotic vascular disease. Other vascular diseases like fibromuscular hyperplasia of blood vessels are more common among women but for unknown reasons. It is interesting to note that surgical menopause produces the same narrowing in risk whether the operation performed is a hysterectomy or a hysterectomy and bilateral oophorectomy (excision of both ovaries) (Gordon et al. 1978).

The difference in risk of atherosclerotic vascular disease between high-risk men and women becomes narrowed after age 60, possible due to the loss of estrogen influence on HDL since the HDL/LDL ratio declines postmenopausally (Kannel et al. 1976). (For further discussion of cardiovascular disease, see chapter 15.)

Falls and Fractures

Falling is a common phenomenon in the elderly. About 20 percent of elderly men and 40 percent of elderly women living at home have experienced a fall. In analyzing each fall as an isolated event, an immediate antecedent process many times can be discerned. Among the diseases predisposing to falls, cardiovascular disease leads the list and underlies approximately one-half of all falls. Syncopy (fainting) due to cardiac arrhythmias (extremely slow or fast heart rate) accounts for a large percentage of falls. These forms of cardiac disease may be obscure and sometimes require an extended period of cardiac monitoring to detect. While evaluation of a person who has fallen frequently is directed toward detecting injuries, there has been recent interest in more-intensive investigation for those in whom the cause of the fall is not absolutely known. Of fifty-nine people living in a residential facility for the elderly, who were studied for two and one-half years, fifty-three of whom were women, thirty-seven had experienced a fall. Twelve were found to have ongoing cardiac arrhythmias that might have contributed to their fall (Gordon Huang and Gryfe 1982). Other forms of cardiovascular disease that predispose to falls include postural hypotension (marked decline in blood pressure upon rising from the seated or lying position), loss of consciousness due to decreased cardiac output associated with aortic stenosis (Stokes-Adams attacks), and so-called drop attacks in which a person falls with transient complete paralysis due to central-nervous-system dysfunction. The other half of falls are due to accidents or a combination of accidents and decline in postural control. Postural control in a standing position is diminished in the elderly and may be diminished even further in elderly women as compared to men. Not only do the elderly sway more than younger people, but women sway more than men with almost twice as great an amplitude (Cape 1978). Part of the explanation for diminished postural control lies in the high prevalence of sensory impairments in the area of joint-position sense. Sensory input to the sense of body awareness and position may be reduced, and hence, elderly people may not be as aware of their body position as younger people. Diminished visual and auditory acuity may allow for failure to identify obstacles in the environment, predisposing to an accident. Central-nervous-system dysfunction in the extrapyramidal and frontal motor-control systems in conjunction with the aforementioned sensory defects result in senile gait disorder (Sabin 1982), where a person may be unsteady while standing, feeling insecure and afraid of falling, with a tendency to fall backward.

It has been suggested that practicing balance exercises may mitigate the high frequency of falls in later life that are due to diminished efficacy of the postural-control mechanism (Cape 1978; Overstall 1980). While far from proven and not normally part of medical practice, such practice makes good sense.

To help prevent falls, the living environment of an elderly person should be set up to eliminate or diminish hazards to ambulation. Throw rugs should be removed as well as loose telephone and electric wires. Halls should be well lit, and the use of nightlights encouraged. Stairways should have banisters on both sides to aid with balance, and bathrooms should have grab bars set up in bathtubs and showers. Nocturnal falls frequently occur due to need to urinate at night—an attempt to get to the bathroom or a stumble over an object in a poorly lit room.

Frequently, a fall may represent an early symptom of a new acute medical illness unrelated to previously recognized physiological abnormalities of cardiovascular and neurological disease, postural instability, or specific environmental hazard. This premonitory fall is one way in which elderly people with new acute illness differ from those younger. Illnesses such as pneumonia, myocardial infarction, and gastrointestinal bleeding may come to medical attention after a premonitory fall.

The effect of a fall or frequent falls frequently makes the person less confident in his or her ability to ambulate resulting in a greatly constricted life-style in addition to the possibility of that person's sustaining severe soft-tissue and internal injury and fractured bones.

Broken bones are a major cause of morbidity and mortality in the aged. In past years, especially before the advent of internal fixation for hip fracture, this type of injury was associated with extremely high likelihood of prolonged hospitalization, immobility, and death. Within the past twenty years, surgical techniques has advanced in conjunction with the physician's ability to effect early ambulation after hip fracture and to lessen the likelihood of poor outcome. It nonetheless remains a serious injury since 12 to 20 percent of elderly people die within 6 months of the injury (Jensen and Tondevold 1979).

Osteoporosis

Men and women affected by osteoporosis are more likely to sustain a fracture after a fall than those with normal bone mass. Osteoporosis, a disease marked by increasing softness of the bones so that they become flexible and brittle and an increased tendency to fall at advanced age, accounts for the increased frequency of fractured bones in the elderly. Since osteoporosis is more common among elderly women than men, it is not surprising that fractures and their subsequent effects on morbidity and mortality are greater in elderly women than men. Osteoporosis is estimated to affect one out of four elderly women. While many women in their fifties experience symptoms as a consequence of osteoporosis, men rarely do before age 75.

In osteoporosis, age-related decrease in bone mass affects both long bones and the axial skeleton vertebrae. Osteoporosis is painless and asymptomatic until fracture of a bone occurs, calling attention to its presence by pain. While sometimes it is discovered by diminished density of bones on radiographic films, osteoporosis needs to be quite severe before it can be detected by standard x-rays because 50 percent of the bone mass has to be lost before it is recognized by characteristic translucence. Other techniques used to identify decreased bone mass are not normally used in medical practice.

Vertebral compression and fracture of the long bones, especially lower forearm and femoral neck (hip), are the major sites of acute bone disease in people with osteoporosis. Vertebral-compression fractures in the elderly usually are atraumatic; typically no immediate preceding event can be identified to have caused the fracture. (In a younger age group, most vertebral-compression fractures are traumatic, due to falls from a height and landing on the feet, transmitting the shock wave to the vertebrae, or direct back injury.) In old age, these fractures most often occur because of diminished ability of the vertebrae to support the body's weight. The fractures produce back pain that may radiate to the front of the body. The pain may be quite severe initially but usually diminishes over the course of a few weeks. Progressive compression of multiple vertebrae leads to shortening of the vertebral column, producing a loss of height. Characteristic postures develop due to compression of the upper thoracic vertebra, producing the so-called Dowager's or Widow's Hump, limitation of chest expansion, and abdominal compression.

Fractures of the forearm occur due to a fall on an outstretched hand. It is interesting to note that both boys and girls have a high frequency of fracture of the distal forearm during childhood and adolescence due to trauma associated with sports, falls, and other injuries. This frequency decreases to a low level during mid-adult years and then increases again in women during the fifties decade, undoubtedly due to osteoporosis weakening of the bone. Fractures of the hip, also much more common in women, become much more prominent later in life (usually age 75) than forearm fractures (Cape 1978). Seemingly minor trauma can produce a hip fracture in someone with severe osteoporosis. External rotation at the hip and shortening of the leg are commonly seen after acute hip fracture, and the person cannot walk.

Healthy bone is in a state of active metabolism; its formation is coupled with resorption. Until approximately age 30, there is a net positive bone balance, resulting in increased bone mass. Afterward, factors influencing resorption and formation are altered to effect a net loss of bone mass of approximately one-half of 1 percent per year (30–40 mg. calcium lost daily) for the remainder of the person's life. For women, net negative bone loss is accelerated during the few years after menopause, reaching a peak of 1 percent per year and continuing at that high level for as long as ten years before returning to the baseline levels. This increase in postmenopausal bone loss, coupled with womens' typically smaller bone mass at maturity, can leave them with a much smaller bone mass than men and underlies the epidemiology of osteoporosis. Approximately 15 million people in the United States have osteoporosis (Harris 1978). Five million have severe osteoporosis and have experienced spontaneous vertebral-body fractures (compression fractures). Between 80 and 90 years of age, the incidence of hip fractures is approximately 10 percent.

Physical activity and diet are factors related to aging that play a major role in determining bone mass. Prolonged immobility leads toward diminution in bone mass, as does dietary deficiency of calcium or malabsorptive states.

Lactase deficiency, causing gastrointestinal symptoms of nausea, belching, flatulence, and diarrhea upon ingestion of milk, is common in the elderly and may lead to selection of a diet deficient in milk and milk products, allowing for poor calcium intake. Lactase deficiency also induces a malabsorption syndrome, that is, any calcium that is ingested may not be absorbed. Up to 30–40 percent of elderly women with osteoporosis have been found to have lactase deficiency. While eight out of thirty women aged 48–82 with osteoporosis were found to have abnormal absorption of ingested lactase, none reported symptoms of lactase deficiency, indicating such an absorptive defect is frequently asymptomatic (Newcomer et al. 1978) While blacks have a greater incidence of lactase deficiency than whites, their increased bone mass at maturity may afford some degree of protection from osteoporosis (Trotter, Broman, and Peterson 1960). Even in the absence of lactase deficiency, calcium absorption has been shown to diminish with age and to be even more greatly diminished in people with osteoporosis (Gallager et al. 1979). Diets low in calcium have been correlated with increased rates of bone fracture (Matkovic et al. 1979).

Various forms of cancer (multiple myeloma, metastatic soft-tissue tumors), endocrinopathies (hyperthyroidism, hyperparathyroidism, hyperadrenalism), and metabolic disorders (renal failure) can also underlie a net decrease in bone mass (Avioli 1978). Most osteoporosis in the United States, however, arises in the absence of these disease states. Its pathogenesis is poorly understood and probably represents a heterogeneous grouping of metabolic alterations leading toward a common disease state (Raisz 1982).

The Use of Estrogens

Estrogenic compounds have been available for clinical use in the United States for approximately the past forty years and, in many parts of the country, are prescribed quite liberally. Until recently, their use had increased markedly; in the 1960–1970 decade, the dollar sales of estrogens quadrupled. As late as 1970, in one study, up to 51 percent of postmenopausal women had used estrogens (Stadel and Weiss 1975). This rate of use was a result of the simplistic view that the postmenopausal state represented an endocrine-deficiency disease, deficiency of estrogens, and was characterized by the plea for "estrogens from puberty to the grave" (Wilson and Wilson 1963).

While the speculation that exogenous estrogen administration was associated with an increased likelihood of developing endometrial cancer had also existed for years, two reports in 1975 called significant attention to the issue (Smith et al. 1975; Ziel and Finkle 1975). Smith et al. related the risk of endometrial cancer to estrogen use in patients with many forms of gynecological cancer. There was a 4.5 times greater risk of a person developing endometrial cancer than other forms of cancer if estrogens were used for at least six months before the cancer was diagnosed. Ziel and Finkle compared the exposure rate to estrogens among patients with endometrial carcinoma and controls with intact uteri. They reported that conjugated estrogen use was found among 57 percent of 97 patients who had endometrial carcinoma as compared to only 15 percent of a control group. The pathologic diagnosis of endometrial cancer in these latter patients was confirmed by a panel of pathologists, removing doubt that the disease in question was cancer and not a lower grade of endometrial proliferation (Gordon et al. 1977).

Since then, many reports have detailed further the associated risks of postmenopausal estrogen use as well as marked conceptual change regarding the postmenopausal years and a rapid decline in the prescription of estrogenic compounds. (Alington-MacKinnon and Troll 1981; Quigley and Hammond 1979; Jick et al. 1979).

Estrogen stimulation to an intact uterus causes proliferation of the endometrium. It is thought that continuous and unopposed estrogen exposure causes the endometrium to develop cancerous changes. That estrogens are in some way related to the development of cancer is indicated by the following observations. In rabbits, for example, endometrial cancer can be induced by exposure to large amounts of estrogenic compounds. The carcinogenic effect of diethylstilbestrol (DES) on the adult female children of women given diethylstilbestrol during pregnancy has been reflected in the development of clear-cell cancer of the vagina. Certain breast-cancer cells may be stimulated by estrogen, and estrogen receptors may have prognostic value in cervical cancer (Martin et al. 1982). The rapidly rising incidence of endometrial cancer in the United States from 1969 to 1973 has exceeded 10 percent per year in some geographic areas. The rates have increased most among middle-aged women (55–64) (Weiss, Szekely, and Austin 1976) but also have increased in older and younger women as well. The rates among middle-aged women parallel the increased use of estrogens in the 1970s.

While it has been argued that much of the increased incidence of endometrial cancer seen in women who use estrogens is due to more-intensive surveillance (Horwitz and Feinstein 1978), such a hypothesis is not tenable. While such screening would detect cancer induced after short-term use, it would have little effect on the total number of cases ultimately diagnosed. In addition, cancer does not occur frequently in those who have used estrogens for a short period of time (Hutchinson and Rothman 1978).

Almost all of the U.S. data relative to estrogen and to risk of endometrial carcinoma have been generated from studies that did not include information as to the concomitant use of progestational agents. U.K. researchers have "labeled American neglect of progesterones as bizarre" (Kaunitz 1980), since the incidence of abnormal uterine histology can be reduced markedly when therapy consists of estrogens followed by progesterone for at least ten days (Patterson et al. 1980). Prospective studies are needed to help define risk using such a corroboration.

Other potential adverse consequences of postmenopausal estrogen therapy include the development of atherosclerotic heart disease, breast carcinoma, and gallstones. These areas in the postmenopausal years have been investigated less thoroughly than has endometrial carcinoma.

Whereas premenopausal estrogen therapy definitely induces atherosclerotic heart disease (Slone et al. 1981), its postmenopausal effects are not clear. Early menopause, especially prior to age 45, predisposes to increased atherosclerotic heart disease (Gordon et al. 1978) and estrogens given to such patients may lessen the risk.

Evidence for the association of the development of breast cancer with postmenopausal estrogen use, while not strong, may be present (Hoover et al. 1976). Fifteen years of estrogen therapy was required before a statistically significant difference could be found between 1,881 women treated with estrogens and a control group. More important was an almost sevenfold increase in cancer found in women who continued on estrogens and who developed benign breast disease while on therapy.

The Boston Collaborative Drug Study (Boston Collaborative 1974) found a 2.5 greater incidence of surgically confirmed gallbladder disease in postmenopausal estrogen users aged 45–69. No significant correlation could be made between venous thromboembolism, newly diagnosed breast carcinoma, or benign breast tumor.

Women at high risk of developing a complication of estrogen therapy include those who already have predisposing features toward such a complication. Specifically, such features include the risk of factors of obesity or hypertension for endometrial carcinoma and preexisting benign breast disease as a risk factor for the development of breast carcinoma.

While there probably is a place for therapeutic estrogen therapy, other than in a few specific circumstances, definite indications are hard to define, especially after natural menopause.

With regard to the older women, the crux of the issue has been that estrogen therapy appears to retard the large net negative calcium balance that occurs in the few years postmenopause (Ryan et al. 1979). In a retrospective study, this translated into a 50–60 percent decreased risk of fracture of hip or forearm in women aged 50–74 who had used estrogen for six or more years and who were still using it at the time of the survey (Weiss et al. 1980). Those who used estrogen for less than six years received less benefit. The decreased risk was observed in women taking relatively low doses daily (0.625 mg. of conjugated estrogens, primarily estrone). The lowering of risk of fracture, however (0.3–3 per 1,000 women per year), was smaller than an earlier projected increased risk of endometrial carcinoma due to estrogens (5–25 per 1,000 women per year).

The benefits accrued from preventing bone loss during estrogen therapy are transient. After therapy is discontinued, a large net negative calcium balance occurs similar to what occurs after menopause.

While the uterine cancers associated with estrogen therapy have been low-grade malignancies with relatively little invasion and while mortality from the disease has not increased, the risk of developing uterine cancers while taking estrogen for a prolonged period of time seems real.

Data available in 1980 permitted an estensive risk analysis of estrogen use in postmenopausal women (Weinstein 1980). Patients who had hysterectomy obviously had no risk of uterine cancer and hence would experience the greatest benefit. Patients with osteoporosis probably would experience a mild benefit; asymptomatic women with intact uteri had little to benefit from therapy. Risk might be diminished by using estrogens in the smallest possible dose cycled with progesterone. Close surveillance for any abnormal uterine or breast sign or symptoms should prompt investigation (Ryan 1982). It is important to note that even topically applied estrogen creams to vulvar and vaginal mucosa can be absorbed systemically and may add to risk of estrogen complication. Long-term maintenance of adequate calcium intake in the form of calcium supplements is probably the safest method of attempting to prevent negative calcium balance.

While estrogen does not produce new bone and does not add strength to already osteoporotic bones, fluoride is a potential stimulator of bone accretion. A combination of calcium, fluoride, and estrogen has been shown to be more effective than four other forms of treatment—placebo, calcium alone, fluoride and calcium, or estrogen and calcium—in prospectively preventing vertebral-compression fractures (Riggs et al. 1982). Thirty-eight percent of the fluoride-treated patients experienced significant side effects of fluoride therapy—notably, gastrointestinal and rheumatic complaints. Of sixty women taking estrogen, eight required therapy for abnormal vaginal bleeding. Obviously, there are great limitations of such therapy. The long-term consequences due to other iatrogenic complications is not known, and the benefits in terms of diminished long-bone fracture have not been defined.

Summary

Many of the health problems common to elderly women relate to the high incidence of falls, osteoporosis, and subsequent bone fracture. The negative psychological effect of falls, distortion of body habitus, pain due to vertebral collapse, and morbidity and mortality due to acute bone fracture figure significantly in their lives. Diminishing the likelihood of falls by careful evaluation for predisposing factors, both physical and environmental, may be beneficial. Current standard medical practice is directed toward the identification of the cause of osteoporosis, looking to find a specific remediable disease, supplementing dietary intake of calcium where appropriate, and prescribing exercise as tolerated (Aloia et al. 1978).

Completely objective criteria have not been defined for the use of estrogens in situations other than therapy of an estrogen-responsive neoplasm or early menopause. Use of estrogens for other than these indications has a great subjective component. A rational decision process to treat with estrogen will take into account each women's individuality coupled with current knowledge of benefits and risks of such therapy.

References

Aldin, E., and Korenman, S. "Endocrine Aspects of Aging." *Annals of Internal Medicine* 92 (1980):429.

Alington-MacKinnon, D., and Troll, L. "The Adaptive Function of the Menopause: A Devil's Advocate Position." *Journal of the American Geriatrics Society* 29 (1981):349.

Aloia, J., et al. "Prevention of Involution Bone Loss by Exercise." *Annals of Internal Medicine* 89 (1978):356–358.

Avioli, J. "What to Do with 'Postmenopausal Osteoporosis'." *American Journal of Medicine* 65 (1978):881.

Boston Collaborative Drug Surveillance Program. "Surgically Confirmed Gallbladder Disease, Venous Thrombo Embolism and Breast Tumor in Relation to Post Menopausal Estrogen Therapy." Report from the Boston Collaborative Drug Surveillance Program, Boston University Medical Center. *New England Journal of Medicine* 290 (1974):15.

Cape, R. *Aging: Its Complex Management.* Hagerstown, Md.: Harper & Row, 1978.

Casper, R; S. Yen; and M. Wilkes. "Menopause Flushes: A Neuroendocrine Link with Pulsatile Lutenizing Hormone Secretion." *Science* 205 (1979):349.

Deftos, L, et al. "Influence of Age and Sex on Plasma Calcitonin in Human Beings." *New England Journal of Medicine* 302 (1980):1351.

Federation CECOS; D. Schwartz; and M. Mayaux. "Female Fecundity as a Function of Age: Results of Artificial Insemination in 1293 Nulliparous Women with Azoospermic Husbands." *New England Journal of Medicine* 306 (1982):404.

Gallagher, J. et al. "Intestinal Calcium Absorption and Serum Vitamin D Metabolites in Normal Subjects and Osteoporotic Patients: Effect of Age and Dietary Calcium." *Journal of Clinical Investigation* 64 (1979):729.

Goldfarb, A. "Geriatric Gynecology." In *Clinical Geriatrics,* edited by I. Rossman. Philadelphia: J.P. Lippincott, 1979.

Gordon, J., et al. "Estrogen and Endometrial Carcinoma: Pathological Support of Original Risk Estimate." *New England Journal of Medicine* 297 (1977):297.

Gordon, M.; M. Huang; and C. Gryfe. "An Evaluation of Falls, Syncope and Dizziness by Prolonged Ambulatory Cardiographic Monitoring in a Geriatric Institutional Setting." *Journal of the American Geriatrics Society* 30 (1982):6.

Gordon, T., et al. "Menopause Coronary Heart Disease: The Framingham Study." *Annals of Internal Medicine* 89 (1978):157.

Harris, L. *Fact Book on Aging: A Profile of America's Older Population.* Washington, D.C.: National Council on the Aging, 1978.

Hoover, R., et al. "Menopausal Estrogen and Breast Cancer." *New England Journal of Medicine* 295 (1976):401.

Horwitz, R., and A. Feinstein. "Alternative Analytic Methods for Case Control Studies of Estrogens and Endometrial Cancer." *New England Journal of Medicine* 299 (1978):1089.

Hutchinson, G., and K. Rothman. "Correcting a Bias?" *New England Journal of Medicine* 299 (1978):1129.

Jensen, S., and E. Tondevold. "Mortality after Hip Fractures." *Acta Orthopaedica Scandinavica* 50 (1979):161.

Jick, M., et al. "Replacement Estrogens and Endometrial Carcinoma." *New England Journal of Medicine* 300 (1979):218.

Judd, H., et al. "Endocrine Function of the Postmenopausal Ovary: Concentration of Androgens and Estrogens in Ovarian Peripheral Vein Blood." *Journal of Clinical Endocrinology and Metabolism* 39 (1974): 429.

Kannel, W., et al. "Menopause and Risk of Cardiovascular Disease: The Framingham Study." *Annals of Internal Medicine* 85 (1976):447.

Kaunitz, A. "Estrogen Use in Postmenopausal Women." *New England Journal of Medicine* 303 (1980):1477.

Martin, J., et al. "Prognostic Value of Estrogen Receptors in Cancer of the Uterine Cervix." *New England Journal of Medicine* 306 (1982):485.

Markovic, V., et al. "Bone Status and Fracture Rates in Two Regions of Yugoslavia." *American Journal of Clinical Nutrition* 32 (1979):540.

Morimoto, S; M. Tysuji; and K. Okada. "The Effect of Estrogens on Human Calcitonin Secretion after Calcium Infusion in Elderly Female Subjects." *Clinical Endocrinology* 13 (1980):135.

Newcomer, A., et al. "Lactose Deficiency: Prevalence in Osteoporosis." *Annals of Internal Medicine* 2 (1978):218.

Overstall, P. "Prevention of Falls in the Elderly." *Journal of the American Geriatrics Society* 28 (1980):481.

Patterson, M., et al. "Endometrial Disease after Treatment with Estrogens and Progestogens in the Climacetric." *British Medical Journal* 280 (1980):822.

Quigley, M., and C. Hammond. "Estrogen Replacement Therapy: Help or Hazard." *New England Journal of Medicine* 301 (1979):646.

Raisz, L. "Osteoporosis." *Journal of the American Geriatrics Society* 30 (1982):127.

Riggs, E., et al. "Effect of the Fluoride/Calcium Regimen on Vertebral Fracture Occurrence in Postmenopausal Osteoporosis." *New England Journal of Medicine* 306 (1982):446.

Ryan, K. "Postmenopausal Estrogen Use." *Annual Review of Medicine* 33 (1982):171.

Ryan, K., et al. "Estrogen Use and Postmenopausal Women: A National Institute of Health Consensus Development Conference." *Annals of Internal Medicine* 91 (1979):921.

Sabin, T. "Biologic Aspects of Falls and Mobility Limitations in the Elderly." *Journal of the American Geriatrics Society* 30 (1982):51.

Slone, D., et al. "Risk of Myocardial Infarction in Relation to Current and Discontinued Use of Contraceptives." *New England Journal of Medicine* 305 (1981):420.

Smith, D., et al. "Association of Exogenous Estrogens and Endometrial Carcinoma." *New England Journal of Medicine* 293 (1975):1164.

Stadel, B., and N. Weiss. "Characteristics of Menopausal Women: A Survey of King and Pierce Counties in Washington 1973-1974." *American Journal of Epidemiology* 102 (1975):209.

Talbert, G. "Aging of the Reproductive System." In *Handbook of the Biology of Aging,* edited by C. Finch and L. Hayflick, pp. 318-356. New York: Van Nostrand Reinhold, 1977.

Trotter, M.; G. Broman; and R. Peterson. "Densities of Bones of White and Negro Skeletons." *Journal of Bone and Joint Surgery* 42 (1960):42.

Weinstein, M. "Estrogen Use in Postmenopausal Women—Costs, Risks, and Benefits." *New England Journal of Medicine* 303 (1980):308.

Weiss, N.; D. Szekely; and D. Austin. "Increasing Incidence of Endometrial Cancer in the United States." *New England Journal of Medicine* 294 (1976):1259.

Weiss, N., et al. "Decreased Risk of Fractures and Lower Forearm with Postmenopausal Use of Estrogen." *New England Journal of Medicine* 303 (1980):1195.

Wilson, R., and I. Wilson. "The Fate of the Nontreated Postmenopausal Woman: A Plea for the Maintenance of Adequate Estrogen from Puberty to the Grave." *Journal of the American Geriatrics Society* 11 (1963):347.

Ziel, H., and W. Finkle. "Increased Risk of Endometrial Carcinoma among Users of Conjugated Estrogens." *New England Journal of Medicine* 293 (1975):1167.

15 Cardiovascular Risk Factors in the Elderly Woman

William B. Kannel and
Frederick N. Brand

While the term *old age* is ambiguous, the age range 65 and over commonly is used to describe an elderly population. If we look at the balance of the sexes among the U.S. older population in 1975, there were 69 men for every 100 women in the age group 65 and over, and the deficit of men increases sharply with advancing age. The main factor determining the sex ratios at each age is the relative level of male versus female mortality. Sex differences in mortality are due mainly to differential rates of coronary heart disease (Waldron 1976). Women fare distinctly better than men.

While the control of undernutrition and infectious diseases now permits a large proportion of the population in affluent countries to reach advanced age, the rewards for reaching this venerable state are too often a cardiovascular catastrophe such as cardiac failure, a coronary attack, or a stroke. However, this is not inevitable since the elderly also have shared in the recent decline in cardiovascular mortality. The 1975 U.S. death rate for heart disease, the leading cause of death, was 84 percent of the rate twenty-four years before; at all ages beyond 45, the rate of death has declined more for women than for men. Thus, it is now known that cardiovascular disease is not merely a matter of chance; it is preventable.

Hypertension is of increasing concern because of its relationship to coronary heart disease and strokes. It is particularly relevant in a discussion of older women and health inasmuch as among women 55 and over the risk of hypertension is greater for women than men, and this difference becomes even more pronounced with age.

Much of the discussion in this chapter is based on findings in the Framingham Epidemiological Heart Disease Study. The Framingham cohort, which has been followed for the past three decades, has now entered the geriatric age range, providing an opportunity to examine the role of cardiovascular risk factors in the elderly, comparing men to women.

The Framingham study was initiated in 1949 to explore the evolution of cardiovascular disease in a general population sample of 5,209 men and women aged 30 to 62 years on entry. In continuous operation since that time, this study examines subjects biennially for the initial development of cardiovascular disease. Detailed descriptions of sampling procedures, response rates, method of examination, laboratory procedures, and the criteria for disease outcomes have been reported elsewhere (Kannel, McGee, and Gordon 1976).

In the course of twenty years of surveillance of the Framingham study cohort, 160 men and 133 women died after having achieved the ages of 65 to 74 years. Women fared distinctly better than men; the average annual mortality rate in women lagged that in men by ten years for overall mortality, cardiovascular mortality, and coronary mortality (see table 15–1). Cardiovascular disease accounted for 50 to 60 percent of deaths in those aged 65 to 74; among women, there was a distinct tendency for the proportionate mortality attributed to cardiovascular disease to increase with age.

Even more important than the length of life is its quality, which is affected severely by cardiovascular diseases. Coronary heart disease, strokes, peripheral arterial disease, and congestive heart failure are distressingly common in both sexes. As may be seen in table 15–2, coronary heart disease, while more common in men, increases with age for women and accounts for the highest incidence of cardiovascular events among them. The incidence of strokes among both men and women increases with advancing age; while women aged 45 to 54 are less likely to have a stroke than men in this age group, the female advantage lessens by age 55 to 64, and by age 65 to 74, women have almost the same annual stroke incidence as men. With respect to peripheral arterial disease and congestive heart failure, the incidence among both men and women increases with age as well, although women maintain a relative advantage over men.

Coronary Heart Disease

The greater resistance of women to coronary heart disease cannot be attributed to a lesser burden of cardiovascular risk factors inasmuch as women have an advantage over men at any level of risk factors, whether singly or in combination (Kannel and Castelli 1972). As shown in table 15–2, the gap between the sexes closes with advancing age, and beyond menopause, the risk appears to escalate two- to threefold for women, and the severity of the clinical manifestations also increases (Bengtsson 1973).

Prior to menopause, the chief clinical expression of coronary heart disease among women is angina pectoris. After menopause, however, myocardial infarction and sudden death predominate in women as well as among men (Dawber and Kannel 1961). Also, for reasons that are not clear, once women develop a myocardial infarction, they fare less well than men chiefly as evidenced by their higher mortality within the first year. The escalation of mortality among women after menopause occurs whether meno-

Table 15-1

Cardiovascular Mortality, Overall and by Age and Sex, of Twenty-Year Follow-Up Patients in the Framingham Heart Study

	Average Annual Mortality per 1,000		
Mortality	*45-54*	*55-64*	*65-75*
Cardiovascular mortality			
Men	4.1	14	17.1
Women	1.4	4	11.6
Coronary mortality			
Men	1.8	4.5	6.2
Women	0.4	1.2	3.5
Overall mortality			
Men	8.4	18	33.3
Women	5	8.2	19.5

Source: Framingham Heart Study, Division of Heart and Vascular Diseases, National Heart, Lung, and Blood Institute, Framingham, Massachusetts. 1949 to present.

pause is surgical or natural; it also occurs whether or not the ovaries have been removed (Hjortland, McNamara, and Kannel 1978).

A possible explanation for the sex difference in the incidence of coronary heart disease is the different endocrine makeup of men and women (Oliver and Boyd 1955). In the Framingham heart study, those women undergoing natural menopause were leaner at exam prior to menopause than a control group who had not yet experienced menopause. Women undergoing surgical menopause with bilateral oophorectomies (removal of both ovaries) weighed more than women experiencing natural menopause but were not otherwise significantly different from the control group of premenopausal women. Hemoglobin levels rose after menopause, and there was also a rise in serum-cholesterol levels between the premenopausal examinations. No significant changes in weight, blood pressure, blood glucose, or vital capacity were found to accompany menopause (Hjortland, McNamara, and Kannel 1978.)

Natural menopause usually is preceded by a general decrease in estrogen concentration that continues for some period after the menopause. On the one hand, the Framingham data clearly suggest that the menopause-related cardiovascular hazards in the postmenopausal women are greatest in close proximity to the onset of menopuase. Premature menopause may be dangerous because the contrast in hormonal status between women who are still menstruating and those who are not is greater on the average at younger ages. On the other hand, most studies of estrogen therapy in men have

Table 15–2
**Average Annual Incidence, per 1,000 Population, of Cardiovascular Events
in Relation to Age and Sex among Men and Women 45–74 Years of Age
Who Participated in the Framingham Heart Study Twenty-Year Follow-Up**

Age	Coronary Heart Disease		Strokes		Peripheral Arterial Disease		Congestive Heart Failure	
	Men	Women	Men	Women	Men	Women	Men	Women
45–54	9.9	3.1	2	0.9	1.8	0.6	1.8	0.8
55–64	20.8	9.5	3.2	2.9	5.1	1.9	4.3	2.7
65–74	20.4	14.5	8.4	8.6	6.3	3.8	8.2	6.8

Source: Framingham Heart Study, Division of Heart and Vascular Diseases, National Heart,
Lung, and Blood Institute, Framingham, Massachusetts, 1949 to present.

found an increased risk of recurrent myocardial infarction (Stamler, Gest,
and Turner 1963; Blackard et al. 1970).

Hypertension

Hypertension is a prominent contributor to overall mortality, approximately doubling the risk of death. It promotes cardiovascular mortality in
particular, where the risk in the elderly is tripled compared to normotensive
persons the same age. Hypertension takes an added significance in the aged
where the absolute risk of dying is greater than in the young. While the
long-term risk is greater over a lifetime in the young hypertensive, the short-
term risk of cardiovascular catastrophes in the hypertensive elderly is for-
midable.

Age Trends in Blood Pressure

Although blood pressure rises with age, particularly in affluent societies,
this is not inevitable and should not be considered a normal or desirable
aging phenomenon. There are some isolated, primitive populations in which
a rise in pressure with age does not occur (Maddocks 1961; Page, Damon,
and Moellering 1974). Longitudinal observation of trends in blood pressure
in the Framingham study indicates a magnitude of rise with age of about
20mmHg systolic and 10mmHg diastolic from age 30 to 64. Longitudinal
biennial monitoring of pressures as persons age indicates that diastolic

pressures in the two sexes are parallel over time, with women's pressures persistently lower than those of men the same age, regardless of their age.

Diastolic blood pressure refers to that existing during the relaxation phase between heart beats, normally about 80 mm. Systolic pressure refers to the greatest force caused by the contraction of the left ventricle of the heart, normally between 100 and 140 mm.

Diastolic pressures rise with age until the mid-fifties and then plateau until about age 65 after which they decline in both sexes. Systolic pressures, in contrast to diastolic pressures, present a different age trend. Among women, systolic pressures initially are lower than for men, but they rise more steeply to converge with those of men at about age 60. The rise in systolic pressure continues unabated at least until age 75. Thus, there is a disproportionate rise in systolic pressure with advancing age, attributed to a progressive loss of arterial elasticity.

Cross-sectional or prevalence-based inferences about age trends in blood pressure are misleading. In the Framingham cohort, cross-sectional data show an apparent crossover in pressures in the two sexes for both systolic and diastolic pressure, with women's pressures initially lower than those of men but higher beyond middle age.

In Western affluent cultures, because blood pressure usually rises with age, it is often considered a normal phenomenon, but unfortunately, what is common is not necessarily optimal in terms of function (Severe et al. 1977). The elderly with lower blood pressures suffer less morbidity and mortality than those with blood pressures closer to the mean for their age. Debate about what is normal pressure in the elderly is pointless unless it is based on morbidity and mortality.

Prevalence

However defined, hypertension is common in the elderly of both sexes. Although common, estimates of the prevalence of hypertension in older persons vary widely, depending upon the upper limits of normal applied and how the pressures were obtained (Koch-Weser 1978; Alderman and Yano 1976). The Framingham study defined hypertension at all ages as above 160mmHg systolic and 95mmHg diastolic (Kannel et al. 1972). By this definition, about 22 percent of men and 34 percent of women aged 65 to 74 were found to be hypertensive. National Health Survey data show that over the age of 65, the prevalence of hypertension is about 50 percent higher in blacks than whites (Niarchos and Laragh 1980; Ostfeld 1978). Data from the Health and Nutrition Examination Survey (HANES) for 1971 to 1974 indicate that among those 18 to 74 years of age, 61 percent of the women as compared to 44 percent of the men had hypertension. While blacks of both sexes have higher rates, the prevalence of hypertension among black women in old age is particularly dramatic: 59 percent of black women aged 65 to 74 as compared to 42 percent of the white women examined were hypertensive according to the HANES study.

For both men and women 65–74 years of age, the average mortality rate increases according to hypertensive status (see table 15-3). Specifically, the relative risk incurred from hypertension is greatest for risk of stroke and least for occlusive peripheral arterial disease but substantial even for the latter, a conclusion based on risk ratios in elderly hypertensives compared to normotensive women to those with normal blood pressures of the same age. In terms of the absolute risk, coronary heart disease is still the most common sequel to hypertension in the elderly of both sexes as in the young.

Although elevated blood pressure is highly prevalent among the elderly, there is no evidence to suggest that the danger is any less than in the younger hypertensive. There is also no evidence that elderly women tolerate hypertension better than men. Relative risks and risk gradients are just as large for women as for men, and the attributable risks in women in the Framingham study are even larger than for men in those over age 65. For risk of strokes and cardiac failure, even the absolute risks are no lower in hypertensive women than men, although they are lower among normotensive women.

Isolated systolic hypertension is the most common variety of hypertension encountered in the aged. This is usually a reflection of diminished distensibility of the aorta and is often considered an innocuous normal accompaniment of advanced age. However, such hypertension is not well tolerated. In the elderly, the risk of cardiovascular sequelae is no more closely linked to the systolic than to the diastolic blood pressure. In the Framingham study, we performed a logistic regression analysis, standardized to place each component of the pressure on an equal footing for the different units of measurement. This analysis revealed no indication of a greater impact of diastolic than systolic pressure for any of the cardiovascular sequlae of hypertension. In fact, analysis of every component of blood pressure, including pulse pressure, mean arterial pressure, as well as systolic and diastolic pressure suggests that nothing is clearly superior to the systolic pressure in predicting cardiovascular events in general and stroke—the most closely related hypertensive event—in particular.

Criteria for defining hypertension traditionally have been based on diastolic pressure. This fact reflects the belief that diastolic-pressure elevation is more pathological than systolic. Recent multicenter clinical trials testing the efficacy of antihypertensive treatment have tended to foster this misconception by basing the indication for treatment on the diastolic pressure regardless of the systolic pressure. Hence, persons with isolated systolic-pressure elevations have been largely ignored.

Table 15–3
Mortality Experience, per 1,000 Population, according to Hypertensive
Status among Men and Women 65–74 Years of Age in the Framingham
Heart Study

	Average Annual Mortality per 1,000			
	Overall		*Cardiovascular*	
Hypertensive Status	*Men*	*Women*	*Men*	*Women*
Normal	23.6	14.5	9.6	3.8
Borderline	37.7	17.8	20.2	9.8
Definite	42.6	24.7	24.5	18.6

Source: Framingham Heart Study, Division of Heart and Vascular Diseases, National Heart,
Lung, and Blood Institute, Framingham, Massachusetts, 1949 to present.

Data from the Framingham study have shown that systolic pressure is
not only a better predictor of cardiovascular disease than diastolic pressure
but also that the predictive value of systolic pressure relative to diastolic
increases with age (Koch-Weser 1978; Kannel 1974).

There is clinical evidence suggesting that isolated systolic hypertension
is a distinct clinical syndrome (Niarchos and Laragh 1980; Koch-Weser
1978). It also has a different population distribution than essential hypertension by age, sex, and race. In contrast to essential hypertension after
age 50, the prevalence of isolated systolic hypertension is greater in women
than men, and the relative risk of this type of hypertension is also greater
in women.

There appears to be some connection between essential hypertension
and isolated systolic hypertension. The Framingham study data show a high
percentage of both women and men have had prior diastolic blood-pressure
elevation. The proportion increases with age, from 24.4 percent among
women aged 35 to 44 to 62 percent among women 65 to 74. Thus, it is
important to keep in mind that it is not particularly helpful to know the
diastolic pressure to assess risk among elderly women or men with systolic
hypertension. In fact, use of the diastolic pressure may be misleading.
Accordingly, not only does systolic pressure improve as a predictor of risk
of coronary heart disease with advancing age, but also it is associated with
an increased risk even when the diastolic pressure is not elevated.

It is conceivable that systolic hypertension is only a sign of arterio-
sclerosis that is responsible for the associated increased incidence of cardiovascular sequelae. The Framingham study pulse-wave data strongly suggest that systolic hypertension is associated with hypertensive as well as

atherosclerotic cardiovascular sequelae whether or not the vessel is rigid. Multivariate analysis, taking age, pulse-wave findings, and systolic pressure into account, indicates that the systolic pressure determines the risk. Thus, it is not likely that isolated hypertension is only an innocent accompaniment of aged, rigid arteries.

Labile Hypertension

Labile hypertension usually is regarded as an innocuous antecedent of fixed hypertension and, hence, unworthy of treatment. This is an especially important consideration in the aged because lability of blood pressure increases with age. To a large extent, this increased lability is a result of the higher pressures normally observed in the elderly. Higher pressures are more labile than low ones so that what has been termed *fixed hypertension* actually has more-labile pressures than so-called labile hypertension (Kannel, Sorlie, and Gordon 1980).

Blood pressure fluctuates physiologically in response to changes in physical activity, mood, wakefulness, and other demands for greater tissue perfusion. Hence, pressures taken under office conditions are sometimes variable. This variability has engendered skepticism about the value of a single office blood-pressure reading. In the Framingham study, 35 percent of male and 27 percent of female hypertensives on one biennial examination were borderline or normotensive on the next. (Kannel, Sorlie, and Gordon 1980). By this criterion, those found to be normotensive might be judged to be very labile and those borderline moderately so. However, this concept of lability is confounded by the statistical phenomenon of regression toward the mean and is thus invalid.

A better indication of the lability of the blood pressure is the standard deviation about the mean of a series of pressures obtained over an hour on a particular examination. The variation in pressure by this criterion in the Framingham study did not appear to be repeatable characteristics of subjects from one examination to another (Kannel, Sorlie, and Gordon 1980), although the blood pressures were highly correlated. Thus, little evidence supports the contention that identifiable persons in a population characteristically have unusually labile pressures on multiple examinations.

So-called basal pressures have been considered the best basis for judging the need for treatment so that those pressures not elevated under these conditions were often thought to be innocuous. As a dangerous extension of this concept, physicians have tended to use the lowest pressure recorded on a patient as the most valid for evaluating risk. It may not be safe to disregard patients whose pressures fail to be elevated persistently on every determination if the average pressure is high.

The risk of cardiovascular disease thus is judged best from the average of a series of pressures. Patients whose pressures are more labile have no lower risk of cardiovascular events than those whose pressures are less variable. In fact, taken alone, the risk of cardiovascular disease increases with the degree of variability in pressure (Tarzi, Magrini, and Dustan 1975). However, this risk reflects the higher average values of those with more-variable values, and when adjusted for the mean level of pressure, there is no relation of variability to risk. This is confirmed in multivariate analysis that has indicated that, for any given average pressure, risk of cardiovascular events is unaffected by the degree of variability of pressure.

Labile hypertension has no distinguishing features that make it unique, and almost all normotensive persons occasionally have pressures above the arbitrary normal limits. Likewise, almost all patients with so-called fixed hypertension occasionally exhibit pressures below conventional hypertensive limits. Casual pressures obtained in the clinic predict cardiovascular events surprisingly well. The only reason that fixed or basal pressure elevation is associated with a higher risk than labile hypertension is that the average pressure is higher. It is therefore more logical to rely on the average pressure than those more-ambiguous indicators.

Determinants of Hypertension

Elevation of systolic or diastolic pressure usually represents primary hypertension in the elderly as it does in the young. Only a small proportion is secondary to some identifiable cause. Only when hypertension involving both components of the blood pressure appears for the first time after age 55 is there a good chance that it is not essential hypertension. Hence, newly developing hypertension in the elderly deserves an investigation for some underlying cause, which usually will be renovascular disease.

Isolated systolic hypertension is not a homogeneous entity. Other causes include aortic valvular insuffiency, atrioventricular conduction disturbance, hyperthyroidism, severe anemia, and Paget's disease. However, these etiologies, which can also cause cardiac failure and other sequelae of hypertension, account for only a small proportion of systolic hypertension in the elderly.

Secondary forms of hypertension occur in the aged as well as in the younger hypertensive person and include undiagnosed renovascular disease, primary aldosteronism (a condition in which the blood contains abnomal amounts of aldersterone, a hormone secreted by the adrenal gland), and pheochromocytoma (a tumor of the adrenal system). However, de novo hypertension in the aged is caused most often by the progressive atherosclerosis occluding one or both renal arteries. This renovascular disease may also produce an acceleration of diastolic-pressure increase in patients with isolated systolic hypertension or cause resistance to treatment in a previously well-controlled subject with essential hypertension.

In the aged as well as in the young, hypertension occurs more often in those who are obese (Kannel and Sorlie 1974). Weight gains and losses normally are mirrored by corresponding changes in blood pressure (Ashley and Kannel 1974), and this occurs independent of salt intake (Reisen et al. 1978). Alcohol intake is also related to hypertension, and it is likely that this aspect also applies in the aged (Kennel and Sorlie 1974). The Framingham study has found that those in the upper end of the normal distribution of blood hematocrit have about twice as much hypertension as those at the lower end (Kannel and Sorlie 1974). Diabetes and gout are more common in the elderly, and those who develop these metabolic problems have more hypertension. There is a tendency for higher pressure as cholesterol values and heart rates rise (Kannel and Sorlie 1974).

High salt intake is believed to play a role in the development of hypertension and very likely in its persistence into advanced age. A high prevalence of hypertension is found in cultures subsisting on more than 5 gm. of salt per day or in those excreting more than 70 mEqs (millequivalents) of sodium (a measure of salt in the blood) (Freis 1976). Those aged who were raised in primitive isolated societies tend to escape hypertension, a protection usually lost on migration to more-advanced civilization (Freis 1976).

There is undoubtedly a strong familial and inherent susceptibility to hypertension, and this very likely applies to the aged as well as the young. However, this susceptibility is only permissive, requiring some environmental cofactor for the hypertension to be expressed. Families share lifestyles as well as genes, and spouses of hypertensive subjects tend to have higher blood pressures (Sackett 1975).

Preventive Management

There is reason to believe that the high frequency of cardiovascular catastrophes and the predisposive risk factors in the aged are not inevitable. Even among the elderly, some are less vulnerable than others. Despite the diminished impact of some major risk factors in advanced age, the standard cardiovascular risk profile efficiently predicts coronary heart disease, brain infarction, occlusive peripheral vascular disease, and cardiac failure in the elderly, identifying high-risk candidates for preventive management.[1]

The vital capacity is a useful addition to the cardiovascular risk profile in the aged. This test provides more-striking predictions for women than men for reasons that are not clear. Although hygienic measures seldom improve vital capacity in the elderly, a low vital capacity does identify persons in need of attention to other modifiable cardiovascular risk factors.

Diabetes is also a stronger cardiovascular risk factor in the elderly woman than in the man. Elderly diabetic women die of cardiovascular disease at four times the rate of nondiabetics. Particularly in women, diabetes makes a contribution to risk that is independent of often-associated low HDL, obesity, poor LDL/HDL ratio, and triglyceride values.

Although there is little demonstrable benefit to quitting smoking beyond age 65 in either sex as regards coronary attacks, overall and cardiovascular mortality was reduced in those who abstained. Additional justification for quitting smoking is found in the demonstrated contribution of smoking to emphysema, bronchitis, lung cancer, and pain in the calves due to inadequate blood supply.

The health consequences of obesity in the elderly are poorly understood. Obesity is a greater hazard in women than in men, and its adverse consequences derive from its promotion of the major atherogenic traits. Because weight control can improve these atherogenic influences, weight control is rational for obese candidates for cardiovascular disease. Overzealous weight reduction in the elderly would not seem wise in view of the finding of excess mortality at low as well as high weights.

There appears to be some benefit to regular exercise beyond age 50. However, it would appear unwise to rely on this fact alone to protect against cardiovascular disease. Moderate exercise may be beneficial as a part of a comprehensive risk-reduction program in the aged.

Summary

On aging, there is a larger duration of exposure to noxious influences promoting cardiovascular diseases and a lessened ability to cope with them. Decline in multiple organ functions occurs as atherothrombotic, embolic, and sclerotic changes close down the circulation. Cardiac reserve declines. The high incidence of cardiovascular disease in the aged is not solely a product of accumulating risk factors as people grow older. However, those who have them do develop more cardiovascular disease, and the risk is compounded when these are multiple. Hence, to identify highly vulnerable candidates for cardiovascular catastrophes, a cardiovascular risk profile should be obtained and multifactorial preventive measures implemented as indicated. Although proof of efficacy in modifying cardiovascular risk factors in the aged is lacking, the recent decline in cardiovascular mortality in the United States, which includes the elderly of both sexes, is encouraging.

Note

1. The serum lipids are not as useful in the aged, and the utility of serum cholesterol is lost beyond age 55. This must be restored by fractioning it into its atherogenic LDL and protective HDL components. However, this partitioning of the serum cholesterol has little utility in stroke or occlusive peripheral vascular disease despite its effectiveness in predicting coronary heart disease. Fortunately, measures advocated to prevent atherosclerotic cardiovascular disease, including weight reduction, avoidance of cigarettes, exercise, and control of diabetes, also raise HDL cholesterol. Subjects who have high triglyceride values tend to have more atherosclerotic cardiovascular disease. However, when concomitant low HDL cholesterol, poor LDL/HDL cholesterol ratios, impaired glucose tolerance, and overweight are taken into account, there is little residual effect. The addition of triglyceride to lipid profiles comprised of HDL and LDL cholesterol does not improve prediction for coronary heart disease. Elderly subjects with high triglycerides should be checked for low HDL values, obesity, and diabetes, and these should be corrected.

References

Alderman, M.H., and K. Yano. "How Prevalence of Hypertension varies as Diagnostic Criteria Change." *American Journal of Medical Science* 271 (1976):343.

Ashley, F.W., and W.B. Kannel. "Relation of Weight Change to Changes in Atherogenic Trends: The Framingham Study." *Journal of Chronic Disease* 27 (1974):103.

Bengtson, H.M. "Ischemic Heart Disease in Women." *Acta Orthopaedica Scandinavica* Suppl. (1973):549.

Blackard, C.D., et al. "Incidence of Cardiovascular Disease and Death in Patients Receiving Diethylstilbestrol for Carcinoma of Prostate." *Cancer* 26 (1970):249.

Dawber, R.T., and W.B. Kannel. "Susceptibility to Coronary Heart Disease." *Modern Concepts of Cardiovascular Disease* 333 (1961): 671–676.

Freis, E.D. "Salt, Volume, and the Prevention of Hypertension." *Circulation* 53 (1976):589–595.

Hjortland, M.C.; P. McNamara; and W.B. Kannel. "Some Atherogenic Concomitants of Menopause: The Framingham Study." *American Journal of Epidemiology* 103 (1978):304–311.

Kannel, W.B. "Role of Blood Pressure in Cardiovascular Morbidity and Mortality." *Progressive Cardiovascular Disease* 17 (1974):5.

Kannel, W.B., and W.P. Castelli, "The Framingham Study of Coronary Heart Disease in Women." *Medical Times* 100 (1972):173–184.

Kannel, W.B.; et al. "Role of Blood Pressure in the Development of Congestive Heart Failure." *New England Journal of Medicine* 287 (1972): 781–787.

Kannel, W.B.; D. McGee; and T.A. Gordon. "A General Cardiovascular Risk Profile: The Framingham Study." *American Journal of Cardiology* 38 (1976):46–51.

Kannel, W.B., and P.D. Sorlie. "Hypertension in Framingham." In *Proceedings of the Second International Symposium on the Epidemiology of Hypertension,* edited by O. Paul. Chicago: Symposia Specialists, 1974.

Kannel, W.B.; P.D. Sorlie; and T. Gordon. "Labile Hypertension: A Faulty Concept? The Framingham Study." *Circulation* 61 (1980): 1183–1187.

Koch-Weser, J. "Arterial Hypertension in Old Age." *Herz* 3 (1978):235–244.

Maddocks, I. "Possible Absence of Essential Hypertension in Two Complete Pacific Islands." *Lancet* 2 (1961):396–399.

Niarchos, A.P., and J.H. Laragh. "Hypertension in the Elderly." *Modern Concepts of Cardiovascular Disease* 49 (1980):43–54.

Oliver, M.F., and G.S. Boyd. "Coronary Atherogenesis—An Endocrine Problem?" *Minnesota Medicine* 38 (1955):794–799.

Ostfeld, A.M. "Elderly Hypertensive Patient, Epidemiologic Review." *New York State Journal of Medicine* 78 (1978):1125–1129.

Page, L.B.; A. Damon; and R.C. Moellering, Jr. "Antecedents of Cardiovascular Disease in Six Solomon Island Societies." *Circulation* 49 (1974):1132.

Sackett, D.L. "Studies of Blood Pressure in Spouses." In *Epidemiology and Control of Hypertension,* edited by O. Paul, pp. 21–35. Chicago: Symposia Specialists, 1975.

Severe, P.S.; et al. "Plasma Noradrenaline in Essential Hypertension." *Lancet* 1 (1977):1078–1981.

Stamler, J.; M.M. Gest; and J.P. Turner. "The Status of Hormonal Therapy for the Primary and Secondary Prevention of Atherosclerotic Coronary Heart Disease." *Progressive Cardiovascular Disease* 6 (1963): 220.

Tarzi, R.C.; F. Magrini; and H.P. Dustan. "The Role of Aortic Distensibility in Hypertension." In *Advances in Hypertension,* vol. 2, edited by P. Milhriz and M. Safar, p. 133. Boehringer-Ingelheim, 1975.

Waldron, I. "Why Do Women Live Longer than Men? Parts I, II." *Social Science and Medicine* 10 (1976):340–362.

# 16 Epilogue

What produces a good old age for women? The authors have delineated a variety of issues and prospects affecting the quality of women's lives from mid-life on. Obvious and fundamental needs have been demarked: an adequate income pre- and postretirement, social interaction, a comfortable home, social-support networks, good health, positive self-regard, and provision of care in infirmity. For many women who are now old, these needs are not met. A recent national survey identified three groups of older Americans[1]:

1. Enjoyers, who report good to excellent health, have relatively low economic stress, have a spouse of equal physical capacity, and are relatively well educated;
2. Survivors, who cope with the lack of one or two of these factors;
3. Casualties, who are in fair to poor health, have relatively high economic stress, and lack a spouse of equal physical capacity.

Significantly, the category of enjoyers was composed primarily of men, casualties were predominantly women, and survivors were more or less evenly found among both sexes. These three categories provide a useful heuristic framework in which to evaluate the importance of health, wealth, and marital companionship as they affect women in particular.

A wide variety of studies have shown us that good health in old age is related to life satisfaction, well-being, and optimism. Women are also less likely to suffer from disabling poor health in old age than men (see chapters 10, 11, and 15). Why, then, are women disproportionately represented among the casualties? The answer would seem to be in both economics and companionship.

For either husband or wife, having a disabled spouse affects marital interaction and companionship. Since U.S. national health statistics show that women are less disabled and live longer than men, older women are more likely to have a disabled or sick spouse for whom they must care. Elderly men are more likely to be dependent upon their wives for health services than women on their husbands; in turn, dependent old women often must rely upon their children. As Turner has pointed out elsewhere[2], the failing health of her spouse increases the power of the wife within the family. However, this power is bought at a heavy price—namely, curtailment of her interests and freedom of movement and alteration of the marital relationship for both.

There is no evidence that the life span or health of older men is likely to change in the foreseeable future. What is needed is greater attention to alternative life-styles for older women to combat some of the vicissitudes they now face as concomitants of their greater life expectancy.

Financial stress, too, is a particular problem for older women (see part II). In general, optimism and economic stress are inversely related. Retirement income for women is lower than for men, and many women who have worked for part or all of their adult lives may, because of the low wages they have received, be better off taking 50 percent of their husband's social security. None of the major retirement schemes including social security currently gives full recognition to women's work as housewives. Clearly, economic insecurity is a problem that adds to misery.

What are the prospects for future old women? Contradictory trends in public policy cloud my view. Through budget cuts and block grants, economic security is being eroded for the now old woman. In March 1981, the Reagan administration proposed elimination of the $122 social-security minimum payment (three-quarters of whose beneficiaries were women), and although Congress restored the minimum, it was saved only for current recipients.[3]

Changes in eligibility requirements for SSI were proposed for fiscal year 1983 that would eliminate age and vocational and educational factors for eligibility as well as abolish the $20 per month income disregard now not counted in eligibility determinations.[4] Copayments for all Medicaid services and for Medicare home health care and hospital stays of two to sixty days also have been proposed, both of which would increase health costs appreciably for old women who currently account for 70 percent of the elderly poor. All federal programs safeguarding the economic security of women have been threatened or cut, and enforcement agencies protecting women against discrimination in employment, promotions, and job training have been weakened.[5] To what extent the political influence of women and the elderly will halt the direction of these proposals remains to be seen.

At present, being old and a woman in the United States and elsewhere has its tribulations—economic insecurity, widowhood, and loss of friends and sexual partners through divorce and illness, or death. Yet most old women are hardy; even in adversity they are brave. They offer us a model from which we can learn about the financial, emotional, and social supports needed by all of us throughout the life course.

Notes

1. Research and Forecasts, *Aging in America: Trials and Triumphs* (New York: Rudder and Finn, 1980).

2. Barbara F. Turner, "Sex Related Differences in Aging." In *Handbook of Developmental Psychology,* ed. B.B. Wolman and G. Stricker (New York: Prentice-Hall, 1982).

3. Carol Mueller, "The Federal Commitment to Women. . . . Twenty Years Later" (Presented at the Conference on Women and Political Power in the United States, 29 April 1981, Boston), p. 3.

4. Women's Equity Action League, *Budget Cuts Hurt Older Women* (Washington, D.C.: WEAL, April 1982).

5. Mueller, "Federal Commitment to Women," p. 3.

Index

Index

About the Contributors

Catherine Adams is an assistant professor in the Department of Nursing at the University of Connecticut, with a background in nursing and a doctorate in counseling psychology.

Donna Anderson is a Ph.D. candidate at the University of Denver. Her current interests are in medical sociology (patient-physician interaction) and marriage and the family, especially the ever-single.

Cleo S. Berkun is assistant professor of social welfare at the University of Maine in Orono. Her research interests include mental health, counseling, and mid-life women.

Rita Braito is an associate professor of sociology at the University of Denver. Her current interests are the ever-single elderly, spouse interaction and mental health, and patient-physician interaction and the terminally ill.

Frederick N. Brand, M.D., is a research associate in medicine at Boston University School of Medicine and has published numerous articles in gerontology as well as on the research on cardiovascular factors from the Framingham Heart Disease Epidemiology Study.

Maryvonne Gognalons-Nicolet is former director of GRAEG, Association de Gérontologie de XIIIe arrondissement, Paris, and is a sociologist at the Centre Psychosociale Universitaire, Geneva. A former visiting Fulbright Fellow at Boston University, her research interests include the social and political implications of mid-life and old age.

Brian Gratton received the Ph.D. in American history in 1980 from Boston University and is currently a postdoctoral research Fellow in social gerontology, Department of Sociology, Case Western Reserve University.

Jennifer Hand received the Ph.D. from the New School for Social Research and is a sociologist at Maimonides Mental Health Center in Brooklyn. Her current research interests include clinical sociology, aging, and sociology of vagrancy.

Beth B. Hess is professor of sociology at County College of Morris in New Jersey. Her recent publications include *Growing Old in America, Aging and*

Old Age (with Elizabeth W. Markson), and *Sociology* (with Peter Stein and Elizabeth W. Markson).

Ruth Harriet Jacobs is chair of the department of sociology and anthropology at Clark University. Her recent publications include *Life after Youth: Female, Forty, What Next?* and *Re-Engagement in Later Life: Re-Employment and Marriage* (with Barbara Vinick). She is a research affiliate at the Boston University Gerontology Center.

Elizabeth S. Johnson coauthored, with John B. Williamson, *Growing Old: The Social Problems of Aging* and she has published in the area of adult-child older-parent relationships. Dr. Johnson is a research associate on the Normative Aging Study of the Boston Veteran's Administration and a research affiliate at the Boston University Gerontology Center.

William B. Kannel, M.D., is professor of medicine at Boston University School of Medicine and former director of the Framingham Heart Disease Epidemiology Study. He has published extensively in the area of cardiovascular epidemiology.

Lawrence J. Kerzner, M.D., is director of the geriatric-education program at Jewish Memorial Hospital, Boston, and assistant professor at Boston University School of Medicine.

Victor W. Marshall is a sociologist in the Department of Behavioral Science, University of Toronto. His research interests focus on the health status and health care of the aged, the social and political implications of population aging, and the importance of the family in the lives of older people. His other research concerns health-care teams and the social psychology of health and illness behavior.

Kay O'Laughlin is a psychotherapist specializing in geriatric psychotherapy with individuals and groups. Her research interests include attitudes toward death, action therapies, and women and depression. She is a research affiliate at the Boston University Gerontology Center.

Ellen Rosen is a sociologist on the faculty of Nichols College, Dudley, Massachusetts. Her current research focuses on employment and unemployment among female factory workers.

Carolyn J. Rosenthal is a postdoctoral Fellow in the Department of Behavioral Science, University of Toronto. A sociologist with particular interests in the fields of aging, the family, intergenerational relations, and health care, her current research concerns ethnic variations in familial-support systems.

Jane Synge is a sociologist in the Department of Sociology, McMaster University. Her research interests include aging, family, social-support systems of older people, and historical sociology of the family.

Maximiliane E. Szinovacz is assistant professor of sociology at Florida State University. Her publications include *The Situation of Women in Austria: Economic and Family Issues* and *Women's Retirement: Policy Implications of Recent Research.*

Barbara F. Turner is an associate professor at the University of Massachusetts, Amherst, where she is also director of the gerontology program. She has published extensively in the fields of gerontology and older women.

Joan Waring is a sociologist at the Equitable Life Assurance Society. She has written extensively in the fields of aging, social change, and the family.

About the Editor

Elizabeth W. Markson is associate research professor of sociology and adjunct associate professor of sociomedical sciences and community medicine at Boston University, where she also is research coordinator for the Gerontology Center. Recent publications include *Aging and Old Age* (with Beth B. Hess), *Public Policies for an Aging Population* (with Gretchen R. Batra, Lexington Books, 1980), and *Sociology* (with Beth B. Hess and Peter Stein). She has taught a course on women and aging at the Boston University Summer Institute in Gerontology since 1978. Her areas of interest include long-term care, women, and social policy.